Conjugal Misconduct

Conjugal Misconduct reveals the hidden history of controversial and legally contested marital arrangements in twentieth-century America. William Kuby examines the experiences of couples in unconventional unions and the legal and cultural backlash generated by a wide array of "alternative" marriages. These include marriages established through personal advertisements and matchmaking bureaus, marriages that defied state eugenic regulations, hasty marriages between divorced persons, provisional and temporary unions referred to as "trial marriages," racial intermarriages, and a host of other unions that challenged sexual and marital norms. In illuminating the tensions between those who set marriage policies and those who defied them, Kuby offers a fresh account of marriage's contested history, arguing that although marital nonconformists composed only a small minority of the population, their atypical arrangements nonetheless shifted popular understandings of marriage and consistently refashioned the legal parameters of the institution.

WILLIAM KUBY is UC Foundation Assistant Professor of History at the University of Tennessee at Chattanooga, where he directs the Africana Studies Program and teaches in the Women's Studies Program.

Cambridge Historical Studies in American Law and Society

Recognizing legal history's growing importance and influence, the goal of this series is to chart legal history's continuing development by publishing innovative scholarship across the discipline's broadening range of perspectives and subjects. It encourages empirically creative works that take legal history into unexplored subject areas, or that fundamentally revise our thinking about familiar topics; it also encourages methodologically innovative works that bring new disciplinary perspectives and techniques to the historical analysis of legal subjects.

Series Editor

Christopher Tomlins, *University of California, Berkeley*

Previously Published in the Series

continues after index...

Conjugal Misconduct

Defying Marriage Law in the Twentieth-Century United States

WILLIAM KUBY

University of Tennessee at Chattanooga

CAMBRIDGE
UNIVERSITY PRESS

CAMBRIDGE
UNIVERSITY PRESS

University Printing House, Cambridge CB2 8BS, United Kingdom

One Liberty Plaza, 20th Floor, New York, NY 10006, USA

477 Williamstown Road, Port Melbourne, VIC 3207, Australia

314–321, 3rd Floor, Plot 3, Splendor Forum, Jasola District Centre, New Delhi – 110025, India

79 Anson Road, #06–04/06, Singapore 079906

Cambridge University Press is part of the University of Cambridge.

It furthers the University's mission by disseminating knowledge in the pursuit of education, learning, and research at the highest international levels of excellence.

www.cambridge.org
Information on this title: www.cambridge.org/9781107160262
DOI: 10.1017/9781316673096

First published 2018

Printed in the United States of America by Sheridan Books, Inc.

A catalogue record for this publication is available from the British Library.

Library of Congress Cataloging-in-Publication Data
NAMES: Kuby, William, author.
TITLE: Conjugal misconduct : defying marriage law in the twentieth-century United States / William Kuby, University of Tennessee at Chattanooga.
DESCRIPTION: New York : Cambridge University Press, 2018. | Series: Cambridge historical studies in American law and society | Includes bibliographical references and index.
IDENTIFIERS: LCCN 2017045842 | ISBN 9781107160262 (hardback : alk. paper) | ISBN 9781316613368 (pbk. : alk. paper)
SUBJECTS: LCSH: Unmarried couples–Legal status, laws, etc.–United States.
CLASSIFICATION: LCC KF538 .K83 2017 | DDC 346.7301/6710904–dc23
LC record available at https://lccn.loc.gov/2017045842

ISBN 978-1-107-16026-2 Hardback

Contents

v

Figures

Acknowledgements

This book arose from my fascination with the personal advertisements in the *New York Review of Books*, and my realization that those outlandish sources just might lend themselves to meaningful historical study. Since that epiphany I have lived in five different cities, taught at four universities, and ever so gradually turned my initial musings into a full-length book. Along the way I have received encouragement and support from so many wonderful people whose inspiration manifests itself on every page.

The project took its earliest form at the University of Pennsylvania, and I am indebted to the many professors who helped me to shape it. I am most grateful to Kathy Peiss, who, simply put, taught me how to be a historian. Her academic guidance, encouragement, and creative insights allowed me to bring my own ideas to light. Moreover, her boundless compassion and generosity motivate me to be a better professor and scholar on a daily basis. I also offer thanks to Barbara Savage, Eve Trout Powell, Walter Licht, Antonio Feros, Stephanie McCurry, Sally Gordon, Sarah Igo, Steven Hahn, and the late Sheldon Hackney for their mentorship and support throughout my graduate school years.

I was fortunate to spend my time at Penn alongside terrific classmates who have gone on to do exceptional things. For their friendship and intellectual companionship, I give thanks to René Alvarez, Dan Amsterdam, Heather Bennett, Marie Brown, Joanna Cohen, Erin Park Cohn, Abby Cooper, Julie Davidow, Elizabeth Della Zazzera, Jack Dwiggins, Rob Goldberg, Cassandra Good, Adam Goodman, Julia Gunn, Richara Heyward, Matt Karp, John Kenney, Reena Krishna, Freddie LaFemina, Zain Lakhani, Jessica Lautin, Andrew Lipman, Erik Mathisen, Jaffa

Panken, Chase Richards, Sarah Rodriguez, Brian Rouleau, Matt Schauer, Katrin Schreiter, Maryan Soliman, and Nicole Myers Turner. The early years of my post-graduate career were somewhat circuitous, but the chaos allowed me to meet superb students and scholars whose support has made this book stronger. I would like to recognize the Women and Gender Studies and African/African-American Studies programs at Eastern Kentucky University, as well as the department of history at Miami University, for research support, mentorship, and camaraderie. Special thanks to Lisa Day, Salome Nnoromele, Sara Zeigler, Tom Appleton, Kathryn Burns-Howard, Gael Montgomery, and Yaroslav Prykhodko.

A stroke of luck brought me to the department of history at the University of Tennessee at Chattanooga, where I have found a vibrant community of creative and compassionate colleagues. I want to thank them for their friendship, patience, and emotional and intellectual support as I have slowly brought this book to completion. I offer special gratitude to Mike Thompson, John Swanson, Susan Eckelmann Berghel, Michelle White, Kira Robison, Aaron Althouse, Fang Yu Hu, Ryan Edwards, Annie Tracy Samuel, and James Guilfoyle. I am also grateful to the nonhistorians in my UTC world: Joseph Jordan, Aaron Shaheen, Jordan Amirkhani, Linda Frost, and Allison Stone. Additional thanks go to UTC's College of Arts and Sciences, Office of Equity and Diversity, and Faculty Grants Committee for generous research support, and to UTC's Office of Research and Special Programs for a Faculty Pre-Tenure Enhancement Grant.

This project has benefited from the help of numerous librarians and archivists. I am grateful to the staff at the University of Pennsylvania, University of Tennessee at Chattanooga, and Howard University libraries, as well as the American Antiquarian Society, American Philosophical Society, Wisconsin Historical Society, American Heritage Center, Social Welfare History Archives, University of Pennsylvania Archives, and the Arthur and Elizabeth Schlesinger Library on the History of Women in America. In addition to offering research aid, the Schlesinger Library awarded me a dissertation grant, which was critical to the project in its early stages. Special thanks also go to Agnes Fellner at the UTC Library's Studio for her friendship and her indispensable help with image scans.

Many kind readers have given me valuable feedback on portions of the manuscript. I received particularly helpful comments from participants in the University of Pennsylvania's Annenberg Seminar in History, and later from participants in the Gender Seminar at the University of Kansas's

Hall Center for the Humanities; thanks to Marie Brown for inviting me to KU, and to Brian Donovan and Katie Batza for their sharp insights. I am indebted to Christina Simmons, who graciously offered commentary at various stages of this project. I have also received valuable feedback from Mathew Kuefler, Robert Lockhart, and Kate Marshall. Thanks as well to my conference co-panelists and commentators, who have given me countless ideas for how to make this book stronger: Ryan Anderson, Alexis Broderick Neumann, Kristin Celello, Rebecca Davis, Megan Elias, Carol Faulkner, Lauren Kaminsky, Alison Lefkovitz, Susan McKinnon, Elizabeth Pleck, Sarah Potter, Susan Randolph, Kimberley Reilly, Renee Romano, Honor Sachs, Christina Simmons, and, especially, Nick Syrett.

It has been a pleasure working with Cambridge University Press. Debbie Gershenowitz and Chris Tomlins saw the potential in this book from the start. As a first-time author, I have appreciated their aid in navigating the publication process, as well as their unyielding trust in my ability to bring the project to fruition. I am also grateful to Kristina Deusch, Josh Penney, Amy Lee, Ishwarya Mathavan, Stephanie Sakson, and to the two anonymous Cambridge University Press readers, whose feedback has been instrumental.

So many other friends and family members have kept my spirits up as I have inched my way toward finishing this book. Special thanks to Chad Simmons, whose love and companionship ensured that the final stretches of manuscript completion would be a joyful time, and not a stressful one; I am so fortunate to have met him. Thanks also to Megan Stevenson, Tom Grosheider, Shannon Riffe, Matt Burton, Catherine Clinton, Renee Romano, Marcus Bachhuber, Mollie Firestone, Rebecca Kirchheimer, Katherine Hill, Amanda Pettit-Shaheen, George and Becky Macko, and Kathy Coykendall for their friendship and loyalty. Additional thanks to Meghan Katzenberger and the entire staff at Niedlov's Breadworks, who have endured my constant presence through the years. I can think of no better workspace, and no kinder souls.

This book would not exist without Mike Macko, who has been my most reliable editor, critic, and cheerleader for nearly a decade. He has read more incarnations of each chapter than any reasonable human should be expected to do, and his unwavering enthusiasm for the project has been its secret lifeline. While our relationship has transformed through the years, my devotion and gratitude remain steadfast.

My brother-in-law, Brian Bockelman, and my sister, Emma Kuby, have been the best sibling-colleagues a young historian could ask for. It has been a particular privilege to tackle the daunting steps of first book production in tandem with Emma, whose encouragement (and commiseration) helped me to push through time and again. Last, I want to acknowledge my parents, Pamela Goldberg Kuby and Mark Kuby. A few lines could never do justice to the two people who have given me everything I have. But for the purposes of this specific project, I want to thank them for showing me the beauty of a loving and selfless marriage while also wholeheartedly embracing my own predilection for conjugal misconduct. This book is for them.

Introduction

This is a book about marriages that breached borders. Some of these marriages involved couples who wed across state lines, literally crossing geographic boundaries to ensure the validity of their unions. Others involved couples who defied legislation in their quest to exchange vows, actively breaching the divide between lawful and unlawful nuptials. All of the marriages examined in this book breached a more abstract set of borders – those ideological boundaries between decent and indecent, reputable and disreputable, moral and immoral. Moreover, all of these marginal marriages sparked extensive backlash, and deepened the early twentieth-century fear that the institution of marriage was in a state of crisis.

Many types of marriages occupied that hazy space between legitimate and illegitimate from the turn of the twentieth century through the Second World War, and *Conjugal Misconduct* examines a diverse array of them. The first type of marital nonconformity in question involves couples who found one another through newspaper personal advertisements and matchmaking bureaus. These individuals looked beyond the geographic borders that typically limited one's spousal options, using the US mails to broaden their romantic possibilities. Critics of such practices accused participants of using an impersonal and immoral mechanism to seek companionship and of letting mercenary motives compromise their quest for love. Meanwhile, the operators of matchmaking bureaus and matrimonial journals faced criticism for exploiting the loneliness of single people and for trivializing the institution of marriage in the name of profit.

The next set of individuals in question took part in a phenomenon known interchangeably as "progressive polygamy," "consecutive polygamy," and "tandem polygamy." A person acquired the label of progressive polygamist after divorcing one partner and remarrying another in rapid succession, flouting the expectation that marriage be a lifelong commitment. In many states, hasty remarriage after divorce was an unlawful practice; as a result, people who longed to marry new spouses in the days or months after getting divorced might elope in neighboring states with looser remarriage codes. Such unions did not always hold up in courts of law after the newlyweds returned home.

Couples might also cross state borders to evade eugenic marriage laws. These laws, which were passed in several states during the 1910s, demanded that couples prove they were free from syphilis, among other physical and mental conditions, before they could exchange vows. Many couples refused to undergo medical testing as a prerequisite for marriage: some were unwilling to pay for expensive antibody tests, others knew they would not pass the doctor's examination, and still others objected to eugenic marriage laws in principle. Still wishing to wed, however, a portion of these noncompliant couples dodged their home states' eugenic requirements by eloping to states with more lenient marriage laws, risking fines and jail time upon returning home.

Another practice that pushed the boundaries of matrimonial propriety was widely known as trial marriage. The term "trial marriage" was used to describe several marital configurations. Some couples were ambivalent about committing to a lifetime together, particularly when they resided in states with stringent divorce codes. Recognizing this reluctance, a set of early twentieth-century scholars argued that childless couples should be able to end their unions without great legal impediment, using the term "trial marriage" to define this arrangement. The expression was also employed to describe the relations of celebrity couples who wed on the condition that they would break off their nuptials if either party became unsatisfied. These provisional unions were particularly popular within upper-class bohemian circles, and they tended to generate extensive – and overwhelmingly skeptical – newspaper coverage. Finally, the term "trial marriage" came to encompass marriages between underage couples, who in some states held the legal option to annul their unions as long as one or both partners remained below the age of consent. Despite the differences between these three domestic models, critics indiscriminately labeled them "trial marriage" as a means of stigmatizing couples who were not committed to permanent wedlock.

Marriage across racial borders also produced great anxiety. Long the source of legal and cultural conflict, black-white intermarriage challenged marital tradition in novel ways throughout the 1920s and 1930s. Thirty of forty-eight states held firm antimiscegenation laws in these years, and many would continue to enforce such laws until the Supreme Court declared them unconstitutional with its 1967 *Loving v. Virginia* decision. Nonetheless, vibrant public debates over interracial intimacy arose in states where marriage across racial lines was legal, and the increasing visibility of mixed-race couples sparked ongoing efforts to erase intermarriage through new legislation and judicial loopholes. Meanwhile, a small but vocal group of writers fed into the debate by advertising widespread interracial marriage as a strategy for dissolving the color line and instilling racial harmony throughout the country.

Challenges to marital convention, what I refer to as acts of conjugal misconduct, fed an ever-deepening fear that the institution of marriage was losing its luster. The unconventional marriages I discuss throughout the book led to ongoing forms of conservative backlash. That backlash manifested itself in the legal sphere, as state and local lawmakers sought to temper conjugal misconduct with restrictions on commercialized matchmaking, hasty remarriage, trial marriage, and other disreputable unions. Backlash also emerged outside the law, culminating in the development of a coercive marriage education and counseling movement that came to prominence in the 1930s. This movement, to be explored in the book's final chapter, arose when a group of educators and social scientists determined that law alone was insufficient to tackle the "marriage crisis" at hand. In response, they devised a program of counseling, coursework, and cultural indoctrination to restore their vision of marital tradition to a society that was exploring new options.

The marital nonconformists profiled in this book received outsized attention for their irregular romantic practices. They were by no means the first to defy marital convention, however, as several nineteenth-century groups had gained notoriety for shunning formal state and religious marriage ceremonies, encouraging nonprocreative intercourse, discouraging monogamy, and establishing large and elaborate kin networks rather than discrete nuclear family units. Some of these groups, such as the Free Lovers, rejected the institution of marriage altogether and publicly argued for its dismantling. Others, among them the Mormons and the

Oneida community, practiced nonmonogamous forms of matrimony. In spite of their many ideological differences, these nineteenth-century groups were united in their self-conscious efforts to create alternatives to monogamous marriage.[1]

Such vocal challenges to the marital status quo would diminish in the late nineteenth century alongside Anthony Comstock's crusade against obscenity and the circulation of information about birth control. Comstock's advocacy led Congress to pass a law in 1873, widely known as the Comstock Act, which criminalized the circulation of any "obscene, lewd or lascivious" materials through the US mails. Radical groups were subject to great persecution under the Comstock Act for publicizing their unconventional views on sexuality and marriage, and as a result of Comstock's persistent attacks, these groups ceased to broadcast their message by century's end.[2]

The relationships examined in this book simultaneously drew from and discarded earlier challenges to traditional marriage. While nineteenth-century radical groups attempted to eliminate major tenets of American marriage such as monogamy and reproduction, the twentieth-century subjects of the book sought to bring their own disreputable romantic arrangements within the confines of marital propriety. And while many nineteenth-century sex radicals wished to eradicate the institution of marriage altogether, the twentieth-century couples hoped to attain marital legitimacy and the social status that accompanied it. Nineteenth-century marital nonconformists ultimately withered under a legal code that deemed their relations immoral and obscene. Later

---

[1] See Helen Lefkowitz Horowitz, *Rereading Sex: Battles over Sexual Knowledge and Suppression in Nineteenth-Century America* (New York: Alfred A. Knopf, 2002); Joanne E. Passet, *Sex Radicals and the Quest for Women's Equality* (Urbana: University of Illinois Press, 2003); John D'Emilio and Estelle B. Freedman, *Intimate Matters: A History of Sexuality in America* (New York: Harper & Row, 1988), 109–138; Nancy F. Cott, *Public Vows: A History of Marriage and the Nation* (Cambridge, Mass.: Harvard University Press, 2000), 105–131; Hal D. Sears, *The Sex Radicals: Free Love in High Victorian America* (Lawrence: Regents Press of Kansas, 1977); Sarah Barringer Gordon, *The Mormon Question: Polygamy and Constitutional Conflict in Nineteenth-Century America* (Chapel Hill: University of North Carolina Press, 2002); Clare Virginia Eby, *Until Choice Do Us Part: Marriage Reform in the Progressive Era* (Chicago: University of Chicago Press, 2014), 7.

[2] D'Emilio and Freedman, *Intimate Matters*, 159–163; Horowitz, *Rereading Sex*, 358–385; Cott, *Public Vows*, 124–131; Christina Simmons, *Making Marriage Modern: Women's Sexuality from the Progressive Era to World War II* (New York: Oxford University Press, 2009), 9.

participants in nontraditional marital arrangements hoped to avoid similar persecution.[3]

* * *

Why, then, did acts of conjugal misconduct spark so much backlash at the turn of the twentieth century? To understand this backlash, one must first understand the broader transformations that the institution of marriage underwent throughout the 1800s. Marriage in the nineteenth century was grounded in the law of coverture. Under that doctrine, a husband and wife were one person in law. Thus, a married woman became a *feme covert* – her rights to own property, to earn wages, and to sue in a court of law were "covered" by the authority of her husband, who in return provided protection and support to his wife and family. Through this arrangement, the husband was expected to function as breadwinner, and the wife to maintain an orderly home. Though a wife might need to earn wages to supplement her husband's income, the law of coverture ensured that those wages remained the property of the husband, even if he was unemployed and generating no income of his own. Laws of coverture thus ensured that the relationship between husband and wife remained one of protector and dependent.[4]

Related to the doctrine of coverture was the idea that marriage served primarily as an economic arrangement. Although Western European and North American couples started to marry for love in the early eighteenth century, economic and political factors continued to play a major role in mate selection throughout the 1800s.[5] Over the course of the nineteenth

---

[3] Eby makes a similar point in her discussion of progressive marital reform: "Unlike more radical experimenters such as free-lovers, Greenwich Village bohemians, Mormon polygynists, or hippies, progressives sought to reform – not replace – long-term, monogamous heterosexual pairings." *Until Choice Do Us Part*, 7.

[4] Amy Dru Stanley, *From Bondage to Contract: Wage Labor, Marriage, and the Market in the Age of Slave Emancipation* (New York: Cambridge University Press, 1998); Norma Basch, *In the Eyes of the Law: Women, Marriage, and Property in Nineteenth-Century New York* (Ithaca: Cornell University Press, 1982); Marylynn Salmon, *Women and the Law of Property in Early America* (Chapel Hill: University of North Carolina Press, 1986); Peter W. Bardaglio, *Reconstructing the Household: Families, Sex, and the Law in the Nineteenth-Century South* (Chapel Hill: University of North Carolina Press, 1995), 31–32; Timothy Marr, "The Shifting Monument of American Marriage," *American Quarterly* 53, no. 4 (2001): 692; Loren Schweninger, *Families in Crisis in the Old South: Divorce, Slavery, and the Law* (Chapel Hill: University of North Carolina Press, 2012), 80–97.

[5] Stephanie Coontz, *Marriage, a History: How Love Conquered Marriage* (New York: Penguin, 2005), 145–146.

century, a marriage was generally considered successful if the bride and groom's families held comparable levels of wealth and similar social positions. A young man from an affluent family could increase his status by marrying a young woman from a similar financial background, and she would benefit in return. By seeking economic equals as marriage partners, wealthy brides and grooms protected themselves from social climbers who saw marriage as a path to high society living.[6] Poorer couples also viewed marriage as a means of consolidating family resources, increasing labor forces, and improving chances for land and property acquisition.[7] For poor and working-class individuals, these practical concerns did not always leave room for questions of romance and personal affinity in the formation of conjugal partnerships.

Gradually the economic model of mate selection faded from view, and by the turn of twentieth century it had been replaced by the notion that romantic love, emotional intimacy, and sexual fulfillment were the staples of a successful union.[8] This shift toward personal choice in mate selection came with risks, however, in allowing the possibility that an individual might select a socially inappropriate partner. What was to be done, for instance, if a young man wed across racial or class lines, or if he wished to marry a woman with a venereal disease? How could the celebration of individual choice be reconciled with the many other social codes that dictated the boundaries of marital propriety? In this sense, the modern ideal of love and personal compatibility stood at odds with the fear that too much free choice prevented individuals from selecting socially appropriate mates.

Accentuating this tension was an underlying social panic over the shifting tides of gender and sexuality. As industrial growth led more

---

[6] See Charlene M. Boyer Lewis, *Ladies and Gentlemen on Display: Planter Society at the Virginia Springs, 1790–1860* (Charlottesville: University Press of Virginia, 2001), 145–150; Elizabeth Fox-Genovese, *Within the Plantation Household: Black and White Women of the Old South* (Chapel Hill: University of North Carolina Press, 1988), 207; Steven M. Stowe, *Intimacy and Power in the Old South: Ritual in the Lives of the Planters* (Baltimore: Johns Hopkins University Press, 1987), 150.

[7] Bertram Wyatt-Brown, *Southern Honor: Ethics and Behavior in the Old South* (New York: Oxford University Press, 1982), 217–222.

[8] George Chauncey, *Gay New York: Gender, Urban Culture, and the Making of the Gay Male World, 1890–1940* (New York: Basic Books, 1994), 117; Lewis A. Erenberg, *Steppin' Out: New York Nightlife and the Transformation of American Culture, 1890–1930* (Chicago: University of Chicago Press, 1981), 155–156. Industrialization and urbanization in the late 1800s played an indirect role in this shift. See William Leach, *Land of Desire: Merchants, Power, and the Rise of a New American Culture* (New York: Pantheon, 1993), 5–6.

and more women into urban employment and recreation, middle-class reformers feared the moral temptations that might entice young women in the public sphere. Between the 1870s and 1910s, state and federal officials made persistent attempts to restrict female sexuality through the enactment and enforcement of laws prohibiting prostitution, contraception, abortion, homosexuality, adultery, and the circulation of obscene materials.[9] In 1910, Congress passed the Mann Act, also known as the White Slave Traffic Act. This law made it a federal offense for men to transport women across state borders for the "purpose of prostitution or debauchery, or for any other immoral purpose," including acts of consensual sex.[10] Thereafter, vice commissioners sought to close down all city brothels in an effort to eliminate venereal disease and other social evils from urban districts.[11]

Adolescents became prime targets of moral reform as youthful sexual experimentation increased in visibility. A growing number of turn-of-the-century brides exchanged vows while pregnant, and studies revealed that more and more adolescents engaged in premarital sexual activity.[12] The issue of youthful sex became all the more prevalent in 1890, when the US Census Bureau added "age of marriage" as a category. Between 1890 and 1930, the census revealed that approximately 343,000 women married at

---

[9] Mary E. Odem, *Delinquent Daughters: Protecting and Policing Adolescent Female Sexuality in the United States, 1885–1920* (Chapel Hill: University of North Carolina Press, 1995); Catherine Cocks, "Rethinking Sexuality in the Progressive Era," *Journal of the Gilded Age and Progressive Era* 5, no. 2 (2006): 93–118; Lawrence M. Friedman, *Guarding Life's Dark Secrets: Legal and Social Controls over Reputation, Propriety, and Privacy* (Stanford: Stanford University Press, 2007), 171–191.

[10] Joanna L. Grossman and Lawrence M. Friedman, *Inside the Castle: Law and the Family in 20th Century America* (Princeton: Princeton University Press, 2011), 110; Angus McLaren, *Sexual Blackmail: A Modern History* (Cambridge, Mass.: Harvard University Press, 2002), 82–92; Jennifer Fronc, *New York Undercover: Private Surveillance in the Progressive Era* (Chicago: University of Chicago Press, 2009), 30, 183–184.

[11] Friedman, *Guarding Life's Dark Secrets*, 186; Allan M. Brandt, *No Magic Bullet: A Social History of Venereal Disease in the United States since 1880*, expanded ed. (New York: Oxford University Press, 1987), 70–77; Timothy J. Gilfoyle, *City of Eros: New York City, Prostitution, and the Commercialization of Sex, 1790–1920* (New York: W. W. Norton, 1992), 177–178, 306–312; Elizabeth Alice Clement, *Love for Sale: Courting, Treating, and Prostitution in New York City, 1900–1945* (Chapel Hill: University of North Carolina Press, 2006), 125–143.

[12] Elaine Tyler May, *Great Expectations: Marriage and Divorce in Post-Victorian America* (Chicago: University of Chicago Press, 1980), 94; Kathy Peiss, *Cheap Amusements: Working Women and Leisure in Turn-of-the-Century New York* (Philadelphia: Temple University Press, 1986), 109–110.

or below the age of fifteen.[13] Reformers worried that teenage sexual activity would increase as unchaperoned young women continued to enter the workforce and to mingle with men in factories and dance halls.[14] To counter these fears, many states raised the age of consent in the early twentieth century, making it illegal for adult men to have sexual intercourse with underage women. While the standard age of consent had been set at ten in the nineteenth century, most states now raised that age to sixteen or eighteen, classifying once-common acts of consensual sex as statutory rape. In altering these laws, legislators affirmed the widespread public belief that young women were engaging too freely in sexual activity.[15]

Anxiety over women's sexual expression also related to marriage, as critics came to resent the gradual embrace of sexuality and camaraderie as tenets of married life – a transformation that culminated with the development of companionate marriage in the 1920s. As historian Christina Simmons notes, supporters of companionate marriage recognized sex as the "glue of marriage," and they therefore advised couples to establish healthy sexual relations as a way to strengthen their unions. Attempting to separate sex from reproduction, proponents encouraged the use of birth control, which allowed couples to enjoy sex without fear of pregnancy.[16] The rise of companionate marriage worried critics in its acknowledgment of women's capacity for sexual pleasure and in its indication that the primary purpose of marriage need not be a procreative one. It also deepened concerns that gender roles within modern marriages had become too equitable.[17]

---

[13] Mary E. Richmond and Fred S. Hall, *Child Marriages* (New York: Russell Sage Foundation, 1925), 57.

[14] May, *Great Expectations*, 94–99. See also Peiss, *Cheap Amusements*; Odem, *Delinquent Daughters*, 2–3, 21–25.

[15] *Conte v. Conte*, 81 N.Y.S. 923 (1903); McLaren, *Sexual Blackmail*, 83–84; Stephen Robertson, *Crimes against Children: Sexual Violence and Legal Culture in New York City, 1880–1960* (Chapel Hill: University of North Carolina Press, 2005), 95–135; Grossman and Friedman, *Inside the Castle*, 110; Friedman, *Guarding Life's Dark Secrets*, 182–183; Odem, *Delinquent Daughters*, 8–37. The age of consent for marriage also rose in many states during these decades: see Nicholas L. Syrett, *American Child Bride: A History of Minors and Marriage in the United States* (Chapel Hill: University of North Carolina Press, 2016), 127–135.

[16] Simmons, *Making Marriage Modern*, 121–137. See also Coontz, *Marriage, a History*, 191–215; Gilfoyle, *City of Eros*, 311–312; Steven Mintz and Susan Kellogg, *Domestic Revolutions: A Social History of American Family Life* (New York: Free Press, 1988), 114–116.

[17] D'Emilio and Freedman, *Intimate Matters*, 266; David R. Shumway, *Modern Love: Romance, Intimacy, and the Marriage Crisis* (New York: New York University Press, 2003), 67–68.

Also central to early twentieth-century anxieties over marriage was the rising popularity of divorce. Between 1870 and 1900, the divorce rate doubled from two of every thousand marriages to four per thousand. Over the first two decades of the new century the rate nearly doubled again, from four divorces per thousand marriages in 1900 to 7.7 per thousand in 1920. By 1924, one out of every seven marriages ended in divorce, approximately fifteen or sixteen times the divorce rate of 1870.[18] Conservative critics castigated divorcees, with particular attention to the moral failings of divorced women; as historian Kristin Celello notes of this era, "'evil' was the word most frequently paired with 'divorce' in the popular press and in religious and legal circles."[19] To many detractors, divorce was a negative consequence of women's entrance into the political realm. In 1912, for instance, Catholic cardinal James Gibbons warned St. Louis men that the passage of a women's suffrage amendment would further exacerbate the divorce rate. "If woman had equal political rights with men there is a probability that on the slightest provocation she would seek divorce," Gibbons insisted. "Women under present conditions are too prone to go to the divorce courts, and political equality might make them more so."[20] In such cases, concerns over divorce reflected a fear that women were fleeing their traditional roles as mothers and wives, and embracing new legal and social opportunities that had formerly been denied to them.[21]

Alongside this preoccupation with the divorce rate was a concern that the American family was under threat. As historian Mary Odem explains, progressive reformers feared that alcohol, poverty, and overcrowding led to the deterioration of family units and contributed to female delinquency. Reformers thus pushed working-class and immigrant families to

[18] William Fielding Ogburn, "Eleven Questions Concerning American Marriages," *Social Forces* 6, no. 1 (1927): 7; Simmons, *Making Marriage Modern*, 112; May, *Great Expectations*, 2; Cott, *Public Vows*, 106–107; Rebecca L. Davis, *More Perfect Unions: The American Search for Marital Bliss* (Cambridge, Mass.: Harvard University Press, 2010), 17–19; Eby, *Until Choice Do Us Part*, 25–35; Mintz and Kellogg, *Domestic Revolutions*, 107–110. On the increasing divorce rate, May writes, "Between 1867 and 1929, the population of the United States increased 300 percent, the number of marriages 400 percent, and the divorce rate 2,000 percent."
[19] Kristin Celello, *Making Marriage Work: A History of Marriage and Divorce in the Twentieth-Century United States* (Chapel Hill: University of North Carolina Press, 2009), 21.
[20] "Gibbons Fears for Women," *New York Times*, 18 Sep. 1912, p. 1.
[21] Robert L. Griswold, *Family and Divorce in California, 1850–1890: Victorian Illusions and Everyday Realities* (Albany: State University of New York Press, 1982), 172–175.

embrace a middle-class domestic structure. They encouraged the formation of nuclear families consisting of a breadwinning father, a stay-at-
home mother, and two or three children, all of whom lived together in a
private home with no boarders. Central to this campaign was the notion
that poor parents were having too many children and that adolescent
daughters growing up in overcrowded households were prone to lives of
sexual depravity.[22]

While some progressives worried that working-class parents were
having too many children, others feared that increasing numbers of
educated white women were abstaining from marriage and motherhood
altogether. In 1906, President Theodore Roosevelt raised the alarm over
educated women's decisions to pursue careers at the expense of family. In
his Sixth Annual Message to Congress, Roosevelt bemoaned the declining
birth rate among white, upper-class women and the high birth rate among
working-class immigrant populations. He chastised unmarried and childless women, arguing that their decision not to procreate would lead to
"race suicide" or the disappearance of the white middle class. He also
denounced those women who opted out of marriage and motherhood as
"race traitors," and he rebuked them for their "viciousness, coldness, and
shallow-heartedness."[23] Such hostilities would persist in the 1910s and
1920s as the white middle-class birth rate continued to fall.[24]

This backdrop of anxiety over shifting sexual, marital, and reproductive mores helps to explain why the subjects of this book received such
outsized attention for nuptials that might strike today's readers as less
than scandalous affairs. The varied marital practices in question here, if
tepid by contemporary standards, fed into broader turn-of-the-century
concerns that the institutions of marriage and family were in states of
decay. Amid public worries over declining sexual values, critics came to
view shifting marital demographics – a decrease in the number of couples
exchanging vows, a mounting divorce rate, and a rising age of first

---

[22] Odem, *Delinquent Daughters*, 104–108.

[23] Laura L. Lovett, *Conceiving the Future: Pronatalism, Reproduction, and the Family in
the United States, 1890–1938* (Chapel Hill: University of North Carolina Press, 2007),
91–93; Jackie M. Blount, "Spinsters, Bachelors, and Other Gender Transgressors in
School Employment, 1850–1990," *Review of Educational Research* 70, no. 1 (2000):
88; Brandt, *No Magic Bullet*, 7–8; Davis, *More Perfect Unions*, 25; Simmons, *Making
Marriage Modern*, 20, 95; Elaine Tyler May, *Barren in the Promised Land: Childless
Americans and the Pursuit of Happiness* (New York: Basic Books, 1995), 61–64.

[24] Wendy Kline, *Building a Better Race: Gender, Sexuality and Eugenics from the Turn of
the Century to the Baby Boom* (Berkeley: University of California Press, 2001), 62.

marriage for men and women – as the stuff of emergency. In this context, any unions that pushed legal and cultural boundaries were vulnerable to backlash.

The phrase "marriage crisis" is one that historians have used to describe this sense of panic over a perceived deterioration in matrimonial standards, and the fear that these shifting marital trends were signs of broader national decline.[25] While the marriage counselors I examine in my final chapter popularized the term in the late 1920s, they did not coin its usage in the United States. Rather, American journalists employed the phrase frequently in the early twentieth century to address European marital patterns. They used it in articles about French women's growing tendency to delay marriage and childrearing, or to reject them altogether; they cited the sharp rise in the German divorce rate, and the accompanying decline in national marriage and birth rates, as signs of a growing marriage crisis; they also used the term in discussing the massive loss of British male life in the First World War, predicting an increase in unmarried English women.[26] As the century progressed, reformers started applying this term to American marriages as well, using it to articulate anxieties over divorce and reproduction, as well as shifting gender roles within matrimony. Though the phrase "marriage crisis" identified a wide and indefinite array of practices, it spoke to a growing sense that American marital trends were taking an undesirable turn, and to the belief that stable family life would be the greatest casualty of these changes.

State legislators responded to the perceived marriage crisis, consistently implementing new laws to prohibit commercialized matchmaking, progressive polygamy, and other forms of conjugal misconduct. The push

---

[25] In their comparative study of global marriage crises, Kristin Celello and Hanan Kholoussy offer a general explanation of why outcries over marriage crisis emerge: "They may arise when marriage or divorce rates are increasing, or when they are declining. Alarm bells may ring because the kinds of unions that are taking place, such as interracial, interreligious, child, and same-sex marriages, are judged not to be in the nation's interest. Some crises are about trying to hold on to 'traditional' forms of marriage, while others are about eliminating nuptial traditions in pursuit of modernity." Kristin Celello and Hanan Kholoussy, introduction to *Domestic Tensions, National Anxieties: Global Perspectives on Marriage, Crisis, and Nation*, ed. Kristin Celello and Hanan Kholoussy (New York: Oxford University Press, 2016), 3.

[26] "France's Marriage Crisis," *New York Times*, 16 Mar. 1902, p. 7; "French Marriage Ideals Some Two Centuries Ago," *Courier Journal* (Louisville), 26 Sep. 1909, sec. 3, p. 3; "Germans Discover a 'Marriage Crisis,'" *New York Times*, 21 Nov. 1913, p. 3; "Germany's 'Marriage Crisis,'" *Washington Post*, 22 Nov. 1913, p. 6; "The 'Marriage Crisis' Abroad," *York Daily* (Pa.), 27 Mar. 1915, p. 4; W. L. George, "Women after the War," *Chicago Daily Tribune*, 18 Apr. 1915, sec. 2, p. 5.

and pull between the couples who defied traditional marital norms and the lawmakers who hoped to temper their defiance is a central topic of this book; attention to both marital nonconformity and the backlash against it allows us to see the ever-fluctuating contours of marriage law, and to recognize the role that acts of conjugal misconduct played in shaping and reshaping those boundaries. Judges also participated in this negotiation over twentieth-century marriage law, and their rulings often illustrate the amorphous legal logic at the heart of debates over matrimony. Amid concerns that marriage had reached a state of crisis, judges frequently centered their decisions about whether to validate or invalidate marriages on the question of whether or not these unions aligned with "public policy." In stating that a marital arrangement was contrary to public policy, judges were able to nullify relationships they deemed inappropriate without offering specific justifications for their actions. This imprecise legal language was grounded not in legislation or judicial precedent, but rather in a broad suggestion that the union in question was morally indecent by its very nature.

Judges applied the term "contrary to public policy" with increasing regularity in early twentieth-century marriage cases. In insisting that particular types of marriage defied public policy, judges sought to rein in the marital relations that offended them or, in the words of historian Hendrik Hartog, "to reimpose marital identities, wifedom and husbandom, on those who had exceeded the limits of normal variation." Judges' public policy justifications raise questions in their general vagueness, their allusion to Christian ideals, and their frequent lack of attention to legal doctrine. In many of these marriage cases, judges presented their rulings as obvious, uncontroversial, and widely agreed upon notions of marital propriety. As Hartog argues, "twentieth-century judges understood themselves as articulating a common sense shared with legislators and the educated public. All knew what was and what was not 'fundamental' to marriage." This assumption of a shared public understanding of marital fundaments allowed courts to dodge legislative intricacies and instead to ground their rulings in more subjective moral codes.[27]

---

[27] Hendrik Hartog, *Man and Wife in America: A History* (Cambridge, Mass.: Harvard University Press, 2000), 302–304. Hartog was not the first scholar to address the ambiguities of public policy rhetoric in judicial rulings. In a 1935 law review article, Walter Gellhorn discussed judges' use of public policy justifications for invalidating contracts. He argued that some courts "have refused to lend their aid to contracts which they deemed to be contrary to public policy. They have exercised their inherent power to avoid permitting their process to be used for antisocial ends – exercised this power not

The sensational press played a role in shaping those moral codes and in feeding the public perception that a marriage crisis was under way. As we shall see, journalists reported widely on varied forms of conjugal misconduct, and their frenzied attention to dysgenic marriages, trial marriages, and the like attached a note of scandal to practices that might otherwise have flown under the radar. The growth of the mass circulation press ensured the proliferation of such stories; the total number of American newspapers rose from 4,051 in 1860 to 18,793 in 1899, and the circulation of major journals increased considerably during these years. Newspaper syndication, which reached new heights of popularity at the turn of the twentieth century, also extended the reach of the press. As more and more local papers began to acquire items from centralized news syndicates, the circulation of information surged. In one literary historian's estimation, a single news story could now reach as many as a thousand newspapers across the nation, thus ensuring that any published account of an unconventional union, however embellished, would find wide readership.[28]

* * *

Attention to the numerous participants in early twentieth-century debates over marital propriety illustrates the necessity of considering both the legal and cultural forces that shaped marital norms. The chapters of this book thus illuminate the ongoing exchange between marital nonconformists and the legal and judicial authorities who sought to repress them. But participants in conjugal misconduct also provoked responses from journalists, as well as clergy, social reformers, and other supporters and

because legislatively directed to do so in a particular case, but because, in their own discretion, they deemed such an exercise necessary as a protection of the public welfare against noxious consequences." In an article from that same year, Blanche Crozier observed, "In the gelatinous territory of public policy the great criterion is reasonableness." Walter Gellhorn, "Contracts and Public Policy," *Columbia Law Review* 35, no. 5 (1935): 684–685; Blanche Crozier, "Constitutionality of Discrimination Based on Sex," *Boston University Law Review* 15 (1935): 753. See also Ernst Freund, *The Police Power, Public Policy and Constitutional Rights* (Chicago: University of Chicago Press, 1904); George W. Wickersham, "The Police Power, a Product of the Rule of Reason," *Harvard Law Review* 27, no. 4 (1914): 297–298; Ray A. Brown, "Police Power – Legislation for Health and Personal Safety," *Harvard Law Review* 42, no. 7 (1929): 866–898; "Marriage, Contracts, and Public Policy," *Harvard Law Review* 54, no. 3 (1941): 473–482.
[28] Charles A. Johanningsmeier, *Fiction and the American Literary Marketplace: The Role of Newspaper Syndicates in America, 1860–1900* (New York: Cambridge University Press, 1997), 1, 17–18.

critics whose voices similarly helped to shape the amorphous boundaries of marriage. A focus on legislation alone prevents us from plumbing the depths of the era's marriage debates.

Furthermore, the very notion of "marriage legislation" is a fraught one, as marriage laws varied from state to state and thus were never a unified force. One state might have denied a man the right to marry a new wife for a year after divorcing his previous one, while a neighboring state might have held no restrictions on remarriage. Some states held strict regulations on racial intermarriage, while others held no antimiscegenation laws whatsoever. The diversity of state marriage laws prevents us from making generalizations about American marriage policy; even more significantly, differences in state laws were one of the primary *causes* of the perceived marriage crisis. The lack of uniformity in state marriage codes incited many acts of conjugal misconduct, as couples took advantage of inconsistent state laws in hopes of attaining the marital status they desired.

In this sense, state borders could serve as battle lines across which two opposing legal definitions of marriage waged war. One common weapon for a state with lenient laws was the presence of a marriage mill near its border. Marriage mills, also referred to as "Gretna Greens" in reference to the Scottish town famous for hosting the nuptials of fleeing English couples, were cities and towns that encouraged easy elopement. They were easily accessible to residents of neighboring states, and they allowed couples to wed quickly and without obstruction. States with marriage mills rarely required couples to announce their intention to wed in advance, and some of them permitted teenagers to exchange vows with relative ease. Therefore, young residents of a state with a high age of marital consent had the option, finances permitting, to take a train or ferry across state borders and to marry at a nearby Gretna Green. The frequency of such elopements became a source of scandal in the early century.

The tangled history of elopement in Pennsylvania, New Jersey, Delaware, and Maryland provides an in-depth example of how disparate state marriage laws intensified the sense of marriage crisis pervading the nation. For several decades, lawmakers in these four states struggled to determine which hoops couples ought to jump through on their paths to the altar, often crafting legislation that directly contradicted statutes in neighboring states. Starting in the 1880s, reporters from Pennsylvania and Delaware complained that Camden, New Jersey, had devolved into the most infamous marriage mill in the mid-Atlantic. This reputation resulted from Camden's proximity to Philadelphia, and from conflicting marriage laws in Pennsylvania and New Jersey. Specifically, Pennsylvania law required that couples attain a license from the state court before they wed, whereas New Jersey law did not compel couples to acquire a marriage license at all. Pennsylvania's requirement thwarted many unlawful unions in that state, particularly ones involving underage couples, who were seldom able to trick court officials into granting them licenses. Meanwhile, the lack of such a requirement in New Jersey meant that two partners could proceed directly to a Garden State justice of the peace if they wished to wed.[29]

While New Jersey officiants knew that they too were expected to uphold the state's marriage laws, a number of Camden ministers gained notoriety for their willingness to join ineligible couples in matrimony for the right price. The mere five miles separating Philadelphia from Camden made it easy for so-called mercenary ministers to arrange an unlawful exchange of vows. Some ministers worked with local taxi drivers to recruit newly arrived couples. Hoping to exploit the Philadelphia couples who took the Market Street Ferry across the Delaware River into Camden, the minsters paid taxi drivers to pick up couples at the ferry landing and to transport them to the altar.[30]

These youthful elopements brought negative publicity to Camden, particularly when they involved criminal activity. One such case emerged in 1894, when Philadelphia Judge James Gay Gordon denounced Reverend William Burrell for overseeing the union of thirty-three-year-old William Eamwood, whom Gordon described as a "full-grown man of degraded appearance" to Dora Hart, a "simple and ignorant child" of fifteen.[31] In apparent response to Camden's ongoing elopement scandals, New Jersey revised its marriage law in 1897, requiring that any out-of-state couple wishing to wed there must procure a license from the clerk of the county where the nuptials were to take place. With these new regulations, Camden ceased to function as a Gretna Green for out-of-state elopers, much to the chagrin of clergymen such as Burrell, who, it was

---

[29] "The Camden Marriage Mill," *The Times* (Philadelphia), 22 Apr. 1894, p. 6; "The Camden Marriage Mill," *The Times*, 17 May 1894, p. 4; "A Mockery of Marriage," *Morning News* (Wilmington, Del.), 23 Apr. 1894, p. 4; "Professional Marriage Mills," *Scranton Republican*, 25 Apr. 1894, p. 4.

[30] "Burrell Boycotted," *The Times*, 13 Feb. 1889, p. 2; "The Jersey 'Marriage Mills,'" *Trenton Evening Times*, 16 Feb. 1897, p. 2.

[31] "Dr. Burrell Gets a Rebuke," *The Times*, 21 Apr. 1894, p. 1; "A Mockery of Marriage," 4; "Professional Marriage Mills," 4.

estimated, would lose between $15,000 and $20,000 per year with the loss of this lucrative marriage market.[32]

Shortly thereafter, ministers in Wilmington, Delaware, began taking advantage of the changes to New Jersey's marriage law. By 1901, newspapers were reporting regularly on Philadelphia couples who made the thirty-mile trip into Wilmington to wed. Though not as convenient as Camden, Wilmington became a popular destination for eloping Pennsylvanians, primarily because Delaware did not require couples to publish their marriage licenses before exchanging vows – a process referred to as "posting the banns." Moreover, in Delaware, couples could buy those licenses directly from justices of the peace, rather than make a separate trip to the courthouse.[33] The Wilmington press quickly launched a smear campaign against the local marriage mill. Journalists wrote disapprovingly that Wilmington had become a hotbed for interfaith marriages, interracial unions, nuptials between first cousins, marriages between teenagers, and – more insidiously – marriages between adults and youth below the age of consent.[34]

Throughout the first decade of the 1900s, Wilmington saw an ever-increasing marriage rate. The city's Board of Health reported 1,061 Wilmington unions in 1901, and that number grew incrementally with each year, increasing to 4,592 marriages in 1910. As these numbers grew, the local press noted the great wealth such unions brought into the pockets of participating clergy, and into the county treasury.[35] Reporters also told familiar tales about the network of entrepreneurs contributing to the marriage mill's operations, with attention to the railroad workers and cab drivers who could spot eloping couples from blocks away. These employers knew where to take the incoming couples

---

[32] "New Jersey's New Marriage Law," *Reading Times* (Pa.), 4 Jun. 1897, p. 2; "No Gretna Green," *Anaconda Standard* (Mont.), 9 Jul. 1897, p. 3; "The Marriage Mill Shut Down," *The Times*, 20 Jul. 1897, p. 4.

[33] "Philadelphians Married," *Morning News*, 21 Jun. 1901, p. 1; "Gretna Green of the East," *News Journal* (Wilmington), 26 Jun. 1901, p. 2.

[34] "Looking for His Daughter," *Morning News*, 19 Aug. 1901, p. 1; "Positive Groom Was a Negro," *Evening Journal* (Wilmington), 11 Mar. 1905, p. 1; The Marrying of Children," *News Journal*, 9 Jul. 1908, p. 4; "Asks Divorce from Relative," *Evening Journal*, 30 Dec. 1909, p. 5.

[35] "Cupid's Busy Year," *Morning News*, 1 Jan. 1906, p. 1; "Cupid Played Many Pranks," *Evening Journal*, 31 Jul. 1906, p. 2; "Nearly 2500 Marriages in Year," *Evening Journal*, 31 Dec. 1907, p. 1; "Real Gretna Green," *Morning News*, 1 Jan. 1908, p. 8; "Death Rate Low; Birth Rate High," *Evening Journal*, 2 Jan. 1909, p. 1; "Many Weddings in Wilmington," *Morning News*, 1 Jan. 1910, p. 8; "Holds Record," *Morning News*, 2 Jan. 1912, p. 9.

for the speedy exchange of vows, and their work ensured the growth of Wilmington's economy.[36]

Such accounts of voracious railroad attendants and cab drivers seized on anxieties over the phenomenon of white slavery, or the abduction of young white women into the world of prostitution and sexual enslavement. Throughout the first two decades of the twentieth century, countless articles, books, films, and plays documented the processes through which hapless adolescent girls were lured into the underworld of commercialized sex after moving to cities. According to these accounts, young women fell into prostitution in a variety of ways – by accepting offers of housing and employment from scheming men, by unknowingly drinking from drugged glasses while amusing themselves in dance halls, or by accepting false marriage proposals from pimps who later forced them into brothels.[37] While such incidents did sometimes occur in major cities, the unrelenting accounts of white slavery reflected a greater cultural anxiety about changing sexual mores. In the words of historian Peter Filene, "The rhetoric was so frenzied, the claims so exaggerated, the descriptions so lurid, that we must suspect something beyond white slavery and prostitution was alarming the reformers. Their sense of social order was threatened not simply by the 'social evil' corrupting fallen women. Ultimately they felt threatened by the sensuality that was running rampant among their own sons and daughters."[38]

Accounts of naïve adolescents descending onto the train platform in a new and foreign city, only to be picked up by a conniving taxi driver and encouraged to commit to a premature marriage, resembled the white slavery narratives that pervaded popular culture. Whereas those stories were concerned with the well-being of impressionable young women, accounts in

---

[36] "Real Gretna Green," 8.

[37] Peter G. Filene, *Him/Her/Self: Gender Identities in Modern America*, 3rd edition (Baltimore: Johns Hopkins University Press, 1998), 93; Odem, *Delinquent Daughters*, 97–98; Pamela Haag, *Consent: Sexual Rights and the Transformation of American Liberalism* (Ithaca: Cornell University Press, 1999), 63–93; Peiss, *Cheap Amusements*, 98; Kevin J. Mumford, *Interzones: Black/White Sex Districts in Chicago and New York in the Early Twentieth Century* (New York: Columbia University Press, 1997), 13–14; Brian Donovan, *White Slave Crusades: Race, Gender, and Anti-vice Activism, 1887–1917* (Urbana: University of Illinois Press, 2006).

[38] Filene, *Him/Her/Self*, 95. On the rhetoric of white slavery, see also Robertson, *Crimes against Children*, 133; Kali N. Gross, *Colored Amazons: Crime, Violence, and Black Women in the City of Brotherly Love, 1880–1910* (Durham: Duke University Press, 2006), 74–76; Joanne J. Meyerowitz, *Women Adrift: Independent Wage Earners in Chicago, 1880–1930* (Chicago: University of Chicago Press, 1988), 62–63.

Wilmington newspapers described the entrapment of impressionable young heterosexual couples who were tempted by a sinister marital scheme. In crossing the Delaware River to elope in Wilmington, these couples became the victims of an immoral culture with the power to seduce them into lives of depravity. By evoking the rhetoric of white slavery, journalists encouraged readers to save young people from meeting such fates.

Therefore, despite the financial benefits elopements brought to the city, many Wilmington residents sought to overturn the city's reputation as a Gretna Green. By 1907, the backlash against hasty nuptials had grown pronounced enough that Delaware legislators started to rewrite the state's marriage law.[39] The first several attempts brought limited results, but the tide turned with the 1912 election of Governor Charles Miller. Upon entering office, Miller committed himself to eliminating hasty unions. State legislators worked to bring his goal to fruition, and a bill sponsored by Senator Thomas Gormley ultimately brought the downfall of Wilmington's marriage mill. Gormley intended for his bill "to break up the traffic in marriage licenses" in Wilmington, insisting that the city's marriage mill was "simply a branch of the white slave traffic."[40] The bill thus stipulated that only clerks of the peace could issue marriage licenses. It required Delaware residents to attain licenses twenty-four hours before exchanging vows, and it demanded that nonresidents acquire theirs ninety-six hours before the wedding ceremony. The bill also required clerks to record license acquisitions in a publicly accessible record book immediately after issuing them so that community members could object to controversial unions before it was too late. Last, the bill required parental consent for the unions of men under twenty-one and women under eighteen.[41] Speaker of the House Chauncey Holcomb conveyed the urgency of more stringent marriage legislation to representatives before

---

[39] "Lawmakers Up against Cupid," *Evening Journal*, 18 Jan. 1907, p. 1; "Bill to Check Reckless Marriages," *News Journal*, 31 Jan. 1907, p. 5; "Against Gretna Green Marriages," *Evening Journal*, 31 Jan. 1907, p. 4; "Licenses to Wed Come Too Easy," *Evening Journal*, 19 Feb. 1909, p. 5; "Change in Marriage Laws," *Evening Journal*, 8 Feb. 1911, p. 1; "Killed Drexler's Marriage Bill," *Morning News*, 22 Feb. 1911, p. 8; "No Gretna Green under This Law," *Evening Journal*, 15 Mar. 1911, p. 10; "New Law Fails to Balk Cupid," *Evening Journal*, 4 Apr. 1911, p. 10.

[40] "Senate Passes Marriage Bill," *Morning News*, 13 Mar. 1913, p. 1.

[41] Ibid., 1; "Outlawing Gretna Green," *Wilkes-Barre Record*, 27 Jan. 1913, p. 8; "Favorable Report on Marriage Bill," *News Journal*, 28 Feb. 1913, p. 1; R. L. Jackson, "Favors Gormley Marriage Bill," *Evening Journal*, 1 Mar. 1913, p. 4; "Parson Asks for Marriage Law Support," *Evening Journal*, 3 Mar. 1913, p. 5; "Timely Warning," *Evening Journal*, 21 Apr. 1913, p. 4.

they voted on the senate bill, insisting, "No bill will do so much to bring back to Delaware the good name she has lost by the ill advised marriages performed in Wilmington."[42] The bill passed in both houses of the state legislature, and Miller signed it into law in late March of 1913.[43]

The new requirement of four-day residency for out-of-state elopers made it nearly impossible for young Philadelphians to come into Wilmington to marry hastily and without parental consent.[44] But the loss of Wilmington as a site for out-of-state elopement led to the emergence of a new marriage mill: Elkton, Maryland. Elkton was only eighteen miles away from Wilmington, and thus easily accessible to Delaware, Pennsylvania, and New Jersey couples hoping to dodge their states' restrictive marriage laws. There was no residency requirement for marriage in Maryland, and the cost of a marriage license was only a dollar – a terrific deal compared with the three-dollar price tag in Delaware. Therefore, out-of-state couples could wed cheaply and swiftly in Maryland.[45]

With the scourge of the Wilmington elopement center finally eliminated, disapproving journalists and clergy from Delaware turned their attention to their Maryland neighbors. One columnist suggested that the city of Elkton ran on "tainted money," arguing that the marriage mill "is so equipped that at one end it pours out mismated husbands and wives upon American society and at the other end pours a flood of money into the deep and open pockets of men of the cloth who profess to see no offense against either heaven or earth in thus commercializing the marriage institution."[46] Other columnists referred to the preachers' actions as "a commercialized perversion of the honorable estate of matrimony" and suggested that marrying ministers viewed the institution of marriage as "a money-grubbing proposition."[47]

---

[42] "City May Pass Out as Gretna Green," *Evening Journal*, 14 Mar. 1913, p. 1.
[43] Ibid., 1; "Senate Passes Marriage Bill," 1; "Delaware No Longer Berks Gretna Green," *Reading Times*, 15 Mar. 1913, p. 1. Untitled, *Morning News*, 26 Mar. 1913, p. 6.
[44] Some 416 couples married in Wilmington during the first four weeks of June in 1912. The following year, the number of marriages during that time period totaled 111. "City Loses Reputation as Gretna Green," *Evening Journal*, 28 Jun. 1913, p. 7; "No Wedding Bells Will Ring To-Day," *Morning News*, 1 May 1913, p. 1; "Gretna No More," *Evening Journal*, 3 May 1913, p. 4; "Gretna Green Closes," *Delaware County Daily Times* (Chester, Pa.), 5 May 1913, p. 2.
[45] "Elkton Is Gretna Green," *Morning News*, 7 May 1913, p. 3; "Elkton Succeeds Wilmington as the New Gretna Green," *Evening Journal*, 6 Jun. 1913, p. 11; "Elkton Thrives as Gretna Green," *Morning News*, 7 Jul. 1913, pp. 1–2.
[46] "Commercializing Marriage," *Evening Journal*, 2 Dec. 1913, p. 4.
[47] "That Disgraceful Marriage Mill," *Evening Journal*, 4 Jan. 1915, p. 4; "'Marrying Parsons' and the Gormley Law," *Evening Journal*, 11 Feb. 1915, p. 4.

One self-identified "Woman Reporter" from Philadelphia took an undercover trip to Elkton to witness the marriage mill in action. Like reporters before her, this writer was struck by the hounding that train passengers received after disembarking in Elkton. Referring to the cab drivers at the station as "a small army of unfed vultures," the author criticized these drivers for "abducting" hapless couples at the station and charging them an exorbitant fee for a ride to the altar. She then discussed the predatory ministers who united couples in matrimony in prompt succession.[48] Two weeks later, the board of the Elkton Methodist Episcopal Church was so alarmed by Reverend Howard Quigg's excessive officiation of marriage vows that they removed him from his sinecure. One account of Quigg's actions noted, "in the midst of a pastoral call, he would leave abruptly when a strange couple walked down the street, to follow them and find out if they were in search of a clergyman, and eager to be married." The board reported that Quigg married between ten and thirty couples a week, and emphasized that he profited mightily from these unions, surrendering only a small fraction of the cost to pay the cab drivers and chauffeurs who transported couples to his parsonage. Despite such criticisms, Elkton remained a popular site for elopement in the decades that followed.[49]

As the above examples illustrate, disparities in state marriage laws prompted a spate of elopements that fueled the growing perception of national marriage crisis. Inconsistent rules about the age of marital consent and the necessity of a marriage license were just two of the factors contributing to the elopement craze. As we shall see, diverse laws on post-divorce remarriage, eugenics, and miscegenation also sparked mass elopement and, in turn, the increased sense of crisis. Inconsistent state divorce statutes further exacerbated the problem. Access to divorce varied from state to state throughout the late nineteenth century, with South Carolina and New York holding the strictest regulations.[50] But states known for their lenient policies – most prominently Indiana in the 1850s and 1860s, Utah in the 1870s, South Dakota in the 1880s and 1890s, and Nevada into the twentieth century – became popular destinations for unhappy

---

[48] "Much Speed, No Privacy in Elkton Marriage Mill," *Evening Public Ledger* (Philadelphia), 1 Mar. 1915, p. 2.
[49] "Marrying Parson at Elkton Shifted from Lucrative Job," *Evening Public Ledger*, 13 Apr. 1915, p. 7.
[50] Divorce was forbidden entirely in South Carolina, and limited to cases of adultery in New York. Nelson Manfred Blake, *The Road to Reno: A History of Divorce in the United States* (New York: Macmillan, 1962), 63.

couples who were willing to spend money and time in distant locales for the sake of severing their unions.[51] As migratory divorces grew in popularity, critics bemoaned the lack of uniformity among state divorce codes, and called for constitutional modifications that would allow federal legislators to enforce national marriage and divorce laws. In 1884, two US congressmen proposed the first of many constitutional amendments that would grant Congress the power to legislate marriage and divorce on a federal level. None of these proposed amendments came to a vote in either house of the Congress, but they captured a sense of great alarm as the twentieth century commenced.[52]

The anxiety intensified as interstate train travel became more affordable and convenient, and as lawyers began to capitalize on increasing migratory divorce rates by moving to divorce capitals such as Reno, Nevada, and advertising for clients in newspapers.[53] Theodore Roosevelt entered the conversation in 1906 with a push for federal marriage regulation in his above-mentioned annual address to Congress. Acknowledging the difficulty of passing a constitutional amendment, Roosevelt nonetheless argued, "The whole question of marriage and divorce should be relegated to the authority of the National Congress. At present the wide differences in the laws of the different States on this subject result in scandals and abuses; and surely there is nothing so vitally essential to the welfare of the nation, nothing around which the nation should so bend itself to throw every safeguard, as the home life of the average citizen." Five years later Franklin D. Roosevelt, then a freshman New York State senator, would continue this fight when he introduced a resolution asking the state's congressional delegation to pursue a similar constitutional amendment.[54]

These battles over divorce further illustrate the role that disparate state legislation played in amplifying proclamations of marriage crisis. They also reveal the vital role that marriage and divorce played in the nation's ongoing legal and culture wars. As couples sought marital arrangements that suited their own personal needs, reformers consistently implemented legal and social mechanisms to limit romantic freedoms and to restore

---

[51] Ibid., 116–129; Lawrence M. Friedman, "A Dead Language: Divorce Law and Practice before No-Fault," *Virginia Law Review* 86, no. 7 (2000): 1501–1508. Whereas most western states required a year's residence before couples could receive divorces, Nevada held only a six-month residency requirement through 1927, at which point it was reduced to three months.

[52] Blake, *Road to Reno*, 133, 145–146; Cott, *Public Vows*, 110.

[53] Blake, *Road to Reno*, 152–153.   [54] Ibid., 146.

their own visions of marital propriety; efforts to enact federal divorce legislation were among those initiatives, as were many of the other forms of backlash profiled throughout this book.

* * *

While I include a broad spectrum of marriage arrangements in my analysis of conjugal misconduct, I have deliberately excluded some, and those decisions require brief explanation. First, I do not consider common law marriage to be a form of conjugal misconduct, primarily because by the nineteenth century's end, a majority of states recognized common law marriage as a form of legitimate matrimony. As legal historian Ariela Dubler indicates, many courts determined that couples needed only to give mutual consent in order to formalize their nuptials. Under this logic, a man and a woman who lived together as husband and wife were legally wed, even if their union had never been licensed by government authorities. Critics of common law marriage argued that the privileges of matrimony should not be granted to couples who had never held wedding ceremonies, insisting that common law marriage granted state recognition to immoral sexual arrangements that were unworthy of marital status. Supporters argued, on the other hand, that common law marriage could act as a civilizing force. It could "bring the untraditional within non-threatening parameters," pushing immoral sexual unions within the boundaries of legal marriage and legitimating the children who might otherwise suffer for their parents' sins.[55]

Proponents viewed common law marriage not as an alternative to traditional marriage, but rather as a means of forcing the obligations of marriage onto couples who had never formally pursued this status. As Dubler notes, Elizabeth Cady Stanton opposed common law marriage for fear that it would impose matrimony upon women who did not desire it. "Nothing could be more reckless than our present system," Stanton argued, "when merely to be seen walking together may be taken as evidence of intent to marry and going through the ceremony in jest may seal the contract." Recognizing the difficulties of acquiring a divorce, Stanton rejected any system in which women were compelled into marriages they could not subsequently escape. Stanton's fears were not unfounded; the indissoluble nature of common law marriage was one of

---

[55] Ariela R. Dubler, "Governing through Contract: Common Law Marriage in the Nineteenth Century," *Yale Law Journal* 107, no. 6 (1998): 1891, 1898–1899, 1904–1906.

the primary reasons that judges tended to support this relation through-out the nineteenth century, particularly because marital status rendered women dependent on husbands rather than on the state.[56]

Common law marriage also served more benign functions. Through-out the nineteenth century and into the twentieth, common law status provided property and inheritance rights to women when their long-term partners died, and it granted legitimacy to children. It also protected participants from acquiring the bad reputations that accompanied unmarried cohabitation and sex out of wedlock. The judges who ruled on common law cases were most concerned that couples publicly present their relationship as marriage – the technical details of the nuptials were less significant.[57]

Common law marriage waned in popularity in the twentieth century, in part because of the bureaucratic complications it caused in regard to inheritance, the distribution of pensions, and divorce cases.[58] While such concerns prompted the decline of common law marriage, it is worth noting that most of these criticisms were made on administrative and not moral grounds. Common law marriage existed by and large as a legitimizing force, which brought informal couples within the boundaries of valid marriage. In contrast, most of the subjects of this book made active attempts to contract valid marriages. They faced great criticism because the disreputable aspects of their relations compromised their claims to marital legitimacy, but they actively sought that legitimacy just the same. Meanwhile, common law marriage foisted legitimacy on couples who in some cases did not even desire it.

Finally, this is a book about nonconforming heterosexual relations, and as such I have held off on discussing same-sex partnerships until the book's Epilogue. My objective here is not to erase same-sex couples from history or to deny the significance of gay and lesbian unions. Rather, my research has revealed that unconventional heterosexual relationships have

---

[56] Ibid., 1908–1910, 1918.

[57] Lawrence M. Friedman, *Private Lives: Families, Individuals, and the Law* (Cambridge, Mass.: Harvard University Press, 2004), 20–25. See also Hartog, *Man and Wife in America*, 90–92; Cott, *Public Vows*, 37–40; Michael Grossberg, *Governing the Hearth: Law and Family in Nineteenth-Century America* (Chapel Hill: University of North Carolina Press, 1985), 67–83; Elizabeth H. Pleck, *Not Just Roommates: Cohabitation after the Sexual Revolution* (Chicago: University of Chicago Press, 2012), 16–17.

[58] Mary E. Richmond and Fred S. Hall, *Marriage and the State: Based upon Field Studies of the Present Day Administration of Marriage Laws in the United States* (New York: Russell Sage Foundation, 1929), 29–30, 338–339; Friedman, *Private Lives*, 46.

long endured a type of scrutiny and backlash that is often associated specifically with same-sex couples. Because same-sex marriage has occupied such a prominent position in recent debates over the boundaries of matrimonial inclusion, it tends to dominate conversations about marital nonconformity, sometimes drawing comparisons to the history of antimiscegnation laws, but rarely yielding broader analysis of the ever-fluctuating definitions of proper matrimony.[59] In a sense, then, this book "queers" the history of heterosexual relations, revealing the many ways in which marital nonconformity has sparked legal and cultural repression, even for straight couples. In other words, the boundaries between proper and improper partnerships have historically involved many more nuances and gradations than a binary heterosexual/homosexual framework permits, and attention to those past practices allows us to see recent disputes over same-sex marriage as but one strand in an elaborate historical struggle over the borders of matrimony.

The existence of these borders makes the history of marriage a rich yet elusive phenomenon. It is nearly impossible to characterize marriage, even in the relatively narrow context of the early twentieth-century United States, when we consider the multitude of boundaries dividing acceptable marital practices from unacceptable ones, the droves of people breaching those boundaries, and the ongoing campaigns to patrol them. Persistent public negotiations over what constituted a proper twentieth-century marriage reveal the amorphousness of the institution. And participants in conjugal misconduct put that amorphousness on display, proving through their unconventional arrangements that marriage could change, while sparking consistent efforts to restore an imagined sense of marital tradition. By tracing the unrelenting battles between marital nonconformists and the people who sought to repress them, this book shows how marriage came to occupy such a meaningful place in American legal culture while simultaneously lacking any inherent meaning of its own.

---

[59] Recent popular and scholarly pieces that compare judicial battles over interracial marriage with battles over same-sex marriage include Amisha Padnani and Celina Fang, "Same-Sex Marriage: Landmark Decisions and Precedents," *New York Times*, 26 Jun. 2015, www.nytimes.com/interactive/2015/06/26/us/samesex-marriage-landmarks .html; Peter Wallenstein, "The Straight Interracial Couple Who Paved the Way for Gay Marriage," *Daily Beast*, 29 Jun. 2015, www.thedailybeast.com/articles/2015/06/29/how-loving-v-virginia-paved-the-way-for-nationwide-gay-marriage.html; Ronald Turner, "Same-Sex Marriage and *Loving v. Virginia*: Analogy or Disanalogy?," *Washington and Lee Law Review Online* 71, no. 4 (2015).

I

Matrimonial Advertisements, Matchmaking Bureaus, and the Threat of Commercialized Courtship

In addition to reporting on current events, newspapers have long provided resourceful single people with an opportunity to expand their dating pool, namely by advertising for mates in the personal and matrimonial columns.[1] As newspaper production and circulation swelled at the turn of the twentieth century, and as business owners began advertising their private matchmaking establishments alongside ads from individuals, commercialized courtship became a source of increased fascination and backlash. The use of personal advertisements and matrimonial bureaus offered men and women the chance to expand their acquaintance pools and to transcend the geographic and class boundaries that had previously delineated their marital options. These industries also provided single people with an opportunity to identify the specific personal qualities they desired in a partner and to highlight their own best physical and personality traits, be they real or imagined (see Figure 1.1). For single Americans, matrimonial businesses offered hope that loving partnership remained possible. Many critics would seek to deflate their optimism.

In 1889, for example, the *Chicago Tribune*'s Willice Wharton wrote a column denouncing the proprietors of matchmaking bureaus, who used newspaper ads to unite single folks in marriage for a small fee. "With the irrepressible 'Bureauist' and matrimonial papers springing up all around,"

---

[1] Matrimonial advertisements began to appear in British newspapers in the late seventeenth century, and were appearing in US periodicals by the beginning of the nineteenth. Pamela Epstein, "Advertising for Love: Matrimonial Advertisements and Public Courtship," in *Doing Emotions History*, ed. Susan J. Matt and Peter N. Stearns (Urbana: University of Illinois Press, 2014), 121.

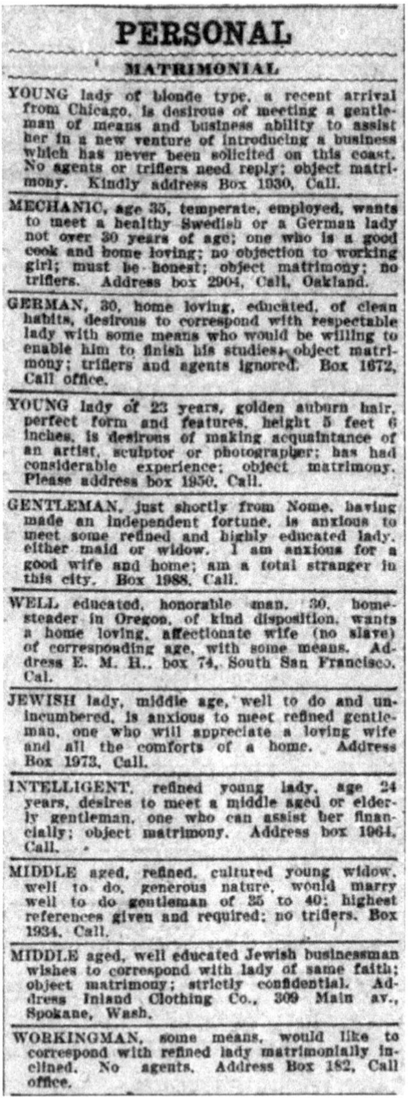

PERSONAL

MATRIMONIAL

YOUNG lady of blonde type, a recent arrival from Chicago, is desirous of meeting a gentleman of means and business ability to assist her in a new venture of introducing a business which has never been solicited on this coast. No agents or triflers need reply; object matrimony. Kindly address Box 1930, Call.

MECHANIC, age 35, temperate, employed, wants to meet a healthy Swedish or a German lady not over 30 years of age; one who is a good cook and home loving; no objection to working girl; must be honest; object matrimony; no triflers. Address box 2904, Call, Oakland.

GERMAN, 30, home loving, educated, of clean habits, desirous to correspond with respectable lady with some means who would be willing to enable him to finish his studies; object matrimony; triflers and agents ignored. Box 1672, Call office.

YOUNG lady of 23 years, golden auburn hair, perfect form and features, height 5 feet 6 inches, is desirous of making acquaintance of an artist, sculptor or photographer; has had considerable experience; object matrimony. Please address box 1950, Call.

GENTLEMAN, just shortly from Nome, having made an independent fortune, is anxious to meet some refined and highly educated lady, either maid or widow. I am anxious for a good wife and home; am a total stranger in this city. Box 1988, Call.

WELL educated, honorable man, 30, homesteader in Oregon, of kind disposition, wants a home loving, affectionate wife (no slave) of corresponding age, with some means. Address E. M. H., box 74, South San Francisco, Cal.

JEWISH lady, middle age, well to do and unincumbered, is anxious to meet refined gentleman, one who will appreciate a loving wife and all the comforts of a home. Address Box 1973, Call.

INTELLIGENT, refined young lady, age 24 years, desires to meet a middle aged or elderly gentleman, one who can assist her financially; object matrimony. Address box 1964, Call.

MIDDLE aged, refined, cultured young widow, well to do, generous nature, would marry well to do gentleman of 35 to 40; highest references given and required; no triflers. Box 1934, Call.

MIDDLE aged, well educated Jewish businessman wishes to correspond with lady of same faith; object matrimony; strictly confidential. Address Inland Clothing Co., 309 Main av., Spokane, Wash.

WORKINGMAN, some means, would like to correspond with refined lady matrimonially inclined. No agents. Address Box 182, Call office.

FIGURE 1.1 "Personal," *San Francisco Call*, 10 Jan. 1909, p. 44.

Wharton scolded, "it is difficult to retain the old belief in the awful sanctity of the marriage relation." She continued, "To bargain over marriage seems as blasphemous as buying one's way into a better world."[2]

[2] Willice Wharton, "Matches Made for Money," *Chicago Daily Tribune*, 25 Oct. 1889, p. 6.

Wharton's words encapsulate several widespread concerns about commercialized matchmaking and the state of marriage itself at the turn of the twentieth century. For Wharton and others, the exchange of funds for possible romance symbolized the reduction of a sacred life event to a mere financial transaction.

Moreover, Wharton's column illustrates the belief that commercialized matchmaking bureaus corrupted marriage by encouraging single folks to pursue wealthy partners and, in Wharton's words, to buy their way into a better world. Too often, opponents alleged, working-class singles used matchmaking services to enter into class circles to which they did not belong. Critics therefore derided individuals who consulted matrimonial pages and marriage bureaus to locate rich spouses, rather than find partners from their own socioeconomic spheres. They also lambasted the proprietors of matrimonial bureaus for attempting to profit from singles' desires for companionship.

In addition to voicing concerns about the place of money in marriage, some critics also deemed commercialized matchmaking services immoral in their tendency to grant women an assertive role in courtship. Others warned of the physical dangers that communication with strangers could bring. A particularly strident set of critics sought to diminish the influence of commercialized matchmaking practices through punitive strategies, including efforts to criminalize the operation of matrimonial bureaus, often on the sketchy grounds that they were contrary to public policy. The blanket claim that such services were inherently fraudulent served to justify the elimination of a major culprit in the ongoing marriage crisis.

Meanwhile, another group of marital traditionalists took a more circuitous approach in their efforts to reform the commercialized matchmaking industry. Rather than reject such channels altogether, these reformers reappropriated them to assert their more conventional ideas about marriage and mate selection. They attempted to move the matrimonial bureau outside the commercial sphere and into the church, the nonprofit sector, and the governmental realm. In doing so, the organizers of noncommercial agencies exploited the popularity of the matrimonial trade, using it to fight *against* the shifting marital patterns they accused commercial agents of perpetrating. The back-and-forth negotiation between the proprietors of commercialized matchmaking industries, the individuals seeking their services, and the reformers attempting to either halt or transform them can inform our understanding of the marriage crisis at hand. In an era of unease over the state of marriage and sexual morals, both the campaign to eliminate matrimonial bureaus and the

effort to modify their uses reflected a celebration of monogamous, permanent, procreative, and love-based marriage by reformers who feared
the institution was in decay.

* * *

In order to understand the backlash against matrimonial brokerage,
we must first recognize the ways in which its late nineteenth-century
incarnation broke from earlier forms of commercial matchmaking. For
generations, Jewish families in Eastern and Central Europe had relied on
matchmakers to find spouses for their children. When families migrated to
the United States, they often brought the tradition of matchmaking with
them. While matchmakers accepted payment for their assistance, they
were nonetheless part of the communities they served. Above all, their
allegiances were to the parents who hired them, and they therefore paid
great attention to questions of familial status and economic standing as
they procured spouses for their clients' children.[3] By the turn of the
twentieth century, however, traditional matchmaking was no longer a
viable career path in the United States, and matchmakers slowly closed
their doors to the public. In the words of Pamela Haag, those who
persisted in serving as matchmakers and employing their services were
considered "malingerers within the modern regime," and matchmakers'
unwillingness to prioritize clients' individual tastes above their parents'
social and economic concerns put them out of touch with the majority of
single Americans.[4] Recognizing this shift, early twentieth-century marriage
brokers applied a different set of principles to their matchmaking. Rather
than cater to parents who sought suitable matches for their children, these
modern brokers helped single people of all ages to locate desirable partners
for themselves. Modern matrimonial bureaus allowed individuals to find
companions with whom they might share romantic and sexual attraction,
and this promise of personal compatibility made them very popular at the
turn of the century. By advertising in newspapers and conducting their
services through the mails, many brokers established national matchmaking networks. In doing so, they vowed to create partnerships that were
based on affinity and not limited by geographical boundaries.

Matrimonial advertisements promised a similar degree of autonomy
and personal choice in mate selection – perhaps even more so, as they

---

[3] Cott, *Public Vows*, 149–51; Clement, *Love for Sale*, 34; "She Persuaded 4000 Hearts to
Beat as 2000!" *Chicago Daily Tribune*, 22 Sep. 1907, p. G3.
[4] Haag, *Consent*, 106.

required individuals to initiate correspondence on their own, without receiving proof of compatibility from a middle person. Matrimonial ads also grew in popularity in the late nineteenth century, due in part to the rise of mass circulation press. As newspapers reached record numbers of readers throughout an expanding geographic range, personal advertisements gained entry into more homes than ever before. With a national rise in the literacy rate, an increase in female newspaper readership, and the proliferation of foreign-language journals, the advertisements also reached many different types of readers, sparking new romantic possibilities for persons of all classes, genders, and national origins.[5]

Closer attention to shifting perceptions on matrimonial advertisements over the course of the nineteenth century provides a deeper sense of why this seemingly innocuous trend became a source of increasing apprehension at the dawn of the twentieth. By the early 1800s, courtship through personal advertisements had become a well-known romantic practice. Early newspaper commentaries presented matrimonial advertising as a quaint novelty. One magazine writer profiled a New England man who had placed a "curious Advertisement" for a wife in the *Charleston Times* in 1805. While the writer found the practice odd, he nonetheless presented it as a potentially useful courtship method. "Though an introduction to the acquaintance of a companion, so novel and unprecedented, may wear with many a theatrical appearance," the columnist wrote, "the writer is conscious of nothing, why it may not be perfectly consistent with every object of Courtship."[6] Commentaries of this nature persisted in the following decades, and for the most part people who placed matrimonial advertisements suffered little editorial abuse.[7] One possible reason for the lack of controversy over matrimonial ads in the early nineteenth century was the relatively unthreatening nature of their content. For decades, male advertisers used particular phrases to describe their ideal mates; "respectable," "of means," "of good character," and "refined" were among these

---

[5] Johanningsmeier, *Fiction and the American Literary Marketplace*, 1–33; Angus McLaren, *The Trials of Masculinity: Policing Sexual Boundaries, 1870–1930* (Chicago: University of Chicago Press, 1997), 45; Robert E. Park, "The Natural History of the Newspaper," *American Journal of Sociology* 29, no. 3 (1923): 274–275; Elmo Scott Watson, *A History of Newspaper Syndicates in the United States, 1865–1935* (Chicago: Western Newspaper Union, 1936), 47–49. The wider circulation of newspapers also raised the profile of matrimonial bureaus, as marriage agents advertised for their services in classified and personals pages.

[6] "A Wife Wanted!!!" *Weekly Visitor, or Ladies' Miscellany*, 27 Apr. 1805, pp. 3, 30.

[7] See "A Wife Wanted," *Philadelphia Album and Ladies' Literary Portfolio*, 7 Jan. 1832, p. 3; "A Wife Wanted," *Workingman's Advocate*, 30 Jul. 1831, p. 1.

popular terms. Frequently, ads would close with the phrase "object matrimony," assuring readers that however outlandish this method of courtship may be, the goal was a respectable marriage.[8]

But as the ads grew in popularity in the 1850s and 1860s, they also became frequent topics of journalistic analysis – and in many cases, disparagement. Newspaper columnists often outright condemned this matrimonial practice. In some cases they illustrated the threat that advertisements posed to innocent young ladies by sharing sensational stories of male swindlers taking advantage of the naïve women they met through matrimonial listings.[9] Matrimonial advertising also came under scrutiny in fictional magazine literature of the era. While short stories on the topic often ended with a happy union between two matrimonial correspondents, their authors nonetheless took many an opportunity to impugn the judgment of characters indulging in such a trade.[10] Critics not only questioned the morality of those who participated in the newspaper matrimonial market, but they also challenged their qualifications for matrimony itself. The author of an 1862 article in *The Knickerbocker* expressed this viewpoint:

No girl of well-regulated mind, and with a proper feeling of delicacy and self-respect, would think of responding to the public overtures of a man whom she had never seen, and of whom she knew positively nothing; and, therefore, the women who usually answer such advertisements may be considered as likely to make undesirable wives.[11]

In the eyes of critics, no woman who responded to or, moreover, placed an advertisement of this sort was worthy of a decent man's attention. Thus, the matrimonial column could never produce a suitable marriage, as no worthwhile woman would deign to partake in this market.

---

[8] Pamela Epstein views the frequently generic language of personal advertisers as an effort to conform to middle-class social and literary convention. Epstein, "Selling Love: The Commercialization of Intimacy in America, 1860s–1900s" (PhD diss., Rutgers University, 2010), 67–68.

[9] "A Warning to Women – Doings of a Matrimonial Swindler – The Effect of Answering Matrimonial Advertisements," *Saturday Evening Post*, 27 Dec. 1856, p. 6. Although allegedly the account of a swindler's actions, this piece ultimately takes the form of a warning to women in search of husbands. It notes that one of this swindler's young victims "is now insane," in an attempt to convey the depths of the harm he has inflicted.

[10] Agnes Leslie, "Advertising for a Husband," *Ballou's Pictorial Drawing-Room Companion* 8, no. 26 (1855): 406; Edwin L. Lothrop, "Advertising for a Wife," *Flag of Our Union*, 6 Feb. 1858, p. 44.

[11] "A Bad Way to Get Married," *The Knickerbocker* 60, no. 4 (1862): 352.

Later commentators argued that women responding to matrimonial advertisements were not inherently depraved, but that instead the ads themselves held the sinister power to corrupt the innocent girls who stumbled upon them. In an 1870 article from *Phrenological Journal and Science of Health*, Howard Glyndon described the process of moral degeneration befalling the "poor little fool" who stumbled into the newsprint matrimonial market:

The personal or matrimonial paragraph, with all its fascination of mystery, is usually – if they who run could read aright – the *Devil's promise to pay*. From reading and becoming interested in such notices there is but one step to answering. Many a girl who would never dare write one is yet bold enough to answer one. Thousands of girls who *do* answer them have no conception of the vile meanings which are hidden beneath the peculiar language in which they are written.[12]

Glyndon continued his narrative of female corruption by suggesting that the moment a "young and unknowing girl" formed a clandestine relationship with a "clever and unscrupulous man, who is her elder in age and in all sorts of experience," her purity would vanish forever. After this fall from grace, only a miracle could halt the woman's descent into hell. Glyndon concluded his article with an impassioned plea for the termination of matrimonial advertisements, "these vile sink-holes of all corruption through which so many thousands of the young of both sexes in our midst disappear from happiness and respectability year after year!"[13]

These dramatic commentaries did little to explain why a person would write or respond to a matrimonial advertisement in the first place. C. G. Horton captured this motivation on the pages of *The Matrimonial Bazar: A Monthly Journal, Devoted to the Interests of Love, Courtship and Marriage*. As editor of this national publication, Horton encouraged singles to utilize matrimonial ads in their quest for the ideal spouse. Horton, who filled his journal exclusively with matrimonial advertisements and articles describing their merits, explained in 1876 that these ads promised to create stronger and longer-lasting partnerships than traditional means of courtship. He maintained that marriage was among the most important events in any person's life, and that therefore all potential brides and grooms must employ great care in selecting mates. Specifically, single people needed to pick from as broad a pool as possible in order to locate partners with whom they shared the greatest

[12] Howard Glyndon, "'Personals' and 'Matrimonials,'" *The Phrenological Journal and Science of Health* 51, no. 2 (1870): 129.
[13] Ibid., 129–130.

compatibility. "To choose wisely," he argued, "it is indispensable to choose widely, for as the ideal standard of merit and temperament, as well as of personal appearance, means and social position, varies with almost every individual, it is obvious that the field for selection should extend beyond the limited sphere of family acquaintance; and for the attainment of that object this organ furnishes unsurpassed advantages."[14]

Horton thus marketed the *Matrimonial Bazar* to "the thousands of marriageable persons in this great country residing in locations wide apart, and who, by reason of the conventionalities of society, and other difficulties, are practically debarred from all social and possible intercourse with each other." He presented his newspaper as a vessel through which singles could overcome these constraints and attain ideal mates. Horton noted in particular the abundance of single men living in remote areas of the West, and the useful role matrimonial advertisements could play in leading eastern women to join them. This was certainly the hope for one twenty-seven-year-old advertiser, "a young gentleman of Dakota Territory" who claimed to be living "among the Indians of the far West." This man wished to correspond with women between the ages of eighteen and twenty-five, with no restrictions on wealth or geographic location.[15] Another advertisement came from a "Gentleman out in the Montana Gold mines," who "wishes correspondence for amusement, and perhaps matrimony."[16] Such ads offered comfort to men who had moved westward to seek wealth and property and who now lacked companionship. Living in regions with few eligible women, these men used matrimonial newspapers to defy geographic limitations and to forge their own romantic opportunities.

Some single women were drawn to this possibility of western migration, and they responded to matrimonial advertisements in hopes of finding husbands in distant locations. A *Chicago Daily Tribune* writer illustrated this phenomenon in an 1884 article on the matrimonial column. The author had placed an advertisement in a Chicago newspaper, claiming to be "A Gentleman engaged in the cattle trade in a

---

[14] "Address to the Public," *The Matrimonial Bazar: A Monthly Journal, Devoted to the Interests of Love, Courtship and Marriage* 7, no. 7 (1876): 2.

[15] Ibid., 2. Meanwhile, Pamela Epstein discusses matrimonial advertisements as a way for urbanites to find intimate connections, combatting the isolation and anonymity that city life often bred. "Advertising for Love," 120–139.

[16] Published in *The Matrimonial News and Special Advertiser* (Chicago), 26 Aug. 1876, p. 3. Horton also seems to have published this journal, which featured numerous advertisements from western men seeking partners from across the country.

Western city, having an income of $5,000 a year." The writer requested correspondence with educated women between the ages of eighteen and twenty-three, "with a view to matrimony." He then published the thirty-six replies he received in an effort to showcase the folly of women who responded to personal advertisements. Despite the unethical process through which the author enticed these women to be subjects for his article, as well as the questionable validity of the conclusions reached, this piece does display the appeal of matrimonial advertisements to women hoping to escape their surroundings. The promise of westward relocation was particularly alluring to many of these midwestern women.[17]

Some of the respondents seemed to care more about leaving home than they did about marriage itself. Several cited interest in "going West" as their primary reason for replying to this advertisement, expressing hope that an epistolary connection would lead to a physical relocation. Others were drawn to the West as an idea. Their letters suggested a desire for mental escape or the opportunity to broaden their worlds by corresponding with a pen pal from an unfamiliar region. One woman admitted to having "a weakness for 'Western' life," which she hoped to satisfy through correspondence with a true westerner. Another woman admitted that she was uncomfortable submitting personal information to a stranger, but that her general distaste for Chicago had nonetheless driven her to correspond with "some one out West." A third respondent hoped "to make the acquaintance of some Western gentleman of education and refinement," but she also noted that she was "very pleasantly situated" in her Chicago flat. While these women were eager to communicate with the advertiser, it seems all three responded less out of the desire to wed a stranger and more from a hunger to learn about life beyond Chicago.[18]

The author estimated that 50 percent of the women responding to such advertisements were "regulars" who "carry on the business of answering personals as a sport." He classified many of these women as married flirts, who gained satisfaction from their anonymous indiscretions. Other respondents wrote out of a thirst for adventure, or the desire to take part in a tawdry but exciting form of heterosocial correspondence. One young woman from St. Paul, for instance, claimed that she devoted most of her time to her academic studies, and that she wrote this letter as a way of

---

[17] "Matrimonial Ads," *Chicago Daily Tribune*, 28 Dec. 1884, p. 12.   [18] Ibid., 12.

temporarily removing herself from the tedium of scholarly life. She acknowledged that matrimonial correspondence was "out of the order of refined social custom," but she believed this questionable activity would offer her a novel form of escape. She closed her letter by stating, "Study, study, and practice all the time one tires and wants reaction." For this young woman, and for others who were dissatisfied with the demands of day-to-day life, personal correspondence provided an inviting sense of release.[19]

The following decade, a similar study yielded even more data. In 1895, personal advertisements made their way into scholarly discourse as sociologist and criminologist Arthur MacDonald published *Abnormal Woman: A Sociologic and Scientific Study of Young Women, Including Letters of American and European Girls in Answer to Personal Advertisements.* This study explored the biological and environmental factors leading to female "abnormality," a trait MacDonald ascribed to any woman who responded to personal advertisements.[20] In order to find subjects for his study, MacDonald placed the following advertisement in newspapers throughout large American cities: "Gentleman of high social and university position desires correspondence (acquaintance not necessary) with young educated woman of high social and financial position. No agents; no triflers; must give detailed account of life; references required."[21] MacDonald received responses from many American women, as well as some Europeans. He did not specify the exact number of responses, but he profiled eighty-eight subjects in the book, and he claimed to have sustained extensive correspondence with a number of them, sharing many of their letters verbatim.[22]

While the "scientific" analysis that MacDonald performed on his female correspondents is of dubious merit – he claimed to use their letters to measure their nervous systems or, more precisely, "to decide

---

[19] Ibid., 12.
[20] Arthur MacDonald, *Abnormal Woman: A Sociologic and Scientific Study of Young Women, Including Letters of American and European Girls in Answer to Personal Advertisements, with a Bibliography* (Washington, D.C.: self-published, 1895), viii. MacDonald was vague in his definition of "abnormality," explaining simply, "The abnormal person of society is in the minority and conforms less to the customs of the community than the average or normal person" (vii).
[21] Ibid., viii.
[22] MacDonald changed the names of persons and places. He dismissed ethical questions about his decision to publish private conversations with the claim that any woman "who answers a public advertisement cannot expect her correspondence with a total stranger to be of a very confidential nature." Ibid., viii–ix.

as accurately as possible the acuteness of the nerves to heat, pain, and locality" – the published exchanges offer insight into the motivations of the women who responded to his ad.[23] These written conversations counter popular representations of women as passive objects of conquest in such exchanges, and they reveal the ways in which women could benefit from matrimonial correspondence. Remarkably, one of the American women MacDonald viewed as a mere subject of his study seemed to be conducting a similar experiment on him. This woman eventually admitted that she was employing matrimonial ads as part of a long-standing effort to understand American men. While this woman's academic approach to the matrimonial column seems to have been unique among the subjects of *Abnormal Woman*, it was nonetheless one of many strategies through which women used these advertisements to their own ends.[24]

MacDonald viewed the women who communicated with him as damaged individuals, labeling them "out of harmony with their present social environment."[25] And indeed some of them were disenchanted or "out of harmony" with the lives they knew. They wrote to MacDonald as a form of escape, if only of the temporary and psychological variety. One American correspondent, the wife of a well-known public figure, expressed loneliness and a hunger for companionship in her letters. She insisted from the outset that no in-person meeting could come of this correspondence, explaining, "my position and surroundings will not permit my ever knowing you, and can give no reason for addressing you the first time, except utter loneliness and a desire to break through conventionalities." This writer noted her lack of friends and her distaste for the high-class company and surroundings her husband's position demanded. She valued her husband's companionship, but felt no romantic attachment to him. A sense of alienation and boredom had propelled her to respond to matrimonial advertisements, despite her unavailability as a bride.[26]

Another correspondent, this one unmarried, expressed similar skepticism about the possibility of a meaningful relationship developing from the matrimonial column. "It seems impossible that any one with 'matrimonial intentions' should advertise in a paper and expect to be suited," she wrote. "I have no matrimonial intentions myself. On the contrary, I prefer liberty and happiness. I think loneliness, however, is terrible, and

---

[23] Ibid., ix.   [24] Ibid., 27.   [25] Ibid., x.
[26] Ibid., 30–33. All subjects profiled in this chapter are American, so from this point onward nationality will not be specified.

I like to talk to and with a refined man, but am sure I am happier now than I would be married to any one."[27] This woman knew she had strayed from convention in responding to MacDonald's advertisement, but she refused to treat this act as a breach of propriety, claiming that her "womanly instincts" assured her she had committed no offense.[28] She noted that while relatives wished her to marry a rich man, she had no interest in doing so. "They would not at all understand why I should prefer to live my own life with my music and books," she explained. "And above all things they would never understand my correspondence with a stranger. They would regard it as one of the 'eccentricities of genius,' and try to save me from such a mad course." But the young woman claimed independence from these stodgy family members, and proceeded in her quest for "intellectual companionship."[29]

Some of MacDonald's correspondents expressed hesitation about the propriety of corresponding through personal advertisements. One letter-writer, who claimed to be in pursuit of "mental improvement," recognized that she might be "treading on 'dangerous ground'" by communicating with a stranger. But defining herself as a woman who was "enchanted with everything that is flavored by mystery," she was willing to take the risk. Not wishing to push social boundaries too far, however, she claimed only to be interested in corresponding with a man of upright moral standing, imploring, "if you are not a perfect gentleman, both morally and socially, please be so courteous as not to answer this (perhaps imprudent) letter."[30]

Another woman was surprised by her desire "to form an acquaintance in this *irregular* manner." After flipping past the matrimonial section time and again, though, she was overtaken by an "insane desire" to respond to MacDonald. To allay any doubts about her moral virtue, she assured him that she was an avid churchgoer.[31] One widow answered MacDonald's ad out of a yearning for adventure, but she simultaneously expressed shame in doing so. "You cannot conceive what an embarrassing thing it is for a lady to do and how it embarrasses me," she wrote. "Besides, it is the first time in all my life that I ever thought of such a thing, much less condescend to write an answer to anything like it."[32] It seems this widow's thirst for new experience outweighed her desire to maintain an air of respectability. Her moral code nonetheless plagued her in her exchange with MacDonald.

---

[27] Ibid., 10.   [28] Ibid., 13.   [29] Ibid., 14.
[30] Ibid., 83–84.   [31] Ibid., 79.   [32] Ibid., 77.

Not all of MacDonald's subjects expressed this reluctance, however, and many saw their communication as a means of escape from unbearable circumstances. One eighteen-year-old woman hoped to meet MacDonald as quickly as possible, explaining, "I am quite unhappy at home, and, having an income of my own, I want to marry, and very soon."[33] Others seemed surprisingly eager to wed MacDonald after having read his one brief advertisement. One woman claimed that her fiancé had died shortly before their intended wedding, and that she hoped to find another companion to ease her grief. Though she knew very little about MacDonald, she vowed to be a good wife to him, or to any other man who would accept her companionship.[34] Alongside all of the other purposes served by matrimonial correspondence – flirtation, the quest for adventure, and the desire for intellectual stimulation among them – the pursuit of love and the escape from loneliness served as one of their central functions.

In general, these particular women paid little attention to financial matters in their letters. While many of MacDonald's correspondents made passing reference to their fiscal circumstances, they did not appear overly concerned about MacDonald's class status. Some of them explicitly rejected money as a meaningful aspect of mate selection, such as a young woman who explained that financial matters meant very little to her and that while she did hold a large sum of money, she was not concerned about her potential husband's income.[35] Matrimonial correspondents in other venues, however, did factor economic questions into their advertising, and on some occasions newspaper advertisers mixed business with romance. One woman who advertised for a husband in an 1895 edition of the *Philadelphia Inquirer* claimed to operate a small business which was "getting too large for her to handle." She hoped to correspond with a gentleman who might relieve her of some of this responsibility: "object matrimony."[36] Men also sought business partners through this medium, including one who advertised in the *Inquirer* for a "plain, good woman, over 35, willing to wed now; must have $250 cash to enlarge business."[37] In some cases male advertisers seemed more interested in their future wife's ability to perform domestic labor than in any personal qualities she might possess. One thirty-five-year-old

---

[33] Ibid., 69.   [34] Ibid., 90.

[35] Ibid., 65. At the same time, this woman recognized that some men used matrimonial advertisements as means of fortune hunting, and she assured any potential suitors that her fortune was so "tied up" that she would have exclusive control of it were she to wed.

[36] G.W., "Matrimonial," *Philadelphia Inquirer*, 22 Feb. 1895, p. 8.

[37] "Matrimonial," *Philadelphia Inquirer*, 28 Apr. 1895, p. 8.

widower wrote, for instance, "Would like to meet widow washerwoman; object matrimony."[38]

Calling attention to the decidedly unromantic nature of these advertisements for marriage, turn-of-the-century critics emphasized the dangers of economic exploitation in their warnings against matrimonial advertising. Specifically, this era witnessed heightened concern over the potential for fraudulent misrepresentation, cases of swindling and robbery orchestrated through phony matrimonial correspondence, and the establishment of marriage bureaus, which capitalized on the popularity of matrimonial advertisements by building entire businesses around them. At the turn of the twentieth century, critics focused more than ever on the fact that matrimonial advertisements could be used as a source of profit for both individuals and corporations. This increasing rejection of marriage as a commercial enterprise yielded criticisms of the matrimonial ad industry and sparked campaigns to destroy it.

* * *

Warnings about the dangers of personal advertising increased in newspapers, magazines, and popular literature over the course of the 1890s. Some articles told stories of couples who had met and married through personal advertisements, only to have one spouse desert the other soon after.[39] Others told of women who had responded to advertisements and subsequently wed, but then learned that their husbands were bigamists with wives across the country.[40] The most dramatic of these cautionary articles involved women whose interest in matrimonial advertisements had led to untimely death. Notable among these was Jennie Warren of Metropolis, Illinois, who responded to an advertisement from Frederick Sanchez of Denver, and relocated there to marry him. Sanchez shot Warren to death for her life insurance; this story served to caution women against following Warren's lead.[41]

Above all, critics highlighted cases in which unsuspecting women responded to matrimonial advertisements and developed a good rapport

---

[38] "Personal," *Philadelphia Inquirer*, 26 Jul. 1896, p. 14.
[39] "His Wife Didn't Suit," *Morning Oregonian* (Portland), 20 Apr. 1890, p. 13; "They Married in Haste," *Aberdeen Daily News* (S.D.), 3 May 1890, p. 4.
[40] "An Atlanta Sensation That Grew out of a Matrimonial Advertisement," *Columbus Daily Enquirer* (Ga.), 21 Nov. 1891, p. 1; "May Be a Bigamist," *Rocky Mountain News* (Denver), 12 Jul. 1892, p. 3; "Her Romance Is O'er," *National Police Gazette*, 4 Nov. 1893, p. 6.
[41] "Fatal Advertisement," *Atchison Daily Globe*, 1 Dec. 1897, p. 3.

with the ad-writers, only to be robbed upon their eventual in-person meetings. These stories were often presented as local topics of interest, such as the account of Widow Schwager of Newark, New Jersey, whose struggles were described in the "Jersey News of All Sorts" column of the *Philadelphia Inquirer* in 1892. This straightforward piece explained that the widow had "published a matrimonial advertisement and secured a husband who robbed her of $2000 and then ran away."[42] Sometimes these stories withheld information about their subjects' identity and location, instead offering brief and generic cautionary tales against using the matrimonial column. One *Idaho Daily Statesman* piece simply stated: "A woman of some means who answered a matrimonial advertisement married the advertiser and was very quickly robbed of all she had. She will know better next time."[43] As it became more common for newspapers to acquire items from syndicates, these local stories were reproduced in journals across the nation.

Although accounts of women robbing men through fraudulent personal advertising were less frequent, they did appear and they often carried even more judgment than when men acted as swindlers. One example from a Mississippi newspaper noted that a "self-styled young widow" in Austin had recently taken advantage of a "silly gentleman" in New Orleans. "Correspondence followed, pictures were exchanged, and he agreed to marry her. He sent $50 to her to pay her expenses to New Orleans. Since then he has not heard of her or his money."[44] Articles like this one suggested that while blind faith in long-distance romance might be understandable in women, men ought to know better than to lose themselves and their money to women they had yet to meet face-to-face. Sometimes the "women" who duped male suitors turned out to be men, describing themselves as attractive ladies who hoped to receive money from their epistolary beaus. Samuel Edwards of Chicago learned this when he responded to an advertisement from Josephine Wickham of Newark. After exchanging several letters, Wickham told Edwards that she would marry him if he paid her fare to Chicago. Edwards complied,

---

[42] "Jersey News of All Sorts," *Philadelphia Inquirer*, 19 May 1892, p. 2.
[43] "Woman; Married," *Idaho Daily Statesman*, 17 May 1892, p. 3. This assertion that swindled women had surely learned their lesson was a common device. See "Current Topics," *The Youth's Companion*, 22 Jun. 1899, p. 318, for a longer cautionary tale that ended in a similar manner: "She has learned by bitter experience, however, that no true gentleman seeks a woman's friendship through an advertisement, and that to enter into such an arrangement is to invite moral disaster."
[44] "Newsy Tit-Bits," *Biloxi Herald*, 22 Aug. 1896, p. 7.

sending $40 to the provided address. When Wickham failed to arrive, Edwards traveled to New Jersey to find her. Eventually Edwards realized he had been duped and that his swindler was a man who had adopted the false identity of Josephine to elicit "fare" from lonely and impressionable suitors.[45]

While these individual cases of swindling yielded dramatic newspaper accounts and criminal investigations, they still served as small-scale examples of marital fraud. But as matrimonial bureaus began to adopt deceitful practices on a much larger scale, state and federal officials intensified their efforts to curtail swindling. This institutionalization of marital fraud would become an even more pressing concern in the early twentieth century, as entrepreneurs capitalized on the popularity of personal advertising for their own financial gain. Marriage brokers won clients by placing advertisements in newspaper personal columns, sometimes disguising them as matrimonial advertisements from individuals and sometimes making it clear that they represented a business establishment. They also solicited clients by responding to individuals' matrimonial advertisements and suggesting that the advertiser enlist their services if the initial ad did not prove successful.[46] After piquing clients' interest, the broker would request an entrance fee, usually between two and five dollars, and vow to put clients in touch with other men and women who wished to wed, generally promising that these potential spouses were affluent and attractive. Such advertisements generated thousands of responses.

In some cases, matrimonial agencies were operated honestly and strove to create successful unions. But as more and more people sought to capitalize financially on singles' desires for partnership by opening matrimonial bureaus, authorities became increasingly concerned about fraud. Officials began leading investigations and raids on these agencies, often uncovering stock photographs of actors that were presented to clients as potential mates, and false biographical information highlighting the beauty and wealth of the client pool. In the eyes of public officials, the

---

[45] "Chicago Man Duped," *Inter Ocean*, 22 Apr. 1893, p. 3.

[46] The above-mentioned author of the 1884 *Chicago Daily Tribune* article on matrimonial advertisements received a solicitation from a matrimonial bureau in addition to the thirty-five responses from individuals. It stated: "If you will please fill out the inclosed blank we can furnish you with a suitable corespondant, that is providing you do not get what you desire from yor add. We have a grate meney young ladies on our books. Yors respectfully. Mrs. S. J. Morrow, Manager Chicago Matrimonial Bureau." "Matrimonial Ads," p. 12.

possibility of fraud came to trump the possibility of legitimate business operations. Matrimonial bureaus were widely pronounced illegal, whether or not they employed fraudulent practices, and their proprietors were frequently brought to federal trial on charges of mail fraud. Between 1900 and 1910, officials arrested the owners of matrimonial bureaus across the nation, including agencies in major cities such as New York, Chicago, Cleveland, Pittsburgh, St. Louis, and New Orleans; smaller cities such as Syracuse, Spokane, and Evansville; and small towns and villages such as Wewoka, Oklahoma; Paducah, Kentucky; Versailles, Missouri; and Richland Center, Wisconsin.[47] Raids on marriage bureaus reflected a desire to crack down on the exploitation of hapless singles. But the indiscriminate haste with which authorities conducted them raises questions about the extent to which questions of fraud truly motivated the war against matrimonial brokerage – or if, instead, anxieties over the commercialization of marital practice and general perceptions of social indecency prompted these crusades.

Authorities often defended their raids on marriage bureaus and match-making services with claims that these establishments were uniformly illegal. And indeed, a number of turn-of-the-century appellate court cases supported this claim with rulings that marriage brokerage was contrary to public policy and that contracts between marriage brokers and their clients were consequently void. In 1883, Judge William Pryor of the Kentucky Court of Appeals held that any agreement in which a third party received payment to bring about a marriage between two other persons was invalid. He stated, "Such contracts, if carried out, result in unhappy marital relations, and have been discountenanced by the law. The elementary authorities, as well as the reported cases, all sustain this view of such a contract." Pryor left no citations to clarify specific examples in which "the law" and "the elementary authorities" had

---

[47] "'Suckers' Not All Dead," *Evening Bulletin* (Maysville, Ky.), 25 May 1901, p. 4; "Cupid's Agent in Toils of Law," *Morning Post* (Raleigh), 6 Mar. 1902, p. 5; "Would Make a Good Wife for a $79,000 Man," *Richmond Dispatch* (Va.), 31 Oct. 1902, p. 1; "Matrimonial Bureau Raided," *Gainesville Daily Sun*, 23 May 1905, p. 1; "Women Held as Defrauders," *Paducah Evening Sun*, 9 May 1907, p. 5; "Accused of Using Mails to Defraud," *Crittenden Record-Press* (Marion, Ky.), 28 Nov. 1907, p. 1; "Hunting Affinities," *Raleigh Herald* (Beckley, W.V.), 5 Nov. 1908, p. 2; "Disguised as a Priest," *Washington Post*, 5 Feb. 1909, p. 3; "He Lived on Love," *Times and Democrat* (Orangeburg, S.C.), 14 Jun. 1910, p. 1; "400 Looking for Wives," *Union Republican* (Winston-Salem), 12 May 1910, p. 1; "St. Paul Man Operated a Matrimonial Bureau," *Bismarck Tribune*, 27 May 1910, p. 8; "Lay Matrimonial Fraud to 3," *Paducah Evening Sun*, 2 Sep. 1910, p. 5.

labeled marital brokerage contracts void, but subsequent cases show that
Pryor's views were common in legal and judicial realms.[48]

In an 1888 New York Court of Common Pleas case, a Mrs. Guion
sued her matrimonial agent, Mr. Wellman, claiming that she had given
him a fifty-dollar deposit, which he had agreed to refund if he failed to
deliver her a husband. After Guion rejected all of the potential husbands
selected by Wellman, she demanded the return of her payment. Wellman
did not comply, and Guion consequently filed suit. The three presiding
judges of the Court of Common Pleas refused to order Wellman to return
Guion's deposit, claiming that the bargain was invalid from the start, and
that "the contract in question [was] void as against public policy." The
justices reasoned that in soliciting the services of a marriage broker,
Guion had acted just as illegally as the broker himself and that she was
therefore not entitled to the funds she had given him.[49]

This ruling was later overturned by the Court of Appeals of New York,
which held that Wellman's actions as a marriage broker were in fact *more
illegal* than Guion's as a solicitor of brokerage services. In ruling that
Guion was entitled to recover her deposit, the court determined that those
who ran marriage bureaus were operating fraudulent businesses, and
therefore persons who enlisted aid from matchmakers were being
defrauded. By drawing this distinction between the defrauder and the
defrauded, the Court of Appeals made an even more damning ruling
against matrimonial brokerage than had the Common Pleas Court, presenting Wellman and his ilk as scheming agents who preyed on the naiveté
of an unsuspecting public. "Where a party carries on a business of
promoting marriage as the defendant appears to have done," the ruling
affirmed, "it is plain to be seen that the natural tendency of such a
business is immoral and it would be so clearly the policy of the law to
suppress it and public interest would be so greatly promoted by its
suppression, that there would be no hesitation upon the part of the courts
to aid the party who had patronized such a business by relieving him or
her from all contracts made."[50] By excusing Guion's poor judgment and
condemning Wellman for exploiting her, the court maintained that the
matrimonial bureau itself was the evil that needed to be rooted out, and it
established a precedent for those district attorneys and vice committees
who would later seek to do just that.

[48] *Johnson's Adm'r v. Hunt*, 81 Ky. 321 (1883).
[49] *Duval v. Wellman*, 1. N.Y.S. 70 (1888).
[50] *Duval v. Wellman*, 124 N.Y. 156 (1891).

In an 1896 Supreme Court of California case, Kittie Morrison filed suit against a man who refused to pay for the matchmaking services she had provided. Morrison claimed that the couple had already decided to marry and that they had enlisted her aid only to help them carry out the agreement. Justice Ralph Harrison still viewed Morrison's participation as illegal marriage brokerage, reasoning that there was no difference between paying someone to facilitate a preexisting marital arrangement and paying someone to locate a previously unknown spouse. As a result, any contracts established between Morrison and her clients were "without legal consideration," and Morrison was not entitled to the payment promised to her through an invalid contract.[51]

While Harrison cited very few precedents to support his claim that marriage brokerage contracts were contrary to public policy, more than anything his ruling rested on the assumption that mere common sense dictated this line of reasoning. In other words, few precedents existed because the illegality of marriage brokerage contracts was "so elementary that but very few cases involving the question have found their way into the reported decisions." In the absence of substantial rulings, Harrison briefly explained the reasoning behind this "elementary" rejection of marriage brokerage; he stated that brokers were driven exclusively by a desire to profit and that their unwholesome motivations deprived couples of "the freedom of choice essential to a happy marriage, and the voluntary selection by each spouse of the person to be his companion for life."[52] Embracing the modern notion that successful marriage was dependent upon individual choice, Justice Harrison accused marriage brokers of denying individuals the chance to select partners on their own terms, and of thus corrupting the institution of marriage with their greed.

An Iowa Supreme Court justice cited the *Morrison* decision in a 1905 ruling against Mary Aldinger, who had accepted $200 from the now-deceased William Grobe to travel to Chicago, where she attempted to coordinate nuptials between Grobe and his desired wife. Aldinger subsequently sought additional money for expenses she had incurred on her trip. Justice Emlin McClain held that it was illegal for a third party to accept funds for the purpose of bringing about a union between two others: "It is contrary to public policy to make such advice or solicitation the basis of an agreement to pay money," McClain concluded.

[51] *Morrison v. Rogers*, 115 Cal. 252 (1896).   [52] Ibid.

Though Aldinger had had every right to help facilitate a union between two adults, she did not have the right to receive compensation for her efforts.[53]

The judges in these cases continually neglected to explain what it meant for a business to be "contrary to public policy," and in many ways they seemed committed to *not* defining the precise meaning of the term. In a 1909 matrimonial brokerage case in the Missouri Court of Appeals, the presiding judge wrote, "A question of what is public policy in a given case is as broad as a question of what is fraud in a given case and is addressed to the good common sense of the court."[54] While the judges may not have been willing to put forth a clear definition, they were unified in their belief that commercialized matchmaking was detrimental to public policy. These legal sentiments provided a rationale for public officials' efforts to cleanse their cities of matrimonial bureaus in the early years of the twentieth century. In Chicago, such efforts were widespread and well publicized, and they were often presented as campaigns against fraud and the swindling of hapless victims. The matrimonial swindle was not a new phenomenon in the early twentieth century – one 1900 *Chicago Daily Tribune* columnist labeled this type of scheme "as old as the oldest." But concerns about the potential social damage caused by marriage bureaus intensified in this era as, in the words of the same columnist, the matrimonial agency swindle "bobbed up anew lately with great vigor."[55]

The writer of this article explained the general scheme through which the managers of marital brokerage firms defrauded their customers. Swindlers would place advertisements in newspapers across the country, claiming that a wealthy young woman hoped to find "a nice agreeable husband." Intrigued by this prospect, men would respond to the listed address, only to receive a reply asking for twenty cents in stamps to pay for postage, and then for a five-dollar membership fee. After paying these costs, the respondents were informed that they had not acted quickly enough, as the woman they pursued was now engaged to someone else.[56] A 1901 investigation of Chicago's Elite Matrimonial association con-firmed this description. Miss E. L. Reading, a former clerical worker at

---

[53] *In re Grobe's Estate*, 127 Iowa 121 (1905).
[54] *Wenninger v. Mitchell*, 139 Mo. App. 420 (1909).
[55] "Swindlers Lack Ideas," *Chicago Daily Tribune*, 12 Aug. 1900, p. 46.
[56] Ibid., 46; Charles L. Benjamin, "Want Ad Fakers Rob Thousands," *Chicago Daily Tribune*, 30 Jul. 1905, p. E3.

the Elite association, disclosed the bureau's fraudulent practices to Chicago's post office investigator, who conducted an official investigation. Reading shared some of the bureau's tricks with the *Daily Tribune*, noting that the agency sought to maximize membership among women by using wealthy eligible men as bait. "When [Reading] was initiated into the mysteries of the work," the article explained, "she says she found that every man on the list was 'wealthy, generous, and kind.'"[57]

The agency's deceit went much deeper than this. According to Reading, while the club promised to provide each member with a unique match for correspondence, in reality members received identical suggestions. As Reading explained, "The height of a man was always given as 5 feet 10 inches, his weight as 180 pounds, dark brown hair. He was in every case a Protestant, did not drink or smoke, was worth over $100,000, and was extremely fond of home life." Similarly, all male clients received the same female match: "Each woman was 5 feet 5 inches tall, weighed 130 pounds, had brown hair and a fair complexion, and was independently rich or had prospects of receiving an inheritance. She was also a Protestant. Her occupation was given as 'lady.'" The alleged mate's age would vary, depending on the age of the client, and eye color was either blue or brown, "the wish of the association's chief official being that the color should make a contrast."[58]

Investigations of Chicago marriage bureaus intensified in 1902, as Detective Clifton Wooldridge led numerous raids on local marital brokerage businesses. The most frequent charge against these firms was mail fraud, with the claim that bureau managers had enticed lonely clients into submitting money through the mails with the false promise that this payment would procure a spouse. In truth, the investigators argued, these "matchmakers" had no intention of matchmaking, and used the promise of marriage – as well as stock photographs and false biographical information – only to take advantage of singles who longed for romantic partners.[59]

These swindlers were most successful in acquiring clients' money by roping them in with the false promise of a wealthy spouse. Many services enticed clients with pamphlets and promotional materials that told of

---

[57] "Agency Secrets Let Out," *Chicago Daily Tribune*, 23 Aug. 1901, p. 3.
[58] Ibid., 3; "Demands $5 or a Wife," *Chicago Daily Tribune*, 6 Sep. 1901, p. 1.
[59] Wooldridge offered a thorough explanation of this swindling process in his memoir. See Clifton R. Wooldridge, *Twenty Years a Detective in the Wickedest City in the World* (Chicago: Chicago Publishing Company, 1908), 119–191.

couples who had found partnership across class boundaries with the help of the marriage bureau. Among the items gathered from a 1902 raid on five separate agencies were promotional materials boasting of cross-class unions. Satisfied clients included "Mrs. Jackson, a Boston widow worth $65,000, married James R. Kelly, a poor man"; "Thomas Schaefer, a poor sailor, married a widow in San Diego, Cal, worth $25,000"; and "Edna Schmidt, daughter of P. G. Schmidt, a Chicago millionaire, married Ernest Wehl, a coachman."[60] Similarly, the Standard Correspondence Club, also raided by Wooldridge, advertised an affluent twenty-five-year-old man hoping to correspond with a "poor girl of good, honest parents, possessing the traits of a good wife, rather than one of wealth without these requirements."[61] As a result of this raid, Hattie Howard, a manager of the "Edna Directory Company," was fined $100 for fraudulent use of the mails. Howard and her colleagues enticed clients with advertisements featuring women "'worth $120,000,' who had married 'kind and loving' coachmen; of daughters of millionaires who eloped with their father's butlers; and of 'proud beauties' who wedded farmers, preferring 'home life to society.'"[62]

In November 1902, Wooldridge raided a matrimonial mail order house, uncovering stacks of stock photos and letters, as well as circulars and advertisements for the service. These circulars encouraged clients to join the club for one dollar, which would provide members with the addresses of wealthy singles who hoped to correspond via mail with a view toward matrimony. Wooldridge seized thousands of envelopes, all containing the same letter from a blue-eyed nineteen-year-old "young lady," who possessed a small fortune and was eager to wed. This stock matrimonial correspondent "desire[d] an early marriage" and "does not care whether you are wealthy or not."[63] That same month, N. C. Clark, head of the Erie Advertising and Introduction bureau in Chicago, was arrested for fraudulent use of the US mails. Clark had similarly acquired fees by emphasizing the wealth and status of her clients. One of her dupes, Mr. D. H. Britt of Raynham, North Carolina, had been matched with "a young widow without children, worth in cash and city property at least $75,000." Britt eagerly wrote the young lady, who knew nothing of

[60] "Raid Cupid and Cupidity," *Chicago Daily Tribune*, 25 Sep. 1902, p. 1.
[61] "Raid on Love's Epistles," *Chicago Daily Tribune*, 8 Nov. 1902, p. 3.
[62] "Court Scores Managers of Matrimonial Bureaus," *Chicago Daily Tribune*, 13 Feb. 1903, p. 7.
[63] "Another Marriage Bureau Is Raided by the Police," *Chicago Daily Tribune*, 21 Nov. 1902, p. 5.

the marriage bureau's existence, had no interest in getting married, and possessed none of the wealth attributed to her by the agency.[64]

Many critics were especially bothered that matrimonial bureaus used claims of wealth, be they true or false, to bait impressionable singles. These commentators also chastised poor individuals for attempting to climb their way into higher classes. One writer highlighted the "mercenary" motives of male matrimonial correspondents, arguing that these men did not want love, but rather capital. "Many of them don't seem to care whether their possible spouses are homely or pretty, old or young, fat or slim, so they have property."[65] The wild popularity of matrimonial organizations – Wooldridge claimed that the month-old Belmont Corresponding Club received an average of 230 letters each day, while it was reported that one agency received $15,000 and 45,000 respondents over six weeks in the spring of 1905, and that another agency in South Bend, Indiana, received an average of 1,400 letters a week – speaks to the allure of this vision.[66]

Wooldridge himself expressed ambivalence about matrimonial agencies, claiming that it was possible to distinguish the good from the bad. "I believe that matrimonial bureaus, with certain restrictions, may be conducted as legitimately as any other line of business," he explained in an interview with the *Tribune*. "They bring together people who would otherwise never have an opportunity of meeting, and happy marriages frequently result." In the same interview, however, Wooldridge bragged that he had broken up more matrimonial bureaus than any other man in the country, and he vowed to close the ones that remained operational.[67] The notion that reputable marriage bureaus could be differentiated from disreputable ones would fade throughout the decade as raids continued, and as critics focused less on the fraudulent acts of individual marital proprietors, and instead embraced the viewpoint that marriage bureaus were uniformly immoral, illegal, and contrary to public policy. Efforts to close marriage bureaus at all costs would overshadow the belief that bureaus could be useful courtship mechanisms when run properly.

The quest to eradicate matrimonial agencies intensified with the September 1907 arrest of Miss Marion Grey of Elgin, Illinois, for

---

[64] "Fee Fails to Bring Wife," *Chicago Daily Tribune*, 16 Feb. 1902, p. 6.
[65] "A Matrimonial Bureau's Letters," *Chicago Daily Tribune*, 21 May 1905, p. B6.
[66] "Take Letters and 'Photos' in Marriage Bureau Raid," *Chicago Daily Tribune*, 18 May 1905, p. 14; "A Matrimonial Bureau's Letters," *Chicago Daily Tribune*, 21 May 1905, p. B6; "Want Ad Fakers Rob Thousands," E3.
[67] "Cupid Dodges 'Hands Up,'" *Chicago Daily Tribune*, 4 Mar. 1903, p. 16.

managing the Search Light Matrimonial Club.[68] Over the course of her subsequent trial in the federal courtroom of Judge Kenesaw Mountain Landis, Grey came to embody the corruption of the matrimonial trade. This process began when Bess Miller, Grey's former assistant, took the stand. Miller testified that she and Grey had sent the same photographs to hundreds of club members.[69] Grey denied defrauding her customers, claiming from the witness stand that it had been her intention "to run a straightforward and honest matrimonial agency and try to find suitable life partners for men and women who wished to be married." She rebuffed Miller's allegations that she had deceitfully circulated the same photograph again and again, insisting that while she had printed a thousand pictures of Kansas City actress Cora Cline, she had included these photographs with her circular letter in the genuine hope of locating a spouse for Cline. She also claimed that she returned the five-dollar membership fee to any clients who did not find romance through her services.[70]

But much more seemed at stake in the jury's decision than precise questions over whether or not Grey's business activities constituted fraud. Instead, Assistant District Attorney Seward Smith Shirer presented this trial as an opportunity to restore order and respectability to the realm of marriage itself. "The sacred institution of marriage is involved in this case," he argued in his closing statement. "Is marriage a traffic in this great and glorious country? Can love matches be made by a paltry $5 policy in an affinity agency? If you permit the operation of this kind of business it will undermine society, break up our homes, and place our wives and daughters in danger." He closed his argument by denouncing Grey herself, asserting, "Miss Grey ran a vicious, disreputable business, and it is up to this jury to stop it. It is a disgrace to civilization – this worldwide hunting of affinities and soulmates. Miss Grey had her chance to lead a respectable life, and since she passed up the opportunity she must suffer for her offenses."[71]

Judge Landis similarly denounced marriage agencies in his charge to the jury. Landis criticized Grey for engaging in "mercenary matchmaking," and he referred to her bureau's promotional materials as "contemptuous," "rot," and "stuff."[72] The Judge's comments did not address

---

[68] "'Cupid's Aid' Has Cash Bond; Marion Gray Still a Puzzle," *Chicago Daily Tribune*, 18 Sep. 1907, p. 4.
[69] "Weeps at Expose of Affinity Game," *Chicago Daily Tribune*, 13 Feb. 1908, p. 3.
[70] "Affinity Finder Reveals Method," *Chicago Daily Tribune*, 14 Feb. 1908, p. 3.
[71] "'Affinity' Girl in Jury's Hands," *Chicago Daily Tribune*, 15 Feb. 1908, p. 3.
[72] "Marian Grey Jury Is in a Deadlock," *Chicago Daily Tribune*, 16 Feb. 1908, p. 1.

questions of the business's legality, but rather they presented a moral condemnation of Grey's entire operation, and on a broader level, of the practice of commercialized matchmaking itself. After these dramatic exhortations from prosecutor and judge, the jury found Grey guilty on charges in connection with William Grable of Missouri. The prosecution had used Grable as its principal witness, claiming that the woman with whom Grey had put him into contact was not the rich and beautiful widow Grey had advertised her to be. Grable had still fallen in love with this woman, but the fact that she lacked the qualities Grey had attributed to her was sufficient evidence for the jury to deem Grey a fraud. She was sentenced to a year in prison (see Figure 1.2).[73]

* * *

This guilty verdict marked a turning point in the crusade against matrimonial bureaus. Following his legal victory, Shirer took it upon himself as Assistant District Attorney to label all matrimonial agencies illegal, whether or not they enticed clients through fraud. Perhaps inspired by New York chief post office inspector Walter Mayer's questionable claim that there were no matrimonial bureaus in New York, Shirer vowed that Chicago would follow a similar path.[74] The next day a grand jury investigated the organizers of a national matrimonial trust, which had allegedly supplied stock testimonials and photographs of Cora Cline to more than a hundred marriage bureaus across the nation – including about twenty agencies in Chicago, Marion Grey's among them. Shirer viewed this investigation as a great development in his case against matrimonial bureaus, and he noted that fifty men and sixty women had been subpoenaed to testify. "We have started a wholesale crusade against matrimonial agencies," he proclaimed, "and are going to drive them out of business in Chicago and elsewhere."[75]

---

[73] "Verdict of Guilty for Marian Grey," *Chicago Daily Tribune*, 17 Feb. 1908, p. 1; "*Grey v. United States* (Circuit Court of Appeals, Seventh Circuit. April 13, 1909. Rehearing Denied May 13, 1909)," in *United States Circuit Courts of Appeals Reports with Annotations*, vol. 96 (Rochester, N.Y.: Lawyers' Co-operative Publishing Company, 1910), 415–417. Grey was acquitted on two additional charges of fraud in connection with other dissatisfied clients. Epstein recounts this trial in detail: see *Selling Love*, 121–129.

[74] "Cupid Must Do Own Work," *Chicago Daily Tribune*, 19 Feb. 1908, p. 18. "Refusal to Halt Anti-Cupid War," *Chicago Daily Tribune*, 29 Feb. 1908, p. 7.

[75] "Inspectors Find Corner in Cupids," *Chicago Daily Tribune*, 20 Feb. 1908, p. 5.

JAIL FOR CUPID'S AID
Marion Grey, Pretty Love Broker, Who
Was Sentenced to a Year in Prison

FIGURE 1.2 Illustration of Marion Grey, in Clifton W. Wooldridge, *Twenty Years a Detective in the Wickedest City in the World* (Chicago: Chicago Publishing Company, 1908), 163.

As weeks passed, Shirer proved correct in his pledge as agency after agency was raided and shut down by authorities, frequently under the investigation of postal inspector James Stuart. In many cases these agencies circulated the exact materials sent out by Grey, furnished by the above-mentioned marital trust. This was the case with "Mrs. Jennie Call," who was arrested in February 1908 for "flooding the mails" with matrimonial advertisements in an effort to entice clients into her matrimonial club. Call, later referred to as Jennie Glinn, had been running the Glinn International Corresponding Association, and had appealed especially to women by offering them a discounted rate of two dollars for club membership. Glinn claimed she had attended every day of the Marion

Grey trial, and in response to the guilty verdict she had revised her business model to conform with the law in every way.[76]

Glinn's trial began in the US District Court for the Northern District of Illinois, Eastern Division. Some witnesses for the prosecution provided no evidence of swindling. Frank Kohler of Sweetwine, Ohio, claimed to have exchanged three or four letters with the widowed Mary Quinn of Clinton, Illinois, after Glinn had given him Quinn's name, but ultimately he "got tired" and married an acquaintance from his hometown. C. S. Runnels, a Nebraska schoolteacher, had received the name of New York's Ida Millner after sending his five dollars to Glinn, and had quickly commenced correspondence. At the time of Glinn's trial, Runnels and Millner were still corresponding. He planned to visit her at trial's end, and to take her back to Nebraska as his wife if the meeting went well.[77]

Despite this less-than-damning testimony, Shirer's closing arguments for the prosecution indicate that the trial served less as an investigation of Glinn's business model and more as an incrimination of all matrimonial bureaus as guilty of exploiting loneliness for financial gain. His statement played to jurors' emotions, focusing on the moral harm matrimonial bureaus inflicted on American society as a whole:

This placing of the sacred institution of marriage on a commercial basis ... will undermine society. It ruins the morals of our boys and girls. My boy or your boy, your daughter or my daughter may answer one of the fraudulent matrimonial advertisements, just for a joke. He or she receives ... a picture of a beautiful woman who is looking for a husband, or of a bachelor who wants a soul partner – poor man or woman not objected to. It is a disgrace that this nefarious business has been permitted as long as it has been.[78]

Shirer concluded by suggesting that the elimination of marriage bureaus was more significant than the specifics of this particular case. He implored, "I demand that you gentlemen, representing the people, help the government break up this traffic in soul partners and this commercial matching up."[79] Judge Solomon Hicks Bethea also deemphasized the details of Glinn's business and focused on the scourge of matrimonial brokerage at large. "This is not simply a case against Mrs. Glinn," he urged the jury, "but a prosecution by government officials to free the

---

[76] "Cupid Promoter No. 2 Taken," *Chicago Daily Tribune*, 26 Feb. 1908, p. 1.
[77] "Affinities on the Warpath," *Chicago Daily Tribune*, 12 Apr. 1908, p. 6; "One Soul Mater Gets Prison Term," *Chicago Daily Tribune*, 16 Apr. 1908, p. 4.
[78] "Love Broker No. 2 Guilty of Fraud," *Chicago Daily Tribune*, 18 Apr. 1908, p. 6.
[79] Ibid., 6.

United States mails of fraudulent enterprises."[80] The jurors conceded by
finding Glinn guilty on all counts after seven minutes of deliberation.
Bethea sentenced her to a year in the Chicago house of correction, stating
that he hoped this sentence would dissuade others from following in
her footsteps.[81]

When the case was appealed the following year to the Seventh Circuit
Court of Appeals, the court affirmed Glinn's conviction of using the
mails to defraud her clients. The court's opinion, however, paid greater
attention to the specifics of Glinn's enterprise; the appellate judges
showed less interest in making an example of Glinn than in determining
whether or not she had practiced mail fraud.[82] Judge Peter S. Grosscup
explained in the opinion that he saw no evidence in the record that Glinn
had ever produced a marriage for any of her approximately six hundred
clients. With that record of failure as a matchmaker, and in light of one
witness's claim that the "wealthy widow" with whom Glinn had put
him in touch actually made a meager living through domestic service,
the appellate court upheld the jury's verdict. Grosscup concluded that
Glinn had never intended to create marriages for her clients; instead, her
only objective had been to receive membership fees from unsuspecting
clients through attractive stock photographs and false descriptions of
potential mates' affluence and affability.[83] Grosscup's precision in
condemning Glinn for her fraudulent marriage brokerage practices,
however, should not obscure the imprecision with which Shirer and
Bethea before him had condemned Glinn for partaking in an industry
of which they disapproved morally.

The raids on matrimonial agencies continued in the months that
followed the trials of Grey and Glinn. Shirer and his colleagues had
succeeded with these two trials in proving that matrimonial brokerage
was in and of itself illegal, with or without fraudulent business practices.
Their campaign received an unexpected boost when the LaPorte, Indiana,

---

[80] Ibid., 6.

[81] "Prison for Agent of Cupid," *Chicago Daily Tribune*, 26 Apr. 1908, p. 3. See Wooldridge, *Twenty Years a Detective*, 159–64, for a less than sympathetic depiction of
Glinn's story.

[82] *Glinn v. United States*, 177 F. 679 (1910). Grosscup mentioned in his opinion that the
defense had assigned "the instructions to the jury" as an error from the district court trial.
One wonders if the defense was referring to what reads today as Bethea's clearly leading
charge to the jury, and his suggestion that the specifics of Glinn's agency were less
important than the idea that someone must be convicted of mail fraud to dissuade future
marriage brokerage.

[83] Ibid.

sheriff uncovered nearly forty bodies on the farm of Belle Gunness, a middle-aged widow and Norwegian immigrant, who had used matrimonial advertisements to attract suitors to her property, only to murder them for their money. The scandal surfaced on 28 April 1908, when a fire destroyed Gunness's home. Four bodies, believed to belong to Gunness and her children, were found in the basement, and Ray Lamphere, formerly Gunness's handyman, was arrested for arson and murder.[84] Sympathy for Gunness herself quickly subsided, however, as suspicions began to encircle the case; skeptics noted that Gunness had executed her will within twelve hours of the conflagration and that the adult body burned in the farmhouse did not have a head. It soon became clear that this case was more complicated than many had initially assumed.[85]

On May 5, investigators found five additional bodies buried in Gunness's yard, and four more the next day.[86] As the body count grew, and as the story began to receive national attention, investigators, journalists, and readers pieced together explanations of what had occurred. Commentators questioned whether or not the decapitated body belonged to Belle Gunness, and assumptions of guilt shifted from Lamphere to Gunness herself. Just days after the initial story broke, newspapers began reporting that Gunness had lured men to her farm through matrimonial advertisements, only to rob and kill them upon their arrival. The LaPorte postmaster claimed that Gunness had been receiving between four and ten letters each day from men across the country since the death of her second husband five years prior.[87]

Journalists reported widely on Gunness's use of matrimonial advertisements, and the *New York Times* published the initial ad she had placed in

---

[84] "Four Die in Fire; Suitor Is in Toils" *Chicago Daily Tribune*, 29 Apr. 1908, p. 3.

[85] "Fire Tragedy Subject Mixed," *Chicago Daily Tribune*, 30 Apr. 1908, p. 5; "Fire Victim's Head Missing; LaPorte Mystery Deepens," *Chicago Daily Tribune*, 1 May 1908, p. 5; Janet L. Langlois, *Belle Gunness: The Lady Bluebeard* (Bloomington: Indiana University Press, 1985), 7.

[86] "Bodies of Five Slain Unearthed in Yard," *New York Times*, 6 May 1908, p. 1; "4 More Skeletons in Indiana Mystery," *New York Times*, 7 May 1908, pp. 1–2; Langlois, *Belle Gunness*, 7–8.

[87] "4 More Skeletons in Indiana Mystery," 2. On Gunness's marriages, see Langlois, *Belle Gunness*, 4–7. Gunness married Norwegian Mads Sorensen in Chicago in 1884. Sorensen died on 30 July 1900, "the one and only day that his two life insurance policies with two different mutual benefit associations overlapped," leaving his widow $8,500. As Langlois recounts, Sorensen showed symptoms of strychnine poisoning, which Gunness attributed to a powder she had given him to help a cold. The death certificate stated that Sorensen had died of natural causes. Belle Gunness married her second husband, Peter Gunness, in April 1902, and he died later that year.

a Chicago newspaper: "A rich and good-looking woman, the owner of a big farm, desires to correspond with a gentleman of wealth and refinement. Object, matrimony. Scandinavian preferred."[88] The postmaster acknowledged that this advertisement yielded numerous responses, especially from the Northwest. But post office employees made light of Gunness's failure to present herself accurately. "It got to be a joke around the Post Office – this flood of mail," Postmaster Small explained to the reporter. "For the advertiser was anything but the comely woman she pretended to be. She was fat, unkempt, and far from attractive in features. But letters came thick and fast, and presently neighbors began to notice strange men appear around the Gunness farm."[89] Other reports paid more attention to the newspapers in which Gunness advertised. Her primary vehicle was *Skandinaven*, a Chicago-area Norwegian daily journal, which allowed Gunness to write in Norwegian and to solicit men of similar ethnic heritage. Ultimately, she was very successful at attracting the wealthy Norwegian farmers she sought.[90] Gunness's ads and the correspondence they prompted would be scrutinized as the case unfolded. Not only did these matrimonial advertisements offer insight into the heinous crimes committed on Belle Gunness's farm; they also provided impetus for additional commentaries on the depravities of commercial marriage and courtship practices (see Figure 1.3).

For many commentators, the murders committed by Belle Gunness seemed less significant than the methods she used to lure men to her property. Detective Wooldridge highlighted this case as the natural culmination of a sinful courtship practice, stating, "In the dread Gunness Farm behold the ripened fruit of the matrimonial agency."[91] For authorities such as Shirer and US District Attorney Edwin Sims, who were already waging a campaign against matrimonial bureaus, the Gunness case offered the perfect example of what might happen if their campaign failed. Just days after the first bodies were uncovered on the farm, Sims demanded the immediate arrest of the managers of every matrimonial bureau in the Chicago district. Meanwhile, Shirer claimed to have acquired evidence against twenty-two of those agencies, many of which had sent young girls "to disorderly places in the red light districts."

---

[88] "4 More Skeletons in Indiana Mystery," p. 2.   [89] Ibid., 2.
[90] "May Have Used 'Ad' to Lure," *Chicago Daily Tribune*, 8 May 1908, p. 3. This article noted that the advertisements in *Skandinaven* were usually placed by farmers who, "after having become well to do, are anxious to marry."
[91] Wooldridge, *Twenty Years a Detective*, 170.

THE DEATH HARVESTER.

A Crop on the Gunness Farm.

FIGURE 1.3 Belle Gunness depicted as "The Death Harvester," in Clifton W. Wooldridge, *Twenty Years a Detective in the Wickedest City in the World* (Chicago: Chicago Publishing Company, 1908), 166.

Arguing that the fates met by Gunness's victims were more common than many assumed, Shirer warned that all respondents to matrimonial ads faced grave danger. He acknowledged that not all matrimonial agencies paved the way for "murder on wholesale style," but he again insisted that all of these agencies were illegal, and he used this incident as proof of the damage they could cause.[92]

At the same time that he condemned matrimonial bureaus for enabling violence and scandal, as evidenced in the Gunness case, Shirer also admonished those people who responded to personal advertisements, branding them "an unintellectual set" and chiding them for carelessly putting themselves at risk of violence and murder.[93] As the body count grew, the media placed greater emphasis on the recklessness of those who

[92] "Her Deeds Hit Love Brokers," *Chicago Daily Tribune*, 8 May 1908, p. 3.
[93] Ibid., 3.

had responded to Gunness's advertisements, criticizing the irrational longings that had inspired so many decent men to risk their lives for material comforts. Expressing little sympathy for the victims of Gunness's matrimonial scheming, one Kentucky columnist joked that "the motto over Mrs. Gunness' door might have been: 'A fool and his money are soon parted.'"[94] After questioning the mental capacity of individuals who responded to personal advertisements, and suggesting that Gunness's victims should perhaps be grateful that death spared them from married life with Gunness, the author closed with a general criticism of matrimonial brokerage as nothing but a scheme for the "robbery of fools." Presenting Gunness as a typical matrimonial agent and categorizing her proprietors as lazy and greedy swindlers, the journalist argued, "If it were not for the people, who hope to get rich without working, and those who try to purchase love, we should have few sensational crimes to report."[95] The proliferation of matrimonial ads allowed acquisitive predators like Gunness to continue preying on foolish victims.

In addition to condemning Gunness for her greed, then, these critics also highlighted the mercenary motives of the people who responded to such ads. While there is no indication that Gunness's victims would have gone to violent extremes to acquire her savings, reports of this case made clear that many of the men who pursued Gunness were as drawn to her money as she was to theirs. As much as Gunness specified in her advertisements that she was seeking a wealthy man to help raise her children, she also emphasized her own wealth as an incentive, and expressed interest in "joining fortunes."[96] But as the identities of the victims emerged, it became evident that many of Gunness's suitors were not as wealthy as they claimed.

For instance, George Anderson was likely spared from death because he lied about his financial status. A Swedish immigrant living in Missouri, Anderson read an advertisement from Gunness in a Scandinavian newspaper in 1906. After a brief correspondence, Anderson paid her a visit in LaPorte, falsely presenting himself as a wealthy farmer. Anderson's narrative faltered when on the second day of his stay Gunness asked him how much money he possessed. Anderson told her that he only had a few hundred dollars in cash, but that he also owned a valuable 320-acre farm. Gunness ordered him to sell the farm, assuring him that if he brought the money back to her they would wed. After a few days away,

---

[94] "The Cupid of LaPorte," *Paducah Evening Sun*, 12 May 1908, p. 4.   [95] Ibid., 4.
[96] "The Lure of Death," *Paducah Evening Sun*, 8 May 1908, p. 1.

Anderson returned to confess that he had lied about the farm and that he was not a wealthy man. The furious Gunness nonetheless instructed Anderson to spend the night at her house, and Anderson complied. He awoke that night to Gunness standing beside his bed bent over him, at which point he spoke to her and she ran out of the room. Terrified, Anderson left early the next morning.[97]

Anderson was not the only suitor to hint that money had driven him to Gunness's farm. John Hunter left his home in Duquesne, Pennsylvania, in November 1907, informing his children that he was heading to Indiana "to marry a wealthy widow." Ludwig Stoll owned a 500-acre farm in Mt. Yeager, Pennsylvania, which he left behind to marry "a wealthy widow in the west." Benjamin Carling of Chicago, another Gunness victim, had informed his sister before leaving that he was headed to LaPorte "to meet a widow with lots of money."[98] The brief examples from Gunness's correspondents indicate that money was often central to this sort of long-distance courtship. For rural Scandinavian immigrants seeking to consolidate their wealth and to find companionship in relatively remote midwestern regions, a matrimonial arrangement based primarily on financial exchanges served a practical function, even if it fell short of satisfying romantic visions of matrimony. For critics like Shirer, however, this explicitly economic motive was unacceptable, and it called for legal intervention.[99]

* * *

In their campaigns to eliminate commercialized matchmaking venues, reformers like Shirer expressed the belief that these courtship mechanisms defied public policy by their very nature: they linked the sacred practice of marriage to greed and financial gain; they left men and women vulnerable to physical and economic exploitation; and they reflected a decline in sexual morals. A different set of reformers shared these apprehensions,

---

[97] "Left Norway to Meet the Woman," *Salt Lake Herald*, 12 May 1908, p. 1.

[98] "Gunness Verdict In," *Washington Herald*, 22 May 1908, p. 3. "Mysteries," *The Stark County Democrat* (Canton, Ohio), 22 May 1908, p. 2.

[99] Three years later, Minnie Murdock of Norfolk, Virginia, drew comparisons to Gunness after similarly murdering the men she had lured to her farm with matrimonial advertisements. Popular accounts of this story reinforced Shirer's warnings that personal ads and matrimonial bureaus could yield deadly results. "No Bodies Yet Found," *Washington Post*, 8 Jun. 1911, pp. 1–2; "Expect to Find More Bodies," *Indiana Gazette* (Pa.), 8 Jun. 1911, p. 2; "Scent New Guinness Case," *Western Sentinel* (Winston-Salem), 13 Jun. 1911, p. 2; "Another Murder Farm?," *Sandusky Star-Journal*, 14 Jun. 1911, p. 7.

but they resisted Shirer's urge to eradicate matrimonial bureaus altogether. These men and women were outspoken in their defense of marriage and family, and they were aware of the threat that matchmaking bureaus placed on their visions of marital propriety. But more than anything, they believed that the institution of marriage itself was in a state of crisis, and they opted to use whatever tools they could to repair it. Therefore, rather than condemn marital agencies and advertisements altogether, these reformers embraced them as a way to promote their traditional family values and to reassert the centrality of marital tradition to American life.

For example, several prominent bachelors from St. Louis established a committee in 1906 to form "The Granite City Matrimonial Bureau." Concerned that their city lacked suitable wives, committee members sought to recruit young women into St. Louis for the purposes of matrimony. The men explained that St. Louis's industrial growth had created an imbalance between the sexes and that without an influx of brides the situation could become dire. As one reporter explained, "Unless marriages are more prevalent in the future, race suicide will play an important part in the history of Granite City." As such, this bureau sought to preserve the institution of marriage and to uphold a steady rate of procreation among the ruling classes.[100] Similarly, the city of Des Moines established a municipal matrimonial bureau "to try to keep the marriages apace with the separations." More than anything, such organizations worried about declining marriage rates, and they insisted that bureaus were necessary for keeping the American population intact.[101]

Some marriage reformers pushed the project of government-run agencies even further, attempting to create state-run marriage bureaus to accelerate the marriage rate amid fears of its decline. Rather than condemn the individuals who utilized matchmaking bureaus, these men created their own, in part to address their fear that the lure of bachelor culture was preventing healthy men from matrimony. In 1909, John Farrell of the Wisconsin General Assembly introduced a bill that would compel bachelors over the age of thirty to pay a yearly tax for failing to wed. Following a similar set of proposals from Missouri representatives, proponents of the Wisconsin bill also sought to form a state-run

---

[100] "Young Women Wanted," *Charlotte News*, 2 Jan. 1906, p. 6.
[101] "Our Envious Neighbors," *Des Moines Register*, 17 Oct. 1911, p. 6; "Lovelorn Lassies Notably Scarce," *Des Moines Register*, 4 Jan. 1910, p. 10; "Matrimonial Bureau Has Been Organized," *Des Moines Register*, 4 Oct. 1911, p. 3.

matrimonial agency to help bachelors find wives, and thus avoid the bachelor tax.[102] Farrell predicted that the creation of a state matrimonial bureau would lead to stronger and longer-lasting unions, without the potential for the fraud that commercial agencies spawned. Farrell acknowledged that some might call his bill "freak legislation," but he warned constituents that a lack of compatibility between partners was contributing to a rising divorce rate, and he believed his proposed solution would lead to fewer doomed marriages.[103] In 1911, another Wisconsin assemblyman, Carl Hansen of Manitowoc, introduced a similar bill that would tax unmarried women over the age of twenty-five and create a government-run matrimonial bureau to facilitate nuptials.[104] Though these bills never became law, their construction reveals an effort by marriage reformers to appropriate the matrimonial bureau phenomenon, transforming sources of profit into mechanisms that would create unions and assist the state in reasserting patriarchal marital tradition.[105]

Church leaders also participated in this conservative appropriation of matrimonial bureaus. Reverend J. F. X. Colman, pastor of St. John's Catholic church in Maryland, preached of his desire to start a matrimonial bureau to reverse declining marriage rates among parishioners.[106]

---

[102] For examples of similar bills in Missouri, see "Bachelors Must Marry," *Leader-Democrat* (Springfield), 2 Dec. 1897, p. 3; "Missouri Legislature," *Scott County Kicker* (Benton), 9 Mar. 1907, p. 2. For background on the creation of bachelor laws and taxes in the early seventeenth century, see John Gilbert McCurdy, *Citizen Bachelors: Manhood and the Creation of the United States* (Ithaca: Cornell University Press, 2009), 50–83.

[103] "Urge Tax on Bachelors," *Salisbury Evening Post* (N.C.), 14 Jan. 1909, p. 5; "Aid to Cupid's Work," *Rock Island Argus* (Ill.), 2 Jan. 1909, p. 3; "The Old Bachelor Must Go," *Charlotte News*, 21 Jan. 1909, p. 4.

[104] "To Tax Spinsters $5 a Year," *Dixon Evening Telegraph* (Ill.), 24 Mar. 1911, p. 7; "Just What It Is Coming To," *Oakland Tribune*, 1 Apr. 1911, p. 12.

[105] Other states to deliberate bachelor tax bills included Georgia, Texas, North Carolina, New Jersey, Pennsylvania, New York, Kansas, Indiana, Delaware, Iowa, Massachusetts, Oregon, Montana, New Mexico, and Minnesota. See "The Old Bachelors' Tax Bill," *Atlanta Constitution*, 9 Aug. 1885, p. 6; "Taxation and Celibacy," *Galveston Daily News*, 14 Mar. 1895, p. 4; "Tax on Single Men," *Trenton Evening Times*, 5 Feb. 1898, p. 5; "Another Bachelor Tax Bill," *Macon Times-Democrat* (Mo.), 29 Apr. 1901, p. 1; "Chicago Teachers after the Bachelors," *Marion Star* (Ohio), 10 Feb. 1903, p. 1; "Oregon News," *Roseburg Review* (Ore.), 6 Jan. 1913, p. 3; "Bachelor Tax Bill Fails in New Mexico," *Oregon Statesman* (Salem), 26 Feb. 1921, p. 1; "Tax for Bachelors," *New Ulm Review* (Minn.), 23 Feb. 1921, p. 4.

[106] "Wants More Weddings," *Minneapolis Journal*, 9 Aug. 1901, p. 5; "Father Coleman on the Married State," *Charlotte News*, 13 Aug. 1901, p. 6.

In St. Louis, Catholic Reverend James Coffey and his female congregants established St. Leo's Matrimonial Club as a church society. Noting a disproportionately high number of female church members, Coffey created this organization to foster lasting nuptials and to encourage male congregants to become "husbands instead of lovers." The agency matched men and women for social activities, sponsored plays and group discussions on the topic of matrimony, and even organized mock weddings. Coffey hoped his interventions would push young men away from bachelordom and spark nuptials among young Catholics.[107]

Following in the footsteps of St. Leo's Matrimonial Club, the Church of the Annunciation in Kansas City, Kansas, opened a matrimonial agency in 1912. Reverend William Dalton created this organization because he worried that young congregants were delaying marriage. Very quickly the organization's reach transcended the walls of the church. In the bureau's first year of operation, Dalton received letters from 17,000 men and women around the world, including correspondents in Jerusalem, Constantinople, Africa, and South America. He employed two stenographers to respond to these letters, instructing them to make matches among people living near one another. Dalton claimed to have produced 400 marriages in the society's first year. In addition to playing matchmaker, Dalton ran weekly marriage education courses, which attracted fifty to a hundred congregants per each "school of matrimony" session.[108]

Dalton charged no fees for his services, thus setting himself apart from commercial matchmakers. Moreover, Dalton used his clerical platform to denounce the greed he believed had overtaken the pursuit of matrimony, both among the people running matrimonial services and their clients. He reserved most of his scolding for those women who let economic factors obstruct their path to true love. "Men really are looking for good wives," he insisted. "But women want to marry money. They ask for rich city men." Dalton repeatedly criticized the entire female sex for letting financial concerns drive their mate selection, while also contending that too many women opted for the frivolities of urban life over the stability of marriage to farmers. He reserved some criticism for men as well,

---

[107] "Young Women Form Club to Win Husbands," *St. Louis Post-Dispatch*, 3 Dec. 1907, p. 1; "Girls Seek Husbands," *Detroit Free Press*, 30 Dec. 1907, p. 3.

[108] "Women Partial to Life in City," *San Francisco Call*, 23 Jul. 1912, p. 11; "Enlisted in the Tribe of Gad," *Inter Ocean*, 24 Jul. 1912, p. 6; "America's Most Remarkable Matrimonial Bureau," *Muskogee Times-Democrat*, 13 Aug. 1912, p. 5; "Matrimonial Bureau of Church a Big Success," *Wilmington Dispatch* (N.C.), 10 Jan. 1913, p. 3.

chastising bachelors for their "irresponsible" unwillingness to provide for a wife and family. "I tell them they are like driftwood on the sea," he declared. "They do not do their duty by staying single."[109] In creating a matrimonial bureau within his congregation, Dalton reasserted his traditional ideas about marriage and gender through a controversial mechanism. He utilized this courtship model to press marriage on the men he believed were shirking their masculine responsibilities and to discourage women from marrying out of greed.

A number of surprising uses for matrimonial bureaus arose from Oklahoma in the late 1910s and 1920s. In 1918, Oklahoma City's J. W. Walden, superintendent of Oklahoma's free employment bureau, launched a state matrimonial agency to find wives for widowed and unmarried farmers. Walden was not the first to propose a state-run marriage agency. As noted above, officials in Wisconsin and Missouri had previously tried to bring this concept to fruition as part of their bachelor taxation bills. Legislators in Washington had also supported a short-lived initiative to form a state-run matrimonial bureau, which they hoped would bring women into Washington to wed its disproportionately male population.[110]

But while these earlier initiatives failed to get off the ground, the Oklahoma state matrimonial bureau gained some traction. Seeking to fend off the labor shortages that accompanied American participation in World War I, superintendent Walden created a marriage bureau that aimed to stop workers from leaving Oklahoma and to entice new workers into the state. The agency helped lonely farmers to find wives, and it also found male partners for women who wished to be farmwives. The *Morning Tulsa Daily World* profiled a local farmer who had written to Walden's agency to find a wife who was "farm broke and a good housekeeper." Walden matched this man with a woman who had contacted the employment bureau for a job – it appears the Oklahoma bureau presumed that a woman pursuing agricultural employment was, in fact, pursuing agricultural matrimony. Walden defended the department's actions by explaining that matchmaking was "a legitimate and

---

[109] "America's Most Remarkable Matrimonial Bureau," 5.
[110] This proposal emerged at the request of Claude Gage, a county marriage license clerk, who claimed to have received more than two thousand letters from women in eastern states, all hoping to move west to wed Washingtonian men. "You'll Find It Here," *Tacoma Times*, 14 Dec. 1912, p. 8; "Here's Your Chance to Wed, Girls," *Tacoma Times*, 31 Dec. 1912, p. 7; "Matrimonial Bureau," *Cincinnati Enquirer*, 2 Jan. 1913, p. 3.

proper function for a free state employment office like this one."[111] A vast departure from the get-rich-quick schemes that drove commercialized matrimonial endeavors, the Oklahoma bureau used marriage to serve the state's own economic interests, utilizing the promise of matrimony to keep Oklahoma's workforce intact.

Following in Walden's footsteps, another Oklahoma institution found an even more unusual use for matrimonial bureaus – as part of a citywide initiative to end suicide. In the early 1920s, the city of Muskogee's Salvation Army established both an antisuicide bureau and a marriage bureau, which operated side by side. Its leaders claimed that the marriage agency would offer hope and romantic possibility to persons who had contemplated ending their lives. As one local journalist explained, the bureau had united several formerly suicidal individuals in marriage, "and the result has been a life filled with love action, rather than loneliness and despair." Adjutant John Howard spoke of a seventy-year-old man whose sense of isolation had nearly led him to kill himself. "We cared for him and tried to fill his time with action," Howard recalled. "Then we found a woman, also aged, who also was alone and lonely. Through our matrimonial bureau they became acquainted and were married. Now they are happy as a couple of kids." In Howard's view, the matrimonial bureau gave desperate individuals a new lease on life, and kept them alive by finding them partners in love and marriage.[112]

The majority of these initiatives took place on local and state levels, but one noteworthy exception arose in 1920 when Alice Robertson, recently elected as the second woman ever to serve in the US Congress, attempted to sponsor a US Bureau of Matrimony. This proposed bureau was the brainchild of the Women's United States Chamber of Commerce, and the committee's members viewed Robertson – from Muskogee herself – as the ideal politician to introduce the initiative. Though Chamber members claimed support from other representatives, they wanted their bill to be sponsored by the only female member of Congress, even though Robertson was unmarried. Proponents of the bill believed that a government-sponsored bureau would save the institutions of marriage and family from deterioration. Chamber secretary Fannie Wolfson argued:

---

[111] "Predicts a Labor Shortage," *Morning Tulsa Daily World*, 5 Dec. 1915, p. 6; "Call for Cotton Pickers," *Haskell News* (Okla.), 28 Sep. 1916, p. 2; "'Jobs' Secured through State at 14 Cents Per," *Muskogee Times-Democrat*, 22 Jan. 1918, p. 1; "State Now Running Matrimonial Bureau," *Morning Tulsa Daily World*, 11 Mar. 1918, p. 3.

[112] "Anti-Suicide and Matrimonial Bureaus Work Side by Side in Muskogee," *Muskogee Times-Democrat*, 27 Jan. 1923, p. 14.

Family life in this country will disintegrate if something isn't done immediately to encourage marriage and stimulate the birth rate. There is nothing ridiculous about our idea. It should be the normal function of the government to raise the standards of marriage and bring together young hearts, and old ones, too, for that matter. Private matrimonial agencies are reaping fortunes, many fleecing the poor souls who apply to them. The safest love broker in the world would be Uncle Sam.[113]

The bill's proponents called for help from eugenicists in guiding the agency's matchmaking practices and in encouraging unions between individuals believed most fit for reproduction.[114]

One might assume that the inclusion of eugenicists reflected anxiety over interracial and interethnic marriage, and it likely did to an extent. While serving in Congress, Alice Robertson expressed disdain for the "poison stream of immigration" that, in her view, tainted the nation with atheism, socialism, and anti-American sentiment.[115] As such, it is probable that Robertson viewed the federal marriage bureau as one way to prevent ethnic groups she deemed undesirable from marrying and procreating with native-born whites. But additional insight into Robertson's commitment to Native American education and assimilation tells an even more complex story about her thoughts on race and marriage. Born in the heart of Indian Territory, Robertson had served as clerk in the Indian Office of the Department of the Interior, administrator at Carlisle Indian School, and field supervisor of Creek Indian Schools. As a proponent of Native American assimilation and Christianization, Robertson made frequent appeals for marriage between whites and Native Americans. In 1889 she had declared that the "Indian question in the Territory is going to be wiped out with blood, *white* blood by intermarriage," and she welcomed this brand of amalgamation.[116]

[113] Mildred Morris, "Girls Want Miss Alice to Abolish Old Maids by Nationalizing Cupid," *Washington Times*, 8 Nov. 1920, p. 1.

[114] Ibid., 1; Alexander Black, "Where John Bull Has Failed Will Uncle Sam Succeed?," *Atlanta Constitution*, 10 Oct. 1920, p. 1; "Marriage Experts Explain the Growing 'Hungry Hearts' Mania," *Ogden Standard-Examiner* (Utah), 18 Aug. 1929, p. 33.

[115] Linda Williams Reese, *Women of Oklahoma, 1890–1920* (Norman: University of Oklahoma Press, 1997), 233.

[116] Quoted in Katherine Ellinghaus, *Taking Assimilation to Heart: Marriages of White Women and Indigenous Men in the United States and Australia, 1887–1937* (Lincoln: University of Nebraska Press, 2006), 170–171; see also Melanie Susan Gustafson, *Women and the Republican Party, 1854–1924* (Urbana: University of Illinois Press, 2001), 174. See Reese, *Women of Oklahoma*, 215–237, for an account of Robertson's career. Reese notes that most of the students Robertson instructed at Minerva Home, a Tulsa boarding school for Native American girls, married white men.

Robertson was not alone in promoting intermarriage between whites and Native Americans. Many white proponents of intermarriage were driven by a hunger for Native lands, a goal that federal Indian policy helped them to fulfill. The Dawes Act of 1887 had divided tribal land-holdings into individual plots to be occupied by nuclear family units, thus breaking up the shared landownership at the heart of many tribal cultures. This measure served as a coercive push for Americanization in its efforts to separate extended families, to assert white gender roles on tribal households, and to link property ownership to monogamous marriage.[117] Some white Americans sought to capitalize on the federal push for Indian marriages by pursuing unions with unwed Native Americans – in great part as a means of acquiring tribal land for themselves.[118] The press reported on this quest for intermarriage, emphasizing the material benefits it brought to white spouses. For example, one North Carolina journalist noted that a Cherokee bride could bring her husband "a dower of 160 acres of fine land and a right to a sum of money that is now held in trust for the members of the tribe in Uncle Sam's strong-box." Ignoring the Dawes Act's assault on tribal culture and landholding, articles like this one served to spark white interest in intermarriage as a path to wealth and property.[119]

Matrimonial advertisements and bureaus played a powerful role in bringing this objective to fruition. Newspapers operating out of Indian Territory published many accounts of marriage brokers and individual advertisers seeking to create interracial partnerships. They often poked fun at the opportunistic white men – and occasional women – who advertised for Native American spouses and sent letters to Indian offices requesting mates. Such articles emphasized advertisers' preoccupation with Native lands, and the mercenary motives that drove their courtship. For instance, the press profiled a Texan who sought correspondence with "young ladies of Indian decent [*sic*], living in Indian Territory. Object, matrimony and business," and a German man who entered the Union

---

[117] Cott, *Public Vows*, 122–123.
[118] Rose Stremlau, *Sustaining the Cherokee Family: Kinship and the Allotment of an Indigenous Nation* (Chapel Hill: University of North Carolina Press, 2011), 50–51. As Peggy Pascoe argues, white-Indian miscegenation law was not widely enacted or enforced until the turn of the twentieth century, when whites owned so much former Indian property that there was little government incentive to encourage these unions. Pascoe, *What Comes Naturally: Miscegenation Law and the Making of Race in America* (New York: Oxford University Press, 2009), 94–108.
[119] "Indian Brides in Demand," *Wilmington Messenger* (N.C.), 5 Sep. 1897, p. 5.

Indian Agency in Muskogee allegedly proclaiming, "I vants to get vone of dese vidows vat iss getting some moneys."[120] Newspapers also referenced the calculated nature of white advertisers' marital choices. For instance, one Tulsa journalist wrote of an Arkansas man, a former occupant of the Benton County poor house, who had approached the Commissioner of Indian Affairs to locate a Creek wife. The article noted his selectiveness in choosing a mate: "He refused to take a Cherokee, because they did not have so much land as the Creeks, and also a Seminole, because their land was not as good as that of the Creeks."[121]

The newspaper-centered pursuit of Native Americans by white singles was prevalent enough to become a source of profit for residents of Indian Territory. In 1900, the Chickasaw tribe passed a law requiring white men to pay a one-thousand-dollar fee for marriage to Chickasaw women, in part as a money-making venture and in part to cut down on the number of exploitative interracial marriages taking place in the area.[122] In 1901, two young women of Seminole descent, Millie and Annie Red Buffalo, were arrested for operating a fraudulent marriage bureau. In a familiar pattern, the women requested five-dollar admission fees from men who wished to find Seminole brides. Emphasizing that prospective wives each held $5,000 to $8,000 worth of property, these women raised a small fortune from land-hungry suitors, for whom they had no intention of providing matches.[123] In 1903, S. M. Brosius, an agent for the Indian Rights Association, discovered that marriage brokers had come into the Choctaw nation to locate potential Choctaw wives for eastern men. They would advertise their bureaus in national newspapers, match Native wives with white husbands, and collect between $25 and $250 for each marriage they created.[124]

---

[120] "Here's Your Chance Girls," *Telephone* (Tahlequah, Okla.), 1 Feb. 1895, p. 6; "Wanted an Indian Widow," *Oklahoma Leader* (Guthrie), 6 Oct. 1904, p. 4.

[121] "Wants Indian Squaw," *Tulsa Daily World*, 4 Apr. 1906, p. 8. See also "Wanted an 'Indian Maiden,'" *Shawnee News* (Shawnee, Okla.), 18 Nov. 1905, p. 5; "Want Indian Brides," *Weekly Times-Journal* (Oklahoma City), 7 Jun. 1907, p. 3; "Seeking Rich Indian Brides," *Tahlequah Arrow*, 12 Oct. 1907, p. 7; "Maine Girl Wants an 'Indian Scout,'" *Chickasha Daily Express*, 27 Nov. 1911, p. 1; "Wants Indian Wife," *Vinita Daily Chieftain*, 15 Aug. 1912, p. 3.

[122] "Chickasaw Girls Object to a Marriage License of One Thousand Dollars," *San Francisco Call*, 6 May 1900, p. 2; United States Department of the Interior, *Annual Reports of the Department of the Interior for the Fiscal Year Ended June 30, 1900* (Washington, D.C.: Government Printing Office, 1900), CLXVIII.

[123] "Seminole Girls Swindlers," *Daily Ardmoreite* (Ardmore, Okla.), 9 Aug. 1901, p. 8; "Matrimonial Bureau," *Tahlequah Arrow*, 10 Aug. 1901, p. 1.

[124] "Brosius Finds New Graft," *Free Press* (Ralston, Okla.), 16 Oct. 1903, p. 8.

As this brief sketch on post–Dawes Act intermarriage indicates, the legacy of white-Indian intermarriage was already a complex one when Alice Robertson proposed the US Bureau of Matrimony in 1920. As a longtime proponent of miscegenation – coming from a region with a long history of racial intermarriages – Robertson may have hoped that the bureau would facilitate more of these unions, bringing the project of Indian assimilation closer to reality while simultaneously eliminating matrimonial swindlers from the region. Fellow supporters of the federal bureau also hoped it would yield eugenically sound unions and higher marriage and birth rates across the nation. In addition, proponents likely believed that the bureau would help to reinforce traditional roles within the family by encouraging female domesticity and subservience and discouraging female entry into the public sphere of labor – these were convictions that Robertson carried into her political career, and convictions that incidentally matched up with the Dawes Act's vision of family propriety.[125] Despite the negative reputation of commercialized matrimonial bureaus, the proponents of the federal bureau were united in the belief that their agency would boost the profile of marriage.

The federal bureau never came to fruition. Its example nonetheless reveals the ways in which Robertson and others seeking to appropriate commercialized matchmaking practices – through bachelors' clubs, religious matrimonial agencies, and state-run marriage bureaus – recognized the popularity of the much-maligned commercial bureau and hoped to capitalize on that popularity in their fight against marriage crisis. Rather than defy public policy, matrimonial bureaus and advertisements could serve the state by restoring interest in healthy and procreative matrimony, populating the expanding nation, and even increasing white access to Indian lands. Unlike the reformers who pushed back against risqué matchmaking venues by shutting down matrimonial bureaus and shaming their clientele, these reformers embraced the agencies in an effort to instill traditional marital values. As their strategies reveal, in the face of a marriage crisis, one reformer's target could quickly become another reformer's weapon.

It is worth noting, however, that both commercialized matchmakers and noncommercial marriage reformers were responding to single

---

[125] Reese, *Women of Oklahoma*, 225. On the domestic model enforced by the Dawes Act, see Rose Stremlau, "'To Domesticate and Civilize Wild Indians': Allotment and the Campaign to Reform Indian Families, 1875–1887," *Journal of Family History* 30, no. 3 (2005): 265–286.

people's quest for new possibilities in courtship. In other words, the popularity of matrimonial advertisements as a strategy for finding partners beyond one's restricted geographical location – or outside one's narrow class or racial designations – displays a crucial feature of modern romance. Innovations in transportation and the wider circulation of newspapers allowed for the formation of partnerships that had not previously been possible. Matrimonial advertising led to exploitation from fraudsters and persecution from overzealous officials. It also prompted the creation of state- and church-centered bureaus as a tactic for fending off marriage crisis. The wide-ranging responses to matrimonial agencies reflect both the excitement and the anxiety that accompanied the expanding geographic and demographic boundaries of mate selection. As we shall see, such apprehension would grow as couples took increasingly to out-of-state elopement to procure the marriage licenses denied to them in their home states. These acts of interstate defiance illustrate the creativity that couples employed in their efforts to wed on their own terms. Such cases also reveal the backlash that marriage could spark when it breached too many legal, cultural, and spatial borders.

2

Hasty Remarriage, Out-of-State Elopement, and the Battle against "Progressive Polygamy"

In April 1904, amid great outcry over Mormons' continued practice of plural marriage, Latter-Day Saints president Joseph Smith issued the "Second Manifesto," formally disavowing polygamy and declaring that persons who continued the practice would be excommunicated from the Mormon faith.[1] As Mormon polygamy faded from view, however, turn-of-the century social reformers identified a new type of polygamy to target amid the official Mormon embrace of monogamy. These reformers campaigned against a concept they referred to alternately as "progressive polygamy," "consecutive polygamy," and "tandem polygamy." They used these phrases to condemn individuals who opted to remarry new spouses after divorce, reserving particular disdain for those persons who remarried quickly after their first unions ended. Criticism of progressive polygamy arose from many circles; Protestant and Catholic clergy preached against it and women's clubs devised strategies for its erasure, while journalists warned readers against its temptations and judges proclaimed its evils in their courtrooms. Even prominent feminist Charlotte Perkins Gilman, herself famously divorced and remarried, contended that

---

[1] B. Carmon Hardy, *Solemn Covenant: The Mormon Polygamous Passage* (Urbana: University of Illinois Press, 1992); Jeffrey Nichols, *Prostitution, Polygamy and Power: Salt Lake City, 1847–1918* (Urbana: University of Illinois Press, 2002), 135–138. For a detailed account of the extended legal battles over Mormon polygamy, see Gordon, *The Mormon Question*. As Gordon explains, four decades of antipolygamy initiatives culminated with a first "Manifesto" in 1890, in which Latter-Day Saints president Wilford Woodruff announced that the Church would no longer encourage plural marriage. That official statement did not, however, prevent "the de facto continuation of plural marriage" within Mormon communities at the turn of the twentieth century (220, 234–236).

remarriage after divorce was "a sort of tandem polygamy rather than a true monogamy," while insisting that permanent marriage was the natural and ideal romantic partnership.[2]

Critics of remarriage after divorce often used the legacy of Mormon polygamy to shape their new moral crusade, presenting progressive polygamy as even more insidious than the "simultaneous polygamy" practiced in Mormon households. These critics noted that while Mormon polygamy was generally limited to Utah, consecutive polygamy existed in every state of the nation, and thus posed an even graver danger. In 1904, Clara Burdette, the first vice-president of the General Federation of Women's Clubs, denounced hasty remarriage along these lines. While she was critical of Mormon polygamy, she was quick to point out that it was now illegal in Utah. Therefore, she believed that reformers should shift their efforts toward eliminating consecutive polygamy, "which exists in several states under the various divorce laws and is more dangerous to the moral life of the nation than the simultaneous polygamy."[3] According to Burdette and critics like her, traditional polygamy was a fading practice; meanwhile, rapid post-divorce remarriage was a growing trend, and it thus demanded the nation's attention.[4]

While Burdette pointed to rising rates of progressive polygamy to argue that it was a more pressing concern than Mormon polygamy, other critics went beyond numerical comparisons to argue that Mormon plural marriage was morally superior to remarriage after divorce. They explained that while polygamous men provided for their multiple wives, progressive polygamists abandoned one wife to pursue another, frequently leaving their first wives and children alone and uncompensated. Congregationalist minister Charles Brown of Oakland voiced this perspective in 1905, declaring that while polygamy in Utah was "abhorrentous," he still

---

[2] Corinne Marie Tuckerman Allen Papers, 1896–1927; Charlotte Perkins Gilman, "Why Marriage Will Keep" (magazine clipping), 1915, A-5, folder #30, Schlesinger Library, Radcliffe Institute, Harvard University.

[3] "News of the Women's Clubs," *Anaconda Standard* (Mont.), 28 Feb. 1904, p. 9. For similar critiques, see "A Shameful Evil," *Lima News* (Ohio), 15 May 1903, p. 11.

[4] "Bachelors and Club Men Are Bandits and Outcasts," *Oakland Tribune*, 25 Feb. 1905, p. 2; "Consecutive Polygamy," *Fort Worth Daily Gazette*, 9 Feb. 1886, p. 8; "Divorce Laws of Indiana," *Indianapolis News*, 1 Jan. 1898, p. 10; "Our Lax Divorce Laws," *Semi-Weekly Messenger* (Wilmington, N.C.), 22 Mar. 1904, p. 4; "Rectors Will Not Marry Divorcees," *St. Louis Republic*, 15 Jan. 1905, p. 1; "Marriage of Corey Called Mormonism," *Daily Review* (Decatur, Ill.), 21 May 1907, p. 2; "Cardinal on Divorce," *Washington Post*, 12 May 1908, p. 3; "Says Fault of Race Suicide Lies with Men, Not Women," *Chicago Daily Tribune*, 14 May 1908, p. 3.

appreciated that Mormon husbands lived with and supported their multiple wives. Brown contrasted this arrangement to progressive polygamy, "where a man merely supported the last wife he chanced to acquire."[5] For Brown and many others, the stability produced in multiwife households, however objectionable, was nonetheless preferable to the instability caused when husbands divorced one wife for another.

Other critics of post-divorce remarriage compared the trend with foreign marriage practices in their efforts to reveal the depth of progressive polygamists' depravity. In a 1910 sermon, Reverend John Reid Shannon of the Metropolitan M.E. Church in Washington, D.C., warned congregants that their marriage habits had begun to resemble those of religious and ethnic communities that Christian Americans should avoid emulating. He declared, "We may abhor the polygamy of Mohammedan Syria, but we have to recognize the fact that there is a progressive polygamy practiced today in certain portions of American society." He continued by castigating those socially prominent men who "get tired of their life partners and they literally swap wives by the so-called 'tandem marriages,' which follow immediately upon divorces obtained when the real reason is preference for another party."[6]

Similarly, in 1922, pastor John Stratton of New York City's Calvary Baptist Church insisted that he preferred the Turkish system of matrimony, in which "the Turks have their wives side by side," to the American practice of consecutive polygamy. Stratton's depiction of Turkey, though simplistic, was not fully inaccurate, as polygamy would not be banned in Turkey until 1926. But the purpose of Stratton's sermon was not to analyze Turkish marital practices, but rather to argue that consecutive polygamy served as an even greater evil than plural marriage in that it denied support to the spouses who had been discarded for new ones. By comparing permissive American attitudes about divorce and remarriage to Islamic nations' acceptance of polygamy, critics like Stratton emphasized the deep moral chasm into which they believed the institution of marriage had plunged itself stateside.[7]

---

[5] "Bachelors and Club Men Are Bandits and Outcasts," 2.

[6] "Divorce Evils Deplored," *Washington Post*, 17 Jan. 1910, p. 5

[7] "Screen and Stage Increase Divorce, J. R. Stratton Says," *Salisbury Evening Post* (N.C.), 24 Apr. 1922, p. 8; "Tandem Polygamy," *Morning Register* (Eugene), 11 Mar. 1923, p. 12. On the illegalization of polygamy in Turkey, see Noel Coulson and Doreen Hinchliffe, "Women and Law Reform in Contemporary Islam," in *Women in the Muslim World*, ed. Lois Beck and Nikki Keddie (Cambridge, Mass.: Harvard University Press, 1978), 40–41;

As this alarmist rhetoric reveals, the rise of the divorce rate generated new questions about divorcees' right to remarry new partners. As
we have seen, divorce itself was a source of great public concern at the
turn of the twentieth century. The rising popularity of the practice, and
the US Census Bureau's success in broadcasting that popularity – in
1909 the agency revealed that 945,925 divorces had taken place from
1887 to 1906 – sparked considerable anti-divorce backlash.[8] Thus, at
the same time that divorce became a more popular and socially
accepted solution to marital incompatibility, the era also witnessed
what historian William O'Neill refers to as a "legal counterrevolution"
against the practice. As O'Neill explains, turn-of-the-century legislators
adopted multiple strategies for reversing the divorce rate. For instance,
the majority of state governments increased their residency requirements from ninety days to six months, thus ensuring that many couples
could obtain out-of-state divorces only if they were willing to live in
their adopted state for half a year. Some states prevented divorce
lawyers from advertising for clients in newspapers, while others
appointed court officials to investigate divorce suits before judges could
rule on them. Certain states decreased their legal grounds for divorce,
while the District of Columbia restricted its grounds to the single cause
of adultery.[9]

In their efforts to curtail the divorce epidemic, state legislators also
created laws to prevent recently divorced persons from remarrying new
partners. Lawmakers hoped that if husbands and wives knew they could
not marry after divorce, they would be less likely to leave their spouses
should a fresh love interest emerge. In 1893, the Oklahoma legislature
passed a law stating that a couple was not officially divorced until six

---

Katharine Charsley and Anika Liversage, "Transforming Polygamy: Migration, Transna-
tionalism and Multiple Marriages among Muslim Minorities," *Global Networks* 13, no. 1
(2013): 62–63. Meanwhile, polygamy remained legal in Syria, though a 1953 Islamic law
demanded that Syrian husbands not take multiple wives if they could not support them
financially. See Noel James Coulson, *A History of Islamic Law* (Edinburgh: Edinburgh
University Press, 1964), 208–209; Jaime M. Gher, "Polygamy and Same-Sex Marriage –
Allies or Adversaries Within the Same-Sex Marriage Movement," *William & Mary Journal
of Women and the Law* 14, no. 3 (2008): 589–592.

[8] Glenda Riley, *Divorce: An American Tradition* (New York: Oxford University Press,
1991), 108–129.

[9] William L. O'Neill, *Divorce in the Progressive Era* (New Haven: Yale University Press,
1967), 26–27. See also J. Herbie DiFonzo, *Beneath the Fault Line: The Popular and Legal
Culture of Divorce in Twentieth-Century America* (Charlottesville: University Press of
Virginia, 1997), 2, 49–51; Riley, *Divorce*, 108–129.

months after being granted a divorce decree, thus preventing separated couples from marrying new people in the interim. Late nineteenth-century Louisiana law stated that if adultery broke up a marriage, the guilty party could not wed the person with whom he or she had cheated for ten months after the divorce. Meanwhile, Maryland and Mississippi denied adulterers the right to remarry altogether.[10] By 1906, fifteen states had placed restrictions on divorcees' remarriages to new spouses, either implementing a waiting period of up to two years during which divorced individuals could not remarry or denying their right to any future marriages whatsoever.[11]

In order to avoid these state restrictions on hasty remarriage, some divorcees left home to marry in other states, where they believed the limits on remarriage did not apply. Due to a dearth of statistics on the prior marital status of early twentieth-century brides and grooms, it is difficult to know how many recent divorcees left their homes to remarry across state lines.[12] But as the cases recounted in this chapter reveal, frequent incidents of hasty migratory remarriage fed into the perception of a marriage crisis in their defiance of standards of lifelong monogamy and in their capacity to expose the porous nature of state marriage laws. A couple's decision to defy a divorce decree and to marry out of state could spark great legal confusion when the new couple returned home, inspiring debate over whether the union was legitimate, void, or even bigamous, and sometimes creating disputes over the legitimacy of children born to remarriage.

Due to the diversity of state marriage laws, courts frequently contested the validity of marriages that defied the home state's mandated delay on remarriage, often reaching contradictory conclusions. Well-publicized instances of hasty out-of-state remarriage led to the creation of stricter laws in some states and sparked efforts to forge uniform marriage and divorce legislation. And while several prominent historians of American divorce have rightly insisted that stricter divorce laws did nothing to slow the divorce rate – that rate continued to grow in spite of the laws intended to reverse it – efforts to stomp out progressive polygamy nonetheless

---

[10] Riley, *Divorce*, 102–103, 125–126.
[11] O'Neill, *Divorce in the Progressive Era*, 7; May, *Great Expectations*, 4–5.
[12] Statistician Walter F. Wilcox addresses the lack of records accounting for newlyweds' previous marital condition (single, widowed, or divorced) in "Proportion of American Marriages Ending in Divorce," *Publications of the American Statistical Association* 14, no. 109 (1915): 483–485.

affected the family lives of countless individuals and couples.[13] These laws brought about the nullification of many second marriages contracted in good faith, the denial of inheritance to longtime spouses, and the delegitimatization of children born of hasty second marriages. Furthermore, zealous warnings against tandem polygamy from religious and moral authorities, and passionate efforts by lawmakers to legislate away this perceived problem, reveal the depths of frustration that many Americans felt as they watched the expectation of long-term monogamy unravel. Ultimately, high rates of post-divorce remarriage fed into wide-ranging concerns about the state of marriage in America and deepened the belief that the institution was in crisis.

* * *

The state of California provides strong examples of the persistent legal disputes and uncertainties surrounding recent divorcees' out-of-state remarriages. In February 1897, the state legislature amended its Civil Code in an effort to slow the rate of hasty remarriage. The amended law specified that if a couple opted to divorce, the estranged spouses must wait a year to marry new partners; remarriages that defied this provision were illegal and void.[14] Shortly thereafter, one California couple put this amended law to the test. In August 1897, Abbie Rose Smith of San Francisco divorced her husband, Robert Smith, in California. Less than four months later, Abbie married prominent lawyer Joseph Wood in Reno, Nevada. Both Abbie and Joseph were California residents, and they wed in Reno specifically to evade the one-year prohibition on Abbie's remarriage in California, returning home immediately after their Nevada nuptials. Within half a year, Joseph Wood had died from a sudden attack

---

[13] For example, Joanna L. Grossman and Lawrence M. Friedman argue, "The formal official law, the law in the treatises, the law mouthed by high court judges, had absolutely no relationship to what was happening on the ground." *Inside the Castle*, 162. See also Riley, *Divorce*, 121–122; May, *Great Expectations*, 5. Moreover, major work on migratory marriage has focused on out-of-state "divorce mills" – with scholars such as Glenda Riley denying their numerical significance and Hendrik Hartog insisting that couples were generally able to attain valid marriages after divorcing, in spite of the questionable legal value of their out-of-state divorces. This chapter, on the other hand, looks at persons who divorced their partners at home, remarried new partners out of state, and then came right back. See Hartog, *Man and Wife in America*, 242–286.

[14] *Estate of Wood et al.*, 137 Cal. 129 (1902); Alicia Barber, *Reno's Big Gamble: Image and Reputation in the Biggest Little City* (Lawrence: University Press of Kansas, 2008), 54–55.

of acute peritonitis; he was survived by his new widow and four children from a previous marriage.[15]

Wood left behind a hefty estate. He appointed Abbie and his daughter, Martha Wood, to be executors of the will, which provided Abbie with a monthly payment of $250 – Wood left only $75 a month for Martha. Displeased with the will's lopsided provisions, Martha and her siblings sought to lower Abbie's monthly allowance to $125. When Abbie refused to accept the lesser sum, the children filed a petition to contest the will on the ground that their father had been "of unsound mind" when he selected Abbie as his primary heir and executor. Although the children did not have the wherewithal to prove their father's mental incapacity, they soon found an even more effective strategy for discrediting their stepmother's right to inherit; they claimed that Abbie Rose Wood was not their stepmother at all.[16]

The children's efforts to reveal the invalidity of Abbie and Joseph's marriage proceeded in a complex, and sometimes contradictory, manner. Martha Wood and her siblings hoped to prove that Abbie Rose Smith had not been eligible to marry their father in 1898 due to her recent divorce from Robert Smith. Therefore, they insisted, her marriage to their father had been illegitimate and she was not, in fact, his widow. In response, Abbie countersued Martha and the Wood estate on the ground that she was owed $10,000 from an agreement she and Joseph had made prior to their marriage. Through this prenuptial agreement, Abbie had surrendered her personal property and property rights to her husband. In return, he had promised to give her $10,000 in gold coins within two years of the wedding – he specified that the executors of his will would grant the sum to Abbie should he die before the two years passed. When the coexecutors of the will refused to grant her this sum, Abbie brought suit before the Superior Court of San Francisco. In his decision, Judge Edward Belcher ruled in favor of the Wood children, declaring that Abbie's hasty remarriage had been illegal in its defiance of California's Civil Code and that she was therefore not entitled to receive the rewards of a prenuptial agreement.[17]

---

[15] *Estate of Wood et al.*, 137 Cal. 129 (1902); "The Passing of Joseph M. Wood," *San Francisco Call*, 18 Jun. 1898, p. 12; "Reno Marriage Declared Illegal," *Evening Sentinel* (Santa Cruz), 13 Dec. 1900, p. 1.

[16] "Last Wishes of Joseph M. Wood," *San Francisco Chronicle*, 21 Jun. 1898, p. 5; "Say He Was Insane," *San Francisco Call*, 26 Jul. 1899, p. 10; "Her Marriage Is Questioned," *San Francisco Chronicle*, 23 Sep. 1899, p. 11.

[17] "Contest over J. M. Wood's Will," *San Francisco Chronicle*, 3 Nov. 1899, p. 14; "The Contest over Wood's Will," *San Francisco Chronicle*, 14 Nov. 1899, p. 7; "Contests His

In explaining why the Nevada marriage was void in California, Judge Belcher stated that lawmakers had passed the 1897 law requiring a year before remarriage "to correct a great public evil which had become too rife." According to Belcher, when divorcees remarried hastily, they took new spouses while the appeal period for their divorce was still under way. Sometimes abandoned ex-husbands or ex-wives successfully appealed a divorce; in such cases, the decree was reversed, reinstating the former marriage and rendering the hasty remarriage bigamous or invalid. "Undoubtedly," Belcher wrote, "it is immoral and against public policy that a divorced person should be permitted to contract a legal marriage pending the right of appeal and while it is yet uncertain what the final judgment will be."[18] Belcher thus hoped to offset the scandal of hasty remarriage with his strict enforcement of the 1897 law, and local reporters helped him to make his case. They explained to readers that Belcher's decision meant that the thousands of Californians who had remarried out of state within a year of receiving their divorce decrees were, like Abbie, not legally wedded to their new partners. While such unions were not punishable offenses, they were nonetheless invalid.[19]

The debate did not end with Belcher's decision, however. A few months later, in September 1900, Abbie Rose Wood and her putative

Father's Will," *San Francisco Call*, 14 Nov. 1899, p. 7; "Pre-Nuptial Contract," *San Francisco Call*, 25 Feb. 1900, p. 26; "Abbie Rose Wood Sues Her Husband's Estate," *San Francisco Chronicle*, 25 Feb. 1900, p. 10; "Abbie Rose Wood's Marriage at Reno," *San Francisco Chronicle*, 5 Apr. 1900, p. 9; "Hundreds Are Not Married," *Oakland Tribune*, 14 Jun. 1900, p. 1.

[18] "That Little Trip to Reno May Have Meant a Ceremony, But It Did Not Mean a Wedding," *San Francisco Call*, 15 Jun. 1900, p. 14. Not all judges in San Francisco's Superior Court agreed with Belcher. In a 1900 case, Judge J. C. Hebbard ruled that the Reno marriage between Frederica and Ben Adler was valid, even though it took place just a month after Frederica's divorce in California from her former husband, Dunbar. Hebbard maintained that since Dunbar had not appealed the divorce, he saw no reason for Frederica to delay her marriage to a new husband. Hebbard disapproved of the 1897 law's tendency to discourage, rather than favor marriage, a position that defied Belcher's call for greater state regulation of nuptials. "Superior Court Judges Differ as to Validity of Reno Marriages," *San Francisco Chronicle*, 8 Jul. 1900, p. 11; "Where Judges Differ on Questions of Marriage," *St. Louis Republic*, 15 Jul. 1900, p. 15.

[19] "Hundreds Are Not Married," 1; "Too Speedy a Wedding," *San Francisco Chronicle*, 15 Jun. 1900, p. 9; "Voids Hundreds of Marriages," *Salt Lake Herald*, 15 Feb. 1900, p. 1; "Reno Marriages," *Evening Sentinel* (Santa Cruz), 18 Jun. 1900, p. 1; "An Important Opinion Filed," *Weekly Gazette and Stockman* (Reno), 21 Jun. 1900, p. 8. Abbie Rose Wood requested a retrial from Judge Belcher, which he refused in October of 1900. She then vowed to take the case to the Supreme Court. "Abbie Rose Wood to Appeal," *San Francisco Call*, 24 Oct. 1900, p. 7.

stepchildren entered the courtroom of Judge Morris Troutt to resolve yet another component of the sticky inheritance case: Abbie's right to her $250 monthly allowance. Once again, Joseph Wood's children claimed that Abbie was not entitled to this sum because her Reno marriage to their father was invalid in its defiance of California's remarriage prohibitions. In response, Abbie's attorney, Timothy Lyons, contended that the California law held no extraterritorial effect and that the state of California did not have the authority to nullify a marriage contracted in another state. Furthermore, Lyons argued that courts should do their utmost to support marriages contracted in the name of true love. He stated, "It is my belief that the policy of the law – and if it is not it should be – is to support marriage wherever contracted ... Marriage, being the foundation of society, is a natural right which the Christian world recognizes can be entered into everywhere." If Lyons's claim lacked legal sophistication, it nonetheless reanimated the long-debated question of whether courts should treat marriage as a "natural right" and encourage its solemnization to all parties who desired it, or rather limit marital status to the parties deemed most deserving.[20]

Judge Troutt did not embrace Lyons's logic, and he denied Abbie Rose Wood the right to her monthly allowance, declaring that the marriage in question was invalid. As Troutt explained, a marriage was not fully dissolved until a year after the issuance of the divorce decree. As such, Abbie was not legally divorced when she exchanged vows with Joseph, and consequently their union had been void from the start. Furthermore, Troutt explained, had the Woods' marriage been declared legitimate, the union would have been polygamous, as Abbie was still legally wed to Robert Smith when she married Wood in Reno. Therefore, he suggested, his decision to void the second marriage protected Abbie from allegations of bigamy. Abbie did not see his ruling as an act of charity, however, and she vowed that she would continue to fight for the right to call herself Mrs. Joseph Wood. Meanwhile, reporters noted that Troutt's ruling confirmed

[20] "Law That Made Nevada Popular Again in Issue," *San Francisco Call*, 20 Sep. 1900, p. 12. See also "Mrs. Wood's Reno Marriage," *San Francisco Chronicle*, 15 Sep. 1900, p. 14. Lyons made even more explicit references to Abbie Rose Wood's Christian right and obligation to marry in his closing statements. He contended, "True, in marriage the law must be obeyed, but Christ has spoken to the world and has absolved the innocent from suffering for the acts of the guilty. To the innocent he has given right and made it a duty to remarry ... Why should those innocent persons who have cast aside a guilty spouse be denied the natural right to enter into a second marriage within one year?" "Nevada Marriages Are Sanctioned by Christ," *San Francisco Call*, 27 Sep. 1900, p. 9.

Judge Belcher's earlier decision on the illegitimacy of Reno marriages, and they asserted that the two decisions against Abbie Rose Wood confirmed the prohibition of hasty out-of-state remarriage for all Californians.[21]

These assumptions proved premature. In August 1902, the California Supreme Court reversed Troutt's decision in a 4–3 ruling, leading journalists to conclude that hasty remarriages were now, in fact, legal. In his opinion, Justice Charles Garouette wrote that Abbie Rose Wood's 1898 divorce from Robert Smith had been absolute because Smith had never appealed the decree. As a result, Abbie was legally unmarried when she wed Joseph Wood, and while California's newly revised civil code prevented divorcees from marrying for a year after their unions had ended, it did not have any extraterritorial operation. In other words, the new California law did not have the power to invalidate hasty out-of-state remarriages, even though those quick remarriages would have been deemed void had they taken place in California. He wrote that if a marriage was valid where contracted – as Abbie and Joseph's Reno wedding had been – then it was valid in California. To support this claim, Garouette cited an 1875 case in which the California Supreme Court had recognized the Utah marriage between an African American woman and a white man, despite the fact that California law prohibited racial inter-marriage at the time. Garouette acknowledged that some California courts made exceptions to this rule when it was clear that a couple had fled to another state deliberately to evade the marriage laws of their home state. Nevertheless, he claimed – perhaps disingenuously – that he could find no evidence that Abbie and Joseph had married in Nevada for the express purpose of dodging California's remarriage law. As a result, their marriage had been valid and Abbie Rose Wood was entitled to her monthly allowance.[22]

A close reading of Garouette's decision reveals a deeper set of social and moral concerns than the mere question of Abbie Rose Wood's right to

---

[21] "Reno Marriages Are Not Valid," *Oakland Tribune*, 10 Dec. 1900, p. 2; "Reno Wedding Is Not Valid," *San Francisco Chronicle*, 11 Dec. 1900, p. 12; "Another Blow Is Struck by Court at the Nevada Weddings," *San Francisco Call*, 11 Dec. 1900, p. 1; "Reno Marriage Declared Illegal," *Evening Sentinel*, 13 Dec. 1900, p. 1.

[22] *Estate of Wood et al.*, 137 Cal. 129 (1902). For the above-mentioned intermarriage case, see *Pearson v. Pearson*, 51 Cal. 120 (1875). Garouette also cited a recent Vermont case, in which the state supreme court had ruled that the state of Vermont was "silent as to marriages abroad" and that therefore a Vermont man's hasty New Hampshire remarriage was valid, even though it defied Vermont laws. See *State v. Shattuck*, 69 Vt. 403 (1897).

inherit. The judge acknowledged that California lawmakers had amended the Civil Code in 1897 in an effort to create a "sound public policy." He disputed the notion that this prohibition on post-divorce remarriage served the public interest, however, by underlining the damage he believed it could inflict on children and families and by noting the law's potential to harm the institution of marriage itself by voiding the unions of romantically committed individuals. He wrote that a ruling against Abbie Rose Wood "would nullify hundreds of marriages, place the stamp of illegitimacy upon scores of children, and change the source of the title to great property interests." For Garouette, it was preferable to keep hasty marriages intact than to strike a widespread blow to marital and familial stability.[23]

Reporters embraced this idea that the state supreme court's ruling marked a victory for the institution of marriage. One writer referred to Garouette as "that gallant promoter of matrimony" who had "tightened the loose marital knots which have been tied in Nevada for persons divorced in California within one year previous to the date of the Nevada ceremony." According to this journalist, Garouette's opinion had brought respectability and legitimacy to all Californians' out-of-state remarriages. The author asserted, "The Reno certificates may now be framed and hung upon the wall without shame. Brides from Reno will be received in company henceforth without raisings of the eyebrow by women whose marriages are not under suspicion."[24] Another reporter wrote that in light of the *Wood* decision, "A Reno marriage is now as reliable, as respectable, as safe and as staid as a church full of guests, a hall full of presents and clothes full of rice. The greatest tribunal of California has said that if a marriage is lawful in Nevada it is lawful here. It has placed its great seal of respectability upon the Reno marriage certificate and has made happy hundreds of anxious hearts."[25] Despite the highly contested path to Garouette's ruling, journalists presented the *Wood* decision as the definitive statement on the legality of out-of-state remarriages in the year following a divorce.

To an extent these commentators were correct. Subsequent appellate cases in California followed the precedent set in the *Wood* case, denying the legality of hasty remarriages contracted in California and validating the ones conducted out of state.[26] At the same time, Abbie Rose Wood's

---

[23] *Estate of Wood et al.*, 137 Cal. 129 (1902).
[24] "Supreme Court Decides Reno Marriages Valid," *Santa Cruz Sentinel*, 6 Aug. 1902, p. 1.
[25] "Reno Marriages All Right," *Oakland Tribune*, 5 Aug. 1902, p. 1.
[26] *Estate of Elliott*, 165 Cal. 339 (1913); *People v. Woodley*, 22 Cal. App. 674 (1913).

case was a lone case in a single state. Her battle to secure an inheritance is useful in revealing the complexities at the heart of early twentieth-century debates over hasty remarriages, and the complications that arose from a couple's decision to evade their home state's laws by marrying elsewhere. The story becomes even more complex, though, when we look beyond California and consider the ways in which legal and judicial authorities across the nation addressed the question of hasty remarriage. Their actions often conflicted with the conclusions drawn by Garouette in his influential California decision. Perhaps more significantly, in some cases judges in a single state contradicted one another in their rulings on this thorny issue, underscoring the lack of legal consensus on divorcees' right to quick remarriage.

* * *

Several states – among them Alabama, Wisconsin, and Tennessee – were particularly strict in their prohibitions on quick remarriage after divorce. Alabama laws forbade all divorcees from remarrying, unless their decree of divorce explicitly permitted them to do so or they had received a court's permission to wed new partners. Defiance of this prohibition on remarriage did not merely render the new union void, but it also made the act of remarrying a felony. As a result, Alabamans who remarried without a court's authorization faced bigamy charges alongside the nullification of their nuptials. Emma Louisa Barfield learned this the hard way when in 1903 she attempted to recover a land inheritance after the death of her husband, W. M. Barfield. The couple had married following Emma's divorce in Alabama from a prior husband, Henry Sellers, who had won that divorce on grounds of Emma's adultery. Now W. M. Barfield's son claimed that Emma had no right to inherit from his father since the couple had never been legally married, despite spending more than a decade as husband and wife. After a circuit court ruled in the son's favor, the case reached the state supreme court, which upheld the lower decision. Chief Justice Thomas McClellan declared that Alabama law forbade Emma from marrying Barfield. Her initial decree of divorce had not given her the authority to remarry, and thus her subsequent nuptials were both void and a felony.[27]

---

[27] *Barfield v. Barfield*, 139 Ala. 290 (1903). The Barfield marriage had taken place in Alabama, and therefore the court did not need to consider the validity of out-of-state remarriages.

Later cases bore similar results, as judges consistently declared Alabamans' post-divorce unions void and bigamous when the remarriages took place in-state. Twenty years after Emma Barfield's court date, for example, the Alabama Supreme Court upheld Clifton Vance's bigamy conviction because Vance had remarried within two months of divorcing his first wife, Minnie. His divorce decree, as well as Alabama statute, dictated that Vance not marry within sixty days of the divorce's formalization, unless he chose to remarry Minnie. Since he defied that prohibition, he was found guilty of bigamy and sentenced to three to four years in prison.[28]

Despite the strictness of Alabama's higher courts in preventing local remarriages too soon after divorce, Alabama judges were less inclined to nullify hasty remarriages conducted out of state, even if the couples returned home immediately after their wedding ceremonies.[29] Wisconsin courts, on the other hand, were quick to deny the legitimacy of all nuptials that defied prohibitions on remarriage, including those conducted in other states. In a prominent 1908 state supreme court case, a recently widowed woman sought the right to inherit from her second husband, James Lanham. This woman had divorced a former husband in order to marry Lanham. Aware that a 1905 Wisconsin law forbade her from remarrying for a full year, she wed Lanham in Menominee, Michigan, less than a month after her initial divorce. The new couple returned home to Monroe County, Wisconsin, immediately after their wedding, and they lived there until the groom's death in 1907.[30]

When Mrs. Lanham's application for support from her husband's estate reached the Monroe County circuit court, Judge John Fruitt ruled that she was entitled to the inheritance. Fruitt noted that the couple had continued to cohabit as husband and wife after the yearlong prohibition on their marriage had lapsed, and as a result they had established a valid common law marriage. The Wisconsin Supreme Court disagreed, however, stating

---

[28] Fortunately for Vance, Alabama Governor W. W. Brandon granted him parole after about a year of imprisonment. *Vance v. State*, 210 Ala. 9 (1923); "Parole Given Talladega Man by Governor," *The Anniston Star*, 24 Jul. 1924, p. 2. For other cases invalidating, and in some cases criminalizing, Alabamans' post-divorce remarriages in Alabama, see *Eldridge v. State*, 126 Ala. 63 (1899); *Gulf States Steel Co. v. Witherspoon*, 214 Ala. 529 (1926).

[29] In a 1918 case, Justice Anthony Dickinson Sayre insisted that Alabama's prohibitions against post-divorce remarriage had "no effect beyond the borders of this state." *McLaughlin v. McLaughlin*, 201 Ala. 482 (1918); see also *Smith v. Goldsmith*, 223 Ala. 155 (1931).

[30] *Lanham v. Lanham*, 136 Wis. 360 (1908).

that evidence of a year's cohabitation was insufficient to legitimize a marriage that had been illegal from the outset. In his ruling, Chief Justice John Winslow acknowledged that in most cases if the marriage was valid where celebrated, it was valid everywhere. Winslow added, however, that there were two exceptions to this rule: "(1) Marriages which are deemed contrary to the law of nature as generally recognized by Christian civilized states; and (2) marriages which the lawmaking power of the forum has declared shall not be allowed validity on grounds of public policy." Winslow did not view the Lanham marriage as contrary to Christian morality – such a categorization was typically reserved for cases of incest. But he did believe that the Lanhams' marriage met the second exception to the "valid where contracted" rule. In his words, it was "against public policy and good morals that divorced persons should be at liberty to immediately contract new marriages." Therefore, despite the fact that the Lanhams' marriage had been legal when contracted in Michigan, it became invalid when the couple returned to Wisconsin.[31]

Winslow did not cite legislation or judicial precedent to justify his assertion that hasty out-of-state remarriages defied public policy. Moreover, his ruling revealed that the 1905 law against hasty remarriage did not address the legality of unions conducted out of state. Through his discussion of public policy, however, Winslow was able to craft a decision that invalidated a type of remarriage he deemed morally reprehensible. He began by articulating his "unmistakable" inference that Wisconsin legislators had "recognized the fact that the sacredness of marriage and the stability of the marriage tie lie at the very foundation of Christian civilization and social order." Accordingly, Winslow explained, these legislators believed that easy divorce and quick remarriage threatened good morals and led to "progressive polygamy," and they had thus amended the state marriage law in an effort to foster family stability. Having declared his certainty that state lawmakers had written the law as a means of upholding public policy, Winslow continued by claiming that Wisconsin legislators had meant for the prohibition to apply to marriages contracted inside and outside the state. He wrote, "To say that the legislature intended such a law to apply only while the parties are within the boundaries of the state, and that it contemplated that by crossing the state line its citizens could successfully nullify its terms, is to make the act essentially useless and impotent and ascribe practical imbecility to the

---

[31] Ibid.

lawmaking power." In Winslow's view, the law would not have been created had its makers deliberately excluded out-of-state ceremonies from their prohibitions on Wisconsinites' remarriages.[32]

Last, Winslow rejected the circuit court's claim that the Lanhams had established a common law marriage by continuing to cohabitate after the prohibition on their nuptials had passed, citing earlier Wisconsin cases to prove that continued cohabitation did not legitimize a marriage that had been invalid in its inception. He thus reversed the circuit court's decision and denied Mrs. Lanham the right to inherit on grounds that she had never been married to the man she called her husband.[33] Subsequent cases in the high courts of Wisconsin yielded similar verdicts, with judges denying the validity of out-of-state marriages contracted less than a year after a partner's prior divorce and rejecting claims that common law marriage entitled plaintiffs to the benefits in question.[34] In all these cases, Wisconsin courts held that laws against hasty remarriage were strong enough to invalidate evasive unions. As long as divorcees remained Wisconsin residents, any remarriage taking place within a year of their initial divorce defied state law and public policy, and was consequently void.[35]

On the surface, Tennessee legislation appeared less strict on hasty remarriage than the laws of Alabama and Wisconsin. Tennessee law stated that couples granted divorces or annulments could marry new partners once their marriages were dissolved, with one notable exception. The law stated, "but a defendant who has been guilty of adultery shall not marry the person with whom the crime was committed during the life of the former husband or wife."[36] Appellate judges were strict in enforcing this law, declaring coadulterers' subsequent marriages void

---

[32] Ibid.   [33] Ibid.

[34] *Severa v. Beranak*, 138 Wis. 144 (1909); *Hall v. Industrial Commission*, 165 Wis. 364 (1917); *White v. White*, 167 Wis. 615 (1918).

[35] One exception to this trend can be found in a 1922 state supreme court case, in which a judge found a Wisconsin couple's Michigan marriage legitimate, in spite of the fact that the couple had wed within a year of the wife's earlier divorce. In this case, however, the wife had received her divorce in the state of Illinois before moving to Wisconsin to live at her new husband's home. It appears that the added complexity of grappling with three sets of state marriage laws led the judge to accept the marriage as legitimate because it was valid in Michigan, where it had been contracted. *Owen v. Owen*, 178 Wis. 609 (1922).

[36] *Pennegar v. State*, 87 Tenn. 244 (1888); see also *Owen v. Bracket*, 75 Tenn. 448 (1881); Frank J. Indovina and John E. Dalton, *Statutes of All States and Territories, with Annotations on Marriage, Annulment, Divorce* (Santa Monica: Law Pub. Co., 1945), 297.

even when they were contracted outside the state. In one 1900 case, Judge R. M. Barton denied the validity of the marriage between Lura and John Newman, who had wed in Texas six months after John divorced his first wife, Mary Glenn. Barton declared their marriage invalid because their adulterous tryst had been the direct impetus for John Newman's divorce from Mary Glenn, who was still living. He wrote, "The policy of the law of this state is to maintain the marriage relation, and to remove all inducements of infidelity on the part of the husband or the wife possible by shutting off all hopes of marriage with a paramour during the life of the wife who has obtained the divorce. It is also a part of the policy of this state to maintain intact the family relations incurred under the first legal marriage, and thereby promote chastity, and also harmony in the family."[37]

Judge Barton acknowledged that if the Newmans had stayed in Texas, the Tennessee courts would have had no power to invalidate their marriage. But the court did have the right to deem the marriage void when the couple promptly returned to Tennessee, and Barton did just that in the name of discouraging adultery and familial decay. Later judgments in Tennessee reinforced this declaration that guilty parties in adultery could not wed their paramours after divorce as long as the betrayed spouse remained alive; this remained the case whether the adulterous couple wed inside or outside Tennessee. Since hasty remarriages often emerged from adulterous trysts, Tennessee's laws sought to discourage married individuals from having affairs altogether by eliminating the exchange of vows founded on infidelity.[38]

* * *

If the higher courts of Tennessee, Alabama, and Wisconsin were especially strict in invalidating marriages contracted after divorce, the states of Colorado and Washington were notably lenient in enforcing restrictions on post-divorce remarriage. Colorado's legislature passed a law in 1908 prohibiting divorced individuals from marrying new spouses within a year of their decree.[39] Some lower court judges did invalidate unions that defied this law – including Denver County Court's John Dixon, who chastised Chaloner Schley for engaging in "progressive polygamy" while

---

[37] *Newman v. Kimbrough*, 59 S.W. 1061 (1900).
[38] Ibid.; *Jennings v. Jennings*, 165 Tenn. 295 (1932); *Bennett v. Anderson*, 20 Tenn. App. 523 (1936).
[39] *Griswold v. Griswold*, 23 Colo. App. 365 (1913).

stating that Schley's marriage was invalid because it had taken place just three days after his wife's divorce was finalized.[40]

The few cases that reached Colorado's higher courts, on the other hand, validated Colorado divorcees' hasty New Mexico remarriages. One 1913 appellate case helps to explain this phenomenon. The case involved a woman seeking divorce from her husband on grounds that he had deserted her after she became pregnant. In response, the husband claimed that no divorce was possible because the couple's union had never been legitimate. He explained that they had married in New Mexico on the same day that the wife's Colorado divorce was finalized, and then they had returned immediately to Colorado to live. Since the couple had deliberately evaded their home state's law forbidding remarriage for a year after divorce, the husband, now hoping to avoid the costs of alimony, claimed to be a single man.[41]

The court rejected this reasoning, ruling that the couple's marriage had been valid when it was contracted in New Mexico, and it was therefore valid everywhere. Judge Alfred King acknowledged Colorado's law forbidding remarriage within a year of divorce, but he stated that the law held no extraterritorial effect, and as such the court did not hold the power to criminalize or invalidate hasty remarriages conducted in New Mexico. King also quoted Charles Garouette's opinion from California's *Estate of Wood* case, rearticulating the justice's concern that the nullification of one out-of-state remarriage could lead to the nullification of countless marriages, many of which had been contracted in good faith. By invalidating these marriages, courts risked creating boundless legal headaches by generating confusion over property ownership, inheritance issues, and the legitimacy of children.[42] Colorado's supreme court reached similar conclusions in other cases involving the New Mexico remarriages of Colorado divorcees, ruling that the marriages were valid when contracted, and thus valid upon the couples' return to Colorado.[43]

The state of Washington's restrictions on post-divorce remarriage had emerged in 1881 with the passage of a law prohibiting divorcees from marrying new spouses for six months after their unions ended. State lawmakers reasoned that during this six-month window, it was still

---

[40] "Progressive Polygamy," *The Sun* (New York), 24 Oct. 1911, p. 2; "Colorado Judge's Divorce Ruling," *Santa Ana Register*, 24 Oct. 1911, p. 3.
[41] *Griswold v. Griswold*, 23 Colo. App. 365 (1913).   [42] Ibid.
[43] *Loth v. Loth's Estate*, 54 Colo. 200 (1913); *Crouse et al. v. Wheeler*, 62 Colo. 51 (1916).

possible that one of the divorced parties would appeal the decree. Therefore, any marriage that either party attempted to contract with a new spouse during the appeal period was void. It was not difficult for courts to enforce this rule against divorcees who married prematurely in Washington, particularly since the state did not recognize common law marriage. While couples may have tried to claim that their hasty marriages became official once the appeal period had ended, courts could reject this logic and deem the marriages void in their defiance of the 1881 law.[44]

Washington courts were often more lenient when deliberating marriages that took place outside the state during the six-month appeal period. While the state's courts were typically stricter than Colorado's on this matter, several major cases reveal efforts by judges to validate unions that appear evasive.[45] The most striking case of this sort involved the 1907 marriage between Dora and Charles Reuben ("Rube") Pierce. The Seattle couple had wed in Victoria, British Columbia, less than six months after Dora's divorce from Albert Porter of Spokane. The couple had returned to Seattle a few days after exchanging vows, and they lived there as husband and wife until Rube deserted Dora in 1909. In response, Dora went before the Superior Court for King County to file a suit for separate maintenance, or a legal separation that would still require Rube, a saloonkeeper, to support her and the couple's two-year-old son. Judge A. W. Frater ruled against Dora, declaring that her marriage to Rube was void because it had taken place less than six months after her divorce from Porter.[46] Though local reporters did not question the legal accuracy of Frater's decision, they raised concerns about its implications by focusing on the fact that Rube and Dora had a young child who, due to his parents' defiance of state law, "has no name, no legal status – he's an illegitimate child." Such articles suggested that this ruling would lead many other innocent children to be labeled illegitimate due to their parents' recklessness.[47]

Dora Pierce appealed Frater's ruling and brought the case before Washington's supreme court, which reversed the lower court's decision. Justice Stephen Chadwick explained his belief that Dora had married Rube in Victoria while under the impression that the couple would reside there

---

[44] *Smith v. Fife*, 4 Wash. 702 (1892).
[45] *State v. Fenn*, 47 Wash. 561 (1907); *Knoll v. Knoll*, 104 Wash. 110 (1918).
[46] *Pierce v. Pierce*, 58 Wash. 622 (1910).
[47] "Many Marriages Invalid," *Wenatchee Daily World* (Wash.), 17 Jan. 1910, p. 1; see also "Child a Victim of Parents' Folly," *Leavenworth Echo* (Wash.), 21 Jan. 1910, p. 2.

after the wedding. A few days later, however, Rube had told her he was unable to find work, and that they must return to Seattle. Justice Chadwick took Dora's testimony as an indication that the couple had married in good faith. In his interpretation, they had not gone to Canada to evade Washington's remarriage laws, which would have rendered their marriage void; rather, they had intended to relocate there indefinitely. Chadwick acknowledged that the testimony in this case was "not altogether satisfactory," but he was willing to give Dora the benefit of the doubt in order to grant financial protection to her son. He wrote, "We know of no public policy which will warrant a court in annulling a marriage between competent parties if there be any evidence to sustain it, and especially so where it appears that the parties have consummated the marriage, a child has been born, and the offending party has been openly acknowledged as a spouse." He therefore reversed the prior judgment and ordered Rube Pierce to support his estranged wife and child.[48]

Justice Chadwick's claim that the Pierces' marriage had been contracted in good faith was a shaky one, and he seemed to recognize that. He was able to rule in Dora's favor, however, by indicating that public policy compelled him to protect innocent children from illegitimacy. This concern over the legitimacy of children born to post-divorce remarriages was central to legal discourse on the validity of such unions in certain states. Most notably, this issue would transform family law in Illinois, helping drive the creation of laws to limit hasty remarriage, and later inspiring their undoing.

* * *

In the spring of 1905, the Illinois state legislature passed a bill forbidding individuals from remarrying for a year after getting divorced – guilty parties in adultery had to wait two years to marry new partners. The consequence of disobeying this law was one to three years in prison.[49] O. L. Hall, a commentator from Chicago's *Inter Ocean*, noted that the law applied equally to men and women, and explained that it sought to reverse the increasing tendency for divorce to serve as "merely a legal means of breaking one marriage contract to assume another." Hall's

---

[48] *Pierce v. Pierce*, 58 Wash. 622 (1910); "Supreme Court Holds for Deserted Woman," *Oregon Daily Journal* (Portland), 10 Jun. 1910, p. 9.

[49] "Divorce and Remarriage, "*Leavenworth Times* (Kan.), 26 Jan. 1905, p. 2; "Aims Hard Blow at Divorce Evil," *Chicago Daily Tribune*, 15 Mar. 1905, p. 5; "New Divorce Bill Passed by House, "*Inter Ocean*, 12 Apr. 1905, p. 3.

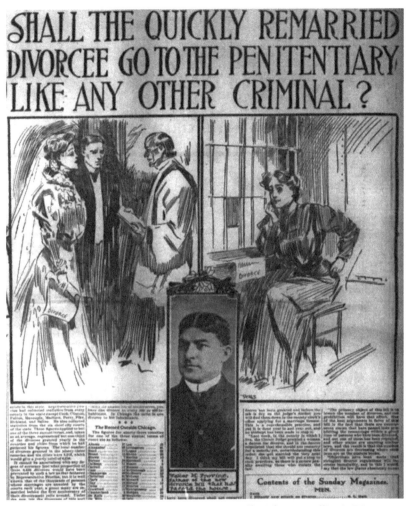

FIGURE 2.1 Illustration accompanying O. L. Hall, "The New Illinois Divorce Bill," *Inter Ocean*, 16 Apr. 1905, magazine section, p. 1.

article featured a large caption, "Shall the Quickly Remarried Divorcee Go to the Penitentiary like Any Other Criminal?" above a larger illustration (see Figure 2.1). Pictured on the left side of that illustration were a bride and groom marrying before a justice of the peace. The bride held a divorce degree in her hand. In an accompanying image, that woman sat behind bars, the same divorce decree still beside her. At the bottom of the illustration was a portrait of Walter Provine, sponsor of the remarriage bill. In case the image and caption failed to convey their point, Hall reminded readers that under the new law, divorcees who remarried too quickly "would find awaiting them not a cozy cottage or flat and the traditional rubber plant, but an unhomelike cell and the traditional corn bread and water."[50]

Supporters of the 1905 law insisted that it would help to keep family units intact, discouraging discontented spouses from ending their nuptials and saving children from broken homes. The law was not retroactive, and therefore it did not criminalize hasty remarriages conducted before its 1 July 1905 enactment. Its proponents believed, however, that it held the promise to save future marriages. This conviction derived in part from the exception the law made for divorced spouses who opted to remarry *one another* less than a year after terminating their unions. Not only did public officials accept these quick remarriages, but they encouraged them. In a newspaper interview shortly after the law came into effect, Illinois Attorney General William Stead bragged that the new restrictions on remarriage would "no doubt tend to reunite many divorced couples," whom he believed were more likely to reconcile due to the limitations the law placed on marriage to a new spouse.[51]

Officials like Stead expressed confidence that this new law would keep marriages intact by making it illegal for discontented spouses to wed new partners in a hasty fashion. Stead's confidence proved hasty in and of itself; following the law's enactment, divorcees continued to marry new partners quickly after abandoning old ones, generally assuming that by marrying in neighboring states they were effectively dodging Illinois's restrictions. In the wake of the new law, however, marriages that had once merely been scorned as acts of "progressive polygamy" were now vulnerable to nullification and the imprisonment of the new brides and grooms. The Court of Appeals of Illinois made this change crystal clear in its landmark 1911 decision, which invalidated a marriage between two parties who had wed out of state to evade the new Illinois remarriage law. This case sent a resounding message to Illinois residents that marriages in defiance of the state's law were not marriages at all.

The case involved a 1909 union between DeKalb County couple John Nehring and Frances Kidd. Frances had divorced her previous husband, Herbert Kidd, a month prior, and the new couple had exchanged vows in

---

[50] O. L. Hall, "The New Illinois Divorce Bill," *Inter Ocean*, 16 Apr. 1905, magazine section, p. 1.

[51] "The Illinois Divorce Law," *Wilmington Journal* (Ohio), 19 Jul. 1905, p. 7; "Law Is Not Retroactive," *Chicago Daily Tribune*, 13 Jul. 1905, p. 2.

Madison, Wisconsin, returning home the following day. Two years later, Frances attempted to divorce Nehring, but he insisted that they had never been legally wed due to Illinois's law against hasty remarriage. Nehring claimed he had not known about his wife's former marriage when they eloped in Wisconsin, and thus he should not be punished for inadvertently violating Illinois's law. While the Circuit Court of DeKalb County dismissed his case, the state's Court of Appeals later vindicated Nehring. In his decision, Judge George Thompson quoted at length from the Illinois statute, noting its restrictions on quick remarriage after divorce, and also highlighting its stipulation that violators of the law should be punished by up to three years of imprisonment, and that "said marriage shall be held absolutely void."[52]

While this law made it clear that hasty remarriages contracted in Illinois were punishable and void, Thompson acknowledged that the law's application to remarriages conducted out of state was less clear. He therefore proceeded by addressing the law's extraterritorial effects. Citing Justice Winslow's ruling from Wisconsin's *Lanham* case, Thompson stated that Illinois lawmakers had passed the new law to discourage divorce and to uphold good public policy. In doing so, they had intended to restrict citizens of Illinois from remarrying too promptly in all states, and not merely in their state of residency. He therefore concluded that the Nehring marriage had been void, as the decision to wed abroad did not free Illinois divorcees from obeying their home state's marriage laws. In Thompson's explanation, the law would hold very little meaning if it applied only to remarriages conducted in Illinois, particularly since modern innovations in transportation made interstate travel quick and easy. With this insistence that the state law held a clear extraterritorial effect, Thompson ruled in favor of John Nehring, concluding that his marriage to Frances had been invalid from the start.[53]

While the court's decision had great personal consequences for Frances Nehring, who lost the right to receive alimony from her estranged spouse, it held even greater implications for the legal status of post-divorce remarriages across Illinois. This ruling served as an indication that any marriage contracted less than a year after one partner's divorce was invalid, with the exception of estranged spouses who remarried one another. News reports indicated that this ruling marked the illegality of

---

[52] *Nehring v. Nehring*, 164 Ill. App. 527 (1911).   [53] Ibid.

all hasty remarriages, with the *Washington Post* estimating that the *Nehring* decision instantly invalidated five thousand Illinois unions.[54]

The case against out-of-state remarriages grew even stronger the next year when the Illinois Supreme Court ruled that marriages conducted less than a year after a partner's divorce were criminal and void. In this inheritance case, Justice Frank Dunn denied Robert Cook the right to receive the homestead of his late wife Mary, due to the fact that he had married her in Missouri just three months after divorcing another woman. Dunn ruled that Cook's recent divorce had invalidated his union with Mary, also citing Wisconsin's *Lanham* case to assert that hasty remarriages defied public policy, and were thus void even when contracted out of state. The Illinois statute had been enacted "for the protection of the morals and good order of society against serious social evils," he explained, and therefore any marriage between Illinois residents that defied this statute would be void, wherever the ceremony took place. Dunn added that the state of Illinois had nullified common law marriages in 1905, and therefore cohabiting couples could not claim to have attained common law status once the restriction on their nuptials had worn off.[55]

As in the *Nehring* case a year earlier, the press seized upon this opportunity to inform readers that any couples who defied the one-year prohibition on remarriage would meet the same fate as Robert Cook. One Chicago writer expressed great satisfaction that the law would affect members of the "best" families. Though the anonymous writer explained that the law "doesn't take any account of race, color or previous condition of servitude," the author nonetheless noted that it would have the greatest impact on members of "high sassiety," due to the fact that many hasty remarriage cases involved inheritance between couples of means. The author proceeded to list the names of high society couples who had married too quickly after one partner's divorce, including the Reverend Albert Dahlstrom, "who married Annie Pedersen a few days – or hours – after he got a decree." The writer maintained that the ruling against Robert Cook rendered these marriages invalid, concluding this gleeful exercise in exposure by stating that any children born of invalid unions would be considered illegitimate as well. Other journalists also

---

[54] "5,000 Marriages Illegal," *Washington Post*, 17 Nov. 1911, p. 1; "Divorcee Marriages Declared Illegal," *Daily Free Press* (Carbondale, Ill.), 16 Nov. 1911, p. 2; "Many Who Think They Are Married Are Sadly Deluded," 17 Nov. 1911, *Inter Ocean*, p. 5.

[55] *Wilson v. Cook*, 256 Ill. 460 (1912).

emphasized that children of hasty remarriages lacked legal standing, and encouraged the partners in these unions to remarry one another immediately in order to grant legal protection to their dependents.[56]

Such court proceedings fed into broader national debates over the status of illegitimate children. While formerly such children had been denied all rights to inheritance, throughout the nineteenth century many states sought to protect the children of unmarried partners and to maintain legal ties between parents and their illegitimate children. These initiatives were driven more by economic concerns than by benevolence; for instance, courts frequently conducted hearings to determine a child's paternity, and called for fathers to support their children financially, even when they were not wed to the child's mother. Though the purpose of these hearings was to place the burden of parental support on individual parents, rather than on public relief, they nonetheless served to lift the stigma against illegitimacy, insisting that children born out of wedlock also deserved the opportunity to prosper. In a further effort not to punish children for their parents' conduct, nineteenth-century legislatures and courts tended to grant the label of legitimacy to the children of annulled marriage, common law marriage, and "putative marriage," in which the parents had falsely believed their union to be valid when they bore the child. Courts also began to grant many illegitimate children the right to inherit from their mothers, and to award mothers custody of those children.[57]

These efforts to protect all children from the dishonor of illegitimacy began to fade in the Progressive Era. As early twentieth-century legislators created new models for offering relief to needy families, they prioritized aid for those families deemed *morally* worthy. This meant that the majority of family pensions went to widows, and most states denied divorced, deserted, and never-married mothers the right to any public aid whatsoever. As mothers often lost custody of children they could not afford to raise, the inequitable distribution of public funds meant that the children of single mothers were disproportionately vulnerable to being removed

---

[56] "High Sassiety Thrown into Big Confusion," *Day Book* (Chicago), 18 Dec. 1912, p. 3. See also "Court Bars Divorcees Fleeing State to Wed," *Belvidere Daily Republican* (Ill.), 18 Dec. 1912, p. 1; "Scores Must Wed Again," *Washington Post*, 19 Dec. 1912, p. 6.

[57] Grossberg, *Governing the Hearth*, 196–233; Mary Ann Mason, *From Father's Property to Children's Rights: The History of Child Custody in the United States* (New York: Columbia University Press, 1994), 69–71; Grossman and Friedman, *Inside the Castle*, 238; John Witte, Jr., "Ishmael's Bane: The Sin and Crime of Illegitimacy Reconsidered," *Punishment and Society* 5, no. 3 (2003): 327–345.

from their homes and becoming wards of the state. Laws against hasty remarriage fed into this trend by foisting the title of "bastard" upon countless children who had formerly been legitimate.[58]

In Illinois, questions over the protection of newly illegitimate children came to dominate public discourse on remarriage after the rulings against Frances Nehring and Robert Cook. Those two high court decisions had made it clear that in-state and out-of-state remarriages were illegal and void when contracted less than a year after divorce. But as the new statute became a recognized component of Illinois family law, critics came to worry that the law was, in fact, harming families in its tendency to deny children legitimacy. This issue became evident in 1913, when Chicago Circuit Court Judge Adelor Petit dismissed a divorce suit from William Marshall, a wealthy horse owner and exhibitor, who sought to sever ties from his wife, Blanche Marshall. The couple – both Illinois residents – had married in Michigan in 1907, just six days after Blanche had divorced her previous husband. Due to the couple's breach of Illinois's remarriage law, Petit explained that their marriage had been invalid from the start, and thus divorce was impossible. Blanche Marshall's attorney, Leslie Whipp, attempted to sway the judge by noting that the couple had a two-year-old son, Willard, who would be denied his father's support should Marshall's decision stand. The judge was unconvinced, responding that he did not have the power to change the Illinois law, even if that law had a harmful effect on the child. According to the *Inter Ocean*, Blanche Marshall responded to the judge's words by "almost collapsing in her chair," and exclaiming, "My child – I didn't know – ." The judge was unmoved, referencing the *Nehring* case to support his claim that the Marshall marriage was unlawful.[59]

After much pleading from Whipp, Petit allowed the attorney to return to court the following day with a new brief on Blanche's behalf, though the judge noted that he was unlikely to change his mind. When the court adjourned the next morning, Whipp brought with him a new strategy. He contended that Blanche Marshall had been only fifteen years old when she

---

[58] Mason, *From Father's Property*, 85–100. Illinois's Mothers' Pension law was amended in 1913 to exclude deserted women, immigrants, the wives of prisoners, and the mothers of illegitimate children. See Joan Gittens, *Poor Relations: The Children of the State in Illinois, 1818–1990* (Urbana: University of Illinois Press, 1994), 53.

[59] "Drastic Divorce Ruling Leaves Baby Nameless," *Inter Ocean*, 9 Apr. 1913, p. 1; "Child Left Nameless," *Alexandria Times-Tribune* (Ind.), 9 Apr. 1913, p. 4; "Divorce Action Dropped in Novel Way," *Charlotte News*, 9 Apr. 1913, p. 9; "Hundreds May Re-Marry in Illinois as Result of Ruling," *Santa Ana Register*, 16 Apr. 1913, p. 4.

married her first husband, and that she had not attained the consent of her parents. As a result, her first marriage had been void under Illinois age-of-consent laws, and her marriage to William Marshall was technically a valid first marriage. Petit was struck by this new testimony, declaring, "Something must be done to protect this innocent child. It must have a name and a social status."[60] Going back on his earlier claim that the Marshall marriage was invalid, Petit resolved to protect young Willard by postponing any ruling on the parents' marriage. Instead, he reversed course entirely by holding the couple in their unhappy marriage for the sake of protecting their son. His efforts proved temporarily successful; William and Blanche reconciled in April of 1914, and William dropped his delayed divorce suit, much to Petit's satisfaction. The couple formally remarried in an effort to prevent further debate over their son's legal status. They divorced for good two years later amid William's realization that his wife had developed a case of "cabaretis" – the strong desire to mingle with men and consume alcohol in cabarets – while he was away on business. Despite the marriage's collapse, however, the couple had managed to protect Willard from the taint of illegitimacy.[61]

Other hastily married couples experienced similar complications. In October of 1913, the *Inter Ocean* reported on two young women who appeared before Municipal Judge Joseph Uhlir, both hoping the judge would uphold the legitimacy of their marriages to recently absconded husbands. Each of these women had married within a year of a prior divorce, and each had borne a child with her current husband. Now those husbands had departed, both of them stating that their wives had remarried too hastily after divorces from other men and that their current unions were thus void and unlawful. In the first of these cases, Judge Uhlir convinced the estranged Stanley Springaski to reconcile with Marie Kozlin-Leonard, and he gave them $1.50 to procure a new marriage license in order to formalize their invalid union. The other couple did

[60] "Mrs. Marshall Fighting to Save Name of Child," *Inter Ocean*, 10 Apr. 1913, p. 3; "Matrimonial Tangle of Illinois Woman Puzzle for Court," *Evening World* (New York), 9 Apr. 1913, p. 2; "Fights for Child's Name," *Chicago Daily Tribune*, 10 Apr. 1913, p. 3; "Society Divorce Case Puzzles Judge Petit," *Indianapolis News*, 9 Apr. 1913, p. 1; "Hasty Wed Unlawful," *Tennessean* (Nashville), 10 Apr. 1913, p. 1.

[61] "Marshalls Drop Divorce Action for Love of Child," *Inter Ocean*, 11 Apr. 1914, p. 3; "News of the Day Concerning Chicago," *Day Book*, 11 Apr. 1914, p. 9. A year later, Leslie Whipp sued Blanche Marshall for an unpaid $600 legal fee from the divorce proceedings. "Sues Woman for $600 Fee," *Chicago Daily Tribune*, 5 Aug. 1915, p. 2; "Wife Has 'Cabaretis,' Horseman Says in Bill," *Chicago Daily Tribune*, 13 Aug. 1916, pt. 2, p. 1.

not offer such an easy solution, as Jack Barrett proved unwilling to reunite with his wife, actress Olga Rommel. The couple had wed in Valparaiso, Indiana, eight months after Rommel's prior divorce. They had lived together as husband and wife for two years, and they now had an eight-month-old baby. Barrett currently provided two dollars each week in child support, but an invalidation of the marriage would relieve him of that responsibility. Judge Uhlir was compelled to deny the validity of the couple's union, and thus to deny the legitimacy of their child. He expressed frustration over his obligation to follow the Illinois law; according to the *Inter Ocean*, he "bitterly assailed" the statute, but insisted that he had no choice but to obey its directives. Contending that Illinois's divorce law was "working a great injustice to dozens of innocent babies and their mothers," and that it was "absolutely wrong," Uhlir nonetheless was forced to leave Olga Rommel and her child to their own devices.[62]

Not all judges felt as beholden as Uhlir to obey the letter of the law in such cases. While one Chicago judge annulled the marriage of Irving and Grace Merinbaum on grounds that both parties had married too soon after their respective divorces, he nonetheless ruled that their three-year-old child would remain legitimate. Another judge refused to deem out-of-state marriages unlawful or invalid, claiming that Illinois courts were powerless to rule on the status of marriages contracted beyond state borders.[63] The majority of recorded rulings on this issue reveal, however, that judges were inclined to invalidate hasty remarriages, to rule that the children they produced were illegitimate, and sometimes to place criminal penalties on the participants in these unions. Judges' skepticism about the law did not, in most cases, stop them from following its mandates.[64]

Still, it was becoming increasingly clear that the law was not having the desired effect of decreasing divorces and minimizing hasty remarriages and, moreover, that it was having the unintended effect of creating

---

[62] "Divorce Act Scored as Unjust to Babies," *Inter Ocean*, 16 Oct. 1913, p. 5; "Judge Uhlir Makes a Sensible Suggestion," *Inter Ocean*, 18 Oct. 1913, p. 6.

[63] "Annuls Marriage; Saves Child," *Chicago Daily Tribune*, 17 Oct. 1913, p. 3; "New Remarriage Opinion," *Daily Book* (Chicago), 23 Sep. 1914, p. 24; "Couple Found Guilty in Illinois Divorce Law Test," *Chicago Daily Tribune*, 7 Oct. 1920, p. 1.

[64] See "Bride Is in Trouble Because She Defied Illinois Divorce Law," *Oakland Tribune*, 30 Jan. 1910, p. 27; "Jail for Defier of Wedding Law," *Chicago Daily Tribune*, 25 May 1913, p. 1; "Married Too Soon after Divorce; Jail," *Inter Ocean*, 8 Jun. 1913, p. 6; "Chicago Bride Arrested for Quick Remarriage," *Chicago Daily Tribune*, 29 Oct. 1914, p. 9; "Warrant for 'Lige' Jones," *Daily Journal Gazette* (Mattoon, Ill.), 22 Jul. 1915, p. 6; "Clinch Legality of Union by Marrying Second Time," *Indianapolis Star*, 2 Nov. 1915, p. 3.

illegitimacy among children.[65] Furthermore, some discontented spouses were taking advantage of the law as a means of breaking up their own unsatisfactory unions. For instance, in 1916, an artist named Ernest Weichsel left his second wife, Anne Hutchinson-Weichsel, for another woman. He had married Anne less than a year after divorcing his first wife, and he highlighted the invalidity of his hasty remarriage to Anne in his effort to convince the court to annul it. In the words of his newly abandoned wife, "He seeks to use one illegal act to make another illegal act possible."[66] Scientist William Gaertner similarly evoked the law to dissolve his 1917 marriage to cabaret star Belle Brown. Gaertner had married Brown in Indiana a month after her divorce from a former husband. Two months after their wedding, Gaertner left his new wife, filing for annulment on grounds that Belle's earlier divorce invalidated their new union.[67] As the Weichsel and Gaertner cases show, Illinois's divorce law did not always achieve its professed goals. Ironically, rather than keeping marriages intact, its restrictions on remarriage gave some dissatisfied spouses an easy excuse to end their unions without legal or economic consequence.

By 1923, a critical mass of lawmakers had come to realize that the 1905 law was not serving its intended purpose – both in its failure to protect the children of hasty remarriages from illegitimacy and in its susceptibility to manipulation by men like Weichsel and Gaertner, who used the law to end marriages they had willingly contracted. In June of that year, the Illinois senate passed the Thon Marriage and Divorce Bill, which repealed the ban on marriages that took place less than a year after one partner's divorce. The law also retroactively validated unions that had defied the remarriage law. The following July, governor Len Small signed the bill. Small's signature legalized hasty post-divorce remarriages and legitimized the children who had emerged from these unions. In the days following the passage of the new law, the Chicago press reported that recent divorcees were now swarming the marriage license bureau to attain licenses. No longer required to wait for a long year to pass after

---

[65] The state's divorce rate rose from 1.0 per thousand people in 1900 to 1.4 per thousand people in 1916. See "100 Years of Marriage and Divorce Statistics: United States, 1867–1967," *Vital and Health Statistics* 21, no. 4 (1973): 34.

[66] "Raises Question on Divorce Law," *Daily Review* (Decatur, Ill.), 5 Mar. 1916, p. 1.

[67] "Scientist and Singer to Test Remarriage Law," *Chicago Daily Tribune*, 16 Sep. 1917, pt. 1, p. 7; "Belle Gaertner, Once a Dancer, Denied Alimony," *Chicago Daily Tribune*, 25 Sep. 1917, p. 15.

getting divorced, these newly single individuals were free to marry their new loves right away.[68]

Illinois judges could still devise their own strategies for slowing the rate of remarriage after divorce. For instance, Chicago's Judge Joseph Sabath vacated a divorce decree he had issued to Josephine Seeberger Lasker after learning that she planned to elope with J. Clark Dean now that her marriage to Howard Lasker was over. He informed Josephine, "I do not want to be a party to hasty remarriage before the ink has dried on a divorce decree," explaining that he would authorize the divorce when he believed the time was right. Meanwhile, he warned Dean against acting rashly: "You can keep company with her," the judge explained, "but do not marry her until I dispose of this motion. If you marry and this divorce is set aside, you will be liable to prosecution on a charge of bigamy."[69] Despite Sabath's personal efforts to prevent quick marriage after divorce, state law now made hasty remarriage possible on a wider level. Illinois divorcees' consistent unwillingness to comply with the one-year restriction on post-divorce remarriage ultimately wore down state legislators, prompting its amendment. Though the restriction was intact for nearly two decades, couples defied it time and again, raising repeated legal and administrative headaches over the fate of illegitimate children. Ultimately, constant disobedience of the law rendered it unsustainable.

* * *

Nebraska courts faced similar concerns over the children of hasty remarriages. The state law, established in 1885, declared it unlawful for divorced persons to marry new spouses before a six-month appeal period had expired, as the divorce could still be reversed within this time frame. Individuals who ignored the law were subject to charges of bigamy. In one 1902 Nebraska Supreme Court case regarding the validity of a marriage contracted only three months after the bride's former divorce, Chief Justice John Joseph Sullivan declared that the state's law was "promotive of social order and sound morality" and that if such marriages were held

---

[68] "Divorce Law Changed by Legislature," *Daily Journal-Gazette* (Mattoon, Ill.), 19 Jul. 1923, p. 6; "Small Makes Less Than Year Matches Legal," *Daily Independent* (Murphysboro, Ill.), 2 Jul. 1923, p. 1; "New Illinois Divorce Law Brings Big Rush to Rewed," *Daily Herald* (Chicago), 6 Jul. 1923, p. 2.

[69] "Judge Blocks Cupid's Plan by Strategic Divorce Move," *Indianapolis News*, 24 Mar. 1928, p. 23.

valid, "the decision would, in our judgment, be a powerful incentive to crime. Such marriages would be multiplied, and the evils resulting from reversed divorces would be incalculable." He thus reasoned, "It may seem harsh and cruel to render a decision which will involve an innocent person in guilt and bastardize after-begotten children, but these consequences are inevitable." Despite his harsh language, Justice Sullivan ruled that the Lincoln couple's marriage was valid because they had continued to cohabit as husband and wife after the appeals period on the wife's former divorce had ended. Though the marriage had been unlawful when contracted, the couple's continued commitment to one another had rendered it legitimate in the long run as a common law marriage.[70]

In using common law marriage as a loophole for validating an unlawful hasty remarriage, Sullivan was able to express his concern over public morals and the growing embrace of divorce, while simultaneously revealing a judicial strategy for protecting spouses and children from illegitimacy charges. Another Supreme Court justice, Jacob Fawcett, validated a Nebraska couple's Iowa elopement by asserting that Nebraska's prohibitions on marriage held no extraterritorial effect, and that since the marriage was legitimate when contracted, it remained legitimate when the couple returned home to Nebraska. Fawcett believed it essential to uphold this union because, in his view, "to hold otherwise would be to render void numberless marriages and to make illegitimate thousands of children the country over."[71] Fawcett recognized the great number of couples who dodged state marriage restrictions to validate their unions in more permissive states. In his view, the nullification of those evasive unions would have disastrous consequences for the children of illicit marriages. Though Nebraska lawmakers and judges did not address children's illegitimacy as extensively as Illinois officials in their debates over hasty remarriage, Fawcett's language illustrates the degree to which the issue of juvenile legitimacy informed remarriage policy in Nebraska. By evoking common law marriage and by denying that marital prohibitions held extraterritorial effects, Nebraska judges could protect families from losing their legal status, even if the bride and groom had defied state law when initially wed.

---

[70] *Eaton v. Eaton*, 66 Neb. 676 (1902); "Rights of Divorced Persons," *Alton Telegraph* (Ill.), 15 Dec. 1902, p. 7; "Nebraska Divorce Law," *Great Bend Weekly Tribune* (Kan.), 26 Dec. 1902, p. 3; "No Legal Marriages," *Wichita Beacon*, 27 Dec. 1902, p. 4.

[71] *State v. Hand*, 87 Neb. 189 (1910); "Marriage Lawful There, Lawful Here," *Nebraska State Journal* (Lincoln), 11 Jul. 1910, p. 12.

Though legal disparities from state to state were at the root of the confusion over the validity of evasive marriages, higher courts within a single state could also disagree over the status of such remarriages. We can see this in Oklahoma, a state whose 1893 law forbade marriage for six months after divorce, pronouncing that any person who defied this restriction would be found guilty of bigamy and that the new marriage would be deemed invalid.[72] Under this statute, W. E. Wilson was initially convicted of bigamy when he married Alphretta Hewett less than six months after divorcing Barbara Wilson in 1916. Since the new couple had married out of state, however, the Criminal Court of Appeals reversed the conviction in 1919, noting that Oklahoma's law carried no extraterritorial effect. As such, the Wilson's remarriage was neither invalid nor bigamous.[73]

Though the state's laws on remarriage remained the same four years later, the supreme court reached a very different conclusion in a 1923 inheritance case. In this case, Justice Franklin Kennamer denied a widow the right to inherit from a man she had wed less than six months after his earlier divorce. The second marriage had taken place in Texas, and under the logic of the *Wilson* case, one would presume it to be legitimate. But Kennamer maintained that Oklahoma's ban on hasty remarriage applied to marriages conducted in all states, provided the couple continued to claim Oklahoma residence. He wrote, "Where a state has enacted a statute lawfully imposing upon its citizens an incapacity to contract marriage by reason of a positive policy of the state for the protection of the morals and good order of society against serious social evils, a marriage contracted in disregard of the prohibition of the statute, wherever celebrated, will be void." Insisting that the state had the obligation to uphold stable family relations in the name of public policy, Kennemar denied the legitimacy of the second marriage. The contrast between the two cases indicates that questions of the law's extraterritorial reach remained unclear.[74]

One particularly complex Oklahoma appellate case from 1925 demonstrates the legal minefield that uncertainties over the legality of hasty remarriages could create. In this case, defendant V. C. Harvey had divorced his first wife in Tulsa in December of 1920. The following February, he married a woman who had herself procured a divorce just

[72] *Niece v. Territory*, 9 Okla. 535 (1900).
[73] *Wilson v. State*, 16 Okla. Crim. 471 (1919).
[74] *Atkeson v. Sovereign Camp W.O.W. et al.*, 90 Okla. 154 (1923).

a day earlier, also in Oklahoma. Both Harvey and his new wife held Oklahoma residency, so to evade the six-month restriction on post-divorce remarriage they had exchanged vows in Missouri, and then they traveled on to Kansas, where they lived for a year. In February of 1922, the couple returned to Oklahoma, and they lived there together until April of 1923, when Mrs. Harvey (referred to in legal documents as Mrs. Harvey II) took a trip to Illinois. While she was away, V. C. Harvey married Inez Vaughn (Mrs. Harvey III), who lived with him as his wife until June, when Mrs. Harvey II returned home. At this point, Harvey was arrested for bigamy. Harvey disputed this bigamy charge. He attempted to use Oklahoma's six-month prohibition on remarriage to his favor, stating that his marriage to Mrs. Harvey II had been invalid because it had taken place less than six months after his divorce from Mrs. Harvey I.[75]

V. C. Harvey's efforts to use the remarriage law to deny his bigamy were unsuccessful. He was convicted in the district court, and the Criminal Court of Appeals upheld that conviction. Referring to Harvey as a "muchly married individual" who, "given time would surpass the record of Henry VIII," Judge Thomas Edwards ruled that Harvey's Missouri marriage to his second wife had been valid. Since the couple had remained in Missouri for a year after their unlawful exchange of vows, Edwards explained, they had entered into a common law marriage once the six-month prohibition on their marriage expired in August 1921. Therefore, V. C. Harvey was legally married to Mrs. Harvey II when he wed Mrs. Harvey III, and his bigamy conviction had been correct. The court did not need to dispute whether Oklahoma's prohibition on remarriage applied to Missouri unions, as the couple's decision to remain in Missouri for an extended period of time eliminated that question. Still, this case serves as another indication of the confusion that divergent remarriage laws could create, and of the ways in which frequently married individuals could capitalize on that confusion in an effort to avoid culpability for their violation of remarriage laws. At the same time, judges could create their own methods for defying efforts to manipulate remarriage law. After providing a technical explanation for why V. C. Harvey had committed bigamy, Judge Edwards added, "We believe there is another reason for declining to hold the marriage void. That reason is based on public policy, on the view that a defendant charged with a crime will not be permitted to take advantage of his own wrong." Ultimately, judges could still rely on

---

[75] *Harvey v. State*, 31 Okla. Crim. 299 (1925).

vague arguments about public policy to invalidate arrangements they believed to be morally indecent.[76]

* * *

As the many above examples illustrate, hasty out-of-state remarriages sparked controversy and legal confusion as courts debated their validity and the legitimacy of the children they produced. Court cases involving these marriages yielded inconsistent rulings across – and sometimes within – state borders. The disparities between marriage laws from state to state generated national conversation on the morality and legality of divorce and remarriage. Moreover, in many cases it was state-to-state legal disparities that *permitted* these ambiguous unions to form, allowing divorced individuals to dodge their home states' restrictions on remarriage and to wed elsewhere. Therefore, as debates over the morality of progressive polygamy intensified, disapproving reformers homed in on these legal inconsistencies, leading campaigns to standardize marriage laws in order to eliminate out-of-state remarriages altogether.

These efforts at standardization took several forms, and they marked the continuation of a reform effort that had begun a generation earlier. Amid late nineteenth-century reports of rising divorce and remarriage rates, government officials had begun proposing solutions to restore the dominance of permanent, monogamous matrimony. As noted, the year 1884 saw the first of many proposed constitutional amendments seeking to grant the federal government the power to create national marriage and divorce laws, and thus to eliminate the trend of migratory divorce and remarriage.[77] National efforts to crack down on divorce and hasty remarriage accelerated in the wake of an 1889 report by US Commissioner of Labor Carroll D. Wright, which illustrated the growth of the divorce rate across the nation, including in rural and politically

---

[76] Edwards offered harsh words to all involved parties, stating, "A mere recital of the facts discloses that the conduct of the defendant is reprehensible in an extreme degree, and that his defense is such that he [is] entitled to only what the cold letter of the law gives him. It also discloses that Mrs. Harvey, II, was an unfaithful wife to her first spouse, and abandoned her own home, and was a particeps criminis in breaking up the home of defendant. What has befallen her is in the nature of retributive justice. As to Mrs. Harvey, III, she apparently knew the marital status of the defendant at the time she entered the marriage relation with him, and is entitled to no sympathy." Ibid.

[77] Blake, *Road to Reno*, 145–146; Cott, *Public Vows*, 110; Riley, *Divorce*, 111. As Riley indicates, proponents of federal marriage legislation continued to push unsuccessfully for a constitutional amendment until 1947. This campaign will be addressed in greater depth in the following chapter.

conservative regions.[78] Wright's research sparked widespread efforts to temper the divorce rate through legislation, including the 1906 formation of the National Congress on Uniform Divorce Law. Participants in this movement blamed disparities in state laws for the nation's rising divorce rate; the initial conference of the National Congress on Uniform Divorce Law thus sought to standardize state marriage and divorce statutes, attracting delegates from forty-two states to undertake this task.[79]

The participants in the Congress on Uniform Divorce Law worked together to write a single set of divorce statutes that they hoped each individual state's legislature would adopt. Historian Glenda Riley has shown that in spite of its members' ambitious goals, the Congress struggled to agree on a single set of grounds for divorce. While the delegates eventually reached consensus on a list of six causes – adultery, bigamy, felony conviction, cruelty, desertion, and drunkenness – their work had limited reach, as only three states adopted this proposed legislation. Subsequent efforts to standardize divorce law across the states proved similarly unsuccessful, in spite of frequent complaints from lawmakers and social reformers that disparate state laws were responsible for the accelerating divorce rate. But while participants in the uniform divorce law campaign had trouble agreeing on the specific grounds for divorce, they were united in their opposition to hasty remarriage. Despite the many clashes that the delegates to the 1906 National Congress on Uniform Divorce Law faced over acceptable grounds for divorce, they agreed that all states should implement a one-year ban on remarriage following an individual's divorce.[80]

Though efforts to create uniform marriage laws failed to materialize into a nationwide policy, efforts to halt hasty remarriage manifested themselves in nonlegal venues. Members of the clergy were among the most outspoken critics of progressive polygamy in the first decades of the twentieth century. Prominent New York priest Louis Lambert criticized Protestant leaders for what he saw as their refusal to wage war on divorce alongside their war on polygamy. In 1902, Lambert had received an appeal for help from Methodist, Presbyterian, and Baptist missionary

---

[78] Riley, *Divorce*, 108–110; Carroll D. Wright, *A Report on Marriage and Divorce in the United States, 1867–1886; Including an Appendix Relating to Marriage and Divorce in Certain Countries in Europe* (Washington, D.C.: Government Printing Office, 1889); Syrett, *American Child Bride*, 127–128.

[79] Riley, *Divorce*, 110–117.

[80] Ibid., 115–127; Mrs. Edward F. White, "Prominent Women Tell of the Need for a Federal Marriage and Divorce Law," *Brooklyn Daily Eagle*, 17 Jun. 1923, p. 2E.

boards, requesting that Catholic leaders stand by Protestant ministers in their efforts to quash the lingering practice of polygamy within Mormon communities. Lambert agreed that Mormonism remained a threat to American sexual morals, but he argued that Protestants played an even stronger role in perpetuating polygamy in their toleration of divorce and their willingness to unite divorced individuals in matrimony. He wrote, "As long as Protestant ministers will continue to officiate at a ceremony providing for the cohabitation of divorced persons, they cannot consistently oppose polygamy." He continued, "We fail to see that tandem polygamy is morally better than the Mormon variety. In fact, we deem it worse because it turns the woman adrift, in many cases unable to fight the battle of life, and deprives the child of the co-operative training of both parents." For Lambert and other Catholic officials, Protestant complicity in the trend toward consecutive polygamy was damaging the soul of the nation and depriving abandoned wives and children of emotional and material support.[81]

Contrary to Lambert's accusations, non-Catholic clergy did speak out against hasty remarriage. In a 1903 interview, New York Episcopal priest Morgan Dix denounced divorce and remarriage in unambiguous terms. "Would it have been possible fifty or even twenty years ago for two divorced persons in fashionable society to have a wedding the very day of the woman's divorce decree, at which five of the ten guests had been themselves divorced?" he asked in reference to an article he had read on the subject. Dix provided the reporter with the name of the hastily remarried woman in question, and he insisted that a generation ago she would have been shunned for her actions. Now, however, the public and press were condoning this behavior, and Dix called for an end to such tolerance. While he did not believe that stricter matrimonial legislation could stem the tide of hasty remarriage, he argued that social ostracism could achieve that end. "The only effectual means I can see is that of cultivating a general public sentiment," he declared. "If people would refuse to receive divorced persons in their drawing-rooms, or to speak to them in the street – there is the remedy. 'I don't want to know you' would be a very powerful hindrance."[82]

---

[81] "Catholic Church and Mormonism," *Intermountain Catholic* (Salt Lake City), 19 Apr. 1902, p. 1; "Cannot Draw Them In," *Deseret Evening News* (Salt Lake City), 24 Apr. 1902, p. 4; "Cardinal on Divorce," *Washington Post*, 12 May 1908, p. 3.

[82] "Rev. Morgan Dix Sick at Heart over Women," *Fort Wayne Journal Gazette*, 13 Dec. 1903, p. 11.

Despite Dix's call for the snubbing of divorcees, a year later the Protestant Episcopalian convention passed a compromise canon permitting the innocent parties in adultery cases to remarry once their divorce decrees had been official for a year. Though the canon gave clergy the right to refuse to conduct these weddings and it compelled the victims of adultery to wait at least a year before marriage, it nonetheless received wide criticism from Catholic officials, including Pennsylvania priest Morgan Sheedy. Sheedy rejected the Episcopalian law, stating that young people needed to be taught to revere marriage and to recognize its sacredness. Sheedy bemoaned the permissiveness of state divorce laws, and like Dix, he called for Christians to ostracize participants in "tandem polygamy" as a means of combatting it.[83]

Several outspoken Protestant ministers heeded Sheedy's call to denounce divorcees and their remarriages. In a 1909 Thanksgiving Day sermon before his New York congregation, renowned Presbyterian minister Charles Parkhurst spoke of several divorced suffrage workers, including Alva Belmont. Parkhurst's primary objective was to undermine the suffrage movement and to fight against female civic engagement. He nonetheless used the accusation of "tandem polygamy" as a tool for discrediting those women who sought the right to vote and for encouraging the public to ignore the rhetoric of remarried women like Belmont.[84] Meanwhile, Reverend R. F. Coyle of Denver's Presbyterian Church cited consecutive polygamy as a notable sign of "the breaking down of woman's modesty and reckless contempt for marital and social laws." Like Parkhurst, Coyle pointed to remarried women as a symbol of the nation's "drift toward grossness and sensuality." In his view, they reflected a troubling breakdown of gender roles and an abandonment of Christian marital principles.[85]

Political leaders could also be outspoken in their desire to stigmatize divorcees, including President William Howard Taft and his wife, Helen Taft. During her husband's presidential run in 1908, Mrs. Taft told an

---

[83] "The New Divorce Canon," *Topeka Daily Capital*, 5 Nov. 1904, p. 4; Rev. Morgan M. Sheedy, "Gravity of the Divorce Evil," *Pittsburgh Daily Post*, 6 Nov. 1904, p. 6.

[84] "Getting Back at Men," *Washington Post*, 26 Nov. 1909, p. 3; "Parkhurst Scores Suffrage Leaders upon Divorce Evil," *Washington Times*, 26 Nov. 1909, p. 12; "Churches Thronged for Thanksgiving," *New York Times*, 26 Nov. 1909, p. 2; "Mrs. Belmont Hurt at Attack," *Pittston Gazette* (Pa.), 26 Nov. 1909, p. 1; "Mrs. Belmont Won't Reply," *Daily Times* (New Philadelphia, Ohio), 27 Nov. 1909, p. 1; "Militant Suffragette Replies to Dr. Parkhurst," *Pittsburgh Daily Post*, 27 Nov. 1909, p. 9; "Society Outside the Capital," *Washington Post*, 29 Nov. 1909, p. 5.

[85] "Feminine Dress Is Scored by Pastor," *Inter Ocean*, 21 Oct. 1912, p. 11.

FIGURE 2.2 Mary Pickford and Douglas Fairbanks at the White House, National Photo Company Collection, Library of Congress, 8 Jun. 1920.

interviewer that she hoped to see an end to the practice of divorce. She regretted the fact that divorcees frequently retained their former social status, expressing alarm that divorce "is countenanced by the so-called highest social circles, and it is made light of, and a woman in many instances is received with as much favor after she is divorced as she was before."[86] William Howard Taft carried on with this campaign when he became president. Taft called for the implementation of uniform divorce laws, insisting that divorced persons who defied their home state's remarriage laws by eloping out of state should be found universally guilty of bigamy.[87]

As public debate over hasty remarriage persisted into the 1920s, the criticism began to focus on the divorces and remarriages of high-profile celebrities. Amid the rise of mass culture and popular cinema, the complicated love lives of Hollywood royalty served to indicate both the immorality and the inevitability of progressive polygamy. In 1920, screen stars Mary Pickford and Douglas Fairbanks each divorced their spouses and wed one another following an extramarital affair. Despite initial criticism, the couple emerged as a beloved pair in the popular press (see Figure 2.2).[88] The marital patterns of superstar Rudolph

[86] "Mrs. Taft on Divorces," *Intermountain Catholic* (Salt Lake City), 4 Jul. 1908, p. 4.
[87] "Upholds President's Views," *Indianapolis Star*, 11 Sep. 1911, p. 7; "Desires Divorce Reform," *Pittsburgh Daily Post*, 11 Sep. 1911, p. 5; "Marriage and Divorce Laws," *Asheville Gazette-News*, 15 Sep. 1911, p. 4.
[88] May, *Great Expectations*, 75–76; Hilary A. Hallett, *Go West, Young Women!: The Rise of Early Hollywood* (Berkeley: University of California Press, 2013), 95–96; Celello, *Making Marriage Work*, 24.

Valentino sparked a more complex narrative. Valentino had married silent screen star Jean Acker in 1919. The couple separated soon after, and Acker attained an interlocutory decree of divorce from Valentino in January 1922. According to California law, neither party could marry until January 1923, when the divorce would be finalized. But Valentino longed to wed his new lover, actress Natacha Rambova (née Winifred Hudnut) right away, and the pair believed they could dodge the restrictions on Valentino's remarriage by exchanging vows in Mexicali, Mexico. They did just that on 13 May 1922, immediately returning across the border to Palm Springs after the celebration had concluded. The following week, a Los Angeles superior court judge questioned the legitimacy of the Mexican marriage, suggesting that Valentino had committed bigamy by remarrying less than a year after receiving his California divorce decree. Amid widespread media reports on this scandalous marriage, Valentino turned himself into the police and was arraigned on two counts of bigamy.[89]

The ensuing bigamy hearing was, in the words of one Valentino biographer, "a living-theater event, a tabloid melodrama." The actor expressed regret at having broken the law, but he insisted that he had done so in the name of love. Ultimately, Superior Court Judge J. Walter Hanby dismissed the bigamy charges, claiming that the prosecution had provided insufficient evidence that Valentino and Rambova cohabitated after exchanging vows, and criticizing California's year-long restriction on remarriage. The couple wed again when the year-long interlocutory period was over, later parting ways in 1925.[90]

Valentino and Rambova weathered the legal and media firestorm that their hasty marriage created; subsequent celebrity couples failed to learn from their struggles. In 1928, film actress Jacqueline Logan eloped to Tijuana with Los Angeles broker Larry Winston just five months after obtaining a divorce from her previous husband. Upon learning of this marriage, Los Angeles Chief Deputy District Attorney Forrest Murray announced that Logan could face bigamy charges if she returned to her home county. After consulting her attorney, Logan learned that since she and Winston had not cohabitated since exchanging vows, she could

[89] Emily W. Leider, *Dark Lover: The Life and Death of Rudolph Valentino* (New York: Farrar, Straus and Giroux, 2003), 197–209.

[90] Ibid., 212–214; Karl K. Kitchen, "Meet the Shiek's Wife," *Oakland Tribune Magazine*, 14 Sep. 1924, p. 6. Nancy Barr Mavity, "When It Comes to a Choice: Babies or a Career and the Society of Puppies," *Oakland Tribune Magazine*, 27 Dec. 1925, n.p.

escape arrest if they continued to live separately until the interlocutory decree expired. At that point, they could wed legally in California. The couple followed through with this plan; Logan's divorce became final in March of 1928, and she legally married Winston the following June.[91] Other celebrities received similar scrutiny for their participation in tandem polygamy, despite avoiding the legal hurdles that Valentino and Logan faced. Lottie Pickford, the younger sister of Mary Pickford, gained media attention in 1929 when news broke of her third marriage; playwright Eugene O'Neill was also the source of much commentary for celebrating his third wedding that year, less than a month after divorcing his second wife. Actors Gloria Swanson, Jean Harlow, John Gilbert, Hoot Gibson, Constance Bennett, Mae Murray, and Adolphe Menjou also received attention for their multiple marriages.[92]

Critics of divorce and remarriage spoke out against celebrity and media culture, arguing that American consumers were less likely to take their marriage vows seriously due to the bad influence of Hollywood stars. Outspoken criticisms of what historian J. Herbie DiFonzo terms "the merry-go-round marriages of stars" and the "celebrity wedding ring-toss" reflected a desire to temper the influence of movie star romances on the impressionable American public. As one *Good Housekeeping* columnist observed, stars who "marry for a season are few in number, but impressive in influence. They belong to the group which sets our fashion in clothes, resorts, amusements; in time, their morality tends to become our own."[93] Similarly, historian Alicia Barber argues that hasty remarriages by celebrities like Pickford and Fairbanks brought "a renewed sense of glamour" to divorce, demonstrating to fans "that marriage need not be permanent and that divorce was often essential to the pursuit of

---

[91] "Another Film Star Marries in Too Great Haste," *Santa Cruz Evening News*, 24 Aug. 1928, p. 13; "Star to Dodge Bigamy Charge," *Oakland Tribune*, 25 Aug. 1928, p. 2; "Jacqueline Logan and Broker to Part to Avoid Bigamy Case," *Brooklyn Daily Eagle*, 26 Aug. 1928, p. 24A; "Mexican Wedding Is Void in California so Pair Live Apart," *San Bernardino County Sun*, 27 Aug. 1928, p. 3; "Jacqueline Logan Gets Final Decree," *Brooklyn Daily Eagle*, 21 Mar. 1929, p. 24; "Jacqueline Logan Rewed to Broker," *Indianapolis News*, 3 Jun. 1929, p. 10.

[92] "Eugene O'Neill Plans His Third Marriage," *Santa Cruz Evening News*, 9 Mar. 1929, p. 11; "Lottie Pickford Reveals Secret Third Marriage," *Brooklyn Daily Eagle*, 24 Jul. 1929, p. 11; "Lottie Pickford Weds Third Time," *Oakland Tribune*, 24 Jul. 1929, p. 3; "O'Neill Weds Actress, Goes on Honeymoon," *San Bernardino County Sun*, 24 Jul. 1929, p. 3; "Queer Laws about Second Marriages," *Journal News* (Hamilton, Ohio), 4 Feb. 1932, p. 7; "Needs a Code," *Daily Mail* (Hagerstown), 15 Sep. 1934, p. 6.

[93] DiFonzo, *Beneath the Fault Line*, 35.

true love." Motion picture studios sought to neutralize the impact of their stars' marriage habits, creating numerous films throughout the 1920s that criticized divorce and remarriage in dramatic fashion. One 1923 film, *Reno*, concludes with the Yellowstone geyser thrusting its much-married lead character to his death on the rocks. In one reviewers' eyes, this karmic punishment for progressive polygamy also served as "propaganda against the conflicting divorce laws of the United States."[94]

But ultimately, the backlash against progressive polygamy from legal and judicial officials, social reformers, clergy, and media only served to highlight its staying power. The disparate state remarriage laws, the inconsistent outcomes of trials over the validity of post-divorce nuptials, the ambiguous marital status of transient couples, and the dubious legitimacy of their children only reinforced the perception that a marriage crisis was under way. Efforts to establish uniform marriage and divorce laws and to ratify a constitutional amendment to permit federal marriage legislation reveal the depths of these anxieties. The eventual failure of such remedies shows that the perceived problem of progressive polygamy was too big and complex to contain with legislation alone. Certainly, many individual couples paid the price for their defiance of remarriage statutes, and their children suffered the social and legal indignities of illegitimacy. But the lack of consistency in rulings on such cases, both across state lines and within single states, only serves to magnify the extent of the problems progressive polygamy caused.

More than anything, the persistence of hasty remarriages exposed the unfeasibility of maintaining any consistent definition of matrimony from state to state and household to household. As clergy preached about the perils of consecutive polygamy and moral reformers maligned Hollywood stars for their frequent divorces and remarriages, their frustration derived in great part from the fact that a centralized legal mechanism was not controlling – indeed, could not control – the romantic inclinations of modern couples across the nation. At the heart of public anxiety over hasty remarriage was the perception that people were no longer

---

[94] Barber, *Reno's Big Gamble*, 93–94, 132. On the influence of the Pickford-Fairbanks marriage and the growing celebration and emulation of celebrity culture in this era, see Lary May, *Screening Out the Past: The Birth of Mass Culture and the Motion Picture Industry* (New York: Oxford University Press, 1980), 144–146. On criticisms that "sinful" Hollywood lifestyles and celebrity culture were having too great an impression on fans, see Robert Sklar, *Movie-Made America: A Cultural History of American Movies* (New York: Vintage Books, 1975), 79–81; Samantha Barbas, *Movie Crazy: Fans, Stars, and the Cult of Celebrity* (New York: Palgrave Macmillan, 2001), 169–172.

exchanging vows with seriousness or a dedication to lifelong monogamy and that there was little the law could do to reverse the trend. Efforts to halt hasty remarriage reflected a widespread fear that long-term nuptials were a thing of the past, and disparities in state laws made it nearly impossible to restore couples' commitment to long-term commitment. But if guardians of marital tradition worried that diverse state laws tore families apart by facilitating easy divorce and hasty remarriage, many were also concerned that inconsistent state laws made it a little too easy for certain people to form family units. As the next chapter's analysis of eugenic marriage debates reveals, disparate state regulations on who was physically and emotionally fit for matrimony added yet another layer of complexity to the marriage crisis at hand.

3

Eugenic Marriage Laws and the Continuing Crisis of Out-of-State Elopement

As we have seen, debates over progressive polygamy reflected above all a concern that Americans had ceased to take their marriage vows seriously. Couples who defied prohibitions on hasty remarriage, exchanging vows with new partners before they were legally permitted to do so, embodied a growing sense that marriage contracts could be broken and rewritten at will. Divorcees' ease in breaching the remarriage clauses on their divorce decrees by eloping to other states revealed the porousness of state borders as well as the obstacles that state legislators faced in restricting their constituents' marital choices. As judges debated the legality of evasive remarriages and as legislators concocted new solutions for minimizing disparities in state remarriage laws, reformers cited the legal confusion such nuptials sparked as yet another indication that the marriage institution was in a state of crisis. By eliminating divorced persons' right to elope across state lines, critics of consecutive polygamy sought to erase the temptation to stray from one partner to another, thus lowering the divorce rate and increasing the rate of successful unions.

Not all efforts to halt elopement were grounded in the desire to keep existing unions intact, however. Many opponents of out-of-state elopement hoped to halt certain people from getting married under *any* circumstances, be it a first marriage or a fifth marriage. While most legislators wanted to encourage matrimony, they were willing to make exceptions when it came to the marriage of individuals deemed physically and mentally "unfit" – among them, persons with venereal diseases, epilepsy, intellectual disabilities, and a host of other real or perceived physical and mental infirmities. Fearing that reproduction among the unfit would yield dire social consequences, many state legislatures passed eugenic laws denying marriage licenses to people believed to possess these conditions. An investigation of eugenic marriage laws, and of couples' active evasion of those laws, adds new layers to the discussion of conjugal misconduct across state borders. The creation of legislation denying marital rights to persons believed physically and mentally unfit for matrimony marked a growing drive to keep the institution pure and to measure the nation's marital success by the quality of the unions it created rather than quantity of vows exchanged. Lawmakers who wished to deny licenses to the unfit knew that they risked decreasing the number of marriages across the nation – particularly as they intensified their quest to prevent "undesirable" couples from eloping across state lines. But if opponents of progressive polygamy wanted to celebrate marriage by compelling couples to honor their vows, proponents of eugenic law wanted to increase reverence for marriage by denying undesirable populations the right to exchange those vows altogether.

This chapter thus explores the creation of state eugenic marriage laws in the 1910s. It considers the restrictive policies themselves, as well as the strategies couples devised to challenge and defy those laws. While most couples conformed with state-mandated marital restrictions, others resisted them, eloping to neighboring Gretna Greens to avoid eugenic regulations. This push-and-pull between the creators and opponents of eugenic marriage legislation yielded consistent renegotiation of the impact public health concerns should have on a couple's freedom to contract marriage. The language of eugenics occupied a forceful role in discussions of marriage law and elopement, and it sparked ongoing campaigns to create uniform marriage evasion legislation to offset marriages that defied eugenic laws, popularly referred to as "dysgenic" unions. Eugenic debates also led to heightened criticism of mercenary ministers and marriage mills, drawing attention to the profits that out-of-state elopements could bring to cities that lacked strict eugenic laws. In prior sections of this book we see expressions of concern that marriage was degenerating into a for-profit industry. Such apprehensions became all the more pronounced as questions about public health entered into statewide and national debates over marriage law. While ministers already faced backlash for marrying out-of-state couples who defied the wishes of their parents or the directives of their divorce decrees, officiants who helped couples dodge state eugenic laws incurred even more disapproval. Not only were they validating marriages that defied abstract notions of public policy; now, noncompliant officiants were also legitimizing marriages believed to threaten the very health of the nation.

Though the strictest eugenic marriage laws emerged in 1913, the ideologies behind them had taken hold of American scientific thought a few decades earlier. The eugenic movement grew from innovations in the fields of evolutionary science and genetics. In the 1850s, English philosopher Herbert Spencer coined the term "survival of the fittest" as a justification for social inequality. Rejecting the belief that poor people were mere victims of chance who could improve their lot with time, effort, and charitable aid, Spencer viewed the plight of the underclass as a manifestation of the laws of nature: "If they are not sufficiently complete to live, they die," he asserted, "and it is best they should die."[1] In 1859, Charles Darwin gave scientific authority to Spencer's theory with the publication of *The Origin of Species*, in which he used the term "natural selection" to explain how organisms compete for limited resources, with the stronger subsisting and the weaker dying out. Darwin did not intend to encompass human life within his writings. The term "Social Darwinism" nonetheless came to signify the notion that weak individuals were not equipped to function in a competitive world, and efforts to preserve their existence defied nature's plan. Gregor Mendel's celebrated experimentation with pea plants further fueled this perception; his work suggested that the most desirable characteristics were inheritable, lending scientific credence to the notion that those lacking such biological traits should not be able to pass their genetic material onto future generations.[2]

These developments in the biological sciences entered the field of marriage law in the later nineteenth century, as genetic arguments were employed to restrict unpopular marital practices. Historian Michael Grossberg reveals this growing connection between biological innovations and marriage law with his analysis of incest in the 1870s. Legal restrictions on incestuous marriages – particularly those between cousins – had slackened over the course of the antebellum period as legislators came to regard marriage as an individual right that fell outside the state's authority. But as scientists began to argue that procreation between blood relatives could produce physically and mentally compromised children, legislators reconsidered the role the state should play in regulating matrimony. Ultimately, many sought to enforce new legal restrictions on

---

[1] Edwin Black, *War against the Weak: Eugenics and America's Campaign to Create a Master Race* (New York: Four Walls Eight Windows, 2003), 12; Harry Bruinius, *Better for All the World: The Secret History of Forced Sterilization and America's Quest for Racial Purity* (New York: Alfred A. Knopf, 2006), 34–38.

[2] Black, *War against the Weak*, 12–13.

incestuous marriage. As Grossberg argues, the passage of these new marriage restrictions revealed "a new inclination to take no chances with heredity." Developments in biology and genetics convinced legislators that Americans could not always be trusted to make their own marital decisions and that the only way to protect future generations from hereditary dangers was through state regulation of marriage.[3]

These growing concerns over the biological consequences of marriage and reproduction found a new outlet with the developing field of eugenics. In 1883, British statistician Francis Galton coined the term "eugenics," which he derived from a Greek root meaning "good in birth." The cousin of Charles Darwin, Galton embraced evolutionary and genetic science in his quest to foster a healthier human race. He believed that eugenicists could improve the physical and mental qualities of the population by giving "the more suitable races or strains of blood a better chance of prevailing speedily over the less suitable," and he proposed concrete steps to achieve that end.[4] Specifically, Galton argued that people possessing the most desirable physical and mental traits should be encouraged to procreate widely, whereas people possessing any physical or mental impairments should not procreate at all. He also called for the regulation of marriage, arguing that society should prohibit eugenically flawed people from exchanging vows and should encourage eugenically sound people to marry and reproduce.[5]

Many state legislatures heeded Galton's call for marriage restrictions at the turn of the twentieth century. As anxieties mounted over growing rates of immigration, racial and ethnic intermarriage, and increasing contraceptive use, reformers worried that the birth rate was declining among the most desirable populations and increasing among those considered racially, ethnically, and socially inferior. As immigrant, African American, and working-class populations grew in urban centers, authorities bemoaned the decline of the middle-class white population. Reflecting on the slowing white birth rate – the average number of children born to white parents declined from 6.14 per household in 1840 to 3.56 in 1900 – President Theodore Roosevelt drew from the work of sociologist E. A. Ross to declare that the white middle class was

---

[3] Grossberg, *Governing the Hearth*, 110–113, 144–146.

[4] Quoted in Kline, *Building a Better Race*, 13; see also Alexandra Minna Stern, *Eugenic Nation: Faults and Frontiers of Better Breeding in Modern America* (Berkeley: University of California Press, 2005), 10–11.

[5] Kline, *Building a Better Race*, 13; Black, *War against the Weak*, 18.

committing "race suicide" in its sluggish rate of reproduction. His words would galvanize legislators' quest to reverse this declining birth rate among the white middle classes and to prevent procreation among those groups widely deemed unfit: immigrants, African Americans, the poor, and the physically unhealthy.[6]

Many Progressive Era physicians believed that the decline of the white birth rate was not a consequence of birth control, but of venereal disease. American dermatologist and syphilologist Prince Alfred Morrow drew from the 1890 census to approximate that one in every seven marriages proved sterile as a result of venereal disease. Morrow thus rejected the common assumption that nonprocreation was a personal decision, and he argued instead that infertility was a tragic and involuntary result of sexual impropriety. Condemning unfaithful men for infecting their unknowing wives with gonorrhea and syphilis, Morrow supported the creation of eugenic marriage laws to prevent the spread of infection among wives and children.[7]

As reformers heeded Morrow's call for an aggressive attack on venereal disease, they also responded to a simultaneous campaign against procreation by the "feebleminded," reflecting the growing perception that intellectual disabilities were inheritable. As legal scholar Christopher Tiedeman argued in 1886, "[If] the blood of either of the parties to a marriage is tainted with insanity there is imminent danger of its transmission to the offspring, and through the procreation of imbecile children the welfare of the state is more or less threatened."[8] This outcry against the feebleminded grew in the early twentieth century, due in part to the scholarship of American psychologist Henry Goddard, who raised apprehension over procreation among mentally unfit populations with his 1908 English translation of the Binet intelligence test, or the IQ test. By circulating and standardizing this system for measuring intelligence, Goddard provided an easy way to differentiate persons possessing "normal" intelligence from those deemed abnormal. Goddard further underscored these distinctions by introducing the term "moron" to describe high-functioning feebleminded people. In declaring that morons possessed a debilitating genetic flaw that must not be passed on to future generations, Goddard identified a new group to target for sterilization, institutional-ization, and eugenic marriage legislation. In the words of historian Wendy

---

[6] Kline, *Building a Better Race*, 2, 11; Stern, *Eugenic Nation*, 13–14; Brandt, *No Magic Bullet*, 7–8.

[7] Brandt, *No Magic Bullet*, 14–20.   [8] Quoted in Grossberg, *Governing the Hearth*, 147.

Kline, "The person labeled mentally deficient was no longer deemed an object of curiosity or sympathy but a threat to the genetic health and stability of the race. According to this new definition, nothing in the environment – no amount of education, training, or nurturing – could alter the destructive potential stored within a feeble mind." As a result, feebleminded persons had to be prevented from marrying and spreading their genes at all costs.[9]

The campaigns against venereal disease and feeblemindedness coalesced as reformers applied new scientific principles to their battles against urban vice. The keepers of homes for the feebleminded often held prostitutes, unwed mothers, and persons with venereal infections as patients, conflating perceived mental and moral disorders within the broader category of feeblemindedness. Other reformers argued that so-called feebleminded women needed to be institutionalized so that they would not engage in promiscuous sex and consequently spread venereal disease to a new generation.[10] Amid these collective fears of excess procreation by the working classes, racial and ethnic minorities, bearers of venereal disease, and the feebleminded, as well as the concern that healthy and prosperous whites were committing race suicide, lawmakers turned to eugenic marriage legislation. By 1914, legislators in thirty-four states and the District of Columbia had embraced calls for marital restriction, passing laws that barred certain parties from getting married as a means of guarding the population from physical, mental, and moral threat. Some of these laws specified venereal disease as their primary target; other laws highlighted more abstract qualities – such as feeblemindedness, poverty, and criminality – as grounds for denying marriage licenses. All eugenic laws drew a divide between those persons viewed as medically and psychologically "fit" for marriage and childbearing and those whose genes were judged unsuitable for future generations.[11]

---

[9] Kline, *Building a Better Race*, 21–25.

[10] Ibid., 24–29, 45–47; Odem, *Delinquent Daughters*, 98. On the broad array of characteristics that eugenicists placed under the rubric of "feeblemindedness" (including perceived promiscuity and sexual degeneracy, homelessness, alcoholism, pregnancy, "wanderlust," and homosexual tendencies), see Paul A. Lombardo, *Three Generations, No Imbeciles: Eugenics, the Supreme Court, and* Buck v. Bell (Baltimore: Johns Hopkins University Press, 2008), 61–62.

[11] Jessie Spaulding Smith, "Marriage, Sterilization and Commitment Laws Aimed at Decreasing Mental Deficiency," *Journal of Criminal Law and Criminology* 5 (1914): 364–365; "State Laws Regulating Marriage of the Unfit," *Journal of the American Institute of Criminal Law and Criminology* 4, no. 3 (1913): 423–425; Matteo Teresi, *Love and Health: The Problem of Better Breeding for the Human Family* (New York:

The first of these laws passed in Connecticut in 1895. The statute barred feebleminded and epileptic men and women under the age of forty-five from contracting marriages, and it punished violators with at least three years in prison. Following in Connecticut's footsteps, the state legislatures of Kansas (1903), New Jersey (1904), and Ohio (1904) passed similar statutes in the years that followed.[12] Other states targeted syphilis and gonorrhea in their eugenic codes, with Michigan passing the first such law in 1899. In 1905, the state passed an additional law preventing any person who had been institutionalized as an epileptic, feebleminded, imbecilic, or insane patient from procuring a marriage license, unless the patient had been "completely cured" of the condition. Other states combined campaigns against venereal disease and feeblemindedness into one law. In 1905, Indiana barred marriage licenses to anyone determined to be "imbecile, epileptic, or of unsound mind." It also prohibited persons with transmittable diseases from exchanging vows. On top of these public health-related concerns, the statute denied marriage to anyone who appeared to be under the influence of alcohol or drugs while seeking a license and to any man who had spent time in a county asylum or a home for indigent persons, unless he proved that he could now support a wife and family. Pennsylvania also incorporated economic stability and moral uprightness into its effort to preserve the physical health of future generations, passing a law that resembled Indiana's in 1913.[13]

The states of North Dakota and Wisconsin created the strictest marriage laws yet in 1913, bringing medical professionals more deeply into the realm of marriage regulation than ever before. North Dakota's legislation forbade the marriage of any man or woman labeled "a common drunkard, habitual criminal, epileptic, imbecile, feeble-minded person, idiot, or insane person." The law barred people with advanced tuberculosis or contagious venereal disease from getting married, unless the bride was over forty-five and thus presumed post-menopausal. In addition, the

---

Shakespeare Press, 1914); Bruinius, *Better for All the World*, 38, 147. On the role of Protestant leaders in influencing state eugenic laws, see Christine Rosen, *Preaching Eugenics: Religious Leaders and the American Eugenics Movement* (New York: Oxford University Press, 2004), 53–67.

12 Grossberg, *Governing the Hearth*, 148–149.

13 Ibid., 150; Smith, "Marriage, Sterilization and Commitment Laws," 365–366; Ruth Velma Schuler, "Some Aspects of Eugenic Marriage Legislation in the United States," *Social Service Review* 14, no. 2 (1940): 301–316; Michael Grossberg, "Guarding the Altar: Physiological Restrictions and the Rise of State Intervention in Matrimony," *American Journal of Legal History* 26, no. 3 (1982): 217–224.

law required that each applicant for marriage file an affidavit from a licensed physician vowing that he or she did not suffer from any of the above conditions. Licenses would not be issued until the county judge received this documentation.[14]

In early August of 1913, just months after the passage of the North Dakota bill, the state of Wisconsin passed a similar law demanding that both partners be free of venereal disease before receiving a license. In this case, only the groom was required to file a certificate from a doctor declaring a clean bill of health no more than fifteen days prior to the application. Like its North Dakota predecessor, this policy took calls for eugenically sound unions to new heights by demanding intimate examinations of the body to prove marital capacity. At the same time, Wisconsin was just one of thirty-four states to regulate marriage on the grounds of physical and mental fitness.[15] Events in Wisconsin thus provide one glaring example of the panic that pervaded the nation as moral crusaders, legislators, and eugenicists fretted that a sacred institution was losing its luster. The Wisconsin law brought a deluge of elopements to Illinois, only adding to the perceived crisis of unlawful out-of-state marriages in the very year that the Gormley bill sought to halt the operation of Delaware's marriage mill. For all these reasons, my discussion of eugenic marital evasions centers on the Wisconsin law. The questions it raised regarding the right of eugenically "unfit" couples to wed in neighboring states added further drama to long-running debates over marriage mills, out-of-state elopement, and the right of justices of the peace to officiate nuptials between unsuitable couples for the sake of

---

[14] "North Dakota: Marriages. Prohibited in Certain Cases. Affidavit of Physician Required. License. (Chap. 207, Act Mar. 1, 1913)," *Public Health Reports* 28, no. 51 (1913): 2810–2811; R. Newton Crane, "United States of America – State Legislation," *Journal of the Society of Comparative Legislation* 15 (1915): 157. As Rosen notes, eugenic scientists themselves were wary of requirements for physicians' certificates, expressing concern that they would control marriage without controlling sex and reproduction – therefore increasing nonmarital sex without serving any eugenic purpose. Protestant leaders and state legislators nonetheless embraced these laws. See *Preaching Eugenics*, 70.

[15] M.K.B., "The Wisconsin Marriage Law Upheld," *Michigan Law Review* 13, no. 1 (1914): 39. The states holding eugenic marriage laws in 1913 were Arkansas, California, Connecticut, Delaware, Georgia, Idaho, Illinois, Indiana, Iowa, Kansas, Kentucky, Maine, Massachusetts, Michigan, Minnesota, Montana, Nebraska, Nevada, New Jersey, New York, North Carolina, North Dakota, Ohio, Oklahoma, Oregon, Rhode Island, South Carolina, Utah, Vermont, Virginia, Washington, West Virginia, Wisconsin, and Wyoming. The District of Columbia also declared voidable "the marriage of an idiot or person judged insane." See "State Laws Regulating Marriage of the Unfit," 423–425.

profit. Added concerns over marriage's connection to public health made the stakes especially high.

* * *

State Senator William Richards of Milwaukee introduced the eugenic marriage bill to the Wisconsin Senate in 1913. An ardent supporter of the bill, Senator George Skogmo argued that the law would improve the quality of marriages and heighten public perceptions of the institution. "This is a case where one should not care [a bit] for constitutionality," he asserted, deflecting any arguments that such a policy would violate the Fourteenth Amendment.[16] In demanding that grooms undergo testing for venereal disease before receiving a marriage license, the bill also stipulated that the person examining the prospective groom be a licensed physician, not under the age of thirty, who would charge no more than three dollars per examination. It also sought to prevent any out-of-state elopements in case a groom did not pass the doctor's examination or opted out of the appointment entirely; a couple that wed in another state with the goal of evading the Wisconsin law would not be legally permitted to return to Wisconsin within a year of the marriage unless that couple filed a certificate of good health with a county district attorney immediately after arriving home. Any out-of-state newlyweds returning to Wisconsin without fulfilling these steps risked a fine and a sentence of one month to one year in jail. Even greater penalties would befall county clerks issuing licenses in violation of the proposed law, as this defiance would be considered a felony punishable by one to five years in state prison. If a dispute were to arise over the physician's findings, the state hygienic laboratory would determine the patient's health status, and the doctor under investigation would risk losing his medical license should any evidence of perjury emerge. The majority of state senators determined Richards's suggestions to be sound, and the bill passed in the senate.[17]

Governor Francis McGovern signed the bill into law several days later, and it quickly became a source of great interest inside and outside Wisconsin. The law, effective 1 January 1914, received the endorsement of a number of powerful public health figures, including Surgeon General

---

[16] "Senate Is in Favor of Eugenic Marriages," *Beloit Daily News*, 24 Jul. 1913, p. 8.
[17] "Bill Provides for Healthy Marriages Here," *Wisconsin State Journal*, 3 Aug. 1913, p. 2; "Senate Is in Favor of Eugenic Marriages," 8.

Rupert Blue, a proponent of marital regulation and sterilization. Embracing the slogan "No one is fit to be married who is unfit to be an ancestor," Blue saw deafness, color blindness, epilepsy, imbecility, delinquency, insanity, and a host of other physical and mental conditions as "a few of the penalties nature inflicts on her children who mismate and who are unfit to be the fathers and mothers of new generations."[18]

Some magazine and newspaper writers heartily supported the law. One editorialist for *The Outlook*, a New York journal, dismissed any criticisms of eugenic marriage law, declaring, "If it is possible to save children from coming into this world maimed and crippled in body and in brain, and at the same time to welcome into the world vigorous children of healthy married parents, surely no doctrinaire theory about 'personal liberty' should stand in the way."[19] Other observers were more conflicted about these issues of personal liberty, raising questions about the state's right to infringe on people's romantic desires. One legal commentator expressed concerns about the cost of the health certificate, arguing that Wisconsin's law was unjust because it did not provide medical examinations at the state's expense, and it therefore discriminated against those who could not afford the three-dollar doctor's fee.[20]

In the days leading up to January 1, the imminent policy shift prompted a series of unusual events. Foremost among these was a threatened strike by Wisconsin physicians, who alleged that the law would ruin them financially. The majority of these indignant doctors supported the principle behind the eugenics law, but they disputed its enforceability, contending that a thorough medical examination would cost much more than the three dollars required by the eugenics law. Doctors were particularly concerned about the Wassermann test, an antibody test for syphilis that cost upward of thirty dollars and that many doctors considered essential for determining a patient's status. Fearing the financial consequences of the new state law, local doctors' organizations began to announce their noncompliance.[21]

---

[18] "Surgeon Blue Praises State's Marriage Law," *Beloit Daily News*, 29 Jul. 1913, p. 8.

[19] "Eugenic Marriage Laws," *Outlook*, 18 Oct. 1913, p. 342.

[20] "Constitutionality of Eugenic Marriage Laws," *Harvard Law Review* 27, no. 6 (1914): 574.

[21] "Local Doctors Dubious about Eugenics Law," *Wisconsin State Journal*, 16 Dec. 1913, p. 1; "Physicians Not to Comply with New Eugenics Law," *Beloit Daily News*, 17 Dec. 1913, sec. 2, p. 7; "Eugenics Law Drawn by Doctor," *Beloit Daily News*, 18 Dec. 1913, pp. 1, 6; "Few Weddings in Wisconsin," *Chicago Daily Tribune*, 20 Dec. 1913, p. 4.

The striking doctors met criticism from legal and medical authorities across the country. Among the harsher critics was Dr. Charles McCarthy, a progressive reformer and head of Madison's legislative reference library, who claimed that these doctors failed to see "that they perform not only private but public functions. Their duty to the state and to the profession in the prevention of sickness is something more than sitting down and getting money out of it."[22] Others came to the doctors' defense, including one columnist who judged the requirement of matrimonial examinations excessive and wasteful, arguing, "It is preposterous to expect any reputable physicians to make such a series of tests for $3. Besides, they have really sick people to look after."[23]

Despite his support for the new law, Wisconsin Attorney General Walter Owen admitted that doctors could not be forced to issue health certificates if they were unwilling to accept the three-dollar fee. He did, however, encourage doctors to comply by stating that many of their fears were unfounded and that the premarital examination need only be as thorough as three dollars would permit. He insisted that the Wassermann test was not an essential part of this effort, thus attempting to bring all state doctors on board, even at the cost of a fully comprehensive examination. Recognizing that no marriage law could be enforced with absolute precision, Owen was most eager for state physicians to help uphold the law's general eugenic principles.[24]

This rally for the support of physicians derived in part from a deeper concern that lack of doctor participation would mark the end of marriage in Wisconsin. Since all marriages would rely on a doctor's approval from New Year's Day onward, physicians' refusal to grant certificates threatened to block countless unions from taking place in the state. In an article published in newspapers throughout the nation, hysterically entitled "Doctors May Stop Weddings," one journalist wrote, "There will be no marriages in Wisconsin after January 1, if physicians in the State persist in their resolve not to perform examinations of men who wish to be married under the new eugenic law for the small prescribed fee of $3." If the doctors continued to protest, the writer argued, couples would seek nuptials across state lines in Illinois, Michigan, Iowa, and Minnesota,

---

[22] "Says Eugenics Marriage Law Can Be Enforced," *Wisconsin State Journal*, 20 Dec. 1913, p. 1.

[23] "Fees and Eugenics," *Los Angeles Times*, 22 Dec. 1913, p. 14.

[24] "Physicians Not to Comply," sec. 2, p. 7; "Few Weddings in Wisconsin," 4. "Holds Eugenic Law Test Easy," *Beloit Daily News*, 23 Dec. 1913, p. 1; "Owen Defines Obligations of State Doctors," *Wisconsin State Journal*, 22 Dec. 1913, p. 1.

despite the possibilities of imprisonment for such elopements.[25] Some journalists tried to alleviate these concerns by assuring readers that noncompliant doctors did not undermine the institution of marriage altogether, as the state board of health could provide medical testing if physicians refused, albeit at a much slower pace. Others expressed more skepticism, predicting that the refusal of legitimate doctors to participate in eugenic marital regulation would provide "a harvest for the quacks" who would "issue certificates for the prescribed fee without making a proper examination of the applicant." Concerns over doctors' participation were rampant in the days leading up to the law's enactment, among both those fearing an end to the exchange of marriage vows and those fearing a surfeit of dysgenic unions.[26]

Adding to the collective anxiety was the concern among engaged couples that doctors' strikes would prevent grooms from receiving the required health examination, delaying weddings indefinitely. Other couples worried that the doctors would *not* strike and that the groom would be doomed to fail the exam. In both cases, couples feared being barred from marriage, and this concern led many to wed before the New Year's Day inauguration came to pass. Throughout December of 1913, Wisconsin newspapers presented a gallery of wedding announcements. The Madison county clerk's office issued ten marriage licenses on December 21, a local record. The following day the office granted seven additional licenses. Joking that Cupid was "getting in his good work before the eugenics marriage law goes into effect," one *Wisconsin State Journal* writer put the irregular situation into perspective by noting that the average number of licenses issued daily was fewer than two. In total, thirty-six licenses were issued during the week of Christmas; only twelve licenses had been issued during this same week in the previous year.[27] Milwaukee County marriage license clerks were even busier. December 31, the day before the new law came into effect, boasted the greatest number of licenses the county had ever issued on a single day. When it was time for the clerk's office to close, eighty-four couples had received

---

[25] "Doctors May Stop Weddings," *Charlotte Daily Observer*, 22 Dec. 1913, p. 4.

[26] Ibid., 4; "Physicians Not to Comply," sec. 2, p. 7.

[27] "Ten Licenses Issued Monday," *Wisconsin State Journal*, 23 Dec. 1913, p. 1; "Cupid Gets in Good Work before New Law Steps In," *Wisconsin State Journal*, 24 Dec. 1913, p. 10; "Couples Storm Clerk Fjelstad," *Wisconsin State Journal*, 29 Dec. 1913, p. 1; "Dane County Issues Many Marriage Licenses," *Wisconsin State Journal*, 29 Dec. 1913, p. 1.

licenses, and the office remained so crowded with applicants that it extended its hours to midnight.[28]

Not all unmarried couples fretted in the face of the looming marriage law. Some heeded the words of crafty entrepreneurs such as Horace Walmsley, a Milwaukee lawyer who claimed to know a way to wed couples without adhering to the eugenic laws. "All that is required in this State," Walmsley argued, "is that two persons who are not married at the time, agree to accept each other as mates ... No service is necessary and the physical examination required by the state law cannot be enforced." Walmsley based this endorsement of common law marriage on a recent state supreme court decision, which declared that any couple could establish a valid marriage contract without a license or a medical examination, as common law marital status came into effect the moment they decided to live together as husband and wife. This recognition of the potential validity of common law procedures empowered couples to take marital routes that rejected the state's meddling in their personal affairs and medical histories.[29]

Common law marriages also offered potential profits to local officials who could receive fees for recording couples' marriages in the county record books. Julius Kroken, register of deeds of Dane County, hoped to profit from common law marriages by charging ten cents per union. Kroken argued that while no paperwork was needed for the marriage to be legal, its legitimacy would be more widely recognized if a contract were drawn up and signed by both parties before two witnesses and a notary public or justice of the peace. "No three-dollar doctor's fee is necessary," Kroken declared, "only 10 cents to register the contract. No marriage certificate, no doctors, no pastor required. The registration of the contract is necessary to obtain recognition in the courts."[30] Unfortunately for Kroken, this advertisement brought in very few dimes once the new law went into effect. On January 11, Kroken complained that he had still not recorded any common law marriage contracts, and when he did receive a request a few days later it was from a gentleman who wished to wed his own niece. Kroken, whose desire to subvert mainstream marriage law went only so far, denounced the arrangement as not only illegal, but an "impolite, indecent and an uncivilized thing to do." The next request

---

[28] "Rush to Beat Eugenic Law," *New York Times*, 1 Jan. 1914, p. 1.
[29] "Wedding Bells Unnecessary," *Los Angeles Times*, 22 Dec. 1913, pp. 1, 6; "Says Eugenic Law Is Useless; Need No Service," *Beloit Daily News*, 22 Dec. 1913, sec. 2, p. 1.
[30] "Offers 10-Cent Marriages," *New York Times*, 8 Jan. 1914, p. 1; see also "County Register of Deeds Offers Aid to Couples," *Wisconsin State Journal*, 7 Jan. 1914, p. 1; "Ten Cents to Marry," *Los Angeles Times*, 8 Jan. 1914, p. 1.

came from an Oklahoma resident, who hoped that Kroken would be able
to file a common law contract within the Sooner State. Kroken could not
assist him.[31]

Despite these early stumbling blocks, Kroken's efforts were not entirely
in vain. Kroken filed his first common law marriage in late February
of 1914, between James Egan and Ethel Barrett. Surprisingly, in their
contract Egan and Barrett described themselves as "free from all venereal
diseases blood or kin and neither of us being an epileptic, idiot, or insane
person."[32] Their reasons for pursuing this back-door entry into
matrimony are unclear. Perhaps they preferred spending ten cents on a
marriage contract to three dollars on a doctor's examination. Perhaps
they objected to the terms of the new marriage laws in principle, believing
that state and medical authorities should not have the right to intervene in
the private matters of mate selection and marriage. But it is striking that
they used eugenic language to characterize a marriage that defied eugenic
regulations. Egan and Barrett were not alone in pronouncing their good
health alongside their desire to evade Wisconsin's new law. Following
the announcement of Egan and Barrett's marriage, Kroken received
additional requests for contracts from couples who believed they would
pass the health exam, if only they would consent to take it. This included
an appeal from a twenty-four-year-old man who longed to wed his
eighteen-year-old fiancée. "We are both stought and hearty," he wrote
to Kroken, "and do not like the eugenic marriage law."[33]

The work of Walmsley and Kroken had its proponents, including
Green County Clerk J. W. Stewart, who was so impressed with stories
of Kroken's marital politics that he implemented an identical system in his
community. Stewart also celebrated open access to marriage in verse,
composing the following poetic lines:

> Let us all work for improvement,
> And for the benefit of everyone
> Encourage matrimony everywhere,
> It's the best thing that can be done.

---

[31] "Common Law Is Not Popular in Madison Society," *Wisconsin State Journal*, 11
Jan. 1914, p. 4; "Kroken May Be Called upon to Record Common Law Marriage,"
Wisconsin State Journal, 13 Jan. 1914, p. 8; "Kroken Receives Application for 10 Cent
Marriage," *Wisconsin State Journal*, 17 Jan. 1914, p. 2.

[32] "Unique Marriage," *Wisconsin State Journal*, 25 Feb. 1914, p. 3.

[33] "Woolworth of Marriage Market," *Wisconsin State Journal*, 4 Apr. 1914, p. 4. This
article describes couples seeking common law marriages as "people who wish to avoid
the eugenics law and still follow the whispers of cupid."

While his reference to "improvement" resembles eugenicists' stated goal of "race improvement," Stewart attempted to establish a healthy and productive human race by encouraging widespread marriage and child-bearing, and not by restricting marital rights.[34]

Most Wisconsinites were less active than Stewart in opposing the new marriage policies, and many resigned themselves to the legal changes, even if the new law prevented them from marrying at their leisure. In the early weeks of 1914, local newspapers highlighted the dearth of in-state marriages taking place. In Milwaukee, "absolute inactivity in the marriage market" characterized the first two days of the New Year, as only one man sought a license, which he was denied when he failed to present a doctor's certificate. In Madison, no licenses were issued by the Dane County Clerk on January 2, even though three had been issued on that day the year prior.[35] As marriage rates slowed, reporters adopted increasingly sinister tones to describe the situation, applying terms such as "race suicide" and penning articles with headlines such as "Fears Race of Badgers Will Become Extinct."[36] Local newspapers cited notably decreased numbers of married couples in the early months of the year; one study indicated that there had been 5,273 Wisconsin marriages from January to May of 1914, compared with the 6,707 unions reported in the same months a year earlier. This disparity led the writer to remark, "The law has either scared a lot of Badgers out of matrimony, showed them to be unfit for marriage or they went out of the state to wed and the fact was not reported by the state board of health."[37] Journalists noted that the dwindling number of marriages in Wisconsin came with a financial cost as well. One reporter estimated that Milwaukee's flailing bridal industry was costing the city ten thousand dollars a day, including lost expenditures for lodging, clothing, flowers, and decorations. Though this high figure was likely an exaggeration, the Wisconsin eugenic law's effect on local business was a stark reality for many.[38]

---

[34] "Green County Clerk Wants to Know All about Common Law Marriages," *Wisconsin State Journal*, 12 Mar. 1914, p. 1.

[35] "One Applicant for a License in Rock County," *Beloit Daily News*, 2 Jan. 1914, p. 5; "Cupid's Stock Takes Slump in Wisconsin," *Wisconsin State Journal*, 2 Jan. 1914, p. 2.

[36] "Fears Race of Badgers Will Become Extinct," *Wisconsin State Journal*, 3 Jan. 1914, p. 1; "One Applicant for a License in Rock County," 5.

[37] "Marked Decrease in Marriage Is Seen in Report," *Wisconsin State Journal*, 26 Jul. 1914, p. 4. See also "Cupid Still Resting; Licenses Fewer in Last Three Months," *Wisconsin State Journal*, 12 May 1914, p. 9.

[38] "Milwaukee's Wedding Famine an Expensive Deal," *Day Book* (Chicago), 10 Jan. 1914, p. 11.

In addition to fears over race suicide and declining commerce, some commentators worried that the new law would create what one reporter termed "irregular, clandestine unions." From this perspective, though the law's intentions had been noble, its restrictions on matrimony were sparking an epidemic of common law marriages and nonmarital cohabitations. While many people accepted that matrimony should be reserved for the most qualified, the actuality of dwindling marriage rates and increases in nonmarital cohabitation made some reconsider the merits of the new legislation.[39]

Other eugenic law skeptics endeavored to show that the Wisconsin statute had indeed sparked a parade of quacks into action, just as critics of the physicians' strike had projected. Their arguments gained traction after a biological Milwaukee woman named Cora Anderson was arrested for adopting a male persona – as well as the pseudonym "Ralph Kerwineio" – and marrying another woman named Dorothy Klenowski in 1914. Klenowski did not know of Kerwineio's female anatomy upon exchanging vows, and neither did Justice of the Peace Edward Burke, who wed the couple.[40] Though this story offers insight into the intersections of same-sex sexuality and transgender identity in the early twentieth century, it also sheds light on the era's eugenic debates. It soon became known that before Kerwineio had married Klenowski, Kerwineio had complied with Wisconsin law and procured a doctor's certificate stating that Kerwineio was physically fit to be a groom. The state of Wisconsin thus validated Kerwineio's gender nonconformity and the marriage of two biological women, casting doubt on the effectiveness of state-sanctioned medical exams. W. J. Scollard, the physician who performed Kerwineio's exam, denied any wrong-doing: "When 'Ralph' made his application for a marriage license certificate I made the customary examination by testing the blood," he explained. "When the examination showed that there was nothing the matter with him I issued the certificate."[41]

---

[39] "Played Havoc with Cupid," *Los Angeles Times*, 25 Dec. 1914, p. 17.

[40] This was Kerwineio's second marriage to a woman. The first wife, Marie White, was aware of her husband's complicated gender identity. The two partners had decided together that Anderson should assume the male role of Kerwineio, in part so that Kerwineio would have broader employment options and access to higher wages. That relationship ended in divorce, and Kerwineio then wed Klenowski. Ida McGlone Gibson, "Amazing Double Life of Cora Anderson; Lived Thirteen Years as Man," *Wisconsin State Journal*, 11 May 1914, p. 2; "Masquerade," *Cincinnati Enquirer*, 4 May 1914, p. 4.

[41] "Eugenic Statute," *Hancock Democrat* (Greenfield, Ind.), 14 May 1914, p. 7. After the marriage to Klenowski ended, Kerwineio once again adopted the female role of Anderson, though this transition may have been motivated by the promise that a return to

Despite Scollard's insistence that he complied fully with Wisconsin's law by testing Kerwineio's blood for syphilis, critics of the eugenic law believed that this case illustrated its futility. Historian Christine Rosen argues that Kerwineio's case confirmed what was "by far the most frequently made criticism of health certificate laws," which was the fear "that prospective brides and grooms could go to 'unscrupulous quacks' who would willingly exchange a health certificate for cash, regardless of the candidate's fitness." News of Kerwineio's marriage and subsequent arrest led many former proponents of eugenic marriage certificates to question their support for Wisconsin's law. Meanwhile, as historian Emily Skidmore explains, in other press circles Kerwineio's perceived deception led to demands for even stricter eugenic marriage legislation, including tests to determine a groom's biological sex before granting him a license.[42] Though responses to the Kerwineio marriage varied, what we see here is that calls for abolishing eugenic laws and calls for expanding them were both grounded in the belief that Wisconsin's requirement of a doctor's certificate was not protecting marriage from the physical and moral threats that lawmakers had sought to quell.

* * *

While members of the medical, religious, and journalistic communities mused on the inadequacies of eugenic marriage law, twenty-nine-year-old Alfred Peterson of Milwaukee took this protest to court. Peterson attempted to wed Hattie Schmidt on 2 January 1914. He did not furnish a physician's certificate, however, and County Clerk Christian Widule therefore refused to issue a marriage license. Peterson claimed he was willing to pursue the needed paperwork, but only from a doctor who would charge no more than three dollars for an exam. Since physicians in Milwaukee had agreed that they would not give a comprehensive test for a mere three dollars, and since Widule demanded that the Wassermann test be included in any marriage examination, Peterson was blocked from taking the steps necessary to attain a license. His attorney thus filed a petition for a writ of mandamus to force Widule to issue a license to

women's clothing would mean the dropping of disorderly conduct charges. See Ida McGlone Gibson, "Cora Anderson Was a Good Man to Both Her Wives," *Wisconsin State Journal*, 12 May 1914, p. 8.
[42] Rosen, *Preaching Eugenics*, 72; Emily Skidmore, "Ralph Kerwineo's Queer Body: Narrating the Scales of Social Membership in the Early Twentieth Century," *GLQ: A Journal of Lesbian and Gay Studies* 20, nos. 1–2 (2014): 151–157.

Peterson without a medical certificate. The attorney argued that the policy was an unreasonable application of police power, that it was discriminatory in requiring medical examinations of men and not women, and that it was unfair to doctors under thirty years old, who were not permitted to perform eugenic examinations. The affidavit was signed by four of the physicians who had refused to examine Peterson.[43]

Judge F. C. Eschweiler heard detailed testimony from local physicians, including Horace Brown, leader of the Milwaukee physicians' strike, before ruling in favor of Peterson and declaring the state marriage law unconstitutional and discriminatory. Noting the law's unreasonable expectation that doctors provide a service that could not be covered by the maximum fixed fee of three dollars, Eschweiler instructed the clerk to resume granting licenses to all candidates, even those who could not provide medical certification. Eschweiler added that if the state desired to prevent unwanted marriages, it could take on the responsibility of extracting unhealthy persons from the marriage pool, but it could not force all citizens seeking this basic legal right to display their fitness for matrimony.[44]

Soon after the circuit court released its decision, Attorney General Owen authorized Assistant District Attorney H. S. Sloan of Milwaukee County to appeal. On 17 June 1914 the Wisconsin Supreme Court overturned the circuit court's decision by a 3–2 margin, ruling in favor of Widule and thus upholding the eugenic marriage law. The ruling, written by Chief Justice John Winslow, began by praising the law's good intentions: "Neither the legislative idea nor the legislative purpose in the passage of the present law can be a matter of serious doubt," Winslow wrote. "The *idea* plainly was that the transmission of the so-called venereal diseases by newly married men to their innocent wives was a tremendous evil, and the *purpose* just as plainly was to remedy that evil so far as possible by preventing the marriage of men who upon examination were found to possess such diseases." Winslow proceeded to refute the argument that the law was discriminatory in forcing men, but not women, to undergo medical evaluation. In theory this was a strong point,

[43] "Eugenic Law to Get Test," *Beloit Daily News*, 3 Jan. 1914, p. 4; "Eugenic Woe Now Appears: Wisconsin Statute to Be Put to Supreme Test," *Los Angeles Times*, 4 Jan. 1914, p. 1; "Eugenics Law Test on Jan. 10," *Beloit Daily News*, 7 Jan. 1914, p. 2.

[44] "Eugenics Puzzles Judge," *New York Times*, 11 Jan. 1914, p. 12; "Eugenic Law in Court," *New York Times*, 14 Jan. 1914, p. 1; "Eugenics Law Is Held Invalid in First Test Case," *Beloit Daily News*, 20 Jan. 1914, p. 5; "Eugenics Law Is Declared Invalid," *New York Times*, 21 Jan. 1914, p. 1.

Winslow observed, as women who transmitted harmful medical conditions to their husbands ought to be held to the same standard as men guilty of the same offense. Medical evidence proved, however, "that the great majority of women who marry are pure, while a considerable percentage of men have had illicit sexual relations before marriage, and consequently that the number of cases where newly married men transmit a venereal disease to their wives is vastly greater than the number of cases where women transmit the disease to their newly married husbands." This disparity justified the divergent expectations along gender lines, even if exceptions would occasionally occur.[45]

Winslow then noted that despite some of its ambiguous language, the Wisconsin bill had been passed with the intent of barring only those with *acquired* venereal diseases from marrying, and not those with congenital conditions – and thus it did not penalize persons for inborn traits, but merely those whose immoral behaviors had borne physical consequences. After this brief exposition, Winslow discussed the weightiest legal concern: the place of the Wassermann test in the doctor's examination. Winslow began this section by stating, "If the law in fact requires the Wassermann test to be made in case of every applicant for a marriage license, the argument is very strong that it requires the absolutely unreasonable." Working with the assumption that Wisconsin lawmakers had been aware of the difficulties of administering the Wassermann test when writing the bill – that they knew of its high cost, that it was a precise and delicate procedure, and that very few physicians in the state could perform it – Winslow concluded that the legislature had never intended for the Wassermann test to be a required component of the exam. Had this been the case, Winslow reasoned, Wisconsin lawmakers would have called for a "practical embargo on marriage" in passing this legislation, as so few intended grooms would ever receive the required test. But as Winslow pointed out, the legislation had not required doctors to utilize "*all* of the recognized tests," but simply "the recognized tests," which may or may not include the Wassermann test. Since there existed several other well-regarded laboratory tests that all physicians could perform for a reasonable fee, Winslow concluded, "it seems quite impossible to believe that the Wassermann test was considered a *sine qua non*."[46]

---

[45] *Peterson v. Widule*, 157 Wis. 641 (1914). "Eugenics Law Test Is Delayed," *Beloit Daily News*, 22 Jan. 1914, p. 5.
[46] *Peterson v. Widule*, 157 Wis. 641 (1914).

The ruling closed with a dismissal of the plaintiff's claim that the law interfered with Wisconsin residents' religious liberty, stating, "We know of no church which desires its ministers to profane the marriage tie by uniting a man afflicted with a loathsome disease to an innocent woman." On all of these grounds, the court ruled that eugenic marital intervention was within the state's police power and was not an intrusion on individual rights. Not all Wisconsin Supreme Court justices shared Winslow's support of the eugenic law, however. Even Justice William Timlin, who wrote a concurring opinion, expressed disdain for the new policy: "I have no sympathy with this statute," Timlin wrote. "I think it tends to discourage marriage rather than to prevent the spread of venereal diseases. All experience goes to show that laws making marriage expensive or difficult or subject to objectionable requirements tend to increase illegitimate sexual intercourse." Despite his disapproval of the law, Timlin concurred with Winslow out of judicial principle, explaining that this issue needed to be dealt with through legislative change and not court interference.[47]

In his dissenting opinion, Justice Roujet Marshall insisted that marriage was a natural right that the government should not police. In creating eugenic obstacles to the exchange of vows, the state weakened the institution of marriage by decreasing the number of couples who could take part in it. Marshall criticized the law for its tendency to "discourage an institution which is absolutely essential to public welfare and so recognized and protected by the fundamental law. By so oppressively interfering with the constitutional right of marriage as to partially or wholly destroy that right, the tendency will inevitably be to promote immorality and social and racial retrogression." The decreasing rate of marriage in Wisconsin throughout 1914 bolstered Marshall's assertion that eugenic laws served to discourage matrimony and to encourage nonmarital cohabitation instead.[48]

While Timlin and Marshall criticized the law's role in decreasing the quantity of Wisconsin marriages, others maintained that it also diminished the *quality* of the vows exchanged. One Christian periodical noted that eugenic barriers had paved the way for common law marriages, as evidenced by Julius Kroken's commitment to registering such contracts.

[47] Ibid.; "Eugenics Law Discouraging Marriage – Timlin," *Wisconsin State Journal*, 18 Jun. 1914, p. 1; "Calls Eugenic Marriage Law 'Silly Legislation,'" *Beloit Daily News*, 20 Jun. 1914, p. 4.
[48] *Peterson v. Widule*, 157 Wis. 641 (1914); "Undue Suspicion of Immorality Cast by Eugenic Law – Marshall," *Wisconsin State Journal*, 19 Jun. 1914, pp. 1, 4.

Couples were now aware of their legal right to wed without holding a public ceremony or enlisting the service of a justice of the peace. In light of this development, the author argued that eugenic marriage law had "cheapened this ancient and sacred rite, [and] desecrated the most solemn ceremony ever devised of God for the unions of hearts and the happiness of man." As these arguments reveal, some people rejected eugenic legislation out of a fear that such laws would weaken the institution of marriage, decreasing the number of couples who could exchange vows and opening new avenues for nonmarital and quasi-marital cohabitation. And as couples devised plans for resisting Wisconsin's law, their defiance created further ammunition for those who feared a marriage crisis was at hand – be they supporters or detractors of eugenic legislation.[49]

* * *

As the above sections reveal, the Wisconsin eugenic marriage law sparked a wide array of moral apprehensions within that state and had a profound impact on the number and nature of nuptials taking place in Wisconsin. It also affected marital culture in nearby states, primarily because after the *Peterson v. Widule* ruling, a spate of noncompliant Wisconsin couples journeyed to neighboring states to exchange their vows in more permissive settings. Some of these grooms had failed to win Wisconsin doctors' approval for a marriage certificate. Others never underwent the examination, because they either knew they would not pass or were unwilling to pay the medical fees. Some couples simply wished to avoid Wisconsin's requirement that they wait five days between the receipt of the marriage license and the exchange of vows, and the state's demand that the couple post its intention to wed publicly during that time to allow for community members to voice objections. Due to Wisconsin's advance notice requirements, certain nearby Illinois cities such as Chicago and Waukegan were already known as marriage mills, with a history of Wisconsin couples at their altars. But interstate weddings took on new meanings with the passage of eugenic regulations.[50]

---

[49] "In the Drift of Current Thought," *Herald of Gospel Liberty* 106, no. 9 (1914): 258.

[50] On Wisconsin's five-day advance notice requirement, see Fred S. Hall and Elisabeth W. Brooke, *American Marriage Laws in Their Social Aspects: A Digest* (New York: Russell Sage Foundation, 1919), 36. Wisconsin was one of eight states to require advance notice before a license could be granted. Of these eight states, Wisconsin was the only one to require that notice be posted for the public to view.

What once had been a short jaunt from Kenosha or Racine to Waukegan for a quick and easy wedding was now a violation of Wisconsin law. It also became a source of great profit for many cities in Illinois and Indiana, which welcomed Wisconsin brides and grooms with open arms. The *Waukegan Daily Sun*, a major news outlet from the suburban Chicago town, teased about the loss of earnings that once-prominent Wisconsin marriage mills faced with the passage of the new law. One article with the taunting title "Milwaukee Is Getting Jealous of Old Waukegan," depicted the woes of a Milwaukee marriage clerk, who dreaded the prospect of boredom and idleness at work as couples took to marrying in Waukegan and Chicago. For those county officials and local business owners who could profit from an increase in local marriages, Wisconsin's loss was Illinois's gain.[51]

Fear of penalty seems to have had little impact on the number of out-of-state weddings conducted in the months following the new Wisconsin law. After the law went into effect, betrothed couples ignored potential consequences and dodged the new rules by seeking nuptials across state borders. The first two Wisconsin couples to wed in Waukegan after the enactment of the eugenic marriage law, Clarence Jansen and Ella Meyers, and George Jacobs and Dorothy Hahn, applied for licenses on New Year's Day of 1914, the very day that the Wisconsin law came into effect. The couples' reasoning is not immediately obvious, as they could have spared themselves the trouble by applying for licenses in Wisconsin one day prior, when the new law had yet to go into effect and they therefore would not have had to submit to a doctor's evaluation. Perhaps they merely wanted to avoid the five-day wait period that Wisconsin required before they could attain a license. Considering the travel and preparation time for a trip across state borders, it is also possible that the two couples made a deliberate decision to take the difficult route. Maybe, like some other Wisconsin couples, they resented that the law discriminated between the sexes by holding men and women to different standards. Or maybe they rejected the idea of government dictating who was worthy of exchanging marital vows. While these examples should not suggest that all couples eloped as a political statement against eugenic marriage policies, they do show us that not all elopers fled Wisconsin because the groom had failed – or feared failing – the doctor's eugenic examinations.

---

[51] "Milwaukee Is Getting Jealous of Old Waukegan," *Waukegan Daily Sun*, 7 Aug. 1913, p. 4.

Other factors contributed to their decisions, and sometimes these involved ideological objections and not just financial or practical concerns.[52]

Aware of the money and notoriety that an influx of brides and grooms could bring, Waukegan authorities eagerly awarded marriage certificates to the visiting couples. While Wisconsin officials risked penalty for marrying couples that had not met eugenic standards, officials in Illinois had little to lose and much to gain. Lake County Clerk Lew Hendee referred to Wisconsinites who wed in Illinois to evade the eugenic law as "the scum of Wisconsin," but he nonetheless defended Waukegan's role as elopement center. His greatest motivation for allowing out-of-state marriages in his community was the revenue they brought to Waukegan. Hendee explained the familiar business model that Waukeganites had devised to take advantage of the situation. Taxi drivers could identify out-of-state brides and grooms with a mere glance, and they were eager to transport these wide-eyed couples to the justices of the peace for a rushed exchange of vows. The system also included a set of "marriage runners," who met all incoming trains and directed eloping couples to the appropriate sites of matrimony. "We have no desire to see the number of Wisconsin marriages curtailed here," Hendee declared, "*because we need the money!* Why, the fees from those Wisconsin marriages support several clerks here." Given that Hendee oversaw three to four hundred marriages a month, of which 75 percent were Wisconsin couples, one assumes that the profits were substantial.[53]

In spite of the profits that out-of-state elopements brought to Waukegan, local media accounts from the 1910s expressed the anxieties these nuptials created for reformers and public servants. Morrow Krum of the *Chicago Daily Tribune* provided a notable example of one Wisconsin couple's quest to wed in Waukegan. Through this account, Krum suggested that the city was filled with swindlers in the form of cab drivers and ministers, all of whom were happy to take advantage of a young couple's naiveté for the sake of financial gain. In ways we have seen before, Krum's article employed white slavery tropes to describe the young couple's potential entrapment by Waukegan officials seeking to exploit them. It depicted the attempted elopement of Joseph "Jeff" Davis and Virginia Lee

[52] "Wed Here; Break Wisconsin Marriage Laws?," *Waukegan Daily Sun*, 2 Jan. 1914, p. 1. On another couple that pursued the common law marriage route on the moral grounds that the Wisconsin eugenics law validated sex discrimination, see "Topics of the Times," *New York Times*, 7 Nov. 1914, p. 10.

[53] "Wed Here; Break Wisconsin Marriage Laws?," 1; Bernard C. Roloff, "The 'Eugenic' Marriage Laws of Wisconsin, Michigan, and Indiana," *Social Hygiene* 6, no. 2 (1920): 235–236.

of Milwaukee, who did not wish to wait five days between receiving a marriage license and exchanging vows, and who thus attempted to dodge that law in Illinois. Davis and Lee stepped onto the platform of Waukegan's train station and were immediately picked up by a taxi driver who knew their kind on sight and who was happy to capitalize on their arrival. The couple's trek to the altar also included a cursory three-dollar doctor's examination – presumably so that the couple would be able to claim a physician's approval if investigated by Wisconsin authorities – and a quick meeting with Clerk Hendee for the granting of the license.[54]

The story ended with Lee backing out of the marriage for fear that her father would disown her if she proceeded to marry in this shameful way, but only after Davis had paid the minister five dollars for his inconvenience. By focusing on the monetary exchanges that accompanied couples' trips to Waukegan, Krum condemned the marriage mill operators for profiting from the desperation of out-of-state couples. Noting that approximately three hundred couples came into Waukegan from Wisconsin each month and that each of these couples spent between fifteen and twenty-five dollars during their stay, bringing the town $50,000 a year, Krum took Waukegan to task for privileging money over morals. He saw further evidence of this greed in the town's record of uniting underage and interracial couples.[55]

While Krum worried that eloping couples put themselves at moral and financial risk, the couples themselves were likely more concerned about the potential legal consequences of their actions. The question of whether a marriage conducted out-of-state remained valid upon the couple's return home was widely contested, yielding inconsistent conclusions from case to case. In the interpretation of legal scholar Herbert Goodrich, the rule most frequently applied to extraterritorial unions was "good where contracted, good everywhere." When out-of-state marriages blatantly defied the laws of the home state, however, judges were more likely to follow a different rule: "If void by the law of the domicile, it should follow that it is void elsewhere as well." In other words, if couples wed out of state for the sole purpose of escaping their home laws, then those evasive unions should be considered void.[56] While elopers from Wisconsin may

---

[54] Morrow Krum, "'Cupid Mills' Make Elopers' Problem Easy," *Chicago Daily Tribune*, 21 Dec. 1919, pt. 1, p. 2.

[55] Ibid., 2.

[56] Herbert F. Goodrich, "Foreign Marriages and the Conflict of Laws," *Michigan Law Review* 21, no. 7 (1923): 750–751.

have determined that judges' vacillations lessened the chance that their out-of-state marriages would be nullified upon their return home, they were also aware that such an offense could lead to jail time. Despite that risk, the desire to avoid the interference of physicians and to minimize wait times was strong enough to lead them into places such as Waukegan for marriage licenses.[57]

The rising number of elopements to Illinois was a source of angst for many. At a time when many states were tightening their restrictions on who was qualified for marriage, a number of prominent Illinois residents wished to follow suit. This even included some employees in Hendee's office, like Bess Bower, who sought to bring Illinois's marriage laws into accord with Wisconsin's. Bower estimated that on average, three to four Wisconsin couples were married in Lake County, Illinois, each day. Troubled by this statistic, Bower worked with Illinois county clerks to replicate Wisconsin's marriage prohibitions in her own state.[58] The Illinois Woman's Christian Temperance Union pursued a similar policy change, resolving at its 1913 convention in Galesburg, Illinois, "We favor the passage of a law requiring that certificate from a reliable physician shall attend application for a marriage license." Union women recognized that their demands for a law resembling Wisconsin's would not immediately be met, but they committed themselves to enforcing the regulation within their own households and families in the meantime. Although it would be two decades before Illinois law required a premarital doctor's examination, Illinois marriage nonconformists, in their numbers and their visibility, spurred those who were bound to more traditional definitions of marriage to push for new legislation.[59]

Reform efforts of this sort took place on the national level as well, specifically in the pursuit of uniform marriage legislation. Similar to the National Congress on Uniform Divorce Law, discussed in the previous chapter, the National Conference of Commissioners on Uniform State Laws was a major force in the quest for standardized marriage and family laws. The Commissioners, a group of lawyers appointed by their respective state governors, attempted to homogenize state laws on various issues, either by collective state legislative enactment or by US constitutional

---

[57] "Bill Provides for Healthy Marriages Here," 2; "Governor Signs Eugenics Bill," *Beloit Daily News*, 2 Aug. 1913, pp. 1–2.

[58] "Miss Bower Now Getting Data on Marriage Statute," *Waukegan Daily Sun*, 25 Aug. 1913, p. 1.

[59] "W.C.T.U. Demands Clean Marriages in State Meeting," *Waukegan Daily Sun*, 13 Oct. 1913, p. 5.

amendment. First meeting as a small assembly of lawyers in August of 1878, the group had grown large enough by 1889 to call yearly conventions to examine the laws of multiple states – all in an effort to bring more uniform policies to these diverse states. By the mid-1910s the group's membership exceeded ten thousand. Members discussed questions of taxes and stock transfer, child labor, and family desertion. They incorporated marriage into their agenda in 1907 due to their growing concern that states held inconsistent policies on common law marriage.[60]

In subsequent years, the Commissioners began a campaign to create homogeneous marriage licensing procedures and a mandatory five-day interval between the application and the issuance of the license in all states. As their attention to marriage law intensified, the Commissioners also sought to implement a rule that would forbid couples from receiving a marriage license outside the county in which one or both of them lived. Illinois Commissioner Ernst Freund recognized that this rule would raise certain complications – it might, for instance, prevent a resident of New York from marrying in the cherished home of her parents in Connecticut. Amid the surge in out-of-state elopements, however, Freund deemed the potential benefits of this policy too positive to deny.[61]

The push for uniform marriage legislation increased as more and more states adopted eugenic marriage laws. Recognizing that eugenic regulations were indirectly yielding higher rates of out-of-state elopement, the Commissioners on Uniform State Laws doubled down on their efforts to forge consistent state laws. The committee adopted a Uniform Marriage Evasion Act at its conference in Milwaukee in 1912, which declared that if a person prohibited from marrying in his or her home state went into another state to contract a marriage, the marriage would be considered null and void in the home state. The Commissioners justified their decision to adopt this act on eugenic grounds. Noting that public opinion had

---

[60] "The Conference of Commissioners on Uniform State Laws," *Michigan Law Review* 2, no. 4 (1904): 299; "The Work of the Commissioners on Uniform State Laws," *Michigan Law Review* 8, no. 5 (1910): 399–400; Ernst Freund, "A Proposed Uniform Marriage Law," *Harvard Law Review* 24, no. 7 (1911): 548; Hon. A. T. Stovall, "Standards Proposed by United States Commission on Uniform Laws," *Annals of the American Academy of Political and Social Science* 38, Supplement: Child Labor Laws (1911): 17; Walter George Smith, "Uniform Legislation in the United States," *Annals of the American Academy of Political and Social Science* 52, Reform in Administration of Justice (1914): 67–69; Walter George Smith and M. D. Chalmers, "National Conference of Commissioners on Uniform State Laws in the United States," *Journal of the Society of Comparative Legislation* 16, no. 2 (1916): 154–155.

[61] Freund, "A Proposed Uniform Marriage Law," 548–545, 552–553.

come to favor eugenic marriage restrictions and the requirement of a physician's certificate before a couple could exchange vows, the committee presented marriage evasion laws as a path toward upholding the nation's health. By crafting uniform legislation that would halt couples from crossing borders to dodge eugenic laws, the Commissioners hoped to close the interstate loopholes that presently allowed couples to marry without medical certification.[62]

The Commissioners on Uniform State Laws expanded these conversations on eugenic marriage legislation at their national conference in October of 1914 amid outcries over the rise in dysgenic elopements. According to Edward Frost, a resident of Milwaukee and the chair of the Commissioners' subcommittee on marriage and divorce, citizens across the country were voicing ever-increasing support for uniform marriage legislation, including eugenic restrictions on matrimony.[63] The 1914 conference featured spirited debate between supporters of stringent eugenic law and their opponents, who worried that eugenic restrictions interfered too greatly with personal liberty in mate selection. Even former president William Howard Taft spoke before the Commissioners, urging stricter marriage laws throughout the states and decrying the "looseness with which the marriage tie is looked upon in many States."[64]

Though they agreed that disparities in state marriage laws led to an undue rise in dysgenic out-of-state elopement, the Commissioners on Uniform State Laws could not reach consensus on the advisability of uniform eugenic marriage legislation. The marriage and divorce committee made no recommendation to the broader commission, stating noncommittally in its report that the subject of eugenic marriage law was "within the scope of uniform legislation concerning domestic relations, and as such legislation is on the increase, the conference has an opportunity to take part in shaping it."[65] The Commissioners did not ultimately

---

[62] Charles Thaddeus Terry, *Uniform State Laws in the United States* (New York: Baker & Voorhis, 1920), 404; National Conference of Commissioners on Uniform State Laws, *Report of the Committee on Marriage and Divorce to the Commissioners on Uniform State Laws in National Conference in re the "Marriage Evasion Act" and the Pennsylvania, Wisconsin and Massachusetts Eugenics Acts.* (Washington, D.C.: n.p., 1914), 1–3.

[63] "Favor Eugenics in Uniform Law," *Oakland Tribune*, 11 Oct. 1914, p. 32; "Commissioners to Discuss Eugenics," *Trenton Evening Times*, 7 Oct. 1914, p. 5; "Need Uniformity of Laws in States," *Philadelphia Inquirer*, 11 Oct. 1914, p. 14; "Lawyers Gather Today," *Washington Post*, 14 Oct. 1914, p. 4.

[64] "Taft Talks about Loose Divorce Laws," *Town Talk* (Alexandria, La.), 20 Oct. 1914, p. 8; "Seek Uniformity in Laws," *Pittsburgh Daily Post*, 20 Oct. 1914, p. 6.

[65] *Report of the Committee on Marriage and Divorce*, 2.

seize upon this opportunity; by one journalist's account, though the majority of members agreed that eugenics was a force for good in building a better race, too many of them worried that forced eugenic marriage regulations were an overextension of the state's police power. These opponents advocated for educational programs, rather than legislation, as a means of shaping attitudes about marriage and public health.[66]

In this regard, the Commissioners on Uniform State Laws did not prove a transformative force when it came to the crafting of marriage laws. Though their discussion of eugenic marriage legislation revealed many members' desire to suppress the growing numbers of out-of-state elopements, the Commissioners' inability to reach consensus on this issue reflected a lingering sense of skepticism over state overreach on public health measures. Still, the Commission was not without its success stories; we can see this with closer attention to the uniform marriage evasion law. Though only Vermont, Massachusetts, and Louisiana adopted the law in the two years after the Commissioners constructed it, two more states joined them in 1915: Illinois and Wisconsin. It is striking that these two states joined the cause just a year after the Wisconsin eugenics law had gone into effect. Once that restrictive marriage law began bringing hordes of engaged Wisconsinites into Illinois for the nuptials denied them in their home state, both legislatures responded by nullifying evasive marriages conducted out of state. Illinois lawmakers explicitly cited the influx of Wisconsin couples entering their state to wed as justification for passing the evasion law. In these cases, couples who defied eugenic marriage laws sparked a backlash that contributed to the adaptation of new restrictive marriage legislation.[67]

This should not suggest that dysgenic marriages were the only force prompting such legal changes, however. Another factor at play in Illinois and Wisconsin's adoption of the Uniform Marriage Evasion Act was the arrest and trial of African American heavyweight boxer Jack Johnson, who in 1913 was convicted by a federal jury of violating the Mann Act, also known as the "White Slave Traffic Act." This 1910 law made it a

---

[66] Charles Henry Adams, "New York Day by Day," *Eagle* (Bryan, Tex.), 28 Dec. 1914, p. 4.

[67] Terry, *Uniform State Laws*, 404; National Conference of Commissioners on Uniform State Laws, *Proceedings of the Twenty-Fifth Annual Meeting of the National Conference of Commissioners on Uniform State Laws* (United States: National Conference of Commissioners on Uniform State Laws, 1915), 140, 170; "Ends Marriages from Wisconsin, Author Asserts," *Belvidere Daily Republican* (Ill.), 28 May 1915, p. 1; "New Laws of Illinois," *Pantagraph* (Bloomington, Ill.), 24 Nov. 1915, p. 11.

federal offense for a man to transport a woman across state borders for immoral sexual purposes. From its inception, the Mann Act was used to criminalize acts of interracial intimacy, and Johnson would become its most prominent victim.[68] Johnson was already viewed by many as a threat to white masculinity in his dominance over the sport; these concerns rose to the fore in his 4 July 1910 victory over white challenger Jim Jeffries. Johnson proved a further threat to white men in his romantic choices, due in particular to his interest in white women. The controversy came to a head when Johnson's first wife, Etta Duryea, killed herself in 1912, allegedly due to her alienation from white and black social worlds as a result of her taboo marriage.[69] This incident prompted vocal condemnations of Johnson, whom many whites judged as responsible for Duryea's untimely death. One Tennessee news editor even created a campaign to have Johnson's name kept out of all southern newspapers, arguing that Jack Johnson's interracial marriage had been "an affront to every white woman in the land."[70] In light of the racial fears unleashed by Johnson's victory over the "Great White Hope," as well as his publicly contested marriage and its tragic end, a large portion of white Americans were eager to bring Johnson down. They succeeded when he entered into another public relationship with a white woman.

A few months after his first wife's death, Johnson became romantically involved with Lucille Cameron of Minnesota, a white woman who had worked as a prostitute in Minneapolis before moving to Chicago with Johnson. The pair soon married, and controversy ensued. As historian Kevin Mumford has argued, white Americans dismayed by their inability to find a white boxer to defeat Johnson now worked "to persecute Johnson within the symbolic realm of sexuality." With aversions to interracial intimacy so strong in both white and black communities, Johnson's critics now saw an opportunity to knock him out in the legal

---

[68] For excellent summaries of the Johnson affair, see Al-Tony Gilmore, "Jack Johnson and White Women: The National Impact," *Journal of Negro History* 58, no. 1 (1973): 18–38; Mumford, *Interzones*, 3–18; Haag, *Consent*, 124–126. On the Mann Act, see David J. Langum, *Crossing the Line: Legislating Morality and the Mann Act* (Chicago: University of Chicago Press, 1994); McLaren, *Sexual Blackmail*, 82–92; Fronc, *New York Undercover*, 30, 183–184.

[69] "Mrs. Johnson Tries Suicide," *New York Times*, 12 Sep. 1912, p. 6.

[70] "Southern Editor Has Amazing Brain Storm," *Chicago Defender*, 21 Sep. 1912, p. 3; see also George Chauncey, *Why Marriage?: The History Shaping Today's Debate over Gay Equality* (New York: Basic Books, 2004), 63–64, for a discussion of the interracial marriage bans that were passed immediately after the Johnson scandal came to prominence.

arena, as they were unable to do in the boxing ring. A US congressman thus introduced a constitutional amendment seeking to ban black and white intermarriage, and state congressmen presented similar bills in at least ten northern states. Federal authorities then accused Johnson of having traveled across state boundaries in 1910 for the purpose of immoral sexual exchanges with a former girlfriend, Belle Schreiber – an offense under the Mann Act. Johnson was found guilty and sentenced to a year in prison, a punishment he dodged by fleeing to Paris and not returning to serve time until 1920.[71]

Johnson's case was just one example of an African American man being accused and convicted of corrupting a white woman under the Mann Act. These cases were widespread in the early 1910s, and they reflected a public preoccupation with black male–white female relationships that pervaded the various regions of the nation. Johnson's case would nonetheless take on a larger-than-life status in subsequent discussions of sex and marriage and in legislative restrictions on the marriage state. The guilty ruling against Johnson, for instance, prompted Assistant District Attorney Harry Parkin of Chicago to declare:

This verdict also will go around the world. It is a forerunner of laws to be passed in these United States which we may live to see – laws forbidding miscegenation. This negro, in the eyes of many, has been persecuted. Perhaps as an individual he was. But it was his misfortune to be the foremost example of the evil in permitting the intermarriage of whites and blacks. Now he must bear the consequences.

Parkin did see a greater good emerging from the fiasco, though, as Johnson's story would "teach others the law must be respected."[72]

The Johnson trial raised anxieties and frustrations that would make their way into legal discussions of marriage, both in and out of Illinois. It triggered new concerns about interracial sex, and it sparked debate about who was entitled to cross state lines for the purpose of exchanging vows. In 1915, many of these questions were answered with the passage of uniform marriage legislation in Illinois. The Johnson case thus complicates the link between dysgenic elopements and the quest for marriage evasion laws. In one sense, its chronological and geographic overlap with the debate over eugenics cautions us against drawing too firm a connection between public health anxieties and the passage of uniform

---

[71] Mumford, *Interzones*, 10–11.
[72] "U.S. Jury Finds Johnson Guilty; May Go to Prison," *Chicago Daily Tribune*, 14 May 1913, p. 1.

legislation. Defiance of eugenic laws was not the lone act of conjugal misconduct occurring in this place and time, and it was not the only factor contributing to the passage of new restrictive legislation. But in another sense, Johnson's story reinforces the role that racial anxieties played in the eugenic marriage debates of the 1910s. The fear of race suicide was grounded in part in the notion that white middle-class civilization was declining due to procreation with physically and mentally unfit individuals; but it also reflected concerns that respectable white citizens were engaging too freely in sexual relations with members of different racial and class groups. It appears that the adoption of uniform marriage legislation in Illinois and Wisconsin sought to address this wide variety of concerns over the future of white civilization.

* * *

Though additional marriage evasion laws failed to materialize in subsequent years, efforts to rein in unadvised elopements took other forms in religious and social reform circles. For instance, fifty California pastors of multiple denominations met in Oakland in 1915 to discuss the problems they believed to emerge from hasty marriage and divorce. Though the ministers focused their energies on California's rising rates of divorce and "consecutive polygamy," they also called for a ten-day waiting period for the receipt of a marriage license following a couple's application, and a campaign to defrock mercenary ministers. The participating pastors saw these initiatives as strategies both church and state could employ to eliminate elopements, forming a clerical committee to continue this work after the conference. Other church groups formed similar organizations to fight against the rising tide of hasty and evasive marriages, including a national Presbyterian committee on eugenics and uniform divorce law.[73]

Female-led social welfare organizations also fought against elopement, often seeking stricter eugenic and marriage evasion policies. At the 1918 convention of the General Federation of Women's Clubs, participants promoted a resolution to support eugenic marriage statutes and the implementation of uniform marriage and divorce laws across the nation.

---

[73] "Clergy to Act on Hasty Marriage; Quick Divorce," *Oakland Tribune*, 19 Jan. 1915, pp. 1, 2; "Pastors United to Fight Divorce Evil in Alameda County," *Oakland Tribune*, 22 Jan. 1915, pp. 1, 2; "United Brethren to Profit by Methodist Convention," *Inter Ocean*, 9 Mar. 1914, p. 10; "Wall Street Hears Gospel," *Scranton Truth*, 15 Oct. 1913, p. 2; "Congregationalists and Presbyterians Active," *El Paso Herald*, 10 Jan. 1914, p. 4C.

Supporters also called for the publication of marriage banns thirty days before the ceremony, and proposed laws compelling both partners to undergo physical and mental examinations before exchanging vows.[74] Meanwhile, Joanna Colcord performed much work on this front as chair of the Committee on Marriage Laws at the Russell Sage Foundation. Troubled by the nation's rising divorce rate and her perception that the institution of marriage was losing its luster, Colcord oversaw a 1920 study of existing and proposed marriage legislation throughout the nation. She conducted this study as both a fact-finding mission and an effort to reform family law. Colcord wrote letters to lawmakers and social organizations around the country to request copies of pending state bills and to collaborate on marriage law reform with other concerned groups. Colcord and her committee shied away from bills requiring health certificates for marriage licenses, noting that such laws caused too many administrative complications to justify their noble intentions – as seen in the ongoing challenges along the Wisconsin-Illinois border. Instead, the committee's work zeroed in on common law marriage, the unions of children below the age of marital consent, the high rates of evasive elopements across state borders, and the operation of Gretna Greens.[75]

The question of elopement and hasty marriage proved troubling to Colcord and the Committee on Marriage Laws. Members were struck by the number of states that did not require a waiting period between the application of a license and the receipt of said license, noting that a mandatory delay would allow family members and acquaintances to intervene in ill-advised local marriages and would make it much more difficult for couples to tacitly elope out of state. The committee's research showed that recent bills mandating a waiting period before the receipt of a marriage license – or between the receipt of the license and the wedding – were failing to pass in state legislatures in the early 1920s. Colcord noted that many lawmakers were voting against these bills due to the extreme

---

[74] "Club Women Tell Needs of States They Represent," *Chicago Daily Tribune*, 16 Jun. 1914, p. 3; "New Commandments," *Dakota Farmers' Leader* (Canton, S.D.), 23 Oct. 1914, p. 9; "Eugenic Law Is Advocated by Clubwomen," *Pittsburgh Daily Post*, 8 May 1918, p. 3.

[75] Meeting of Miss Colcord's Committee on Marriage Laws and Administration, Minutes, March 1920. Letter from Committee on Marriage Laws to American Association for Organizing Family Social Work, 15 Mar. 1920. Both items from Family Service Association of America Records, Box 13, Folder 39. Social Welfare History Archives, University of Minnesota. On Colcord's and the Russell Sage Foundation's work on child marriage, see Syrett, *American Child Bride*, 172–195.

measures they proposed; while nine states already held laws requiring up to a five-day delay before the issuance of a license, newer bills demanded notice of ten, fifteen, and twenty days. Other bills called for the county issuing the license to pay to have the marriage announcement posted in local newspapers before the couple could wed. Still others demanded that counties provide judicial proceedings for the airing of objections to an impending marriage. While Colcord saw value in these measures, she believed that they overreached, sparking opposition from legislators who would gladly support less elaborate and extensive laws, but who balked at the extremity of the ones before them.[76]

The work of committees like Colcord's help to reveal the extent of the backlash that out-of-state elopements provoked, illustrating the unpredictable measures that state lawmakers took to rein in the perceived crisis of hasty and unsanitary marriage. As Colcord's work revealed, some officials were so disturbed by evasive marriages that they proposed corrective measures that were too extreme to pass through state legislatures, such as twenty-day wait periods before the issuance of a license. The fact that so many bills *failed* helps us to see the passions elopement sparked. In their efforts to put an end to such elopements, concerned lawmakers overextended themselves by seeking overly aggressive, often implausible solutions. Their continued efforts to implement stricter premarital health examinations and longer waiting periods, however ill-fated, demonstrate the intensity of the concerns that dysgenic unions and evasive elopements generated.

Perhaps the most dramatic initiative proposed was not a state bill, but rather a federal measure. In 1921, 1923, 1925, 1927, and 1930, Kansas Senator Arthur Capper – in collaboration with the General Federation of Women's Clubs – sponsored the Capper Amendment, a bill proposing a constitutional amendment that would grant Congress the right to enact federal marriage and divorce laws. Capper sought support for this bill by noting that disparities in state laws facilitated elopements by underage partners and the physically unfit. Capper insisted that in addition to creating a uniform age of consent for men and women, a constitutional amendment would enable the adoption of a law forcing couples to wait two weeks between the application and issuance of a license and requiring them to publicly announce their intention to wed. It would also force both

---

[76] Joanna C. Colcord, "Why Marriage Bills Fail Which Provide for Advance Notice," *The Family* 3, no. 4 (1922): 83; Report of the Committee of Marriage Laws for 1923, Family Service Association of America Records, Box 13, Folder 41.

prospective spouses to submit affidavits proving their physical and mental fitness for matrimony, thus helping to alleviate the nation's eugenic anxieties.[77]

This amendment never passed, and even Colcord's Committee on Marriage Laws could not reach consensus on the measure, with some deeming it essential and others insisting that marriage legislation should remain the prerogative of individual states. And as long as states remained responsible for their own marriage laws, legal differences across state borders would prompt continued elopements, followed by consequent efforts to tweak legislation. For example, Nebraska passed a law in 1923 requiring a ten-day notice before the issuance of a marriage license. The state repealed this law shortly thereafter following a campaign from jewelers and other retailers, who bemoaned the loss of business they were experiencing as couples fled into nearby states with fewer restrictions on acquiring licenses. The fear of financial loss – or the desire for financial gain – made some state legislators reluctant to duplicate the laws of neighboring states. In many cases, it was that very resistance to duplication that allowed for marriage mill cities to keep their budgets intact.[78]

It was also the desire for profit that pushed many Gretna Green operators to ignore their states' increasingly strict laws and to look the other way on questions of eugenics and evasion. We see this when we return to Wisconsin, where couples continued to defy eugenic legislation by eloping in Illinois, even after both states passed evasion laws. One reason these couples were able to maintain their defiance was that county officials like Clerk Lew Hendee continued to welcome them, in spite of legal interventions to the contrary. Sparked by a desire to maintain the profits that the Waukegan marriage mill had long reaped from dysgenic elopement, Hendee did his best to keep the Gretna Green in operation. Claiming support from Illinois Attorney General Edward Brundage in issuing whatever licenses were requested of him, Hendee argued in December of 1919, "A county clerk is an administerial not a judicial officer ... and if a couple under oath declare they are not violating the marriage laws of the state in which they intend to live the clerk can do nothing but issue the license. He cannot refuse to issue a license just

---

[77] Syrett, *American Child Bride*, 184; "Senator Capper on the Need of One Divorce Law," *Springfield Missouri Republican*, 18 Jul. 1923, p. 7.

[78] "Report of the Committee of Marriage Laws," 9 Jun. 1925, Family Service Association of America, Box 13, Folder 41.

because he may think any member of the contracting party is not telling the truth. If they swear falsely it is their lookout." With this profession of willful ignorance, Hendee and his colleagues reaffirmed their commitment to validating evasive interstate unions, in spite of legislative efforts to stop them.[79]

Eugenic marriage restrictions remained a fixture in Wisconsin law in the decades that followed. Throughout the 1920s state legislators proposed multiple amendments to require women to provide doctor's certificates before they could wed; such amendments were unsuccessful, and it remained the exclusive responsibility of men to prove their freedom from syphilis.[80] Mass elopement across the Illinois-Wisconsin border came to an end in 1936 when the Illinois legislature passed a law requiring couples to undergo examinations for venereal disease before receiving their marriage licenses, and demanding that couples file notices of their intention to wed three days before the intended nuptials, thus preventing the covert exchange of vows. But rather than terminate dysgenic elopements altogether, these laws brought eloping couples, now from Wisconsin *and* Illinois, to the marriage mills of Indiana, such as Crown Point and Valparaiso. Through this example, we can again see a familiar cyclical pattern that exemplified the relationship between elopement and eugenic marriage laws through much of the twentieth century: with the closing of one marriage mill came the opening of another. As one state's laws came to encourage premarital exams, noncompliant couples found new options in other states.[81] For example, when a 1935 Pennsylvania law implemented a three-day wait between a couple's application for and receipt of a marriage license, many impatient couples opted to wed in Maryland – specifically in Elkton, which remained a popular elopement site two decades after its debut as a Gretna Green.[82] Many residents of Elkton

---

[79] "Cites Brundage Ruling to Back 'Marriage Mill,'" *Chicago Daily Tribune*, 25 Dec. 1919, p. 23. As Syrett illustrates, justices of the peace similarly feigned ignorance when asked about their willingness to wed underage individuals who lied about age. *American Child Bride*, 179.

[80] "Woman Solon to Urge Eugenics Law for Women," *Anniston Star* (Ala.), 18 Jan. 1925, p. 12; "Eugenics," *Reading Times* (Pa.), 19 May 1925, p. 4.

[81] "Cupid's Arrows Hit Mark 260 Times at Crown Point Range," *The Times* (Hammond, Ind.), 26 Jul. 1937, p. 9; "Join in Campaign against Crown Point Marriage Mill," *Garrett Clipper* (Ind.), 11 Oct. 1937, p. 2; "Fifty Couples Married at Valparaiso Thanksgiving," *Garrett Clipper*, 29 Nov. 1937, p. 2; "Kill Indiana Marriage Mills," *Chicago Daily Tribune*, 12 Jan. 1938, p. 1.

[82] "Law to Curb Elopements," *Los Angeles Times*, 2 Jun. 1935, p. 31. "Aims at 'Gretna Greens,'" *New York Times*, 24 Mar. 1937, p. 27.

continued to embrace their town's appeal as a marriage mill, seeking to capitalize on the economic benefits that couples brought as they entered the city to dodge eugenic regulations. Among those to welcome such defiant couples was the Reverend Charles Cope, known as one of Elkton's "marrying ministers." Cope did not try to hide his attraction to the revenue this practice generated. Rather, he attempted to profit in as many ways as possible. A retired Baptist minister, Cope was also on the payroll of the local taxi company that transported couples from the Elkton train station to his house, where he would also receive pay for presiding over the wedding.[83]

Like Wisconsin and Illinois marriage mills in prior years, Maryland cities lost their Gretna Green status in 1937, when a new Maryland law called for forty-eight hours' notice before marriage licenses could be issued.[84] This time cities in Virginia, most prominently Alexandria, capitalized on the changes to marriage law. Virginia did not require any delay between the application for a license and its issuance, provided that the couple applied at the county seat during daylight hours. Without this demand for a waiting period, and in the absence of a health certificate requirement, Virginia became a new haven for the couples who could no longer marry with ease in neighboring states. These disparities in marriage law across state borders allowed for couples to defy the laws of their home state and marry elsewhere if they were unwilling to submit to the eugenic testing or to endure the waiting periods dictated by their states of residence.[85]

When new eugenic laws forced the closure of marriage mills, some couples tried their luck in neighboring states, while others resigned themselves to nonmarriage, common law marriage, cohabitation, or compliance with the eugenic rules of the day. When Illinois began requiring health certificates for marriage in 1935, the days of the Waukegan marriage mill were numbered. But the loss of this site of legal evasion does not negate the countless acts of conjugal misconduct performed there in the years preceding its collapse. The people who eloped to Waukegan to avoid policies they did not wish to follow in their home states, and the county employees like Hendee who defied widespread moral beliefs by

---

[83] "Elkton Checks Ads of Marrying Clergy," *New York Times*, 6 Aug. 1935, p. 19.

[84] "Aims at 'Gretna Greens,'" 27. "Gretna Green Is Curbed by Voters in Maryland," *New York Times*, 10 Nov. 1938, p. 12; "The Nation," *New York Times*, 13 Nov. 1938, p. E2.

[85] Blair Bolles, "A 'Gretna Green' for Virginia," *New York Times*, 4 Dec. 1938, sec. 2, p. 1.

keeping the mill running in the face of strident criticism, were in many ways responsible for the later acts of legislation that sought to bring eugenic marriage laws into new states, to target elopement centers, and to render marriage laws uniform across state borders. But in their efforts to chart their own marital paths, even if it meant defying state or medical authorities, these couples revealed the limitations of marriage law in shaping the course of human desire. As distraught minister Amos Keiser claimed when shotgun weddings were outlawed in his home state of Pennsylvania, "It's a great law, if it was adopted in all states. It won't stop elopements though. Love always finds a way. It has lots of loopholes, too."[86]

---

[86] Paul F. Ellis, "Squires Find Going Tough," *Ogden Standard-Examiner* (Utah), 31 May 1931, p. 9.

4

Trial Marriage and the Laws of the Home

The forms of conjugal misconduct we have seen thus far involved individuals who bridged geographic divides in their mate selection techniques, and partners who breached state borders to formalize otherwise unlawful marriages. Couples who took part in "trial marriage," the next arrangement in question, did not necessarily cross physical borders in forging their controversial unions, but they nonetheless pushed the boundaries of marital propriety in meaningful ways. While its definitions varied from person to person, at its foundation the trial marriage was a union that couples entered into with an eye toward impermanence. Men and women would get married – sometimes formally, and sometimes through common law arrangements – with the agreement that after a fixed period of time they would part ways if one or both partners was unsatisfied, provided the couple remained childless.

In practice, the term "trial marriage" had wide application, as critics used it to describe a broad set of marital behaviors; specifically, it encompassed marriages between childless spouses that ended in divorce, provisional or noncohabitative unions between bohemian couples, and annullable marriages between adolescents. In sum, the term came to characterize partnerships that defied traditional notions of marriage as an indissoluble contract. Opponents feared that trial marriage, in its varied forms, reflected the diversification of an institution that ought to remain uniform. They thus used the ambiguous phrase to disparage couples who opted to dictate the parameters of their own relationships and whose marriages failed to meet long-time standards of permanency and propriety.

Though we cannot know how many couples described their unions as trial marriages in the early decades of the twentieth century, it is clear that this was not a common tendency. In spite of its rarity, the topic of trial marriage received outsized attention from the law, church, and media, even becoming a popular topic in literature, drama, and film.[1] This very incongruity – the small number of couples defining their relationships as "trial marriages" versus the dramatic outcries against them – speaks to the historical significance of the phenomenon. The subject thus adds another layer to the complex legal and cultural discourse surrounding sex, marriage, and family in the early twentieth century, and it reveals the deep sense of panic over shifting social and sexual mores, all feeding into the perception of a marriage crisis. Critiques of trial marriage also reveal a public preoccupation with the sexual and marital arrangements of working-class individuals, whom critics feared would embrace trial marriage with disastrous effects. In many ways, trial marriage came to symbolize conservative critics' more abstract worries that the sacred institutions of marriage and the family were under attack and that poor individuals were procreating indiscriminately. Amid rising alarm over prostitution, contraception, divorce, and a host of other perceived sexual and moral ills, occasional examples of trial marriage encapsulated moral reformers' concerns over the public embrace of marital choice and sexual freedom.

The study of trial marriage also helps to illuminate the role of the legal and judicial profession in the regulation of early twentieth-century marriage and divorce. During this era, the phrase "trial marriage" entered into courtrooms as judges presiding over divorce and annulment cases used it to describe the broken unions they encountered. Applying the term to ill-conceived nuptials between couples who were typically young and inexperienced, these judges joined the fight against the marriage crisis they believed to be at hand when they refused to dissolve the unions before them. As we shall see, critical judges tended to rely on the claim that trial marriage was "contrary to public policy" as a way of denying annulments to young couples who pursued them. Rarely citing specific laws or court cases to support their claims, these judges used the

---

[1] Burns Mantle, "The 'Trial Marriage' Takes Place in Woods," *Chicago Daily Tribune*, 13 Nov. 1912, p. B1; Mantle, "A Wronged Heroine Who Spurns Marriage," *Chicago Daily Tribune*, 15 Dec. 1912, p. B3; Percy Hammond, "The Taliaferros Make Fun of Advanced Feminism," *Chicago Daily Tribune*, 26 Feb. 1914, p. 7; "'Trial Marriage' Arrives," *New York Times*, 1 Feb. 1927, p. 24; Mae Tinee, "Tropic Islands, Girl Violinist, Handy Villains," *Chicago Daily Tribune*, 25 Feb. 1930, p. 29.

language of public policy to explain that marriage was too sacred an institution to disrupt at the behest of dissatisfied spouses. The vague legal language that judges often used to justify their rejections of trial marriages seems more than anything to betray their deeper moral and religious concerns. In this sense, court rulings on trial marriage tended to blur the boundaries between civil law and moral perception, as judges used the language of public policy to grant legal authority to their personal views of sexual propriety. But in labeling failed unions "trial marriages" and in refusing to annul them, these judges reinforced the currency of the phrase, while simultaneously intensifying the fight against the marriage crisis.

The earliest noted conversations about trial marriage took place in academic circles. British sexologist Havelock Ellis defined the phenomenon in the 1890s as a nonbinding relationship between two childless partners. Ellis supported trial marriage, arguing that the state should not force marriages between couples with no children to raise and that divorces should be available whenever childless couples desired to end their unions.[2] Despite Ellis's outspokenness on the subject, the concept of trial marriage did not enter popular American consciousness until it appeared in the much discussed – if less frequently read – 1906 academic treatise *The Family* by Elsie Clews Parsons, a prominent New York anthropologist and sociologist. In this book, Parsons offered a brief suggestion that some societies might benefit from providing childless couples with easier access to divorce. Although Parsons expressed this idea as just one possibility among many for improving the quality of marriages, and although it came in a short passage toward the end of her nearly four-hundred-page text, it was enough to prompt public condemnations from clergy, legislators, and social reformers.

Similar condemnations would emerge more than twenty years later, when Colorado Judge Ben Lindsey, along with coauthor Wainwright Evans, proposed a similar idea in the 1927 book *The Companionate Marriage*. While Lindsey did not embrace the term "trial marriage," elements of companionate marriage aligned notably with the model put forth by Parsons two decades prior. Lindsey argued that in order for marriage to remain the sacred institution he believed it to be, young married couples without children should be granted easy access to divorce

---

[2] Rebecca L. Davis, "'Not Marriage at All, but Simple Harlotry': The Companionate Marriage Controversy," *Journal of American History* 94, no. 4 (2008): 1143.

if their marriages proved unsuccessful.[3] Lindsey's push for companionate marriage met with the same vitriolic criticisms that Parsons before him had endured. As we shall see, the two decades between the publication of *The Family* and *The Companionate Marriage* were marked with consistent negotiation over couples' right to establish provisional marital arrangements. As couples from all class backgrounds ignored the public outcry and established their own trial marriages, legislators devised new strategies for eliminating such unions. By looking at actual trial marriages in the context of these academic discourses, we come to see the wide-ranging effects that trial marriages played in remapping the boundaries of marital propriety in the early twentieth century.

* * *

Elsie Clews Parsons based *The Family* on a sociology course she taught at Barnard College from 1902 to 1905. She had married Herbert Parsons, a prominent lawyer – and soon-to-be Republican congressional representative – in 1900, to the surprise and disappointment of many colleagues, who generally assumed that this would be the end of her promising professional career. Parsons defied those assumptions by remaining in her job for the next five years, despite becoming pregnant within six weeks of her wedding, and then again in October of 1902.[4] Well aware that most affluent women resigned from their jobs after marriage, and certainly after childbirth, Parsons rejected this convention, seeking to lay out a new set of personal and professional opportunities for married women. According to Parsons biographer Desley Deacon, "Much of the happiness Elsie did experience in the early years of marriage came from the sense of accomplishment she felt in demonstrating the possibility of a new sort of marriage that widened women's capacities rather than narrowed them." This desire to expand the opportunities available to modern women would drive Parsons's academic work.[5]

---

[3] Judge Ben B. Lindsey and Wainwright Evans, *The Companionate Marriage*, 2nd ed. (Garden City, N.Y.: Garden City Publishing Co., 1929). I attribute passages from *The Companionate Marriage* to Lindsey, despite his shared authorship with Evans. The text is written in Lindsey's voice, and it quotes conversations in which Lindsey partook. Evans's contribution to the writing process was significant, but the text's perspectives come across as uniquely Lindsey's.

[4] Desley Deacon, *Elsie Clews Parsons: Inventing Modern Life* (Chicago: University of Chicago Press, 1997), 49–51, 56–59, 61.

[5] Ibid., 55.

Among Parsons's greatest concerns was the silence surrounding sex and sexuality, and women's inability to express autonomy in their own sexual lives. As long as women lacked proper sex education and the freedom to discuss sexuality at will, Parsons saw no potential for gender equality. Furthermore, in the words of Deacon, Parsons argued that "without frank discussion and acceptance of the moral and physical aspects of sex relations . . . girls develop a general hostility toward marriage and sexuality as personally confining and physically unaesthetic."[6] Parsons believed that the way to address unsavory modern marital and sexual trends, including increased rates of divorce and prostitution, was to discuss them openly and to devise strategies for reversing them. With the publication of *The Family*, she hoped to offer solutions to these perceived problems. Ironically, the very forces she sought to conquer conquered her instead.

Parsons's offending statement appeared in her discussion of strategies for eliminating prostitution. She briefly considered the possibility that increased tolerance of sexual activity among the young and childless might allow for the scourge of prostitution to dissipate. She argued: "It would therefore, seem well from this point of view, to encourage early *trial* marriage, the relation to be entered into with a view to permanency, but with the privilege of breaking it if it proved unsuccessful and in the *absence of offspring* without suffering any great degree of public condemnation."[7] Parsons never claimed to support this point of view with conviction, and two pages later she wrote that childless marriage was "a progressive substitute for prostitution; but, like prostitution, it is a social evil, in so far as it is a check upon the development of personality."[8] But the uncertainties and nuances of her argument, and her traditional views on childless marriage, rarely entered into the public debates this passage inspired.

On 18 November 1906, one day after the publication of *The Family*, Reverend Morgan Dix of New York's Trinity Church commenced the assault on Parsons's work. Despite admitting that he had not read the book, Dix saw the publication of *The Family* as an opportunity to preach a sermon on the deterioration of the home. On the subject of trial marriage, Dix asserted, "The idea of men and women living like animals,

---

[6] Ibid., 64.

[7] Elsie Clews Parsons, *The Family: An Ethnographical and Historical Outline with Descriptive Notes, Planned as a Text-book for the Use of College Lecturers and of Directors of Home-reading Clubs* (New York: G. P. Putnam's Sons, 1906), 348–349.

[8] Ibid., 351.

separating at will, and contracting new alliances, leaving the children to be nobody's children, and to be cared for by the State, is barbarous."[9] Dix either did not know or did not care that Parsons suggested trial marriages only for childless couples. He blamed her for disseminating these "simply outrageous" ideas just the same, and he prepared his sermon with the intention of doing "everything in my power to counteract the bad effects which are bound to come from Mrs. Parsons' remarks."[10] On the potential harms of Parsons's work, Dix argued: "Few persons know, and very few reflect, to what an extreme the radicals of the day are pushing their schemes of social revolution. When so much is bad, it is hard to say what is the worst; but perhaps the worst is the plan to abolish marriage and break up the home. It is in the mind of these fanatics that marriage shall cease." He proceeded with an attack on "radicals" and "anarchists" like Parsons for challenging the institution of marriage with their morally bankrupt ideas.[11]

Dix was quickly joined by scores of clergy in excoriating *The Family*, and while perhaps some of these ministers had quickly purchased and read the dense text in its entirety, we can assume that the majority of criticisms were not grounded in actual exposure to the book. Many of them took the greatest issue with the fact that its author was a woman, including the Reverend Henry Barber of New York's Beloved Disciple Episcopal Church, who argued that the content of *The Family* was "utterly abominable, and, coming from the pen of a woman, makes it doubly atrocious."[12] Perhaps Parsons's most rabid clerical critic was the Reverend Charles Parkhurst of New York, who deemed trial marriage a form of progressive polygamy and argued in his 1906 Thanksgiving Day sermon at Madison

[9] "Dr. Dix on Trial Marriages," *New York Times*, 18 Nov. 1906, p. 12.
[10] "All Rally Round the Wedding Ring," *Chicago Daily Tribune*, 18 Nov. 1906, 3. This article quotes a number of ministers who planned to preach against Parsons the following day. Among them was Rev. Charles McCready of New York's Roman Catholic Church of the Holy Cross, who claimed, "From what I read of Mrs. Parsons' book in the papers I believe it to be indecent. I believe it will tend to spoil the family, and deserves the condemnation of every decent man and woman." Rev. Sidney Herbert Cox of Bethany Congregational Church compared Parsons's ideas to the "customs of the savages, where the chief took numerous wives on trial, and when he tired he would have them put to death. These theories do not come under the law of civilized society." Several of Parsons's critics ignored her stipulation that trial marriage be available only to childless couples, dismissing her proposal as indecent in its disregard for the children of broken homes. See also C.M., New Jersey, "Correspondents," *Phrenological Journal and Science of Health* 120, no. 5 (1907): 165.
[11] "Dr. Dix Speaks Out to Save the Home," *New York Times*, 19 Nov. 1906, p. 5.
[12] "All Rally Round the Wedding Ring," 3.

Square Presbyterian Church that "a consecutive harem is no improvement on a simultaneous one." Parkhurst did note Parsons's tentativeness in proposing this solution, but in his eyes, Parsons's very mention of the term "trial marriage" as a potentially positive good demanded reproach.[13]

The following February, the *New York Observer and Chronicle* published an anonymous critique of trial marriage that bore a suspicious resemblance to the sermon presented by Parkhurst a few months earlier. Its author viewed trial marriages as one of many man-made obstacles created to drive people away from traditional marriage as it had been defined by God and to alter the course of an institution that had endured for centuries in its ideal, unimpeachable form. Perhaps the author recognized that in making this charge, he invited a history lesson on the changing paths that marriage had taken across nations and throughout the course of human civilization. He therefore proceeded to attack academic scholarship on marriage as inherently immoral in its dispassionate examination of a sacred ritual. The reviewer criticized *The Family* for being "rigidly scientific." He argued, "It is cold, hard and bloodless. Facts of the most repulsive nature are handled without delicacy or reserve. The facts with which the authoress deals seem to have no interest for her except as facts." He viewed this scholarly detachment as the most insidious characteristic of *The Family*, for its matter-of-fact tone tended to "give to matrimonial looseness of life a standing of respectability."[14] To this critic, marriage was out of bounds as a subject of academic inquiry. His rejection of scholarship on marriage allowed him to maintain his religious view of the institution as a universal creation of God, which was both strong enough to have resisted change over centuries and vulnerable enough that Parsons's work threatened its foundation entirely.

The war waged on *The Family* was not limited to clergy. The secular press and a host of social reformers also played a pivotal role in publicizing and denigrating Parsons's book. Among these critics was suffragist and Populist activist Mary Elizabeth Lease. While Lease was known for her vulgar and unfiltered rhetoric, once being labeled by a Republican editor a "petticoated smut mill" for her "venomous tongue," she was appalled by *The Family*'s "trial marriage" argument.[15] For Lease, marriage called for a greater degree of delicacy than did other subjects of

[13] "Trial Marriage Idea Denounced in Churches," *New York Times*, 30 Nov. 1906, p. 6.
[14] "Sanctity of the Marriage Tie," *New York Observer and Chronicle*, 21 Feb. 1907, p. 239.
[15] O. Gene Clanton, *Kansas Populism: Ideas and Men* (Lawrence: University Press of Kansas, 1969), 76.

social and political debate. "It is preposterous and disastrous," she charged, "to present as a remedy for admittedly existing chaotic conditions in the marriage relation any scheme of reform ... which will permit wider scope and fuller license to the animal propensities of man." Ignoring Parsons's stipulation that trial marriages be available only to childless couples, Lease predicted that the system would turn the children of divorced parents into wards of the state and would bring further social scorn upon women. Echoing Barber's comments on Parsons's lack of feminine propriety, Lease expressed regret that an allegedly respectable woman would propose such an objectionable system.[16]

Some of the most outspoken commentators on the Parsons controversy were newspaper readers, whose letters to the editor were published liberally. These letters often expressed disgust at Parsons's ideas, while failing to display any real understanding of what those ideas indeed were. One of her earliest critics was J. H. Lord, who wrote a letter to the *New York Times* to express shock that "such a scandalous and immoral project as the 'trial marriage' should be exploited, even in these times of riotous thinking, by a woman, and especially by a woman of the breeding and education of Mrs. Parsons." Arguing that monogamous marriage was ordained by God and existed as "the very fountainhead of all social morality," Lord feared that Parsons's work served to undermine marriage altogether. Without showing any signs of having read the text or of understanding just what Parsons meant in her passing reference to "trial marriage," Hall emphatically declared that the "invention of this scheme must have taxed the ingenuity of Satan, and if society would adopt it his kingdom would soon come on earth."[17] Equally dramatic in his criticism of a book that he admitted to not having read, Philip Swain of New Jersey scolded the editor of the *New York Observer* for daring to publish a review of *The Family*. Swain described trial marriage as a "horrible, earthly, sensual, devilish" doctrine that "makes a shudder come over one the mere mention of it."[18]

Parsons's detractors were male and female; many of them were members of the clergy, but they also included journalists, social reformers, and concerned citizens with no professional obligation to comment. The majority of them displayed limited understandings of Parsons's

---

[16] "All Rally Round the Wedding Ring," 3.
[17] J. H. Lord, "The Trial Marriage," *New York Times*, 21 Nov. 1906, p. 8.
[18] Philip Swain, "No Trial Marriage for Him," *New York Observer and Chronicle*, 21 Mar. 1907, p. 374.

scholarship, and several admitted to not having read *The Family* at all. Though their specific arguments against Parsons varied from sermon to sermon and letter to letter, they were united in their general concern that marriage was changing rapidly and that its moral and religious obligations were lost on those who exchanged vows without committing fully to a lifelong union. *The Family* sparked a firestorm that would not go away with the mere passage of time (see Figure 4.1). While media attention to Parsons herself faded as 1907 came to an end, concerns about trial marriage as a new menace to moral society bubbled beneath the surface, ready to boil over with the slightest provocation.

This conflict would play itself out in a variety of ways over the next two decades. At the same time that Parsons was creating a stir with her reflections on trial marriage, the Iowa legislature was dealing with the issue on a more concrete level. In February of 1907, state legislators introduced a bill for trial marriages. The bill, modeled on a similar measure presented in the South Dakota legislature weeks earlier, provided that a marriage contract could be entered into by a man and a woman for the length of five years, at the end of which the couple would be free to part ways or to renew the contract if they so desired.[19] While the Iowa bill was not adopted into law, this very possibility created great angst for some commentators, leading one reporter to fume, "Compared with this Iowa dream, Utah really stands out in conspicuous boldness for the high moral plane on which the marriage relations are placed by the Mormons."[20] Some of Parsons's critics cited the situations in Iowa and South Dakota as evidence of the general decline in morals that had led to the anthropologist's endorsement of trial marriage.[21]

While these legislative affairs received just a fraction of the public attention thrust upon the unsuspecting Elsie Clews Parsons, they nonetheless triggered some bizarre acts of opposition among local Iowa politicians. The first occurred in March 1907, just a month after the proposal of trial marriage legislation in Iowa. With the support of the Fort Dodge city council, mayor S. J. Bennett passed a city ordinance declaring that every resident of the Iowa town aged twenty-five to forty must be married in the next sixty days, or pay a fine of between ten and one hundred dollars. Bennett also announced that he would perform free marriage ceremonies

[19] "Wants Wedlock Probationary," *Los Angeles Times*, 13 Feb. 1907, p. 1; "Down a Moral Niagara," *Los Angeles Times*, 14 Feb. 1907, sec. 2, p. 4.
[20] "Down a Moral Niagara," sec. 2, p. 4.
[21] "Trial Marriages," *New York Times*, 2 Dec. 1906, p. 6.

"TRIAL" MARRIAGE

Bridegroom of a Week: SORRY YOU MUST BE GOING. NICE TO HAVE HAD THIS GLIMPSE OF YOU.

FIGURE 4.1 Otho Cushing's comedic commentary on trial marriage graced the cover of *Life* magazine a month after the publication of Parsons's book. *Life,* 27 Dec. 1906.

for any unwed couples hoping to escape the fine; in the two days following this declaration, the mayor officiated thirty-three weddings.[22] In the weeks

[22] "Pass Law That All Must Wed," *Los Angeles Times,* 21 Mar. 1907, p. 1; "Mayor and Bachelors of Fort Dodge Worried by Enforced Marriage Law," *Chicago Daily Tribune,* 22 Mar. 1907, p. 6; "Marrying Mayor Busy," *New York Times,* 23 Mar. 1907, p. 1.

before the ordinance went into effect, Bennett's mailbox was flooded with letters from angry protesters across the country, including members of the Chicago Bachelors' Club. Meanwhile, local spinsters waged a boycott against Fort Dodge's Grand Leader Department Store, whose manager had openly supported the new policy. As tension mounted and threatening letters continued to arrive, Bennett's commitment to the ordinance increased. Where he had initially presented the decree as a positive and encouraging effort, which was "in the interest not only of good morals, but of a sound public policy," his devotion to the cause took on an increasingly militant tone as opposition grew. Just ten days later he declared, "This ordinance will go through ... When it becomes a law, I propose to see that it is enforced if it takes the entire police force." Bennett's enthusiasm for this ordinance likely faded, however, when his young daughter eloped in Des Moines with an older chauffeur who did not want to pay the fine.[23]

That same year, Judge Zell Roe of Des Moines began to officiate marriage ceremonies that were "divorce-proof." He publicly asked of each bride, "Do you, Mary, solemnly agree that you will never bring an action for divorce against John except for a statutory offense?" He demanded the same pledge from the groom. To demonstrate his commitment to eternal unions, Roe stated that if one of these couples brought a divorce suit during his lifetime, he would return the fee that the bride and groom had given him for the marriage, and pray to God for forgiveness.[24] While we cannot know all of the factors that drove men like Bennett and Roe to devise such unusual regulations, the context does provide some hints. It is telling that these zealous commitments to enduring marriage arrived in Iowa in 1907, just months after the "trial marriage" bill came under consideration. Although this bill was never enacted into law, it is probable that Bennett's and Roe's efforts to sanction ubiquitous and eternal marriage derived in part from the anxieties unleashed by the proposed policy. As scholars and state legislators called for a form of provisional marriage that, it seemed, would further raise an ever-increasing divorce rate, men like Bennett and Roe did what they could to maintain some semblance of the institution they believed so vital to their communities.

---

[23] "Marrying Mayor Busy," 1; R. E. Sherman, "Mayor Fighting for Marriage," *Los Angeles Times*, 31 Mar. 1907, sec. 4, p. 12; "Pass Law That All Must Wed," 1; "Elopes to Wed Chauffeur," *Washington Post*, 8 Oct. 1907, p. 1; "Sire Said Wed; They Did It," *Wichita Daily Eagle*, 20 Oct. 1907, p. 8.

[24] "New Marriage Vow," *Los Angeles Times*, 24 May 1907, p. II16.

Fears perpetuated by trial marriage were not limited to Iowans, however, and as the 1910s came to an end, newspapers across the country devoted increasing attention to the phenomenon, spreading news of these provisional unions to an ever-increasing reading public. Some of these articles featured diversionary stories about the eccentrics who embraced the trend – including Elmer Thayer, a Massachusetts war veteran who had placed a personal advertisement for a housekeeper. At the end of three months' employment the successful candidate would be eligible to become his trial wife, and three months after that his permanent partner.[25] Other writers pondered the demographic consequences of trial marriage, such as a Connecticut columnist who worried that an increase in trial marriages in Hartford would greatly limit birth rates among the more affluent residents of the city.[26]

Often these articles made tenuous connections between support for trial marriage and other morally questionable activities. Among the most egregious of these pieces was a *Los Angeles Times* article highlighting predatory photographer J. T. Valpey's preoccupation with trial marriage. Valpey was detained in 1915 for enticing young women into posing for nude photographs with promises that French film directors would be drawn to the risqué shots. Subtitled "Girl Says Photographer of Nudes Talked Trial Marriage," the article suggested that the photographer's affinity for provisional marriage had fed his indecent urges. Quoting Valpey's portrait subject as saying, "He discussed poetry with me, and eugenic marriages, and said he believed the only way for two persons to decide their fitness to become man and wife is to have a trial marriage," the article suggested that photographic exploitation and affinities for trial marriage were both products of the same indecent mindset. The writer did not address Valpey's suggestion that trial marriage might be an effective way of ensuring eugenic fitness.[27]

Most stories on trial marriage profiled the success or failure of various couples' experimental arrangements without providing details about the legal status of the marriages in question. While it is not always clear whether the featured couples married legally or were involved in non-marital cohabitation, their presence in national newspapers brought the phrase "trial marriage" into homes across the nation. Journalists presented readers with diverse perspectives on the plausibility and morality

[25] "Ad for a Wife on Trial-Marriage Plan," *The Herald* (Carroll, Iowa), 31 Jul. 1907, p. 3.
[26] "Trial Marriages in Capital City," *Bridgeport Herald*, 23 Dec. 1906, p. 12.
[27] "Poetry and Odd Morals," *Los Angeles Times*, 2 Aug. 1915, pt. 2, p. 2.

of such unions. While articles titled "Trial Marriage Fails" appeared more frequently than ones titled "Trial Marriage Succeeds," some writers suggested that provisional unions could bring couples happiness. Among these was a profile of William and Mary Glover, who in 1909 decided to formalize the trial marriage they had entered into ten years prior with an official marriage ceremony. The New Jersey couple had kept the conditional nature of their union private, and had not disclosed that they were only provisionally married until announcing their second, more permanent exchange of vows. "Had their trial marriage proved a failure they never would have publicized the fact," the author assured the reader, highlighting the taboo that surrounded this type of experimental endeavor, particularly when it led to separation.[28]

Another success story involved Mr. and Mrs. Archibald Robins of San Francisco. While the two were deeply in love, the bride "held advanced ideas on the subject of binding herself for life," and had thus insisted on drawing up a five-year marriage contract, at the end of which the couple would separate if not mutually satisfied. After five years together, during which the Robinses had experienced marital harmony and run a vegetarian restaurant together, they nonetheless opted to live apart for a year. But when a fire destroyed their restaurant, "Mrs. Robins came and wept on the shoulder of her husband-friend and they decided to break the contract." From this point onward, the couple lived together as husband and wife without any stipulation – the sort of eternal attachment that, the writer suggested, all marriages ought to replicate.[29]

Most trial marriages profiled in newspapers were less successful. Some of the featured marriages lasted only briefly – including that of Kentuckian Jane Parks, who had provisionally married Charles Caldwell because he could provide her with a home, but who left Caldwell within a week because she did not love him.[30] Others lasted much longer before the bride and groom decided to take advantage of their separation clauses. Among the long-lived trial marriages was that of Nina and William Fonda, a New York couple that parted ways twenty years after initiating a trial marriage. While the marriage had only been formalized with the entry of the two names into the family Bible, and it had initially been intended as a conditional and voidable arrangement that could be broken if either husband or wife desired separation, after twenty years those

[28] "Trial Marriage Proves Happy," *Los Angeles Times*, 30 May 1909, p. 1.
[29] "Trial Wedlock O.K.," *Los Angeles Times*, 30 Nov. 1909, p. 3.
[30] "Trial Marriage Lasted a Week," *Columbus Daily Enquirer* (Ga.), 14 Jan. 1909, p. 4.

conditions had changed. Now Nina demanded, and ultimately received, a legal separation, which would force William to pay fifty-dollar counsel fees and eight dollars per week in alimony, in part to support the couple's fifteen-year-old son.[31]

Other writers focused on the more sensational elements of trial marriage. A 1914 article titled "Bullets End Trial Marriage" told of Martha Boltze, a twenty-six-year-old San Francisco woman who was shot by husband James Dakas after breaking off her trial marriage with him. Dakas then shot himself in the head, and both were in critical condition at press time. The writer claimed that Dakas became violent because he feared being separated from Boltze's three-year-old son, the product of a previous trial marriage whom Dakas wished to raise as his own. Three months prior an attorney had drawn up a contract for the couple, stating that Dakas and Boltze would live as husband and wife with the understanding that either of them could break the contract at will. When Boltze sought to do just that, the tragic conflict ensued. Lurid stories like this one served as cautionary tales. Depicting the people indulging in the practice as violent, irresponsible, fickle, and both mentally and morally unsound – it could not have been incidental that the author chose to highlight Boltze's former trial marriage and the hopeless situation into which her actions had thrust her young son – authors of these stories used shocking narrative to urge readers against a worrisome practice.[32]

* * *

The above accounts represent a sampling of the many articles that pervaded newspapers on the subject of trial marriage. Despite their ubiquity, these accounts were fleeting human interest stories, with near-anonymous characters whose names would likely never see newsprint again; indeed, the *Los Angeles Times* did not even bother to inform readers whether Boltze and Dakas died from the injuries reported in the initial piece. Rarely did these stories become sustained topics of interest that went beyond one short article. The primary exception to this rule was a well-known couple whose literary and artistic achievements had placed them in the public eye long before news of their trial marriage broke. They were

[31] "Trial Marriage Fails," *Los Angeles Times*, 4 Aug. 1914, pt. II, p. 6. See also "Trial Marriage Fails after Five Years," *Chicago Daily Tribune*, 11 Aug. 1907, p. F2; "Trial Marriage of a Week; Woman Then Leaves Husband," *Chicago Daily Tribune*, 12 Jan. 1909, p. 2; "One Trial Marriage Fails," *New York Times*, 15 Sep. 1909, p. 1.

[32] "Bullets End Trial Marriage," *Los Angeles Times*, 14 Mar. 1914, p. 2.

FIGURE 4.2 "Noted Novelist and 'Friend Husband' Confess of Their Experimental Marriage." Photo of Jacques Danielson and Fannie Hurst from World Wide Photos, 5 May 1920.

New York writer Fannie Hurst and pianist Jacques Danielson (see Figure 4.2), whose 1915 marriage was kept secret until 1920, when Hurst announced that she and Danielson had wed, but that the first year of their union had been probationary and that they still maintained separate residences. In an interview with the *New York Times*, Hurst explained that before meeting Danielson she believed she would never succumb to married life. A romance with Danielson made her reconsider this plan, but not enough to challenge her conviction that she was not cut out for a traditional marriage routine. She explained that upon meeting Danielson, "I found my youthful determination that marriage was not for me suddenly undermined. But my determination that marriage should never lessen my capacity for creative work or pull me down into a sedentary state of fat-mindedness was not undermined."[33]

Arguing that nine out of ten of the marriages around her were "sordid endurance tests, overgrown with the fungi of familiarity and contempt,"

[33] "Fannie Hurst Wed; Hid Secret 5 Years," *New York Times*, 4 May 1920, p. 1.

Hurst sought an arrangement whose luster would not wear off after a few months and become "as a breakfast cloth, stale with soft-boiled-egg stains." In order to avoid that staleness, Hurst and Danielson opted to test out married life for a year, and to part ways if the arrangement proved unpleasant. Five years later, the experiment was still working, and the happy pair decided to publicize their status. The couple emphasized their vow to never cohabitate. They spent as much time together as they saw fit, but neither party felt guilt in dining alone or in making separate social arrangements when the need arose. "We decided that seven breakfasts a week opposite to one another might prove irksome," Hurst explained. "Our average is two." Though childless, Hurst vowed that she and her husband would maintain separate apartments should they bear children, explaining that any child of theirs would take Danielson's name "until reaching the age of discretion, when the decision would lie with him."[34]

Hurst insisted that her marriage was "neither the result of a fad or an 'ism'" but that it was instead a personal effort by two people to forge an arrangement that suited their unique needs. Despite the pride she expressed in having found a setup that worked for her, Hurst displayed a defensive quality when discussing the arrangement, repeating at the end of the interview her "freedom from faddism." "Neither my husband nor I lives in Greenwich Village or wears horn-rimmed spectacles," she assured readers. "My hair reaches to my waist. His is clipped. We believe in love but not Free Love. Rather, we are willing to pay the price in mutual sacrifices toward the preservation of one another's individuality."[35]

This language illustrates Hurst's awareness that her unconventional marriage left her vulnerable to criticism, and she therefore attempted to downplay the radical nature of the relationship. In denouncing free love, she took great pains to present her own romantic arrangement, despite its eccentricity, as more decent than relationships between people who discarded marriage and monogamy altogether. In describing her long hair and her husband's short hair, Hurst made it clear that while she and her husband challenged marital convention, they had no interest in challenging *gender* convention. If anything, their adherence to respectable gender norms allowed them to be bolder in publicizing their alternative marital arrangement. Recognizing the strident condemnations that challenges to

---

[34] Ibid., 1. Hurst and Danielson never had children and thus never tested this theory.
[35] Ibid., 1, 5.

marital permanency, monogamy, and cohabitation could provoke, Hurst sought to avert the media attack she sensed coming her way.[36]

Danielson also deemphasized the radical qualities of the trial marriage. When news agencies began to profile the couple's union, Danielson tended to rearticulate Hurst's stance on the marriage, assuring interrogators that this was a mutual choice that benefited both spouses.[37] His arguments took on a defensive tone a few days later, as he became aware that his domestic situation was attracting great media attention. "In the face of the deluge of comment aroused by Miss Hurst's and my marriage announcement," Danielson wrote in a letter to the *New York Times*, "I find myself constrained to make the following statement, to avoid growing misconceptions on the part of a public apparently eager to stamp with sensationalism the slightest departure, no matter how seriously and conventionally undertaken, from the beaten matrimonial trail."[38]

Following this biting introduction, Danielson painted a picture of his marriage as hardly a departure from the beaten matrimonial trail at all. In emphasizing the amount of time he and Hurst spent at work each day, Danielson presented the desire for labor efficiency as a central reason for this domestic arrangement. "We are both workers," he wrote, "and must devote long evenings to study and reading and practice, so, all in all, I hardly think we can be classified as a pair that has thrown off the responsibilities of the usual marriage ties in order that we may play promiscuously." Danielson then enumerated the standard marital responsibilities in which he and his wife gladly partook. In particular, he stressed Hurst's willingness to tend to him, noting her talent in serving him the homemade dinners prepared by her cook, the comfort she offered him when he came by for an evening visit, and her devotion to nursing him when he was ill.[39]

In addressing his critics, Danielson lodged a critique against those who located radicalism where none existed. He quietly condemned those persons so tied to tradition and appearances that they failed to see the ways in which his marriage fell within their traditional framework. In the process, he highlighted the irrationality of moral crusaders by

---

[36] On other unconventional couples' insistence that they did not support free love, see Eby, *Until Choice Do Us Part*, 51–55.

[37] "Fannie Hurst Secretly Wed," *Los Angeles Times*, 5 May 1920, p. 5.

[38] "Living Apart Cheap, Danielson Says," *New York Times*, 7 May 1920, p. 12.

[39] Ibid., 12. On similar marital experiments that nonetheless reinforced traditional gender roles, see Christine Stansell, *American Moderns: Bohemian New York and the Creation of a New Century* (New York: Henry Holt, 2000), 226–227.

emphasizing the tameness of the arrangement against which they were crusading. While this tactic may have undersold the elements that made his arrangement a true departure from traditional marriage, it also expressed a criticism of those people who would find moral fault with any marriage that did not adhere strictly to Victorian domestic expectations. Furthermore, this stance alerts contemporary readers to the notion that participants in trial marriage, despite the unconventionality of their arrangements, were not necessarily attempting to pose a challenge to traditional matrimony. Rather, Hurst and Danielson defined their trial marriage by contrasting it to free love and bohemianism, arguing that unlike these radical movements, their union posed no threat to sexual and gender convention. They hoped to create a marriage that served their personal needs and to incorporate their trial marriage within the bounds of marital propriety. They had no interest in upending the institution of marriage itself.

Despite Hurst and Danielson's efforts to represent themselves as a typical couple, most commentators denounced the pair for challenging marital convention and for setting a poor example for impressionable young people. In one editorial, writer Corra Harris expressed disdain for this "hocus pocus marriage" and insisted on referring to Hurst as "Mrs. Danielson," even though Hurst had continued to publish under her maiden name. Condemning Hurst and Danielson for their unwillingness to cohabitate, Harris argued that their marriage would have harmful social effects. She maintained that the duty of any married couple was "to live with one another and bear with one another in the customary manner, because if you do not others will follow your example and make a mess of what you claim to have made a success." She continued: "Not even Mrs. Danielson will claim that the way she lives her married life should be the accepted universal way of living in the married relation. She is petting herself, making an exception of herself because she is a professional woman with a career to keep. Nobody's career is so important as one marriage well made."[40] In Harris's view, the potential damage this personalized marriage could inflict upon the greater public outweighed whatever joys Hurst and Danielson culled from it.

Editorialist Edwin Slosson of the *Independent* also worried that Hurst and Danielson's example would cause a moral collapse if it spread too widely. "However well satisfied the couple in question may be with a

---

[40] Corra Harris, "That 'Secret' Marriage," *Independent*, 5 Jun. 1920, pp. 311, 342.

marriage divorced from domesticity," he asserted, "it would be very unfortunate if their example were generally followed, for it would mean the abolition of one of the ancient and valuable institutions of society, the family."[41] Slosson predicted that one couple's decision to rewrite the rules of marriage would lead others to follow suit. While Hurst and Danielson might be able to handle this unconventional arrangement due to their childlessness and affluence, Slosson feared that less advantaged folk were doomed to fail in their efforts to emulate it.

Some critics scoffed not only at Hurst and Danielson's romantic arrangement itself, but also at the couple's wealth and artistic sensibilities. They suggested that no real couple would be able to live this way – just a rich bohemian one. A *Los Angeles Times* columnist took Hurst and Danielson to task for not having children and for claiming that they would hire a nurse to care for any children they might have in the future. Arguing that the challenge of raising a child would make the couple's arrangement impossible, the author noted with sarcasm: "Oh pshaw! That couple never took each other 'for better or worse, for richer or poorer, in sickness or in health, till death do them part.' Real love doesn't shirk tests; it invites them ... And the couple that talk about professional nurses for babies have not enough love."[42]

It was not merely the lack of children that rendered Hurst and Danielson an incomplete couple, this author argued. It was also their upper-class surroundings and their self-imposed shelter from the rougher aspects of New York life. The columnist proclaimed that a marriage could be considered authentic only if a couple endured a wide array of hardships. If during these five years of marriage Hurst and Danielson had "lived together, had three babies, survived the pins and pricks of a scant purse, annual spring cleanings, done the laundry at home, weathered a maidless era, bad cooking, overdue bills, in-laws and several illnesses; if they had seen each other under every handicap, faced a few calamities together, built and paid for a home out of scant earnings – and kept their sweet

---

[41] Edwin E. Slosson, "Semi-Detached Marriage," *Independent*, 8 May 1920, p. 209.

[42] "Marriage a la Mode," *Los Angeles Times*, 8 May 1920, pt. 2, p. 4. The author's hostility toward Hurst and Danielson's childlessness resembles the language of late nineteenth-century critics of abortion and contraception who criticized "fashionable" couples for limiting their procreation. In 1869, for example, writer James Dabney McCabe criticized upper-class couples with few or no children for attempting "to enjoy the blessings of the married state, and to avoid its responsibilities," and he worried that this selfish behavior would lead to the diminution of the native white race. Quoted in Friedman, *Guarding Life's Dark Secrets*, 181.

tempers through it all, with love unimpaired, they might have something to brag about." In the absence of these qualifications, the author concluded, Hurst and Danielson were not married; rather, "so far they have only got a deferred license."[43] In this author's eyes, a childless marriage was not a valid one, nor, it seems, was one between people with enough money to avoid a dirty house, poor health, and a host of other daily struggles.

Some commentators compared Hurst unfavorably with another female celebrity whose marriage had come under fire: movie star Mary Pickford. Pickford, discussed above for her hasty marriage to Douglas Fairbanks after a mutually adulterous affair, was able to improve her public image as a result of these comparisons. As historian Hillary Hallett has noted, Pickford benefited from a public relations campaign that pitted Pickford's commitment to traditional family and domesticity against Hurst's more experimental route. After returning from her honeymoon with Fairbanks, Pickford assured interviewers that her marriage would feature consistent cohabitation and daily family meals that she herself planned to cook. This strategy allowed Pickford and Fairbanks to regain the public's favor, revealing their commitment to marital bliss in spite of their past indiscretions. It simultaneously served to further marginalize Hurst and Danielson, painting their noncohabitation and intermittent contact as an affront to the institution of marriage.[44]

Newspaper columnists were not alone in asserting that a marriage license was insufficient proof of a genuine marriage. Some of the most vocal critics of Hurst and Danielson were prominent members of the legal profession, and they condemned the couple not for breaking formal law but for skirting social convention. One such critic was Chicago judge John McGoorty, who regularly presided over divorce courts. McGoorty denounced the Hurst-Danielson marriage not because it violated state or federal law but because it went against a different type of legal code, "the laws of the home." He considered the marriage "subversive to the building of homes, contrary to the laws of the home and a dangerous proposition viewed from any angle . . . The state of marriage brings with it companionship, cooperation, love and the rearing of children, and Miss

---

[43] "Marriage a La Mode," pt. 2, p. 4
[44] Hallett, *Go West, Young Women!*, 95–96; Gaylyn Studlar, *Precocious Charms: Stars Performing Girlhood in Classical Hollywood Cinema* (Berkeley: University of California Press, 2013), 42–47; "Home Life in California," *New York Times*, 3 Jun. 1920, p. 10.

Hurst's ideas are contrary to the ideal of the home."[45] McGoorty's concerns about the demise of the home reveal the broad social consequences he feared would accompany trial marriage – specifically, a decline in procreation, childrearing, and family life. His remarks illustrate the blurred boundaries between moral and legal critiques of trial marriage. While McGoorty knew that the Hurst-Danielson marriage fit within the boundaries of civil law, he argued that there was a greater moral code that ought to dictate the parameters of private romantic life. His perception of the laws of the home – grounded in his own ideas about gender roles and family structure – trumped his understanding of marriage as a contract between individuals. In other words, his ideological response to the Hurst-Danielson union seems to have overshadowed his knowledge of marriage law itself.

* * *

The wealth of commentary on Hurst and Danielson made them the unwitting sign-bearers of the trial marriage phenomenon. The charges leveled against them emphasized their rejection of proper family life and the economic privilege that allowed them to experiment with marriage and not suffer any material consequences. Sensationalistic news reports on the Hurst marriage and others like it applied the term "trial marriage" to discredit the outlandish romantic trends emerging from rich bohemian circles and to warn the masses against emulating these arrangements. Rather than adopt the term themselves, however, some young working-class couples found the phrase imposed upon them by unsympathetic legal authorities. Early twentieth-century legal records reveal that legislators and judges used the term "trial marriage" to describe nuptials between teenagers who had married hastily and who now hoped to dissolve their unions. At the same time that critics attacked elite couples' trial marriages as exercises in privilege and frivolity, they attacked young working-class couples for entering matrimony prematurely and without sufficient understanding of its obligations. Judges used the phrase "trial marriage" to castigate these teenagers for their impulsiveness and to justify their own decisions to deny young couples the divorces and

---

[45] "Chicago Women Let Miss Hurst Have Her Way," *Chicago Daily Tribune*, 5 May 1920, p. 5. Judge Kenesaw Mountain Landis expressed his opposition to the Hurst-Danielson marriage in a less nuanced manner. When asked if he had an opinion on the marriage, he replied, "I am afraid that under the present postal laws you could not print it if I told you."

annulments they sought, often insisting that the dissolution of these marriages would oppose public policy. At times, judges struggled to reconcile the law's acceptance of some forms of trial marriage with their personal distaste for the practice; the rhetoric of public policy could help them to dodge this dilemma.

In the eyes of jurists, "trial marriage" referred to a union that could be annulled without consequence if the couple ceased cohabiting before the petitioner reached adulthood.[46] Annulment existed as a legal loophole through which couples could terminate their marriages in states with strict divorce laws, such as New Jersey and New York. A husband pursuing annulment alleged that his wife possessed a defect that rendered the marriage invalid. Had he known about this defect from the start, he argued, he would never have exchanged vows. Grounds for annulment might include a wife's premarital pregnancy or unchastity, a husband's bigamy, a spouse's dishonesty about his or her racial identity, an undisclosed physical or mental deficiency, or a mate's frigidity or impotence.[47] In some states, couples could also file for annulment on grounds of infancy, or the argument that one or both spouses had been too young to consent to marriage. Distraught parents sometimes pursued annulments on their children's behalf, insisting that they had not provided consent for their children to marry – often a requirement for minors – and that the young partners were thus not legitimately wed. As more and more underage couples sought annulments on these grounds, legislators began referring to premature unions as trial marriages.[48]

---

[46] See Richmond and Hall, *Child Marriages*, 20. The age of "adulthood" varied from state to state. In their 1925 study, the sociologists indicated that in Kentucky, Louisiana, Virginia, Florida, Maine, Pennsylvania, Rhode Island, Tennessee, Colorado, Idaho, Maryland, Mississippi, New Jersey, and New York the legal minimum age for marriage was fourteen years for boys and twelve for girls. With parental consent, any child could marry after reaching these ages. Until girls turned twenty-one and boys eighteen, the legal exchange of marriage vows required the consent of parents. Young couples were often able to subvert these requirements, however, through both their own designs and the general ineptitude of license bureau workers. See also Syrett, *American Child Bride*.

[47] Joanna L. Grossman and Chris Guthrie, "The Road Less Taken: Annulment at the Turn of the Century," *American Journal of Legal History* 40, no. 3 (1996): 307–330; Grossman and Friedman, *Inside the Castle*, 180–187. See May, *Great Expectations*, 4–5, on the stringency of divorce law in New York and New Jersey.

[48] Grossman and Guthrie, "The Road Less Taken," 315–318. As the authors note, from 1895 to 1906, 28 percent of annulment plaintiffs filed on the grounds of infancy or lack of parental consent. May also indicates that many young men initiated divorce and annulment proceedings because the bride's parents had coerced the groom into marrying their "ruined" or pregnant daughter. *Great Expectations*, 99–100.

The New Jersey Court of Chancery used the term in its 1907 divorce law, noting: "Young men under eighteen years of age are thus permitted to contract a 'trial marriage,' and if the wife be above sixteen years of age, it will be optional with the husband alone to affirm or disaffirm the marriage when he shall reach the age of eighteen years or at any time before."[49] In New York State, a man or woman who separated from a spouse before turning eighteen was permitted by the state's Code of Civil Procedure to annul the marriage, even if parents had given consent to the union.[50] While the New York code did not explicitly label these annulments "trial marriages," several state judges described them as such, often with hostility.[51] As the century progressed, judges displayed a persistent concern over the declining state of marriage and sexual morals in their rulings on youth annulment cases. Just as companionate and bohemian couples had unleashed criticism from journalists for dismissing the permanence of marital vows, this distinct type of "trial marriage" generated similar condemnation from members of the legal profession.

Judges' preoccupation with adolescent marriages fits within a greater context of anxiety over the sexual and romantic lives of young adults. More specifically, an examination of youth trial marriage cases displays a particular uneasiness over the marital practices of young couples from working-class and ethnic communities. The language that judges used in interpreting the annulment laws, and the ways in which this language changed between the 1900s and the 1920s, helps us to see the growing hostility toward the marriage practices of the nonaffluent. As divorce rates rose, and fears over ethnic and working-class proliferation grew, annulments for the underage became less and less common. In the end it was young, inexperienced, and often impoverished brides and grooms who would bear the brunt of these mounting anxieties.

Despite the seemingly straightforward language of the New Jersey divorce law in permitting men under eighteen to dissolve their unions, state judges used discretion in dispensing annulments to minors. For instance, while Vice-Chancellor Eugene Stevenson accepted the right to underage annulment as part of New Jersey's state divorce law in the 1910 case *Titsworth v. Titsworth*, he was reluctant to declare a young

---

[49] *Titsworth v. Titsworth*, 78 N.J. Eq. 47 (1910).

[50] *Mundell v. Coster*, 142 N.Y.S. 142 (1913); Amasa J. Parker, Jr., *Supplement (1907–1912) to the New York Annotated Codes* (New York: Banks Law, 1912), 373–374.

[51] See *Mundell v. Coster*, 142 N.Y.S. 142 (1913); *Lazarczyk v. Lazarczyk*, 203 N.Y.S. 291 (1924).

male plaintiff's marriage voidable, and he found a way to dismiss his petition for annulment. Stevenson admitted that as a husband under the age of eighteen, the plaintiff should have been entitled to an annulment. He contended, however, that the high stakes of this case – particularly the burden that annulment might thrust upon the abandoned bride – left it open to increased scrutiny. He explained: "Where a petitioner in a case like this invokes this statutory remedy which disrupts the marriage relation under the common law and the law of nature, while it leaves his perhaps innocent victim bearing a heavy burden, which may greatly mar her entire life, public policy demands that the case must be clearly proved, and the best evidence of the pre-eminently essential fact must be presented." With this caveat, Stevenson ruled that David Titsworth had not submitted sufficient evidence to verify that he was underage and that therefore he could not be granted an annulment in good confidence.[52]

Admitting that the law permitted trial marriage for minors, Stevenson rejected the plaintiff's position on evidentiary grounds. His language suggested deeper motivations. He reasoned: "The effects of a decree of nullity in a case like this upon the defendant and upon society, upon the institution of marriage as heretofore recognized by our laws and customs, are too important and far reaching to permit such a decree to be based upon the testimony of interested witnesses."[53] One might view Stevenson's concerns about the case's effects on society and the institution of marriage as an indication that moral concerns trumped his desire to let the New Jersey divorce law of 1907 dictate the case's verdict. His language suggests a tension between the law's acceptance of changes to the marriage state and his own belief that it was in the interest of public policy to preserve marital tradition. Expressing regret over the growing embrace of dissolvable marriage, Stevenson used his judicial authority to keep one particular marriage intact.

Other New Jersey judges were more willing to accept the divorce law of 1907 without qualification. In a 1917 Court of Appeals case, Justice Thomas Trenchard reversed a lower court ruling and granted an annulment to the male plaintiff, who had been shy of eighteen when he married his twenty-year-old wife. The couple did not cohabit after the ceremony. Previously the lower court had dismissed the petition, holding that because the plaintiff's parents had consented to his marriage, it was no longer voidable. Trenchard and the Court of Appeals disagreed, citing the

---

[52] *Titsworth v. Titsworth*, 78 N.J. Eq. 47 (1910).   [53] Ibid.

1907 divorce law to explain that a husband was legally entitled to annul his marriage if he had wed under the age of eighteen. In this straightforward ruling, Trenchard acknowledged the place of underage annulment within New Jersey's family laws.[54]

With this ruling, Trenchard maintained that civil law ought to overshadow public policy concerns. He insisted that the New Jersey divorce code was clear in allowing underage annulments, and he thus warned judges against letting moral concerns overshadow the straightforward letter of the law.[55] But not all New Jersey judges agreed that the law spoke for itself, and one ruling in particular displayed the range of factors that shaped annulment decisions. In an opinion issued in an early stage of the 1921 case *Gibbs v. Gibbs*, Vice-Chancellor Malcolm Buchanan questioned the male petitioner's right to an annulment. Charles Gibbs had married the older Carcline Jablowski before he turned eighteen. He had falsely claimed to be twenty-two years old, and now he wanted the marriage voided on grounds that he had wed while below the age of consent. In assessing the plaintiff's allegations, Buchanan stated that the divorce law did not automatically nullify minors' marriages. "The purpose is to discourage marriages in which one or both parties are of immature age," he maintained. "But it is only to discourage – not prohibit, inasmuch as the statute does not make them void ... Indeed, in certain instances, such as seduction cases, the state by its statutes encourages the marriage."[56] Buchanan did not accuse Gibbs of seduction, the act of enticing a woman to consent to sexual intercourse with the false promise of marriage.[57] He did, however, accuse Gibbs of deceit. Presuming that Jablowski would not have married Gibbs had she known of his youth – and had she thus realized she was entering into a trial marriage – Buchanan refused to grant an annulment to a young man whose nuptials were founded on lies.

Most striking here is Buchanan's discussion of the fate that would befall the bride were she to become a young divorcee. Reflecting widespread anxiety over mounting divorce rates, Buchanan envisioned a bleak future for a divorced Carcline Jablowski:

A certain "loss of caste" is, under the conditions of our social fabric, almost inevitably visited upon a divorced wife, even though she be entirely free from guilt

---

[54] *Taub v. Taub*, 87 N.J. Eq. 624 (1917).   [55] Ibid.

[56] *Gibbs v. Gibbs*, 92 N.J. Eq. 542 (1921).

[57] Haag, *Consent*, 3–24; Stephen Robertson, "Seduction, Sexual Violence, and Marriage in New York City, 1886–1955," *Law and History Review* 24, no. 2 (2006): 334.

or wrong of any kind ... Common report or gossip ... concerns itself much with the fact that a woman has been divorced, but concerns itself little, if at all, to spread the fact of her innocence in regard to such divorce. Again, even if there be no child of the marriage, her subsequent opportunity for marriage is very greatly decreased. Many men from religious belief or personal grounds will decline to entertain the idea of marriage with one who has been the wife of another.[58]

As this case shows, New Jersey judges could use discretion in granting annulments to underage couples, in spite of the trial marriage loophole in the state's divorce law. While judges like Trenchard viewed the youth annulment provision as a law to be applied with uniformity, others allowed public policy concerns – such as the future marital prospects of divorcees – to shape their interpretations of marriage law.

In some cases, judges' personal objection to the idea of "trial marriage" seems to have had the greatest influence on their annulment rulings. An examination of New York underage annulment cases helps to demonstrate this growing legal and judicial resistance to trial marriage as an option for youth. A pair of cases from 1909 and 1912 reveals judges' initial belief that divorce and annulment could rescue young people from impulsive romantic decisions. In the first of these cases, New York Supreme Court Justice Charles Wheeler granted an annulment to plaintiff Marion Mitchell, a teenage bride who had fled to Canada to wed Elton Mitchell before returning to New York. Wheeler asserted that marriage was central to the foundation of the family and civilization at large and that the public ought to hold a deep interest in the maintenance of pure marriages. As such, he believed that society would benefit from the dissolution of this particular union. He wrote: "This State has seen fit, in its wisdom, to discourage marriages contracted by immature persons, who have not reached the age of consent, and has provided for the annulment of such marriages under certain circumstances and conditions." In Wheeler's view, the termination of this inappropriate marriage would serve the interests of the imprudent couple, the members of their community, and the institution of marriage itself.[59]

Three years later, New York Court of Appeals Judge Albert Haight similarly ruled that Anna and William Cunningham could have their brief marriage annulled. The New York couple had wed in New Jersey in 1910 – he was around forty years old, and she had yet to turn eighteen. Haight prefaced his ruling by noting that marriage contracts "have

---

[58] *Gibbs v. Gibbs*, 92 N.J. Eq. 542 (1921).
[59] *Mitchell v. Mitchell*, 117 N.Y.S. 671 (1909).

always been considered as involving questions of public policy, and the interests of others than those of the contracting parties"; his decision therefore needed to consider the well-being of the public and not just the needs of this specific couple. In the end, Haight sought to satisfy both interests. Noting that the bride had wed while under the age of legal consent, without parental approval, and outside her home state, Haight ruled that this intergenerational marriage was "repugnant to our public policy and legislation," and he cleared the path to its dissolution.[60] As these cases illustrate, questions about public policy factored into 1910s annulment rulings, and judges tended to present annulment of underage marriage as a socially beneficial act that freed the public of immoral and inappropriate unions. While some of these judges acknowledged the controversy surrounding underage annulments – among them Justice Daniel Cohalan, who admitted that the policy was "to all intents and purposes providing in such cases for trial marriages" – their rulings reflected the belief that it was better to erase these youthful mistakes than to prolong them.[61]

But as public concern over trial marriage mounted, and as sensationalistic news stories about the phenomenon began to circulate with regularity, New York's laws changed to subdue the practice. Responding in part to the growing concern that divorce and annulment rates had gotten out of hand, the New York State legislature amended its Domestic Relations Law in 1922 to make trial marriage a less feasible option for underage partners. The amendment stated that a bride's or groom's minor status alone could no longer justify the annulment of a marriage; thereafter the judge needed to consider the marriage as a whole, the circumstances that had led to matrimony, and the case's influence on society before deciding the couple's fate. In 1923's *Todaro v. Todaro*, the first prominent New York case of this nature to arise in the wake of the amendment, Justice

---

[60] *Cunningham v. Cunningham*, 206 N.Y. 341 (1912).

[61] *Mundell v. Coster*, 142 N.Y.S. 142 (1913). There were exceptions to this general tolerance for underage annulment in New York in the 1910s. Judge Vernon Davis avoided placing his stamp of approval on trial marriage in one 1918 case. Despite his view that trial marriage or, as he called it, "legalized concubinage for an indefinite period" was "abhorrent to the well-recognized sanctity of the marriage status," Davis admitted that he was required to recognize it if claims of underage marriage were legitimate. Fortunately for Davis, the male plaintiff had lied about his age, telling his wife that he was twenty-one when he was really just twenty and therefore, according to New York State law, a minor. Davis dismissed the husband's complaint on the grounds that this deceit invalidated his right to an annulment. *Bays v. Bays*, 174 N.Y.S. 212 (1918).

John Tierney refused to grant an annulment because he believed the couple in question could find contentment with proper effort. In this case, Rose Todaro sought an annulment from her husband, Giovanni Todaro. She had married at the age of fourteen, but with her mother's advice she had informed the officiator that she was nineteen. At age seventeen Rose wanted legal leave of her nuptials.[62]

Tierney was unsympathetic to Rose's request. Invoking the amendment to the Domestic Relations Law, Tierney explained that the state legislature aimed to decrease the number of trial marriages and that marriages between minors could no longer be annulled merely at the couple's insistence.[63] While he did not explain why the preservation of this unhappy marriage was beneficial to public policy, he used his judicial authority to keep it intact. Noting that Rose Todaro had not been seduced, entrapped, or coerced into marriage, the judge saw no justification for an annulment apart from her youth, which under the new law was insufficient to terminate a marriage. Chastising both the plaintiff and her mother for lying about the bride's age, Tierney saw no reason why husband and wife should live apart. "If this marriage is entitled to be annulled because of the plaintiff's non-age," he wrote, "the amendment of the statute would be futile and the law might as well have been left as it was." With that he dismissed Rose's complaint.[64]

Perhaps the definitive case on the subject, tried by the New York Supreme Court of Oneida County in December of 1923 and then again in February of 1924, involved the marriage of Lottie and Stanislaw Lazarczyk. In this case, Lottie, the daughter of Polish immigrants, sought an annulment after having married and given birth before reaching the age of eighteen. In his ruling on the first trial, Judge Louis Martin, like Tierney before him, noted that the amendment to the New York Domestic Relations Law had endeavored to dissuade couples like the Lazarczyks from ending their marriages on a whim. Lottie would therefore need to illustrate grounds for annulment that went beyond the question of age, as her youth was not, under the new amendment, sufficient cause for her marriage to be deemed voidable. The fact that Lottie had borne a son only

---

[62] *Todaro v. Todaro*, 200 N.Y.S. 567 (1923).

[63] Ibid. Tierney wrote: "It is obviously the intention of the legislature to abolish the license afforded by the prior state of the law to permit persons under eighteen years of age to make trial marriages which they could repudiate without penalty. It recognizes that a marriage may be validly contracted by a person under that age that public policy dictates should not be annulled at the mere desire of the parties."

[64] Ibid.

damaged her case, further convincing the judge that husband and wife could not separate without creating disastrous social repercussions.[65]

In his ruling, Judge Martin noted that before 1 September 1922, the court had been beholden to rule in favor of any underage plaintiff pursuing annulment, assuming that there had been no cohabitation after the eighteenth birthday. Martin viewed the amendment to the Domestic Relations Law as a strict response to the chaos that ensued. In the days before the amendment, he explained, "Special Terms and official referees were burdened with a large number of this class of cases. It was practically putting the official approval of the court on trial marriage. Young people of immature age had no restraint; they would contract a marriage and if not suited with the result, would, after a time, apply to the court and obtain an annulment on statutory grounds." According to Martin, this practice "resulted in lowering the standard of the marriage contract, made it a farce, and was in direct conflict with the teachings of the church to which many participants belonged; a condition in society that courts would not tolerate if they had the power to prevent." This statement is striking in its appeal to religious principles as a driving force for legislative and judicial action. Furthermore, it illustrates a common fear that the marriage contract itself was altered, and in this case cheapened, by the rise of provisional marital practices. This simultaneous recognition that marriage could change, coupled with a conviction that it ought not to, drove legal and judicial minds to beat back the rule-breakers at all costs. If the law permitted or encouraged the cheapening of the marriage contract, then the law must be changed.[66]

It should thus be no surprise that Martin denied Lottie Lazarczyk's motion. Citing the *Todaro* case and praising the Domestic Relations Law's efforts "to remedy this growing evil," Martin maintained that there had been no fraud in the Lazarczyks' procurement of their marriage license; Stanislaw had not seduced, deceived, or coerced Lottie into marrying him, and she had attained consent from her parents due to her underage status. Neither Lottie's youth nor her general unhappiness in the marriage concerned Martin. "The unfortunate disagreements are not serious," he concluded, "but are the direct results of two young people entering into a solemn contract, the continuing of which is not

---

[65] *Lazarczyk v. Lazarczyk*, 201 N.Y.S. 816 (1923); 1930 U.S. Federal Census, Lottie Szablak, Utica Ward 11, Oneida County, New York. Accessed through Ancestry.com (database online).

[66] Ibid.

surrounded by that romance which they had anticipated. Neither party was properly fitted by training to enter upon the marriage relation, and assume the burden of married life; but having assumed it, they must abide by the result." Satisfied with his findings, Martin provided these parting words to judges who might face similar questions in future cases: "Courts should in the future, and no doubt will, exercise extreme care in these cases, and unless sufficient facts and circumstances surrounding the marriage are shown to justify a finding of annulment, outside of mere nonage, will refuse a decree." Amid growing demands for divorce and annulment, Martin hoped to deter other judges from enabling future trial marriages between young and naïve couples.[67]

Although Martin refused to grant Lottie Lazarczyk the annulment that she pursued, he did permit her to bring a second action due to her claim that she could offer new evidence. The case was retried two months later in the courtroom of Judge Ernest Edgcomb, who rejected upfront Lottie's new allegation that Stanislaw had used fraud and duress to attain her consent. He did, however, investigate Lottie's claim that Stanislaw had been violent on one occasion, but he did not view this occurrence as a detriment to the marriage, stating that one act of violence did not jeopardize Lottie's general safety, nor did it portend future violence. Like Martin, he denied that "misunderstandings, bickerings and quarrels between a married couple" were sufficient grounds for the dissolution of a union.[68] As in previous cases, which Edgcomb noted had "become altogether too frequent of late," the plaintiff's youth was insufficient to win her an annulment, and charges of abuse and irreconcilable differences did nothing to enhance her case in the eyes of the court.[69]

Moving quickly from these technical points, Edgcomb proceeded with a lecture on the deteriorating state of marriage. He praised the 1922 amendment for denying underage couples the right to engage in trial marriage, insisting that the court was obligated to preserve permanency and monogamy as the marital status quo:

Public policy demands that the court should refuse to put its stamp of approval on trial marriages. The marriage contract is looked upon by the law as the most sacred one which can be made. It should be kept inviolate. Without marriage, and

---

[67] Ibid.
[68] Here Edgcomb quoted his own ruling from two months prior, in which he had denied a petition by a wife seeking legal separation from an allegedly abusive husband. *Wendt v. Wendt*, 202 N.Y.S. 46 (1923).
[69] *Lazarczyk v. Lazarczyk*, 203 N.Y.S. 291 (1924).

without the sanctity of the contract there can be no ideal family or family life. The home and the family are the very basis upon which our civilization rests ... No community can long endure where family ties are forgotten and where marriages can be dissolved for the asking, and where free love runs rampant.

Refusing to let sympathy for Lottie Lazarczyk's misfortune overwhelm his desire to maintain the vision of marriage dictated, in his mind, by church and state, Edgcomb rejected her complaint, stating: "It is better that a few be made to suffer and to lie in the bed which they voluntarily made, than to break down the walls which the church and civilization has built up about the marriage contract." He concluded that despite her being sixteen at the time of marriage, Lottie had made a conscious decision to exchange vows, and she should not be treated as a victim for a choice that she alone had made. He did not offer any judicial precedent to explain the court's responsibility to preserve his vision of civilization and proper family life. By vaguely attributing his ruling to the demands of public policy, Edgcomb was able to grant judicial authority to his views about marriage, sexuality, and Christian morality and to fend off threats to these personal ideologies.[70]

It is clear from Edgcomb's ruling that he wished to make an example of a foolish young couple, revealing that adolescent mistakes still had consequences and that marriage must not be entered into impulsively. He also expressed concern that the marriage of underage women was a problem that primarily plagued "a certain class of foreigners, who now constitute a large portion of the inhabitants of many of our cities." While Stanislaw Lazarczyk's origins are unclear, and Lottie was born in New York, perhaps her status as the daughter of Polish immigrants and the ethnic sound of her surname were sufficient grounds for Edgcomb to include her among the "foreigners" who disrupted the marital order. The judge's statements here reveal a greater concern with increased rates of separation among immigrants and their descendants, which Edgcomb hoped to temper by forcing long-term unions.[71]

---

[70] Ibid. Edgcomb invoked the language of public policy again in a 1927 case, in which he denied another underage woman the right to an annulment. He wrote: "Public policy will not permit one to grasp the benefits of a marriage contract with no intent to live up to its obligations, and the next minute throw it aside and ask for a destruction of the very status which he has insisted upon creating." In a later passage he stated: "To dissolve this marriage under the circumstances would, in my opinion, have a tendency to be injurious to the public good." In neither passage did he explain how the public would suffer from the annulment of this union, nor did he present any legislation or judicial precedent to support these assertions. *Smith v. Smith*, 221 N.Y.S. 672 (1927).

[71] See Richmond and Hall, *Child Marriages*, 36–40. Statistical information on underage marriage among immigrants does not bear out these concerns. The authors examined the

Judges like Edgecomb were likely driven to some extent by economic motivations in denying divorces and annulments to underage couples. Perhaps they worried that if a marriage were terminated, the former wife, possibly a mother, would become a public charge who depended upon the state for a living wage. Marriage, which obligated the husband to fill a breadwinning role whether he wanted to or not, prevented this dependence on public charity and compelled the wife to rely on the private support of her husband. The youth, poverty, and lack of formal education that many plaintiff wives displayed may have only bolstered judges' assumptions that with the loss of marital status, these women would soon be reliant upon the state for sustenance.[72]

The rhetoric applied in these judicial rulings indicates, however, that judges were driven by more than just financial concerns. Edgecomb's claim that "no community can long endure where family ties are forgotten and where marriages can be dissolved for the asking, and where free love runs rampant" illustrates a moral justification for the denial of underage annulments. Like the clergy, columnists, and social reformers who denounced Elsie Clews Parsons's writings out of the belief that they endangered the standard of monogamous marriage, Edgecomb denied Lottie Lazarczyk her annulment out of conviction that the dissolution of marital ties would lead to social chaos and moral decay. Strikingly, this fear of disorder seemed to wane when 1920s New York judges made underage annulment rulings on marriages that did not involve two working-class individuals. For instance, Judge William Dowling expressed little reservation in annulling the marriage between college-bound Geraldine Mathewson, daughter of a prominent physician, and Edward Mathewson, a high school dropout who sold household appliances for a living. Dowling emphasized the fact that Geraldine had only

---

1920 census to approximate the percentage of women who married between the ages of fifteen and nineteen within broad ethnic categories. They found the rate to be 13.3 percent among the white daughters of native parents, 6.3 percent among the native white daughters of foreign parents, 14.3 percent among foreign-born white immigrants, and 20 percent among the black population. The authors questioned the accuracy of the statistical data on African American marriages.

[72] See Anna R. Igra, *Wives Without Husbands: Marriage, Desertion, and Welfare in New York, 1900–1935* (Chapel Hill: University of North Carolina Press, 2007), 42–44. Igra emphasizes reformers' desire to return fugitive husbands to the homes they had fled so that their wives and children would cease to be public charges of the state. As only the most impoverished women were eligible for anti-desertion support, the greatest efforts to maintain stable marriage were directed toward poor communities, frequently ones with high immigrant populations.

been seventeen when she married the twenty-year-old Edward, insisting that the bride "did not know her own mind; that she was really beside herself in her mad infatuation for him; that there was never any real love existing between them; that she is only a child."[73] Lottie Lazarczyk's youth did not seem to arouse these compassionate feelings in the judges who ruled on her case.

In Dowling's eyes, the marriage between Geraldine and Edward was inappropriate due to the couple's divergent class backgrounds. Dowling repeatedly cited this distinction in family wealth and education, declaring, "The difference in status of this couple is such now that a successful marriage resting on a true family relation is impossible." He thus granted the couple an annulment, suggesting that the two could remarry in a few years if Edward returned to school and used his education to attain a white-collar job. Dowling concluded by stating that an annulment would serve the best interests "of this young couple, of their parents and of the public."[74] In light of the general hostility with which New York courts viewed underage annulment in the 1920s, it is striking to see a judge's suggestion that a cross-class union would have an even more negative impact on public policy than its termination. The sympathy shown to Geraldine Dowling puts the opposition that Lottie Lazarczyk encountered into sharp focus. It helps us to see the role that class resentment and nativism could play in shaping trial marriage rulings, and it emphasizes judges' efforts to regulate the sexual behaviors of poorer Americans – both by halting their unions to more affluent partners and by forcing them to remain wed to their economic equals.

* * *

It was from this messy context that Ben Lindsey emerged with his push for companionate marriage. Though his home state of Colorado permitted judges to annul weddings between partners who had not yet reached the age of twenty-one, Lindsey likely would not have approved of the Lazarczyks' separation for the simple fact that Lottie and Stanislaw had a child.[75] But Lindsey stood to empower a different type of couple with his

---

[73] *Retan v. Mathewson*, 226 N.Y.S. 80 (1927).
[74] Ibid. See also *Foley v. Foley*, 203 N.Y.S. 674 (1924). This case permitted an annulment between a couple due to religious differences, displaying another instance in which a judge viewed a marriage between two inappropriate partners as even more harmful to society than its dissolution.
[75] Lindsey and Evans, *The Companionate Marriage*, 74, 172.

call for friendship, intimacy, and communication between husband and wife, enjoyment of sex, and use of birth control. As long as the husband and wife remained childless, Lindsey argued, they should be entitled to divorce, generally without payment of alimony, if the relationship soured.[76] He also called for sex education and the recognition of sexual intimacy as a central part of any romantic relationship, and not just a procreative act. According to historian Christina Simmons, this system encouraged couples to marry early, before the husband had necessarily adapted to the breadwinner role he would be expected to fill once children came along. In the meantime, women were permitted to seek education, to work, and to retain some independence before devoting themselves to childcare. Once the husband and wife had become comfortable in their married roles, they would begin to have children and to live as a traditional couple.[77]

Lindsey was adamant in proclaiming that companionate marriage was not the same as trial marriage. "*Technically* the Companionate and Trial Marriage have certain features in common," Lindsey admitted, "but *one* is not the *other*. Both would normally avail themselves of Birth Control and divorce by mutual consent. Both would place a minimum of obstruction in the way of childless couples wishing a divorce. And both recognize the fact that when men and women marry they can never be perfectly certain that their marriage will turn out to be a permanent success. But there the similarity ends." Lindsey explained that couples would enter companionate marriages with the full intention of making the relationship permanent. Divorce would remain an option for childless spouses, but unlike trial marriage, the couple would not view the union as an experiment and would strive for a lifelong union.[78]

---

[76] Davis, "Not Marriage at All," 1142–1143.

[77] Simmons, *Making Marriage Modern*, 121–122.

[78] Lindsey and Evans, *The Companionate Marriage*, xxiv–xxv. In a later passage, Lindsey referred to trial marriages as "free love unions," taking great pains to differentiate this practice from companionate marriage: "I trust I make it clear why I object to having the Companionate confused with this kind of thing. *The Companionate is legal marriage; and every childless marriage wherein, by mutual agreement, the parties can obtain a divorce if they want it, is a Companionate.* In other words, the Companionate is a firmly established, perfectly respectable institution among us right now. Childless couples are socially respectable, and they are as much married as any one else. There is no 'trial marriage' about it" (ibid., 140–141). See Davis, "Not Marriage at All," 1144, for further examination of Lindsey's efforts, in Davis's eyes less than successful, to distance "companionate marriage" from "trial marriage."

In this way, Lindsey presented companionate marriage as a happy medium between the crushing strictures of traditional marriage and the formless free-for-all of trial marriage. Noting the allegedly impure intentions of folks establishing trial marriages, he presented his own program as a sane alternative in its dedication to marital success. In articulating the merits of companionate marriage, Lindsey explained that if a young husband and wife took time to get to know one another and to verify their compatibility before having children – knowing that an escape route existed if the effort proved a failure – they would have a greater chance of finding long-term happiness together. In predicting this hypothetical couple's happy ending, Lindsey wrote: "When they finally did have a family, the chance of that home breaking up would be very slight indeed. Thus the number of marriages would *increase*; and the number of divorces and broken homes would *decrease*. At present divorces are increasing. Here is a way to stop it."[79]

As this brief passage demonstrates, Lindsey viewed the spread of companionate marriage as an antidote to the spread of divorce. A wide array of critics feared that his work would have the reverse effect. Opponents of companionate marriage – which they tended to conflate indiscriminately with "trial marriage," despite Lindsey's protestations – included Catholic, Protestant, and Jewish clergymen, university professors, and jurists. In a speech given to commemorate the one hundredth birthday of the late Morgan Dix, that fierce critic of Elsie Clews Parsons twenty years prior, New York Episcopal Bishop William T. Manning called upon his parishioners to uphold Dix's legacy of fighting against all challenges to the marriage institution. Manning proclaimed that "the Apostles of Liberalism," namely those fighting for companionate and trial marriages, were "an outrage against the law of God, a shame and dishonor to the time in which they live and an insult to all decent manhood and womanhood." He evoked Morgan Dix's "fearless and constant witness for the sacredness of marriage and the home," and he recalled Dix's warnings against the crumbling standards of marriage and the ever-growing divorce rate. Nearly twenty years after Dix's death, Manning saw further signs that matrimony was in decline through young couples' embrace of companionate marriage. It was up to God-fearing Christians to defy these temptations and renounce Lindsey's message.[80]

---

[79] Lindsey and Evans, *The Companionate Marriage*, 138.
[80] "Manning Assails Trial Marriages," *New York Times*, 7 Nov. 1927, p. 32.

Other critics spoke in similar moral terms. Rabbi Nathan Krass took companionate couples to task for being concerned merely with their own gratification and for ignoring marriage's greater purpose of serving God and community. He argued, "The chief purpose of marriage is not personal happiness, but the dedication of one individual to another and of two individuals to the good of society and to divine law." In Krass's view, semi-committed couples were not fulfilling those obligations.[81] In a 1928 lecture to Chicago's Sunday Evening Club, New York Baptist Minister Harry Emerson Fosdick similarly suggested that companionate marriage was bred in the selfish notion that marriage was first and foremost for personal pleasure and contentment. Relating the trend to the purchase of shoes, he explained, "If at first one does not get a good fit, he tries again until he does. The companionate marriage ... has slipped until it is now only a trial marriage, an experimentation in sexual experiences."[82] Lindsey's belief that marriage ought to be a pleasurable experience for husband and wife and that sex could serve the purpose of leisure, and not merely procreation, was a great departure from the traditional notion of marriage as a sacred, communal obligation. His acceptance of pre-procreative divorce only further enraged marital purists.

Criticism like this was not limited to the clergy, and professors and legal scholars were often the most dramatic in their attacks on companionate marriage. W. H. P. Faunce, president of Brown University, argued, "That kind of marriage means woman reduced to slavery [and] children left to public asylums," ignoring Lindsey's desire that divorce be available only to childless couples.[83] Judge Joseph Sabath of Chicago, who had overseen numerous divorce trials, also rejected Lindsey's agenda. Like the judges who spoke out against the Hurst-Danielson marriage, Sabath evoked religious dogma to make his case. He advised, "My warning to young people and the parents who may approve and encourage Judge Lindsey's theory is to disregard it and continue to look upon marriage as the most sacred institution on God's earth." While he admitted that divorce was appropriate in some cases, he worried that Lindsey's idea would increase the nation's divorce rate to alarming heights.[84]

---

[81] "Rabbi Denounces Companionate Marriage," *New York Times*, 28 Nov. 1927, p. 24.
[82] "Fosdick Raps 'Trial' Union," *New York Times*, 30 Jan. 1928, p. 8.
[83] "Companionate Tie Is Called Slavery," *New York Times*, 20 Aug. 1928, p. 14.
[84] "Judge Sabath Scores Lindsey Marriage Plan," *Chicago Daily Tribune*, 26 Nov. 1927, p. 17.

But Lindsey had stated all along his intention to reduce the number of divorces. While he and Sabath disagreed over which methods should be applied to this end, they both desired the same results. As opposition grew, Lindsey's claims to the conservatism of his agenda only increased. He admitted that he saw imperfections in the form that marriage was taking, but it was his very belief in the centrality of the institution that led him to seek improvements. "Because I care so much for the sanctity and permanence of the American home," he explained in an editorial, "I am bitterly opposed to 'free love,' and so called 'trial marriage' as they exist under the present marriage code. Most of the present marriage code I of course heartily approve."[85]

Lindsey's insistence that his plan would yield happier marriages and lower divorce rates provided little comfort to critics, who scoffed at the very idea of easily attainable divorce. In this regard, Lindsey's ideas suffered the same fate as Elsie Clews Parsons's brief musing on trial marriage two decades prior. As Parsons had learned in 1906, the notion of conditional marriage – a childless cohabitation with an aim toward permanent union – would be met with scorn from those seeking to temper the divorce rate and who failed to recognize that Parsons sought the very same objective. Twenty-one years later, Ben Lindsey would fall into the same trap. His vision of widely available birth control, marital intimacy, and easy access to divorce for childless couples would be excoriated by critics who refused to acknowledge that Lindsey's larger goal of creating happy and long-lasting unions often resembled their own. In some ways, then, moral authorities undermined their own quest to improve the quality, quantity, and duration of marriages by rejecting the ideas of scholars who sought creative means to similar ends.

An aversion to divorce and a sense of panic over changing gender conventions and sexual morals lay at the root of efforts to eliminate all relationships that might be identified as trial marriage. The term itself did not distinguish between the varied forms of provisional matrimony. Again, it encompassed conditional unions between childless individuals, as proposed by Parsons and Lindsey; it could serve as an experimental or noncohabitative substitute for the stifling bonds of traditional matrimony, as practiced by Hurst and Danielson; or it could describe an escape from vows that had been hastily exchanged before the parties had even reached the age of consent, as we know from Lottie Lazarczyk's efforts at flight.

---

[85] "Editorials by Our Readers," *Independent Record* (Helena), 3 Feb. 1927, p. 5.

Despite the vastly different experiences and worldviews of the various champions of trial marriage, their actions and words prompted the same hostile outcries from conservative critics. Rarely was "trial marriage" a phrase that actual couples chose to label their exploits. But the consistent return to the term as a public demarcation of social and sexual depravity linked these diverse intentions and behaviors in their general opposition to public policy.

Class distinctions ensured that couples would experience the effects of anti–trial marriage sentiment in different ways. Lindsey's vision would have encompassed the Hurst-Danielson arrangement but would have denied divorce to Lottie and Stanislaw Lazarczyk, who had borne a child and who therefore, in accordance with Lindsey's theory and, more importantly, with New York state law, were obliged to remain married. While Hurst and Danielson had access to contraception throughout their years together, birth control was less often a possibility for working-class couples, who often lacked the funds to purchase condoms and diaphragms or lacked access to adequate medical information about contraceptive options.[86] Unequal access to birth control across class lines ensured that poorer couples would bear more children, and the birth of children almost guaranteed that couples like the Lazarczyks, despite their youth and the legal right to annulment on the grounds of non-age, would be forced to remain legally married.

While public discourse on trial marriage centered on academic figures like Parsons and Lindsey and celebrities like Fannie Hurst, trial marriage was perhaps most relevant to women like Lottie Lazarczyk, who at sixteen had the most at stake in her efforts to become a single woman. Hurst was financially and socially stable to the degree that, had her marriage to Danielson imploded, she would have possessed the resources to fend for herself without fear of becoming a dependent of the state. Critics therefore could not treat her as an economic risk, but they could question her moral judgment and raise concerns that her view of marriage would lead to crisis if embraced by too many impressionable and disadvantaged persons. When sixteen-year-old Lottie married Stanislaw Lazarczyk in 1922, the chances that the example set by Fannie Hurst and Jacques Danielson factored into her plans are remote. But in a way, Lottie's later effort to annul the marriage could be used as evidence of columnist Edwin Slosson's prophecy that trial marriage among the elite

---

[86] Leslie J. Reagan, *When Abortion Was a Crime: Women, Medicine, and Law in the United States, 1867–1973* (Berkeley: University of California Press, 1997), 40–41.

paved the way for trial marriage among the masses.[87] And these connections, however artificially drawn, vindicated efforts by New York lawmakers to tighten the divorce code and to put an end to one specific form of trial marriage in an effort to make marriage itself that much more resistant to collapse. It would be the penniless, and not the cultural elites and subjects of gossip columns, who would struggle most in the face of these legal changes.

By denying underage couples the opportunity to contract trial marriages, Judge Edgcomb and his robed colleagues did their part to warn young people against forming reckless unions and to fend off the "free love" principles that threatened to overtake traditional romantic values.[88] A judge's refusal to grant an annulment meant that the couple would for the time being remain legally married. It did not mean, however, that the couple would continue to live as husband and wife.[89] Despite Edgcomb's belief that Lottie and Stanislaw could work out their problems and live happily together, Lottie refused to reconcile. Six years after Edgcomb issued his verdict, Lottie was living as a single woman in her parents' home. Her family provided the 1930 census with her maiden name, Lottie Szablak, and offered no indication that she had ever been married. Under the category of "marriage condition" Lottie had offered an "s" for single. She provided no response to the question of "age at first marriage," suggesting that none had ever taken place. Perhaps in the years between the trial and census Lottie had attained an annulment or a divorce in a different state, but her employment at a suspender factory would suggest an absence of funds for a costly, migratory divorce.[90] More likely, in refusing to reunite with Stanislaw, Lottie granted herself an annulment of the psychological variety. As she ceased to honor the marriage contract that Edgcomb and Martin had declined to terminate, she decreed that her marriage was indeed a trial marriage, with or without validation from the court.

In 1930 Lottie Szablak viewed herself as a single woman, and at age twenty-four she was living in her parents' home, with no husband to speak of. As for her child, there is no clear evidence. Maybe Stanislaw had taken

---

[87] Slosson, "Semi-Detached Marriage," 209.

[88] *Lazarczyk v. Lazarczyk*, 203 N.Y.S. 291 (1924).

[89] See Hartog, *Man and Wife in America*, on the limitations of formal law in dictating the actual marital arrangements that nineteenth-century couples constructed.

[90] 1930 US Federal Census, Lottie Szablak, Utica Ward 11, Oneida County, New York. Accessed through Ancestry.com. On migratory divorces, see Blake, *The Road to Reno*, 116–129; Hartog, *Man and Wife in America*, 258–286; Friedman, "A Dead Language," 1501–1508.

over parental duties, or maybe the child had died in the six years after the trial. Perhaps Benjamin Szablak, listed in the 1930 census as the child of Alexander and Paulina Szablak, was not Lottie's brother but, in fact, the son from her former union, being raised by her parents as their own. One can only speculate, but the point is that in spite of Judge Edgcomb's orders that the marriage remain intact, Lottie and Stanislaw's broken union could not be reconstructed with mere orders from the court. In the wake of a ruling that denied her the right to reclaim her person from the grips of a marriage she did not want, Lottie was able to create some sort of familial arrangement that defied the judge's orders and that, one hopes, provided her more satisfaction than life as a captive bride ever could have.[91]

As the above array of examples illustrates, anti–trial marriage rhetoric reveals the threat that provisional nuptial arrangements posed to traditional conceptions of marriage. Opponents of trial marriage sought to condemn those couples who shaped the parameters of their own relationships and who claimed the right to end their marriages should the romance fade. For Lottie Szablak, the only way to carve out a domestic arrangement that defied public policy was to withdraw into the private realm – to impersonate the unmarried status she so desired and to hope that naysayers overlooked her indiscretions. In this regard, it would be too optimistic to view Lottie's extralegal separation as a victory narrative. Her very need to devise this creative solution reveals the intransigence of New York's court system – represented in this case by a pair of judges more interested in maintaining their own visions of sexual and familial propriety than in assessing the legality of her request. But if judges could use the rhetoric of public policy to dodge the nuances of formal marriage law, then women like Lottie could respond by dodging the judges' rulings. By making her trial marriage vanish into thin air, Lottie Szablak realigned herself with the demands of public policy. In doing this, she proved that marriage could be as illusory and amorphous as the language used to justify its existence.

---

[91] 1930 US Federal Census, Lottie Szablak. Hartog argues that women who escaped traditional marriages – by legal or illegal means – typically did so with the intention of forming new romantic relationships that "were by and large conventional, that conformed to the norms of the traditional law of husband and wife, that would be, they hoped, 'real' and permanent." Lottie Szablak's case does not necessarily challenge this assertion, as it is conceivable that Lottie did remarry in later years. Her experiences nonetheless raise the possibility that some once-married individuals viewed singlehood as a worthy end, particularly after escaping unsatisfying unions. Hartog, *Man and Wife in America*, 286.

5

Black-White Intermarriage, the Backlash against Miscegenation, and the Push for Racial Amalgamation

Of all the controversial marriages discussed in this book, unions across the black-white divide are the most familiar in scholarship and popular culture. Historians of the United States have rightly framed debates over intermarriage as indicators of the nation's racial climate throughout the nineteenth and twentieth centuries. As historian Renee Romano notes, the question frequently posed to white parents in the Civil Rights era – "Would you want your daughter to marry one?" – was widely perceived to be the "final question" on the pathway toward racial equality. According to this logic, the embrace of marriage across the color line could lead to the disintegration of that line altogether.[1] As such, the shifting tides of miscegenation law and public perceptions of interracial marriage have long served as barometers for understanding the state of race relations.

But in addition to raising anxiety over the fluid meanings of race, debates over intermarriage also fueled the ongoing marriage crisis, for the increasing visibility of marriage across the color line served as yet another indication that the institution of marriage was under threat in an era of increased sexual freedom. Like unions established through commercialized matchmaking services, hasty remarriages, dysgenic partnerships, and trial marriages, interracial unions raised concerns that the institution of marriage was losing out to a culture of permissiveness. Some lawmakers addressed these multiple threats collectively as they endeavored to reform marriage. For example, US Senator Arthur

---

[1] Renee C. Romano, *Race Mixing: Black-White Marriage in Postwar America* (Cambridge, Mass.: Harvard University Press, 2003), 196.

Capper's 1923 uniform marriage and divorce bill sought to illegalize nuptials between black and white Americans alongside its many other initiatives – minimizing grounds for divorce in every state; raising the age of marital consent; forbidding epileptics, the feeble-minded, and persons with communicable disease from marrying; and eliminating marriage between blood relatives.[2] As Capper's efforts reveal, attacks on interracial marriage could function within a broader campaign to undo changes to the institution of marriage at large. In this way, an examination of black-white intermarriage in the context of marriage crisis reminds us that proponents of anti-miscegenation measures were attempting both to maintain their visions of racial purity *and* to monitor the institution of marriage from the harms they believed miscegenation would cause. At the same time, this topic brings the racialized dimensions of marriage crisis into greater focus, reminding us that anxieties about modern marriage were often deeply intertwined with anxieties about whiteness.

Apprehensions over intermarriage manifested themselves in many ways during the 1920s and 1930s. Perhaps most visibly, public accounts of black-white intimacy sparked ongoing efforts to create miscegenation laws in states where they did not exist. But the extent of unease over racial intermarriage becomes all the more apparent when we look beyond the realm of lawmaking. By considering the lived experiences of partners in black-white marriages, as well as the strategies that dissatisfied spouses and their disapproving families used to dissolve those unions in courts, we can see the elaborate patterns of backlash that mixed marriages provoked in the 1920s and 1930s. Condemnations of intermarriage reflected a desire to preserve racial purity and an effort to halt individuals from challenging marital convention.

This era also witnessed new political strategies intended to counter the backlash against intermarriage. Organizations such as the National Association for the Advancement of Colored People (NAACP) successfully fought against anti-miscegenation bills by arguing that such bans led to the exploitation of black women and harmed the institution of marriage itself by encouraging immoral nonmarital sex across racial lines.

---

[2] *Fourteenth Annual Report of the National Association for the Advancement of Colored People for the Year 1923* (New York: NAACP, 1924), 42; James Weldon Johnson, "Views and Reviews," *New York Age*, 3 Feb. 1923, p. 4; "Kansas Solon Seeks to Make Marriage Laws," *Oakland Tribune*, 16 Dec. 1923, p. 12A. The stipulations against interracial marriage were eventually removed from the unsuccessful bill.

Meanwhile, a more radical set of African American intellectuals and race leaders encouraged interracial marriage as a political tool for bridging the nation's racial divide. Proponents of racial "amalgamation" were well aware of the white supremacist ideologies driving opposition to intermarriage. But they were also aware of ever-present concerns over the state of matrimony itself, and they consequently adopted the rhetoric of marriage crisis in their appeal for widespread miscegenation. Countering the argument that black-white nuptials weakened the institution of marriage itself, these men and women insisted that loving interracial unions *strengthened* marriage when they united the best types of people. In this sense, the perception of a marriage crisis could be used both to discourage and to encourage love across the color line.

* * *

Unlike the developments examined in prior chapters, the relationships in question here did not present a completely new challenge to the institution of marriage; indeed, black-white marriage had sparked controversy for decades. Yet several factors changed the conversation about intermarriage in the 1920s, and as a result, mixed-race nuptials posed a different type of threat to marital tradition than they had in generations past. Part of this change can be attributed to the tremendous media attention on the subject. The issue received great publicity, for example, with the 1924 New York production of Eugene O'Neill's *All God's Chillun Got Wings*, a controversial play that explored the marriage of a white woman to a black man.[3] In addition, newspaper coverage of the infamous 1925 Rhinelander annulment trial, in which wealthy white New Yorker Kip Rhinelander sued to end his marriage to Alice Jones, a working-class African American woman, forced the phenomenon into readers' homes. Tabloid accounts of interracial celebrity couples, such as African American track star Phil Edwards and his white German wife, also familiarized readers with the concept.[4]

Social contact across the black-white divide escalated during these decades, particularly in urban areas, as thousands of African Americans

---

[3] One *Chicago Defender* columnist criticized the play as serving no purpose but to "intensify racial consciousness, to fan flames much too high for the nation's good." "Legislative League Acts," *Chicago Defender*, 15 Mar. 1924, p. 6. See also Mumford, *Interzones*, 121–132.

[4] "Lawmakers Legislate, Lynchers Lynch, but Interracial Love Affairs Go On," *Afro-American* (Baltimore), 1 Jul. 1933, p. 13.

relocated from the South to northern metropolises.[5] The Great Migration changed the face of northern urban centers, bringing unprecedented numbers of African Americans into the industrial labor force and creating new opportunities for interracial contact in labor and leisure. The growing presence of a vibrant black community sparked the interest of young white urbanites; as historian Elizabeth Smith-Pryor notes, white Americans were "attracted to the other side of their constructed color line as they tanned, listened to jazz, and danced black-inspired dances."[6] In some cases whites and blacks partook of these cultural activities side-by-side, specifically in frequenting dance halls and black-and-tan cabarets.[7] These increasing interracial contacts raised concerns among the guardians of white purity. While only 0.5–1 percent of African Americans had white spouses in the 1920s and 1930s, legislators consistently introduced new anti-intermarriage bills for ratification. These bills failed to become laws in the North, but perhaps as effective as formal legislation in halting interracial marriage were extralegal violence, the discriminatory enforcement of morals laws, and public sentiment, which overwhelmingly opposed black-white marriages. Throughout the 1920s, northern whites boosted their efforts to halt interracial romantic unions and to prevent African Americans from pursuing "social equality" as they sought economic opportunity in their new northern homes.[8]

Eugenicists took part in this exchange as well. Fearing that increased interracial contact would heighten rates of miscegenation, race scientists

---

[5] Around 500,000 southern African Americans moved to northern cities from 1916 to 1919, and another million joined them in the 1920s. James R. Grossman, *Land of Hope: Chicago, Black Southerners, and the Great Migration* (Chicago: University of Chicago Press, 1989), 3–4; Tera W. Hunter, *To 'Joy My Freedom: Southern Black Women's Lives and Labors after the Civil War* (Cambridge, Mass.: Harvard University Press, 1997), 232.

[6] Elizabeth M. Smith-Pryor, *Property Rites: The Rhinelander Trial, Passing, and the Protection of Whiteness* (Chapel Hill: University of North Carolina Press, 2009), 41–42.

[7] African American writer Chandler Owen described the black-and-tan as "America's Most Democratic Institution." Owen, "The Black and Tan Cabaret – America's Most Democratic Institution," *The Messenger* 7, no. 2 (1925): 97, 100; Chad Heap, *Slumming: Sexual and Racial Encounters in American Nightlife, 1885–1940* (Chicago: University of Chicago Press, 2009); Simmons, *Making Marrige Modern*, 90; Rachel F. Moran, *Interracial Intimacy: The Regulation of Race and Romance* (Chicago: University of Chicago Press, 2001), 5.

[8] Paul R. Spickard, *Mixed Blood: Intermarriage and Ethnic Identity in Twentieth-Century America* (Madison: University of Wisconsin Press, 1989), 272–273; Pascoe, *What Comes Naturally*, 163–204; Robert P. McNamara, Maria Tempenis, and Beth Walton, *Crossing the Line: Interracial Couples in the South* (Westport, Conn.: Praeger, 1999), 31–32; Simmons, *Making Marriage Modern*, 88, 259 fn. 90.

warned of the disastrous results they feared would arise from intimate contact across the color line.[9] Albert Edward Wiggam advised communities to establish local eugenic societies to discourage race-mixing and to slow the influx of immigrants from Eastern and Southern Europe, suggesting that such societies offer lectures on "how the supposed 'melting pot' does not melt."[10] These eugenic notions gradually seeped into the realm of federal politics. The Johnson-Reed Immigration Act of 1924 responded to the fear that "racial purity" was under threat by restricting the number of immigrants who could enter the United States from any given country per year, severely limiting immigration from Eastern and Southern Europe and the West Indies, and effectively barring Asian migration.[11]

While this act did not specifically involve African Americans or black-white intermarriage, it did reflect a growing national desire to maintain the racial integrity of the native white population. With the Virginia Racial Integrity Act of 1924, eugenic thought once again inserted itself into state marriage law, barring the marriage of a white person to any person with the slightest trace of African American, Native American, Asian, or Malaysian ancestry. This act encoded a "one-drop" definition of race into Virginia law, raising concern over miscegenation's threat to white racial purity and strengthening the division between "white" and "nonwhite" persons as distinct parties that should not engage in social and sexual intercourse.[12] The removal of the category "mulatto" from the 1930 census also served to erase the nation's history of racial mixture and reflected the Jim Crow era trend

---

[9] In his call for the preservation of white supremacy, Lothrop Stoddard bemoaned the dissolution of the geographic barriers that had once separated discrete racial and ethnic groups. He believed that interracial social contact encouraged whites to engage in interracial sex, which led to the birth of physically and mentally deficient children. In this regard, Stoddard argued, "crossings with the negro are uniformly fatal," and white civilization was at risk of being "vanquished." Stoddard, *The Rising Tide of Color against White World Supremacy* (New York: Scribner's, 1921), 300–302.

[10] Albert Edward Wiggam, *The Fruit of the Family Tree* (New York: Blue Ribbon Books, 1922), 365–370.

[11] Jane Kuenz, "American Racial Discourse, 1900–1930: Schuyler's *Black No More*," *NOVEL: A Forum on Fiction* 30, no. 2 (1997): 178–179; Stern, *Eugenic Nation*, 16–17; Smith-Pryor, *Property Rites*, 46–48.

[12] Pascoe, *What Comes Naturally*, 140–150; Lisa Lindquist Dorr, "Arm in Arm: Gender, Eugenics, and Virginia's Racial Integrity Acts of the 1920s," *Journal of Women's History* 11, no. 1 (1999): 143–166; Peter Wallenstein, *Tell the Court I Love My Wife: Race, Marriage, and Law – An American History* (New York: Palgrave Macmillan, 2002), 137–141.

to downplay distinctions of color among black Americans.[13] As legal historian Ariela Gross has explained, judges and juries helped to construct a post-emancipation narrative that erased the nation's legacies of antebellum intermixture and that divided Americans into discrete racial categories. According to this legal fiction, miscegenation was a rare occurrence, and race was easily identifiable by a person's appearance and the company he or she kept. This "racial common sense" – or the belief in the obviousness of racial identity – denied the existence of mixed race individuals and racial passing and perpetuated the belief that deliberate love across the color line was impossible, despite mounting evidence to the contrary.[14]

At the same time that these theories of immutable racial difference tightened their grip on state and federal legislation, ideas about race were changing in intellectual circles, and these shifting ideologies called barriers to racial intermarriage into question. The work of anthropologist Franz Boas played a major role in reshaping ideas about racial difference in the early twentieth century. Nineteenth-century racial science had treated race as a biological reality, contending that whites were inherently superior to members of "lower" racial groups. But the 1920s ushered in an outspoken group of "liberal environmentalists," who argued that race was a cultural construction. With Boas at their forefront, liberal environmentalists contested the belief that African Americans were innately inferior to whites, explaining instead that blacks' degraded social status resulted from a history of oppression and limited opportunity. In arguing that race was a social construction, these thinkers disputed the "racial common sense" that pervaded courtrooms. Their arguments did not undo essentialist racial classifications – if anything, as Peggy Pascoe argues, the notion that a person's race could be determined by mere observation was more prevalent than ever in 1930s legal culture. Still, liberal environmentalists' recognition of the permeability of racial categories weakened the case against racial

---

[13] Kuenz, "American Racial Discourse," 177. Smith-Pryor, *Property Rites*, 46–48, 54–55; Haag, *Consent*, 124; Moran, *Interracial Intimacy*, 54. As Greg Carter explains, W. E. B. Du Bois and other prominent black thinkers also encouraged the removal of the "mulatto" category from the census, in part to build solidarity among individuals identified as black. Carter, *The United States of the United Races: A Utopian History of Racial Mixing* (New York: New York University Press, 2013), 111, 129.

[14] Ariela J. Gross, *What Blood Won't Tell: A History of Race on Trial in America* (Cambridge, Mass.: Harvard University Press, 2008), 90–110. See also *Haag*, Consent, 121–132.

intermarriage, as it challenged the notion that love across the color line involved the unnatural union of two scientifically distinct parties.[15]

Amid these elaborate disputes over the measurability of racial identity, the concept of interracial marriage adopted a new set of meanings. The growing presence of African Americans in the North, the development of the thriving literary and intellectual movement of the Harlem Renaissance, and the increasing acceptance of race as a cultural category bolstered eugenicists' fears that white dominance was under threat and that miscegenation was the culprit. In addition to generating eugenic screeds and sparking legislative efforts to prevent further race mixing, these fears of miscegenation heightened the Ku Klux Klan's efforts to injure and intimidate married black-white couples, as well as couples in pursuit of marriage licenses.[16] As debates raged between eugenicists and Boasian cultural relativists over the construction of racial identity, and as African American migration sparked anxiety over the perceived black quest for "social equality," actual intermarried couples bore the brunt of these cultural clashes.

Ethnographic and sociological studies from the 1920s and 1930s shed light on the difficulties that black-white couples faced, highlighting their social alienation and the economic hurdles they often encountered. Two of these studies stand out for their extensive documentation. The first is George Schuyler's *Racial Intermarriage in the United States*. Schuyler, a prominent African American journalist and satirist who himself wed a white woman, Josephine Lewis Cogdell, in 1928, published this study as an article the year of his marriage, and as a pamphlet in 1929. A decade later, Robert Edward Thomas Roberts, an anthropology student at the University of Chicago, completed "Negro-White Intermarriage," his master's thesis, based on approximately 250 interviews he conducted in 1936.[17]

---

[15] Pascoe, *What Comes Naturally*, 124–130; Pascoe, "Miscegenation Law, Court Cases, and Ideologies of 'Race' in Twentieth-Century America," *Journal of American History* 83, no. 1 (1996): 46–61; Mia Bay, *The White Image in the Black Mind: African-American Ideas about White People, 1830–1925* (New York: Oxford University Press, 2000), 187–202; Lee D. Baker, *From Savage to Negro: Anthropology and the Construction of Race, 1896–1954* (Berkeley: University of California Press, 1998), 99–126; Herbert S. Lewis, "The Passion of Franz Boas," *American Anthropologist* 103, no. 2 (2001): 447–467.

[16] Smith-Pryor, *Property Rites*, 44, 163; George Schuyler, *Racial Intermarriage: One of the Most Interesting Phenomena in Our National Life* (Girard, Kans.: Haldeman-Julius Publications, 1929), 20–22.

[17] Robert Edward Thomas Roberts, "Negro-White Intermarriage: A Study of Social Control" (master's thesis, University of Chicago, 1940), 3, 8–9.

As these studies reveal, couples faced great consequences when they defied anti-miscegenation laws in their home states, ranging from the simple voiding of the marriage contract in Arizona, Arkansas, Missouri, Nebraska, California, Utah, and Colorado to a fine of $3,000 and a ten-year prison term in North Dakota.[18] While interracial couples were legally permitted to wed in states that lacked miscegenation laws, they often encountered great social and physical barriers in their efforts to exchange vows. Schuyler told of a group of white men from Montclair, New Jersey, who in 1925 had burned a cross on the front lawn of a prosperous African American man after he was spotted applying for a marriage license in New York City with a young blond-haired white woman. He also wrote of Klan members threatening engaged couples in New York, a young white woman from New Jersey who was found "mentally incompetent" and committed to a home for the feebleminded when she sought to wed a black man, and Christian clergy refusing to marry a mixed-race couple in Connecticut.[19] Often the struggle to procure a license only marked the beginning of a couple's difficult married life. To make this case, Schuyler noted that many interracial couples resisted appearing together in public out of fear that passers-by would react with hostility or physical violence, and that in many parts of the country the threat of harassment, arrest, and mob violence kept mixed couples from taking vacations and traveling together in public.[20]

In addition to suffering physical and verbal abuses, these couples also struggled to procure housing, since landlords frequently refused to rent homes to mixed-race couples.[21] Some couples dodged this dilemma by having the white party secure the property without mention of a black spouse; landlords rarely reacted well upon learning of their tenants' marriages, however, and the discovery often led to a "none-too-polite request to move." Other couples devised creative ways to cohabitate despite widespread disapproval of their marriages, such as one New York couple, "a Jewish man and a brown woman, both people of refinement and intelligence," who were able to acquire

---

[18] Schuyler, *Racial Intermarriage*, 15. In a later article Schuyler added that mixed-race couples also faced "savage fines and long prison sentences in such progressive commonwealths as Maryland, Mississippi, Indiana, Alabama, Florida, the Dakotas, Texas, Tennessee, Nevada, Colorado, Georgia, Idaho, Louisiana, Virginia and West Virginia." Schuyler, "When Black Weds White," *Modern Quarterly* 8 (1934): 13.

[19] Schuyler, *Racial Intermarriage*, 20–22.   [20] Ibid., 26.

[21] Ibid., 23–24; Roberts, "Negro-White Intermarriage," 85, 90–94.

a lovely apartment facing Central Park when she pretended to be his housekeeper.[22]

As painful as these physical and material threats must have been, they were often outweighed by the emotional anguish that participants in racial intermarriages experienced when separated and disinherited from disapproving families. Some of Roberts's respondents had been the ones to sever ties with parents and siblings, not wanting their own marriages to mar loved ones' reputations. One white woman kept her marriage a secret and cut off correspondence with her large family, even as both parties continued to live in Chicago. "They never knew much about Colored," she explained. "I'd much rather they didn't know where I am than know the truth."[23] Whether this secretive approach was bred in shame, fear of confrontation, or a desire to protect families from criticism, it speaks to the anxieties that lingered for intermarried couples after they exchanged vows. The majority of Roberts's interviewees had informed their families of their marital status, however, and they suffered greatly for their honesty. Many white partners in mixed marriages were completely disowned by their families after marrying black spouses, several of them using phrases like "to them I am dead" to emphasize the irreversibility of this disinheritance. Indeed, these white relatives rarely even attended the funerals of their estranged intermarried family members.[24] On the whole, African Americans in mixed marriages endured fewer familial separations, but they nonetheless experienced great tension in their dealings with relatives who opposed their marriages. Respondents also claimed to have lost the majority of their friends, black and white, after marrying across the color line, and as a result their social contacts were composed almost exclusively of other interracial couples.[25]

As these examples reveal, legal prohibitions were not necessary for the subjugation of interracial couples. In the absence of statutes prohibiting racial intermarriage, northerners crafted their own social mechanisms to ensure that the racial separation mandated in the South would occur naturally in the North.[26] Residential and recreational segregation limited opportunities for interracial bonding and courtship, and when interracial couples broke through these barriers and exchanged vows, they faced a

---

[22] Schuyler, *Racial Intermarriage*, 23–24.
[23] Roberts, "Negro-White Intermarriage," 68.   [24] Ibid., 71–73.   [25] Ibid., 75–76, 79.
[26] On the creation of these extralegal codes against "race mixing," see Kathy Peiss, "Love across the Color Line," in *Love across the Color Line: The Letters of Alice Hanley to Channing Lewis*, ed. Helen Lefkowitz Horowitz and Kathy Peiss (Amherst: University of Massachusetts Press, 1996), 58–59.

host of other daily struggles and humiliations. Knowledge of these social consequences served as a disincentive for many interracial couples contemplating marriage, ensuring that intermarriage remained infrequent, even where legal.

Nonetheless, many black-white couples who defied these social hurdles were very happy in marriage. Schuyler closed his pamphlet by claiming that, as per his research, mixed-race marriages typically lasted longer than did unmixed marriages.[27] He thus sought to understand why so many interracial couples were willing to stay together despite barriers to their happiness and social inclusion, particularly in an age in which "orthodox marriages" were dissolving at unprecedented rates. His respondents emphasized their fervent love for one another, as well as the idea that having already sacrificed their entire social worlds to be together, they had no desire to abandon the havens they had created to shield themselves from a disapproving public. One white woman described the insulated life she shared with her black husband, despite their residence in a major northeastern city. "Our social life centers in our home," the woman admitted. "We are forced to really *live* here instead of using it as merely a lodging place." Schuyler viewed this confinement as both a tragedy and a boon to their relationship. He commented, "Realizing their status in society, cognizant of the added strain upon their relationship and aware of the greatly increased opportunities for developing flurries of temper, they seem to make unusual efforts to be as pleasant and inoffensive as possible to each other. Knowing that they are two against the world, they cling the closer together."[28] Many other racially intermarried couples made similar efforts to bind themselves more closely together as the outside world conspired to tear them apart.

As these examples suggest, the visible element of racial difference rendered these relations threatening and transgressive in a way that the other marginal marital arrangements addressed in this book were

---

[27] The US Census Bureau estimated in 1926 that fifteen of every hundred marriages ended in divorce, but Schuyler believed that the rate was much lower for interracial couples. He did not support this hypothesis with compelling evidence – he claimed to have drawn his conclusions from "a perusal of newspaper files for the past fifteen years." But there is some reason to his argument that due to the controversy of these marriages, reporters would have jumped at the opportunity to publicize their failures. Schuyler thus assumed that newspapers had reported on every instance of divorce and annulment among interracial couples, and the dearth of such reports signified their general success. Schuyler, *Racial Intermarriage*, 27–28.

[28] Ibid., 29.

not, chiefly because black-white couples were less able to hide their marital nonconformity from the public than were couples with like complexions.[29] While the unconventional couples described in prior chapters were often susceptible to legal backlash and condemnation from editorials and pulpits, they were generally able to conceal the nonconformity of their marital arrangements when they so desired. Interracial couples, on the other hand, were rarely granted that luxury. In this regard, legislators and judges were not needed to keep these couples in their places, as regular citizens took it upon themselves to police marriage along racial lines.

*   *   *

To escape this policing, many interracial couples turned inward, removing themselves from public view in hopes of finding private tranquility. But racial intermarriage remained an inescapable topic, as newspapers frequently brought the stories of high-profile mixed-race couples into homes across the nation. All too often these stories depicted the perils of racial intermarriage, only enhancing readers' negative perceptions of the phenomenon. One well-documented case was the 1927 marriage between Helen Lee Worthing, a white film actress and former Ziegfeld Follies star, and Eugene Nelson, an eminent African American physician (see Figure 5.1). As news of the marriage spread, and as former friends began to snub Worthing and Nelson for their union, Worthing turned to drinking and drug use to temper her disillusionment.[30] Gradually the couple's love soured, and media coverage increased as the marriage deteriorated, culminating when Worthing initiated divorce proceedings in December

---

[29] This should not suggest that racial identity is discernible by mere physical appearance or that all "interracial" couples possessed strikingly different phenotypical characteristics. The point here is that those couples recognized as possessing distinct racial characteristics or who did not "pass" as members of the same race could not obscure the fact of their conjugal misconduct from a judging public in the way that like-complexioned couples could.

[30] Helen Lee Worthing, "Hollywood's Most Tragic Marriage," *Ebony*, Feb. 1952, pp. 30–31. After a public appearance with Nelson, in which she was ignored by former friends and mocked by members of the crowd, Worthing developed an alcohol dependency. She wrote: "I had never drank before except a few sips of champagne occasionally at a party. But suddenly, I wanted liquor – I wanted the sour, stinging, bitter taste of it burning my throat. I drained the glass and asked for another." She would continue to turn to alcohol to cope with the hurt that accompanied the loss of friendships and career opportunities. See also Donald Bogle, *Bright Boulevards, Bold Dreams: The Story of Black Hollywood* (New York: One World Books, 2005), 58–59.

FIGURE 5.1 Helen Lee Worthing and Eugene C. Nelson, New York
World-Telegram and the Sun Newspaper Photograph Collection, Library of
Congress, 20 Jan. 1933.

of 1930. Major newspapers profiled the decline of this marriage, emphasizing the problems Worthing and Nelson encountered after separating. It
is possible to read this method of reporting as a type of cautionary tale, or
a suggestion that marriage across the color line inevitably led to the sort
of drama, addiction, and mental illness that Worthing, as the wife of a
black husband, came to know. While national news writers initially had
little to say about the exchange of vows between a white film star and a
black doctor, they were quick to depict each moment of the marriage's
demise and to hold it up as an example of the dysfunction that ensued
when mixed-race couples wed.[31]

　　If media commentary reflected public discomfort with racial intermarriage, this unease becomes all the more apparent when we examine legal
culture. Peggy Pascoe has meticulously documented the rise in miscegenation legislation, as well as its intensified enforcement, throughout the
first half of the twentieth century. Pascoe also describes the exhaustive
efforts by legislators to bring miscegenation laws into new states and the

---

[31] "Ex-Follies Girl Here Incognito," *Los Angeles Times*, 30 Dec. 1930, p. A5; "Denied
Divorce," *Pittsburgh Courier*, 13 Dec. 1930, p. 1; "Asks Divorce," *Chicago Daily
Tribune*, 22 Apr. 1931, p. 18.

District of Columbia, as well as the many successful campaigns by the NAACP to block these laws from entering northern regions. This battle between proponents and critics of intermarriage bans became especially pronounced in the 1920s, as a revitalized Ku Klux Klan began to push even harder for such laws.[32]

Discussion of state legislation is vital for understanding the anxieties that black-white marriages provoked in the decades after emancipation, as lawmakers devised new ways to enforce white supremacy in the shadow of slavery. But an exclusive focus on the successful or unsuccessful passage of miscegenation laws obscures the complex role that courtrooms played in dissuading black-white marriages, even in states where such unions were legal. Though courts could not make miscegenation laws materialize where they did not exist, they could provide regretful spouses – or more frequently, their disapproving families and friends – with opportunities to dissolve such unions on grounds of fraud and deceit. Courtroom efforts to terminate intermarriages, as well as the media accounts that accompanied them, helped reinforce the notion that such marriages were inconceivable, and could thus only result from trickery, intoxication, or mental illness. Though the outcomes of these divorce and annulment cases varied, each one hinged on the premise that black-white marriage could only result from the black partner's deception and the white partner's mental ineptitude.[33] Ultimately, these courtroom proceedings fed the myth that consensual interracial unions were not possible, while simultaneously putting those very unions on display for public scrutiny.

In states where black-white marriage was legal, a partner did not have the right to terminate a marriage on the grounds that his or her partner belonged to a different racial group. It was possible, however, to claim that a marriage had been contracted under fraudulent circumstances – that had Partner A known of Partner B's hidden racial identity, then the marriage would never have taken place. In this way, efforts to annul interracial marriages often came in the form of fraud allegations. An impressive amount of scholarship has focused on one such annulment case as a lens into race relations, sexual politics, and miscegenation law in the 1920s. This case, the above-mentioned marriage and near-annulment

---

[32] Pascoe, *What Comes Naturally*. On the rebirth of the Klan, see Lynn Dumenil, *The Modern Temper: American Culture and Society in the 1920s* (New York: Hill and Wang, 1995), 250–302.

[33] Pamela Haag makes a similar argument in *Consent*, 127.

of Alice Jones and Leonard "Kip" Rhinelander, is a worthy vantage point. Rhinelander, the son of a preeminent white Manhattan family, married Jones, a working-class woman from New Rochelle, New York, in 1924. The union provoked controversy from its outset due to the bride and groom's disparate class status; newspapers frequently emphasized Kip Rhinelander's society upbringing and hearty inheritance alongside descriptions of Alice Jones as a "cabman's daughter."[34]

The couple's notoriety grew alongside reports that Alice's father, born in England, had declared himself a "colored man" when taking his oath of US citizenship. Amid great media hoopla, Kip, succumbing to pressure from his disapproving parents, petitioned for annulment on grounds that Alice had withheld her nonwhite status from him. In a much-publicized case before New York Supreme Court Justice Joseph Morschauser, Alice Jones denied that she had misled her husband. Insisting that Kip had known about his wife's race from the start and had married her nonetheless, Alice's attorneys sought to prove that Kip had loved Alice for who she was, and only now claimed otherwise due to pressure from his father. After several days of dramatic testimony, including the public reading of love letters describing the couple's private sexual encounters, the case reached its dramatic peak when Alice's attorney, Lee Parsons Davis, had her disrobe before the jury. Davis hoped to show jurors that Alice's "colored" skin was unmistakable and that Kip therefore could not have been ignorant of her racial identity. This strategy was successful, albeit at a great cost to Alice Jones's dignity. The jury ruled in Alice's favor, agreeing that she had not deceived Kip and that the couple had deliberately contracted an interracial union. While the jurors in Morschauser's courtroom kept the marriage intact, Alice and Kip would never live together again.[35]

The Rhinelander trial illustrates one elaborate negotiation over black-white marriage in a state where it was legally permissible but culturally intolerable in most circles. This case highlights many social divides that

---

[34] "Daughter of Taxi Man Wed to Rhinelander," *Chicago Daily Tribune*, 14 Nov. 1924, p. 1; "Society Youth Weds Cabman's Daughter," *New York Times*, 14 Nov. 1924, p. 1.

[35] Earl Lewis and Heidi Ardizzone, *Love on Trial: An American Scandal in Black and White* (New York: Norton, 2001); Smith-Pryor, *Property Rites*; Angela Onwuachi-Willig, *According to Our Hearts: Rhinelander v. Rhinelander and the Law of the Multiracial Family* (New Haven: Yale University Press, 2013). By predicating the verdict on the belief that the jury could identify Alice's race from looking at her unclothed torso, Davis reinforced the "common-sense" notion that race was identifiable on sight. See Gross, *What Blood Won't Tell*, 96–99.

racial intermarriage brought to the forefront – not only racial divides, but also ones of gender, class, and generation. But too great a focus on this single trial prevents us from seeing the extensive reach of the debates it captured and obscures similar – if less publicized – annulment cases from the historical record. In many ways, what is exceptional about the Rhinelander case is that it was not exceptional. Though it was the most dramatic and well-publicized trial of its type, it was nonetheless one among many, and attention to this wider range of attempted interracial marriage dissolutions offers insight into the cultural anxieties that racial intermarriage provoked.

Five years before the Rhinelander trial became a source of public fascination, another interracial annulment dispute graced Justice Morschauser's courtroom. In this case, Sybil Neale, a white woman from New Rochelle, discovered that her husband of two years, Theodore Neale, whom she had believed to be a white man with Spanish, French, and Native American heritage, was instead "a negro of light complexion." Sybil Neale had made this discovery when she noticed that beneath her mother-in-law's braided wig was what one *Washington Times* reporter described as "a patch of black kinky hair characteristic of the negro."[36] While Sybil had approved of the ethnic heritage that Theodore had claimed was his, she could not tolerate the idea of being married to a "mulatto." Shocked and confused about the implications of her mother-in-law's hair, she went directly to her attorney, Burton Meighan, who advised her to leave the apartment she shared with her husband right away so that he could investigate Theodore's racial background. Sybil took Meighan's advice, leaving home immediately and never returning to the apartment.[37]

The ensuing investigation and subsequent judicial battle relied on pseudoscientific analysis to determine Theodore Neale's racial identity. Investigators examined Theodore's brother, Arthur, for clues. They analyzed his skin color, as well as his eye color, the shape and size of his nose and lips, the texture of his hair, and the thickness of his beard to come to the conclusion that Arthur Neale was indeed "colored" and that his brother must therefore be as well. Meighan relied upon "expert"

---

[36] "How She Proved Her Husband Was a Negro," *Washington Times*, 25 Jan. 1920, "American Weekly" section, p. 7; "Asks Divorce from Her Negro Husband," *New Castle Herald* (Pa.), 1 Nov. 1919, p. 6; "Marriage Annulled Because Mulatto Concealed His Race," *St. Louis Post-Dispatch*, 6 Jan. 1920, p. 8.

[37] "How She Proved Her Husband Was a Negro," 7.

testimony from Harvard sociologist Earnest Albert Hooton, who concluded that Arthur Neale had "a decided and unmistakable admixture of negro blood."[38] Sybil's legal team brought Hooton's statements into Morschauser's courtroom, claiming that Arthur Neale's racial identity was a clear indicator of Theodore Neale's and insisting that the marriage would have never taken place if Theodore had admitted his black heritage. Embracing this logic that race could be determined through an examination of physical features, Morschauser agreed that Theodore Neale had defrauded his wife, and granted Sybil the annulment.[39]

One striking element of this case is the matter-of-fact way in which Sybil Neale discussed her decision to pursue annulment; more precisely, Sybil presented this legal path as not a decision at all, but a common-sense solution to a marriage that was, in her mind, inconceivable once its interracial composition became known. After the trial, she told reporters that she had already forgiven her husband and his family for their supposed indiscretions, stating, "If I could spare any of them sorrow I would be willing to do almost anything to help except continuing to live with him." Sybil proceeded to tout her magnanimity in forgiveness, presenting herself as a victim of the Neale family's calculations. She concluded by declaring that she now saw it as her responsibility to speak publicly about her experience to protect unsuspecting whites from suffering similar indignities. Sybil Neale's statements reinforced the court's suggestion that a clear and indisputable racial divide separated her from Theodore. In doing so, she presented intermarriage as an inconceivable phenomenon, despite having participated in one for two years.[40]

Another case highlighting the supposed impossibility of black-white intermarriage took place in Philadelphia in 1930. This case involved the marriage of Beatrice Ingham, a white nurse, to H. Harry White, a "light-skinned Negro" who allegedly represented himself to Ingham as white. When Ingham heard a rumor that her husband was not fully white, she launched an investigation to determine his race. She located his birth certificate, which stated that he and his parents were African American. At this point White acknowledged his racial background, admitting that he had lied to Ingham because he loved her too much to risk the rejection he knew would come when she learned the truth. Unmoved, Beatrice

---

[38] Ibid., 7.
[39] "Annuls Marriage," *Wilkes-Barre Times Leader*, 6 Jan. 1920, p. 5. Smith-Pryor, *Property Rites*, 179.
[40] "How She Proved Her Husband Was a Negro," 7.

Ingham went to live with her parents and initiated divorce proceedings immediately; she won her case on grounds of fraud and deceit. Following Sybil Neale's lead, the Ingham family denied any hard feelings toward Harry White. Beatrice's father, Joseph Ingham, told the press that Harry was "an awfully nice fellow," whom his daughter continued to hold in high regard. Nonetheless, the realization that White was not, in fact, white rendered his marriage to Ingham inconceivable in the eyes of his ex-wife and her parents. Racial fraud justifications for divorce and annulment allowed women like Beatrice Ingham to rely on the notion that interracial marriage was impossible, even when it was legal.[41]

Of course, Kip Rhinelander's example should give us pause before believing a white spouse's claims of ignorance over a partner's nonwhiteness. Knowing that parental pressure led Kip to disavow his knowledge of Alice Jones's race, we should recognize the possibility that Sybil Neale, Beatrice Ingham, or any number of the other white spouses claiming to have been tricked into marrying a nonwhite spouse were, like Kip, falsely claiming fraud and deceit to escape marriages that family and friends had rejected. But whatever the actual motivations behind efforts to dissolve marriages on grounds of racial deceit, what is clear is that such allegations carried cultural and legal weight. Claims of racial misrepresentation were sufficient to bring Neale's and Ingham's marriages to an end, and would have done the same for the Rhinelander marriage had not Kip's own misrepresentations been so clear. Sympathy for the white "victims" of duplicitous black spouses could be so strong in northern courtrooms that it led judges to sacrifice the well-being of children in the name of protecting a white parent. Such was the case with Bernice Seeney of Battle Creek, Michigan, who learned after five years of marriage that her husband, Orval Seeney, was black. Appalled by this discovery, and ostracized by friends and family, Bernice pursued and won a divorce on grounds of "extreme cruelty." She also surrendered all parental claims to the two children she and Orval had borne, with circuit judge Blaine Hatch affirming her belief that a white woman could not be a parent to nonwhite children.[42]

---

[41] "Nurse Granted Divorce from Negro Husband," *Evening News* (Wilkes-Barre), 3 Sep. 1930, p. 2; "Nurse Given Divorce from Hubby Who Posed as Nordic," *Pittsburgh Courier*, 13 Sep. 1930, p. 8.

[42] "Relinquishes Negro Husband, Children," *Daily Times* (New Philadelphia, Ohio), 18 Sep. 1929, p. 5; *Michigan, Divorce Records, 1897–1952* (database online), Ancestry.com, 2014. Not all judges were willing to break up families due to race. For instance, one judge in Omaha refused to annul the marriage between Francis and Clara Dwyer when

The above cases offer just a few examples of white individuals seeking to end their marriages by claiming that their spouses had fabricated whiteness. Claims of racial deceit, be they true or false, were an effective means of terminating an interracial marriage in the absence of miscegenation laws.[43] These stories indicate the role that divorce and annulment statutes could play in combatting marriages that defied public policy, if not state law. If annulment loopholes troubled judges and lawmakers in their capacity to facilitate progressive polygamy and encourage trial marriage, they could also help to restore traditional marriage by erasing unions that traversed racial lines. But while Bernice Seeney and other discontented white spouses used the courts to undo their marriages, other interracial couples fought legal authorities – as well as meddling friends and family members – to keep theirs intact. Often such cases involved white teenage women whose disapproving parents turned to the criminal justice system to "rescue" their daughters from the scourge of interracial love.[44]

Such was the case with Margaretta McClintock (see Figure 5.2), a white sixteen-year-old from Uniontown, Pennsylvania, who startled her parents when she wed Roosevelt Williams, a black twenty-seven-year-old, in 1934. Margaretta had met Roosevelt while he lived in her mother's home as a boarder. The two had married at the Uniontown courthouse. Though there was no law against interracial marriage in Pennsylvania, the couple knew that marriage license clerks in the area typically denied licenses to couples of different races, and so Margaretta reported her age as twenty-one and her race as "colored." She also provided a false last name, Nuce. When Margaretta's mother, Caroline McClintock, learned of her daughter's marriage to a black man, she pressed charges against both husband and wife, citing her daughter's false representations and her

the doctor who delivered their child suggested to Francis that his wife might be part black. The judge insisted that there was no proof of the wife's blackness, and moreover stated his refusal to place "the stigma of bastardy" upon an "innocent and helpless child, the offspring of this marriage." "Refuse to Annul Marriage," *Lincoln Evening Journal*, 3 Jul. 1919, p. 4.

[43] See also "Seeks Divorce; Says Wife Has Negro Blood," *Washington Times*, 18 May 1920, p. 9; "Girl Seeks to Be Freed from Negro Husband," *Oshkosh Daily Northwestern*, 9 Dec. 1921, p. 1; "White Girl, Who Wed Race Man, Seeks Decree," *Pittsburgh Courier*, 1 Sep. 1923, p. 1; "Marriage Annulled after Sensational Story Told in Court," *Pittsburgh Courier*, 28 Nov. 1925, p. 1; "She Deceived Me!" *Pittsburgh Courier*, 1 Jun. 1940, pp. 1, 4.

[44] There are parallels between families' efforts to terminate their young daughters' interracial marriages, and working-class Progressive Era parents' use of the court system to "rescue" their daughters from consensual sexual relations, public amusements, employment, and self-sufficiency. See Odem, *Delinquent Daughters*.

FIGURE 5.2 Press photo of Margaretta McClintock, Acme Photographs and the Newspaper Enterprise Association Reference Department, 21 Jul. 1934.

son-in-law's efforts to encourage Margaretta's dishonesty. The two were arrested and indicted on charges of perjury and deceit, and they spent their honeymoon behind bars in the county jail. The furious Margaretta declared her continued loyalty to her husband, telling reporters, "I don't care if we do have to go to jail – I'll still love Roosevelt and nothing will change that." Though she admitted to lying about her race, age, and name, she justified her actions in the name of love. "I love him," she told District Attorney Wade Newell. "I intend to stay with him always. I don't want anyone else." The couple beseeched Newell to free them and let them leave the county for a more welcoming location.[45]

Margaretta's tone softened, however, after nine days in jail. At this point the couple's attorney, William Crow, announced that both

[45] "Doesn't Want Anyone Else but Her Negro Husband, Girl Says," *Daily Courier* (Connellsville, Pa.), 20 Jul. 1934, p. 1; "White Bride Protests Love for Negro Hubby," *Evening Standard* (Uniontown), 20 Jul. 1934, p. 1; "Mixed Marriage Comes in Court," *Evening Standard*, 24 Jul. 1934, p. 1; "Sentence Day in Local Court," *Morning Herald* (Uniontown), 7 Aug. 1934, p. 5.

Margaretta and Roosevelt believed they had been hasty in exchanging vows. They were now willing to annul the marriage. Perhaps nine days in jail had led the couple to reevaluate their devotion to one another. More likely, the threat of more jail time caused the newlyweds to consider whether their union was worth the price they were paying for it. Also, Caroline McClintock's promise to drop her perjury and conspiracy charges if the couple broke off the union likely played a role in their decision to pursue annulment, not only by providing Margaretta and Roosevelt an escape route from their legal troubles, but also by reminding them of the litigation and jail time that might result should they reject this olive branch.[46]

Caroline McClintock's offer to have the charges dropped did not materialize. This may have been due to the fact that County Detective J. A. Hann had filed his own charges against the couple. In addition, Ms. McClintock was arrested for running a "bawdy house" just a week after announcing her willingness to drop the charges, likely undermining whatever authority she had in shaping her daughter's legal fate.[47] Margaretta and Roosevelt were thus indicted for perjury and conspiracy, and they pled guilty, throwing themselves at the mercy of the Fayette County Court and vowing never to see one another again. In the end, Margaretta was sentenced to three months in jail, and Roosevelt was sentenced to six months and forced to pay a hundred-dollar fine. The couple's attorney had requested leniency from the judge, blaming Caroline McClintock for taking in a black boarder, and thus initiating the romance.[48] Crow's strategy is telling, for it indicates that the marriage itself, and not the perjury that had facilitated it, was the greatest source of angst in the courtroom. Margaretta had broken the law by misrepresenting her name, age, and race. At the same time, the age of consent in Pennsylvania was sixteen, and black-white unions were legal.[49] All this to say, despite the couple's untruths in acquiring a marriage license, their marriage ought to have been legitimate. But perjury charges served to tear the couple apart and to penalize a relationship that may have been legal, but was

---

[46] "Ardor for Her Negro Rapidly Cools," *Morning Herald*, 1 Aug. 1934, p. 11.

[47] "Mother of White-Black Bride Held as 'Madam' of Leith Bawdy House," *Evening Standard*, 9 Aug. 1934, p. 1; "Grand Jury to Finish Big Job Late Saturday," *Evening Standard*, 31 Aug. 1934, p. 1.

[48] "Couple Plead Guilty," *Morning Herald*, 6 Sep. 1934, p. 4; "Girl, Negro Mate Plead Guilty to Perjury Charge," *Daily Republican* (Monongahela, Pa.), 6 Sep. 1934, p. 1; "Girl, Negro Sentenced," *Morning Herald*, 17 Oct. 1934, p. 10.

[49] Odem, *Delinquent Daughters*, 15.

nonetheless deemed unacceptable in the courtrooms and living rooms of Pennsylvania. The couple had succeeded in defying marriage license clerks, who themselves defied state law in their refusal to grant marriage licenses to couples of different races – one Uniontown newspaper referred to this common denial of interracial marriage licenses as an "unwritten law" that clerks knew to obey.[50] Margaretta and Roosevelt had deliberately broken that unwritten law, and now they had to pay the price.

That same year, another mother sought to annul her white daughter's marriage to a black man, similarly exploiting the criminal justice system in order to dissolve a legal marriage of which she disapproved morally. Doris Chase, a white seventeen-year-old resident of Sioux City, Iowa, had married longtime acquaintance Hartwell Bonner, a twenty-three-year-old man described by the press as a "mulatto pool-hall janitor."[51] The bride and groom did not deny their races when acquiring their license; on the couple's marriage certificate, Doris is listed as "white" and Hartwell as "colored." The couple likely did lie, however, in stating the bride's age as nineteen.[52] When Doris's mother, Florence Chase, learned of her daughter's union, she initiated Bonner's arrest for "contributing to child delinquency," and she saw to her daughter's arrest on charges of "incorrigibility." Doris was despondent over her mother's efforts to end the marriage, and she could not understand why she had been arrested. "This is my life, and I don't see why it is anyone's business whom I marry," the teen bride declared from prison. "He is a wonderful man. No matter what they do to him or me, I still love him. Race? That's all bunk. When you love someone, you don't pay attention to that."[53]

Unlike Caroline McClintock before her, Florence Chase was unsuccessful in bringing an immediate end to her daughter's marriage. The couple remained legally wed, and had a child shortly thereafter. The 1940 census indicates that five years later, the two had separated. Doris, now twenty-two, lived with her parents and her four-year-old daughter, Joanne Bonner. Hartwell was listed as a "lodger" in the home of a

---

[50] "Miscegenation Raises Rumpus," *Daily News Standard* (Uniontown), 19 Jul. 1934, p. 1.

[51] "Love," *Logansport Pharos-Tribune* (Ind.), 11 Jan. 1935, p. 2.

[52] Marriage Records for Hartwell C. Bonner. *Iowa, Marriage Records, 1880–1937* (database online). Ancestry.com, 2014.

[53] "Bride Asserts Love for Negro," *Muscatine Journal* (Iowa), 10 Jan. 1935, p. 1; "Love," p. 2. "White Bride Resents Mother's Racial Hate," *Pittsburgh Courier*, 19 Jan. 1935, p. 13; "Jailed in Sioux City, Iowa White Girl, Negro Husband," *New York Age*, 19 Jan. 1935, p. 5; Florence Chase also filed charges against William B. Payne, an African American witness to the marriage.

woman named Amy Gardner. His race was listed as white, which raises the possibility that he opted to pass for white following the legal struggles emerging from his interracial union. Both Doris and Hartwell claimed to still be married, but by 1944 she was wed to another man, suggesting that her marriage to Hartwell was legally dissolved shortly after the census. Though Doris Bonner would serve time in the Iowa State Penitentiary in 1941 on a six-month sentence for "lewdness and vagrancy," it appears that her mother's initial use of the criminal justice system to break up her marriage was unsuccessful. Nonetheless, this case exemplifies white parents' efforts to use the court system to terminate legal interracial unions – sometimes at great cost to their own children's reputations.[54]

Sometimes friends and kinfolk disapproved so deeply of loved ones' interracial marriages that they sought to have intermarried family members declared insane – a strategy they hoped would prompt annulment. In 1925, Henry Faison, a white World War I veteran and son of a former North Carolina congressman, married Annie Nelson, an African American cook at his District of Columbia boardinghouse. Faison's friends and family jumped to action, claiming that Faison must have been suffering from shell shock and that he therefore was not in control of his faculties when he married Nelson. An uncle traveled to Washington and had his nephew admitted into the Gallinger Municipal Hospital Psychopathic Ward, and then to St. Elizabeths Hospital, for psychological observation. Faison's inner circle hoped that a diagnosis of mental illness would lead to the annulment of a marriage they could not accept. Whether or not they themselves believed Faison was mentally unsound, these prominent white citizens knew that insanity was a viable justification for dissolving an unthinkable union.[55]

Though Faison was not declared insane, his relatives succeeded in making him second-guess his nuptials. Just a few days after the uncle's intervention, Henry Faison submitted his own petition for annulment, stating that for the six months leading up to the wedding, Nelson had

---

[54] *1940 United States Federal Census* (database online). Ancestry.com, 2012; *U.S. Social Security Applications and Claims Index, 1936–2007* (database online). Ancestry.com, 2015; *Iowa, Consecutive Registers of Convicts, 1867–1970* (database online). Ancestry.com, 2015.

[55] "Annulment Sought of Mixed Marriage," *Evening News* (Wilkes-Barre), 29 Jan. 1925, p. 10; "Former Tar Heel Weds Negro Woman," *Albemarle Press* (N.C.), 29 Jan. 1925, p. 1; "Son of Late S.C. Congressman Weds Pretty Colored Girl in Washington," *New York Age,* 31 Jan. 1925, p. 1.

kept him continuously intoxicated with liquor, depriving him of his capacity to say "I do" with any conviction. Annie Nelson refuted Faison's description of events, telling reporters that the two had been in a loving relationship for a year before they had exchanged vows, and presenting Faison's love letters as evidence. Faison continued to send her such letters as he underwent mental observation, and she visited him regularly during his hospital stay. The minister who presided over the couple's nuptials also insisted that Faison had been lucid and enthusiastic at the ceremony. A letter Faison sent his wife from the hospital helps to explain his seeming change of heart. He wrote, "I hardly know what to do, as they are raising so much hell here and are going to continue to. I guess the best thing we can do is to annul the marriage. With lots of love and kisses from yours."[56] If love brought this young white man into a union with a black woman, coercion from family members led him to backtrack and to concoct a damning story that would facilitate the legal termination of that marriage.[57]

Similar stories made their way into newspapers in subsequent years, featuring family members' insistence that their white relatives' interracial marriages were the result of mental illness. Sometimes this strategy reflected a desire to prevent black spouses from inheriting white family fortunes. Such was the case with the estate of James Banks, a seventy-nine-year-old lawyer from Atlanta who married Dolly Gardner, his long-term African American partner, in Chicago in 1927. The couple had loved one another for over four decades, and had cohabitated openly for thirty years in Atlanta without any backlash from Banks's kin. Only after the pair moved to Chicago to wed and start a home away from anti-miscegenation laws did the Banks family commence its fight against the relationship. Concerned that Dolly would inherit Banks's fortune, the family attempted

[56] "Washington 'Scandal' Love Bark Wrecked, Annulment Sought," *Pittsburgh Courier*, 7 Feb. 1925, pp. 1–2; "North Carolinian Asks Annulment of Negro Marriage," *Index-Journal* (Greenwood, S.C.), 1 Feb. 1925, p. 1.

[57] Faison was not the only white participant in an interracial marriage to claim a black spouse had used alcohol or drugs to facilitate an unwanted union. Dolores Elizabeth Ford, the white daughter of a wealthy manufacturer, sought to end her marriage to Harlem cabaret performer Eugene Newton by claiming that he had used narcotics and alcohol to trick her into matrimony the night they met. Though Newton and his friends claimed that the two had known one another for months, Ford's story prevailed in the courtroom and the marriage was annulled. "Eloping Heiress Is Taken Home," *Harrisburg Telegraph*, 20 Jul. 1929, pp. 1, 14; "'She Loves Me,' Says Hubby," *Pittsburgh Courier*, 27 Jul. 1929, pp. 1, 5; "Heiress Weds Poor Plumber," *Oakland Tribune*, 20 May 1930, p. 1.

to have the marriage declared null on grounds that Banks had lacked the mental capacity to consent due to age and dementia.[58]

Though the desire for inheritance drove the Banks family's lawsuit, their legal strategy relied on the assumption that an affluent white man would never wed a black woman of his own free will, and therefore only mental incompetence could explain Banks's decision. Meanwhile, the family presented Dolly as a scheming younger woman, who had taken advantage of Banks's senility as a way to win his fortune. To challenge the authenticity of the marriage, Fannie Calloway, Banks's sister and the chief complainant in the case, described Dolly as Banks's "secretary," despite her knowledge of their enduring romance. Dolly Gardner Banks countered that Calloway and her relatives had accepted the relationship for over forty years and had acknowledged her as a "real wife" to James, even if Georgia law had forbidden them from marrying.[59] James Banks also fought to save his marriage from annulment, asserting that the union was genuine and denouncing his relatives' greed. "No one made any trouble until we were married," he told reporters. "We lived together many years before that. But after the marriage they began worrying about my money."[60]

The couple fought relatives' efforts to annul their marriage for the next two years, until James Banks died in 1932. Though rumored a million-aire, Banks's estate had declined to only $800 at his time of death, leaving Dolly poor and ill with a nervous condition, which she had acquired during the three years of litigation.[61] Ultimately, her struggle to prove her husband's mental soundness had threatened her own emotional stability. Other couples similarly struggled to maintain equanimity when faced with hostility from friends and family. When Laura Stedman Gould Dees, a descendant of President Grover Cleveland, hanged herself in 1939, the question of white spouses' mental aptitude became all the more prevalent. The police concluded that Dees had committed suicide in response to the isolation that marriage to Milton Dees, an African American chauffeur, had brought her. Rebuffed by friends and family after marrying across the color line, and relegated to an unfamiliar black

---

[58] "Colored Wife, White Relatives Battle for Man's Million," *Afro-American*, 13 Apr. 1929, p. 5; "'Cannot Annul Our Marriage,' Says Banks," *Afro-American*, 8 Feb. 1930, p. 1; Haag, *Consent*, 127–128.

[59] "Colored Wife, White Relatives Battle," 5.

[60] "Cannot Annul Our Marriage," 1.

[61] "Banks, Thought Millionaire, Dies Broke," *Afro-American*, 16 Jan. 1932, p. 19; "Million Dollar Estate Shrinks to Just $800," *Afro-American*, 10 Dec. 1932, p. 10.

neighborhood in Long Island, Laura Dees had fallen into a state of depression that ultimately led to her suicide. Her family sought to spin the story differently. Rejecting the popular narrative that seclusion and social scorn had exacerbated Dees's depression, family members argued that Dees was a "lunatic" whose mental incapacity had caused the controversial marriage. Upon learning that Laura Dees had left her full estate to her husband, cousin Mary Nixon sought to have the marriage annulled retroactively. In her desperate effort to lay claim to the family fortune, Nixon fell back on the familiar claim that interracial unions derived from mental illness, reinforcing the perception that only psychologically unsound white individuals wed across the color line.[62]

Laura Dees's social prominence added to her sense of alienation as a partner in an interracial marriage and placed further scrutiny on her personal and romantic life. But if public notoriety denied Laura and Milton Dees the ability to function as a private couple, it could also protect intermarried couples from backlash. Such was the case with Herbert Newton and Jane Emery, a well-known communist couple who attracted both scorn and support for their marriage. Emery, the white partner, was the daughter of John Emery, an American Legion commander. After two short-lived marriages to white men, Emery turned to communism in the early 1930s amid the depleted economy of the Great Depression. In 1932, Emery began a romantic relationship with Newton, an African American communist. The couple wed and gave birth to a child in 1933, basing their new family in Chicago. Herbert Newton was the only black resident in the South Side apartment building they inhabited, and in 1934 the building's white owner evicted the couple for their interracial cohabitation – an action that municipal judge Thomas Green upheld. After being removed from their home, the Newtons returned their belongings to the unit, an act of defiance that sparked their arrest and brought them back before Judge Green. Green gave both partners a fine of two hundred dollars; when neither could pay, he ordered them to jail.[63]

---

[62] "Does Intermarriage Pay – Or Doesn't It?" *Pittsburgh Courier*, 10 Jun. 1939, p. 3; "Relative Claims Socialite Suicide Was Mentally Weak," *New York Age*, 19 Aug. 1939, p. 6; "White Wife Was Crazy, Kin Says," *Afro-American*, 26 Aug. 1939, p. 8.

[63] David Beasley, *A Life in Red: A Story of Forbidden Love, the Great Depression, and the Communist Fight for a Black Nation in the Deep South* (Winston-Salem: John F. Blair, 2015); Stephen Breszka, "Whites Stunned When They Learn Girl Prodigy Is Race Man's Wife," *Pittsburgh Courier*, 22 Dec. 1934, p. 4.

Here the story took a twist. As Jane was being taken to her cell, a lawyer in the courtroom recognized her as the daughter of John Emery, and he informed Green of the young woman's family connections. Now the judge reversed course. As one journalist explained, Green had been eager to put Jane behind bars when he viewed her as a "nondescript white girl." His outlook changed, however, when he realized she "was a somebody in the white world." Suspending Jane's sentence for a week, the judge ordered that she undergo psychiatric evaluation to determine her state of mind when marrying Herbert Newton. As Jane explained to a reporter, "Now that they've found out my respectable background, I'm to be given special consideration – a psychiatric examination and that sort of thing. I'm to be considered not quite in my right senses for my marriage and the Communistic principles I profess." Jane's noncommunist friends and members of the Emery family shared these concerns about her mental well-being.[64]

The trial and investigation of Jane Emery Newton reflected a number of social anxieties. As Newton biographer David Beasley has pointed out, this case encapsulated a wider fear of communist infiltration and a belief that the party was using young women like Jane to "bait" black men into the cause.[65] But beyond questions of political affiliation, this case serves as another example of the argument that psychologically stable whites did not consent to marriages with black partners; any such marriages were therefore the product of mental instability, and thus nonconsensual. Unlike some of the cases mentioned above, it was the fidelity of Jane Emery Newton's parents that preserved the union. Though the psychiatric director of the Chicago Municipal Court initially diagnosed Jane as schizophrenic and ordered her commitment to the Cook County Psychopathic Hospital, John Emery hired stellar legal representation for his daughter. Jane's defense team brought in a new set of psychiatrists to assess her condition, and they concluded that she was "not only sane, but exceptionally brilliant." After four days in a mental hospital, Jane was permitted to return home to resume her life.[66]

Jane Emery Newton's parents were by no means the only white parents to support a son or daughter's interracial nuptials in the face of legal

---

[64] Beasley, *Life in Red*, 77; Breszka, "Whites Stunned," 4; Haag, *Consent*, 127.
[65] Beasley, *Life in Red*, 78–79.
[66] Ibid., 79–82; "Efforts to Send White Woman to Asylum for Marrying Negro Fails," *New York Age*, 29 Dec. 1934, p. 1; "White Wife of Race 'Red' Adjudged Sane," *Pittsburgh Courier*, 29 Dec. 1934, p. 13.

challenges. One set of parents in Seattle went so far as to tell a marriage license clerk that their fourteen-year-old daughter was in fact eighteen so that she could marry a thirty-eight-year-old black man; in the end, the state superior court annulled the marriage and sentenced both parents to prison for perjury.[67] But media accounts of contested interracial marriages indicate that white parents were more often than not the ones initiating efforts to dissolve the unions. Such was the case with Mary Loney, a white woman from Larksville, Pennsylvania, who endured mental examination when her parents attempted to annul her marriage to her African American boyfriend of five years.[68] Similarly, Leon Lazarus, a white New York insurance broker, claimed that his daughter, Sylvia, suffered from a mental disorder after she wed William Stewart, a black resident of Harlem, in spite of the officiating reverend's claims that she had appeared fully cogent at her wedding. Though the twenty-seven-year-old Sylvia insisted she was happy in her marriage, the elder Lazarus traced his daughter to Chicago and had her forcibly transported to New York, where she was declared insane and committed to a sanitarium.[69] Sylvia Lazarus had in fact suffered a nervous breakdown as a college student, and it is possible she was having a relapse, as her father claimed. Still, in many ways Sylvia's situation mirrors that of Jane Emery and many others who faced similar coercion from family members, court officials, and health professionals, all of whom used psychological diagnoses to quash unions that sparked their moral indignation.

Even sympathetic media accounts of beleaguered interracial marriages perpetuated troubling racial assumptions. Such stories typically neglected the perspective of the black partner in the marriage or made false assumptions about his or her motives. For instance, reports on the Newton marriage offered little insight into Herbert Newton's stance on the marriage. If a white woman's devotion to a black husband called for mental evaluation, a black man's dedication to his white wife called for no

---

[67] "Jail Negro Husband of White Girl," *Brooklyn Daily Eagle*, 2 Mar. 1937, p. 8; "Marriage of Girl to Race Man Annulled," *Pittsburgh Courier*, 16 Oct. 1937, p. 23.

[68] "White Girl Is Negro's Bride," *Plain Speaker* (Hazleton, Pa.), 13 Jul. 1937, p. 11; "Bride of Negro Held by Police," *Wilkes-Barre Times-Leader*, 13 Jul. 1937, p. 3.

[69] *Papers of the NAACP* (Microfilm Collection), Part 11, Series B, Subject File: Kidnapping; Edgar T. Rouzeau, "Interracial Romance Hits Snag; Wife Called 'Insane,'" *Pittsburgh Courier*, 30 Apr. 1938, pp. 1, 4; "Tear Girl from Negro Husband," *Times* (Hammond, Ind.), 20 Apr. 1938, p. 1; "Park-Ave. Socialite 'Kidnapped' from Negro Husband in Chicago," *Washington C.H. Record-Herald* (Washington Court House, Ohio), 21 Apr. 1938, p. 1.

explanation. The press could assume that it was grounded in love, lust, or the pursuit of status. Whatever the motive, a black partner's mental stability did not come into question. When gender roles were reversed, this model stood. As we saw with Dolly Gardner Banks's inheritance case, disapproving family members relied on the fiction that a black woman was interested only in her white husband's money, in spite of their knowledge that the couple had loved one another for decades. Courts and newspapers could perpetuate the belief that sane white Americans would never marry across the color line; accusations of insanity did not, however, fall on black partners in interracial unions.

* * *

As the preceding examples illustrate, the decision to partake in a lawful interracial union sparked a wide range of legal and extralegal consequences. The marriage could yield discrimination, harassment, and violence, and it could also entangle two spouses in a judicial system that worked to erase their legitimate nuptials. Meanwhile, high-profile interracial marriages often inspired new anti-miscegenation bills in states where laws did not exist. In many ways, this pattern is similar to what we have seen in previous chapters; marginal marital arrangements sparked social and judicial backlash, offered new visions of marital possibility, and prompted constricting legislative initiatives. What sets black-white marriage apart from other forms of conjugal misconduct is that the backlash it provoked in turn provoked its own backlash. In other words, the campaign to eliminate racial intermarriage inspired even stronger campaigns to protect interracial couples from persecution. Many critics of anti-miscegenation initiatives emphasized that their efforts did not mark an endorsement of black-white marriage, but rather an attempt to guard mixed couples from abuses. Another, much smaller group of critics actively promoted race-mixing as a means of weakening the nation's racial divide. Both sets of these activists embraced the language of marriage crisis to make their cases. In their own particular ways, they suggested that anti-miscegenation law was hostile to the institution of marriage and that social hierarchies ought to be drawn not along racial lines, but rather along marital ones.

Before exploring the strategies used to fight bans on racial marriage, one should recall that any perceived endorsement of miscegenation could threaten a person's physical and social well-being. In a nation where lynching had long served as a deterrent to interracial socializing, the slightest show of support for black-white marriage was an act of

bravery, and race leaders were well aware of this risk.[70] Recognizing
the dangers that racial intermarriage posed to its participants and
supporters, many African Americans expressed ambivalent feelings
about marriage across the color line. Some black leaders, such as
Howard University sociologist Kelly Miller, viewed African Americans
who married whites as devoid of racial pride and self-respect. Other
leaders, including Booker T. Washington, warned against intermarriage
for more practical reasons – among them the fear that such marriages
would anger white critics of miscegenation, increasing white resentment
toward African Americans and compromising the quest for black
economic advancement.[71]

Despite personal distaste for racial intermarriage, many race leaders still
opposed anti-miscegenation statutes on a political level. While W. E. B. Du
Bois maintained that most African Americans did not wish to marry across
the color line, and in fact he discouraged them from doing so, he nonetheless insisted that the NAACP fight against anti-miscegenation laws, which
he deemed unconstitutional and discriminatory toward African Americans.
As Du Bois argued, "To prohibit such intermarriage would be publicly to
acknowledge that black blood is a physical taint – a thing that no decent,
self-respecting black man can be asked to admit."[72]

Another reason for strong black opposition to anti-miscegenation laws
was the belief that these statutes permitted the sexual exploitation of
black women by white men. With anti-intermarriage laws in place, white
men could seduce or impregnate black women without supporting them
or any children the encounter created – indeed, where anti-miscegenation
statutes existed, legitimizing a mixed-race child through marriage was
forbidden by law. With interracial marriage legal, however, black women

---

[70] In describing middle-class black resistance to interracial intimacy, Rachel Moran notes,
"For blacks, interracial sex threatened their fragile hold on respectability and their
freedom to build communities of color without fear of racial violence." Moran, *Interracial Intimacy*, 65. On the connection between lynching and alleged interracial intimacy,
see Leon F. Litwack, *Trouble in Mind: Black Southerners in the Age of Jim Crow* (New
York: Knopf, 1998), 280–325.

[71] Spickard, *Mixed Blood*, 297–298.

[72] Ibid., 298–299; Mumford, *Interzones*, 163. While the NAACP was initially uninterested
in getting involved in the quest to overturn anti-miscegenation laws, the public outrage
and prejudicial legislation generated by the Jack Johnson scandal inspired the organization to join the struggle in 1913. Francesca Gamber, "The Radical Heart: The Politics of
Love in the Struggle for African-American Equality, 1833–2000" (Ph.D. diss., Southern
Illinois University, Carbondale, 2010), 206–210; Pascoe, *What Comes Naturally*,
169–170.

would have some judicial recourse available when they bore children with white men, as they could use the courts to pursue financial support or to compel marriage with the fathers of their children.[73]

The NAACP embraced this argument in its fight against anti-miscegenation laws. Between 1913 and 1929, the organization mounted at least twenty-nine successful campaigns to block proposed bans on intermarriage, and their efforts intensified in the mid-1920s as Ku Klux Klan activity rose. The NAACP's success derived from its insistence that a very small number of interracial unions occurred in northern states, and its assertion that the continued legalization of interracial marriage would minimize illicit sexual activity between white men and black women. Meanwhile, organizers argued, indecent sexual contact remained rampant in southern states where intermarriage was forbidden. These arguments helped to block anti-miscegenation legislation, not due to widespread popular support for interracial marriage, but because such rhetoric emphasized the sacredness of marriage and disavowed immoral sexual relations. Du Bois illustrated this elevation of marital relations when he wrote, "If two full-grown responsible human beings of any race and color propose to live together as man and wife, it is only social decency not simply to allow, but to compel them to marry." As this statement reveals, supporters of intermarriage could gain allies by emphasizing the moral superiority of marriage to cohabitation, regardless of each partner's color.[74]

The NAACP was thus able to block anti-miscegenation bills by shifting the conversation away from racial amalgamation and toward the promotion of marriage itself. But if the organization's rhetoric appears markedly traditional in its celebration of marriage and the protection of womanhood, it was nonetheless quite provocative in the challenge it posed to the "racial common sense" so often on display in divorce and annulment proceedings. Within a legal culture of denial over the possibility of mutually consensual interracial marriages, the NAACP argued that genuine love across the color line was a rare but real phenomenon and that mixed-race couples ought to have the right to wed – particularly if the alternative was unmarried cohabitation or exploitative sexual relations. Their efforts acknowledged that white partners could and did consent to interracial

---

[73] Gamber, "The Radical Heart," 213; Michele Mitchell, *Righteous Propagation: African Americans and the Politics of Racial Destiny after Reconstruction* (Chapel Hill: University of North Carolina Press, 2004), 215–216; Spickard, *Mixed Blood*, 298–299.

[74] Pascoe, *What Comes Naturally*, 169–180.

unions and that such nuptials were likely not the result of intoxication, insanity, or manipulation, despite vocal claims to the contrary.

In addition to lobbying against anti-miscegenation bills, the NAACP offered members the opportunity to debate the merits of intermarriage in the pages of *The Crisis*, its official magazine. A series of letters in several 1930 issues illustrates a range of views on the subject.[75] The discussion began when a young white man requested advice from Du Bois, the magazine's founder and editor. The letter-writer was in love with a woman he described as "a light mulatto." The two had fallen in love in college, but since then they had struggled to define the terms of their relationship. His parents disapproved of the pairing, as did black and white friends. Therefore, the letter-writer had not seen the woman he loved in six years, but the two had maintained correspondence and their love burned strong.[76]

The letter-writer assured Du Bois that no "immoral" relations had passed between the pair. "I am conservative," he pledged, "and my ideas of love, marriage and divorce and religion by the modern flaming youth would be considered hopelessly mid-Victorian, Puritanical, old fogey and all the other scornful terms applied to such. I do not smoke, drink, dance, play cards, rarely go to a movie and my relations with her were just as 'narrow.'" Despite these conservative sexual and social values, the gentleman could not escape his love for the young woman, and he hoped to marry her. This admission required some unusual rationalizing on his part, however, as he explained to Du Bois, "I do not advocate racial intermarriage in general. But, Mr. Du Bois, since she is more white than Negro why should she not marry white?" With this explanation of his circumstances, the letter-writer requested advice from Du Bois on his romantic quandary.[77]

Du Bois responded that the young man and woman should marry if they so desired, but then he proceeded to list the difficulties they would face after exchanging vows:

You are going to have restricted social intercourse, naturally so far as the whites are concerned; but also, so far as the colored people are concerned. In this matter, they are just as prejudiced as the whites. You are going to meet more or less insult and embarrassment in public places, if your wife is dark enough to have her color

[75] *The Crisis* controlled its editorial content, so these letters do not represent the entirety of its readers' views. They nonetheless offer a compelling cross-section of perspectives, presumably from middle-class black readers.
[76] "Postscript," *The Crisis*, January 1930, p. 28.   [77] Ibid., 28.

noticeable; and finally, (perhaps this is the most serious), you are going to have difficulty in finding work or in keeping it if people know that you have married a colored woman ... If, before you had fallen in love you had consulted me as to the possibility, I should have pointed out these facts and emphasized them and advised you to go no further. But now the question simply is, are both of you ready, in the face of this situation, to face a world "well lost for love"?

With this candid response, Du Bois asked *Crisis* readers to share their thoughts on the matter of racial intermarriage, promising to publish select letters in future issues.[78]

Respondents expressed an array of opinions on the topic. Some of them reiterated Du Bois's message about the challenges interracial couples faced in a society that spurned their unions, noting that the pair would need to be ready to serve as "martyrs" if they wed. "A Colored Woman of Texas" opposed the marriage, arguing that it would be cruel for the man to burden his wife with the inevitable struggles she would face. "If he loves her as he claims he does," she wrote, "he will not want her to suffer martyrdom in seeing her children boycotted by both his race and her race."[79] "A Colored Man from New York" expressed this view in even stronger terms: "How *dare* this young man expose this young woman (and the reverse holds true) to a position so horribly invidious, and exclaim 'I love you' at the same time?" the writer scolded. "This young man and woman propose to ignore Society and live for themselves. Impossible."[80]

If critics denied the possibility that mixed couples could withstand the social obstacles thrust upon them, others argued that marriage could be a tool for combatting those very obstacles. Robert Carter of Massachusetts suggested that the marriage would serve as a respectable counterpoint to the "100 per cent white gentlemen in the Southland who are ever ready to disgrace young colored girls." His words echoed the NAACP's critique of those white men who adamantly opposed interracial marriage, but who eagerly contributed to the mixing of the races through exploitative sexual encounters.[81] E. David Craig of Chicago reinforced this point with his claim that while he did not encourage black-white unions, he believed interracial couples should be able to legitimize their relationships. "This is not a plea for amalgamation," he insisted. "Amalgamation needs no plea.

---

[78] Ibid., 29.   [79] "Inter-Marriage: A Symposium," *The Crisis*, February 1930, p. 50.
[80] Ibid., 50, 67.
[81] "Inter-Marriage: A Symposium," *The Crisis*, March 1930, p. 91. On this phenomenon, see Randall Kennedy, *Interracial Intimacies: Sex, Marriage, Identity, and Adoption* (New York: Vintage Books, 2003), 76–77.

While we sit wondering, amalgamation moves on with irresistible force. The question is: should it go on endlessly through the shameful channel of bastardy, or should it be brought within the bounds of law by racial intermarriage?" Here was a chance for interracial sexual relations – so often sites of exploitation – to receive the stamp of legitimacy. Craig implored this couple to seize the opportunity.[82]

If the above commentators grounded their support for racial intermarriage in the NAACP's language about the protection of black womanhood, others went further in suggesting that intermarriage could serve a positive social good. "A Colored Man of Colorado" argued that racial intermarriage would gain social acceptance only when strong-willed men and women came forth as "martyrs willing to offer themselves in the clinic of social investigation and research."[83] A contributor from Philadelphia encouraged the couple's union with the claim that intermarriage "tends to increase the bond of fellowship between races, destroys prejudices and often produces clever and beautiful offspring."[84] Corris Richardson, an African American woman from New Rochelle, claimed that black-white intermarriage could be an effective means of destabilizing the color line. She argued, "We who call ourselves Christians should do all that we can to break the barrier that separates the two races."[85]

While unconventional, the suggestion by several readers that intermarriage held the power to conquer America's racial divide was not a new one. A number of early twentieth-century writers, scientists, clergy, and politicians had presented black-white marriage as a necessary step toward racial harmony in the United States. Reverend Robert Bryant of Rockford, Illinois, attracted the attention of journalists in 1903 when he encouraged marriage as a remedy for racial conflict, expressing hope that racial blending would make color distinctions vanish completely. Bryant noted that such intermingling already occurred at a faster rate than critics would admit.[86] Dr. G. Frank Lydston presented a similar perspective at a

---

[82] "Inter-Marriage: A Symposium" (Mar. 1930), 89.
[83] "Inter-Marriage: A Symposium" (Feb. 1930), 50. Having read the young man's explanations of his general opposition to racial intermarriage, however, the Colorado writer did not believe this particular gentleman was qualified to represent the cause.
[84] Inter-Marriage: A Symposium" (Mar. 1930), 91.
[85] Ibid., 89. On additional debates over interracial romance among readers of the black press, see Kim Gallon, "'How Much Can You Read about Interracial Love and Sex Without Getting Sore?': Readers' Debate over Interracial Relationships in the *Baltimore Afro-American*," *Journalism History* 39, no. 2 (2013): 104–114.
[86] "Marriage with Negroes Urged to Solve Problem," *Chicago Daily Tribune*, 10 Mar. 1903, p. 2.

1903 Chicago Physicians' Club banquet, arguing that miscegenation was the only solution to the "negro problem."[87]

Prominent white Chicago lawyer Clarence Darrow drew ire in 1910 when it was reported that he had advocated racial intermarriage at a National Negro Committee conference. "It may be a long way in the future," an Associated Press dispatch quoted Darrow as saying, "but intermarriage between the races finally will settle all difficulties as it has in the case of the Irish and Germans and other people who formerly had to be kept apart in order to preserve the peace."[88] This statement generated fervent criticism, including an attack from *Watson's Magazine*, the literary vessel of populist ex-presidential candidate Tom Watson and the platform for his anti-Semitic, anti-Catholic, anti-socialist, and pro–Ku Klux Klan screeds.[89] Perhaps in response to such criticism, Darrow rescinded the offending statement. Though he admitted remarking that amalgamation was inevitable in a nation where blacks and whites dwelt side by side, he denied that he had presented this inevitability as a positive good, or an outcome to which Americans should aspire. While the content of his initial speech remains unclear, it is striking that Darrow, known for his progressive stances, equivocated in this discussion of interracial marriage – a topic so politically charged that he struggled to discuss it with candor.[90]

Franz Boas also predicted the amalgamation of the black and white races. In a 1910 lecture, Boas argued that racial antagonism would gradually dissipate as more and more black-white marriages came to exist. While Boas recognized that this process would be stalled by anti-miscegenation legislation, he believed that legal barriers to miscegenation could not withstand the force of human desire.[91] George Burnham Foster, professor of religious philosophy at the University of Chicago, spoke with

---

[87] "Race Problem a Puzzle," *Chicago Daily Tribune*, 31 Mar. 1903, p. 1.

[88] "Advises Negroes to Marry Whites, "*Chicago Daily Tribune*, 13 May 1910, p. 5. See also "Darrow Urges Intermarriage," *Boston Daily Globe*, 13 May 1910, p. 9; "Race Amalgamation Urged by Darrow," *Atlanta Constitution*, 13 May 1910, p. 10. On white ethnic assimilation and intermarriage, see David R. Roediger, *Working toward Whiteness: How America's Immigrants Became White* (New York: Basic Books, 2005); Matthew Frye Jacobson, *Whiteness of a Different Color: European Immigrants and the Alchemy of Race* (Cambridge, Mass.: Harvard University Press, 1998).

[89] Thomas E. Watson, "Reasoning with an Old Populist Who Now Calls Himself a Socialist," *Watson's Magazine* 5, no. 1 (1910): 540.

[90] "Darrow Says He Never Said Blacks Should Wed Whites," *Chicago Daily Tribune*, 20 May 1910, p. 1.

[91] "Prof. Boas Predicts Race Amalgamation," *New York Times*, 15 May 1910, p. 2.

conviction about the radical potential of interracial marriage. In a 1913 speech before the NAACP, and again in a 1914 speech before Chicago's all-white Grace Methodist Episcopal Church, Foster visualized a world free of racial distinctions, expressing his belief that love and marriage held the power to unite the races, both spiritually and phenotypically.[92]

Calls for interracial marriage dwindled in the 1910s and 1920s amid the negative publicity surrounding Jack Johnson's marriages. But cries for amalgamation resumed as the twenties came to a close. These arguments now reflected the growing recognition of race as a cultural category, and they noted the arbitrariness of the racial boundaries that so often restricted social and romantic interaction. In 1931, for example, journalist Caleb Johnson cited a study conducted by the Carnegie Institution, which refuted popular assumptions that mixed-race children were less fertile than their "pure white or pure black" parents. Analyzing this data, Johnson envisioned a time in the not-so-distant future when African Americans would be "completely absorbed into the general body of mixed bloods of all races which will constitute the American people of the future."[93]

The work of natural and social scientists on the topic of interracial marriage and procreation sparked further debate about the possible benefits of marriage between the races. The editorial pages of African American newspapers became particularly vibrant sites for discussion of the social consequences of racial intermarriage. In 1929, Baltimore's *Afro-American* published an editorial supporting intermarriage as a positive force. Acknowledging that the majority of whites and African Americans opposed marriage across racial lines, the editorial staff still believed that intermarriage might solve the problem of the races.[94] In subsequent months, the *Afro-American* would provide a space for discussion of the merits of racial intermarriage as a means of assimilation, often publishing letters that encouraged a rapid and inclusive amalgamation

---

[92] "Professor Foster Preaches Amalgamation," *The Chicago Defender*, 14 Nov. 1914, p. 1.
[93] Caleb Johnson, "Crossing the Color Line," *Outlook & Independent*, 26 Aug. 1931, pp. 526, 543. In 1931, Earnest Hooton argued that intermarriage and racial amalgamation could create impressive physical results, as in many cases the children of mixed parentage were taller and healthier than unmixed children. "Says There Are No Pure Races," *Pittsburgh Courier*, 20 Jun. 1931, p. 6. Other social scientists made similar claims: Edward Byron Reuter, *Race Mixture: Studies in Intermarriage and Miscegenation* (New York: Whittlesey House, 1931), 153–154; E. Franklin Frazier, "Children in Black and Mulatto Families," *American Journal of Sociology* 39, no. 1 (1933): 19–27.
[94] "Amalgamation," *Afro-American*, 5 Jan. 1929, p. 6.

process. For instance, Catharine Jones, a teacher of home economics, pledged her unequivocal support to the blurring of racial lines. "As soon as amalgamation of the races occurs," she argued, "the economic and social condition of the race will be changed, prejudice will be broken and there will be no race problem." Several other letters in that very issue echoed Jones's points.[95]

The most vocal proponents of black-white intermarriage as a political tool, often referred to as amalgamationists, sought to reverse eugenic assumptions that racial intermarriage would prompt the degeneration of the human race, arguing instead that interracial unions could *improve* the social order. By embracing this connection between mate selection and the future of human civilization, and by encouraging marriages among specific groups of people as a social duty, amalgamationist thinkers adopted a positive eugenic model of their own, albeit one that was at odds with mainstream eugenic thought. Voicing their theories in African American journals such as *The Messenger*, black writers and intellectuals including George Schuyler, J. A. Rogers, and Thomas Kirksey embraced the Boasian argument that there were no inherent differences between the races, and they argued that marriage across the color line could challenge arbitrary racial classifications.[96] Writing in the midst of the Harlem Renaissance, Schuyler was troubled by what he viewed as the development of "Negro Social Consciousness," or an artistic and intellectual celebration of blackness as a defining and unifying characteristic. Arguing that the "laudation of things Negro" only proved the white supremacist assumption that the races were distinct and should occupy separate social worlds, Schuyler encouraged intermarriage as a method of uniting disparate racial groups in their shared American identities. In the process,

[95] Catharine Jones, "Amalgamation Means an End of Prejudice," *Afro-American*, 19 Jan. 1929, p. 6. Other letter-writers were less supportive of calls for amalgamation and interracial marriage. John Harris encouraged African Americans to follow the lead of Marcus Garvey in combatting interracial marriage and in developing a deeper sense of race pride. J. Stanley James of Worton, Maryland, criticized race leaders for prioritizing the quest for racial intermarriage over efforts to acquire education and employment for destitute African Americans. See Harris, "The Man Who Makes Himself White to Gain Natural Advantages Does Not Despise His Color," *Afro-American*, 26 Jan. 1929, p. 5; James, "An Eastern Shore Reader Gives His Reasons for Opposing Amalgamation," *Afro-American*, 2 Feb. 1929, p. 5.

[96] George Hutchinson, "Mediating 'Race' and 'Nation': The Cultural Politics of *The Messenger*," *African American Review* 28, no. 4 (1994): 532–536; Hutchinson, *The Harlem Renaissance in Black and White* (Cambridge, Mass.: Harvard University Press, 1995), 289–312.

divisive cultural differences would dissipate, and race would cease to be a defining social categorization.[97]

Schuyler's calls for interracial marriage became fixtures in the *American Mercury* and in his "Views and Reviews" column in the *Pittsburgh Courier* in the late 1920s. In a 1927 essay, Schuyler presented what he believed were the three possible solutions to the "so-called Negro problem" in America. The first was the emigration of black Americans to foreign nations. The second was the total segregation of African Americans into their own neighborhoods, or into a separate colony within the United States. The third possibility, and in Schuyler's eyes the most feasible, was the amalgamation of blacks and whites through "social intercourse" between the two racial groups. Schuyler did not explicitly recommend interracial sex and marriage in his call for socialization across the color line, but he hinted at this possibility with references to black-and-tan cabarets and dance halls as "exceedingly valuable" in establishing contact and affinity between the races, and in his claim that Americans "must become one people socially and physically, as economically we are already."[98]

Schuyler accused African Americans of hypocrisy in their attitudes toward interracial marriage. He denounced middle-class black men for treating mixed-race couples with hostility while at the same time insisting on extremely light-skinned African American women for their own wives. Schuyler spoke highly of the mixed-race couples he had encountered in his hometown of Syracuse, emphasizing that these couples held legal marriages, had successfully raised children, and ran respectable households. He noted their payment of taxes, their lack of prison records, their career success, their efforts to educate their children, and their commitment to being good neighbors. Despite these fine qualifications, such couples were snubbed by black society. Schuyler believed, however, that the public had much to learn from their subversive yet traditional unions.[99]

In later columns Schuyler called more explicitly for interracial marriage as a means of easing racial conflict. In a 1929 piece, he held little back in declaring, "It is eminently desirable from a social, economic, and anthropological point of view that the Negroes and Caucasians in the country should amalgamate." He argued that since miscegenation had been "the

[97] Hutchinson, "Mediating 'Race' and 'Nation,'" 535–536; Simmons, *Making Marriage Modern*, 90.

[98] George Schuyler, "Views and Reviews," *Pittsburgh Courier*, 11 Jun. 1927, pt. 2, p. 8.

[99] Schuyler, "Views and Reviews," *Pittsburgh Courier*, 4 Feb. 1928, pt. 2, p. 8.

order of the day since the first dawn of history," he saw no reason for resistance to racial intermarriage in the present.[100] Schuyler also noted that the majority of these marriages took place between "middle-class folk or better," so critics could rest assured that class barriers were rarely breached with intermarriage and that future mixed-race couples would be composed primarily of "good citizens" of both races.[101] Like eugenicists who encouraged marriage between persons who were physically healthy, financially mobile, and morally upstanding, Schuyler called for prosperous and principled couples as participants in his amalgamationist campaign.

With his emphasis on the general wealth and respectability of couples who wed across the color line, and his suggestion that middle-class status entailed good citizenship, Schuyler appealed to conservative critics of racial intermarriage, assuring them that the amalgamation of the races would not blur class boundaries or challenge the American social order. But Schuyler's argument was more complex than this, and he proceeded to make an impassioned case for black-white intermarriage that was unlikely to appease critics. "Not only is it eminently desirable that the two 'races' lose their racial identity," he argued, "but it is absolutely necessary if the Negroes are to attain the objectives for which they now strive. The cult of things African can only keep the Negroes in ghettos as they are at present." In Schuyler's view, the only way for African Americans to attain social and economic equality with whites was to become one with them in marriage and in rearing mixed-race children, who would know greater opportunities than their darker-skinned counterparts. It ultimately did not matter to Schuyler if readers agreed that amalgamation was desirable or necessary, for in his view the process was inevitable, and had long been under way. "It will happen in spite of all the yelpings of white and black race patriots," he predicted, "and it will be a good thing for all concerned."[102]

Schuyler's writings exemplify the difficulties of labeling amalgamationist thinkers either "conservative" or "radical" in their opinions on marriage across the color line, for Schuyler incorporated ideas from both of

---

[100] Schuyler, "Views and Reviews," *Pittsburgh Courier*, 27 Jul. 1929, p. 12. In one piece Schuyler noted some of the more prominent figures of mixed descent to illustrate the potential benefits of intermarriage. They included Alexandre Dumas, Frederick Douglass, Booker T. Washington, W. E. B. Du Bois, Alexander Pushkin, and Samuel Coleridge Taylor. *Racial Intermarriage*, 30–31.

[101] Schuyler, "Views and Reviews," *Pittsburgh Courier*, 27 Jul. 1929, p. 12.

[102] Ibid., 12.

these political poles into his call for interracial marriage. In advocating for intermarriage, Schuyler challenged black and white opponents of miscegenation to release their prejudices and to look to one another as social equals. In doing so, however, he rejected the notion that there was anything inherently valuable about African American culture itself, dismissing black struggles to retain community and cultural heritage as "the cult of things African." His efforts to present amalgamation as a means of uplift particularly appropriate for respectable and middle-class couples indicates an adherence to class strictures that seems at odds with his call for the destabilization of racial boundaries.

Moreover, while Schuyler dismissed critics of racial intermarriage as prejudiced and ill-informed, his case for intermarriage included his own condemnation of the romantic arrangements he deemed damaging to the institution of marriage. He argued that in spite of criticisms directed against intermarried couples, these marriages were "nearer the ideal matrimonial state than is usual in this day of progressive polygamy." He continued, "The great trouble with our modern social structure is that the family is disintegrating and the wise men are scratching their polls trying to figure out ways and means of saving it ... And yet this monogamic family is the cornerstone of all present and much of past civilization ... [and] we ought to encourage any step that will prolong it."[103]

With these words Schuyler simultaneously contested and reinforced the boundaries of marital propriety. He encouraged a practice that was widely believed to challenge the institution of marriage by claiming that committed racial intermarriages could *strengthen* the standard of monogamous marriage and save the deteriorating family structure. He agreed that monogamous marriage was under threat and he saw the acceptance of respectable intermarriage as a remedy that could fortify marriage as the cornerstone of civilization. Opponents of racial intermarriage had long argued that the practice would challenge "the purity of public morals."[104] And while Schuyler dismissed these critics, he simultaneously applied their rhetoric in denouncing changes to modern marriage as damaging to the public good and in arguing that monogamous marriage was essential to the function of American society. In this way, Schuyler showed that he was as invested in preserving the marital status quo as

[103] Schuyler, "Views and Reviews," *Pittsburgh Courier*, 4 Jan. 1930, p. 6.
[104] A Virginia court applied this phrase in 1878 as it voided the marriage of a black man and a white woman. Pascoe, *What Comes Naturally*, 1–2.

he was in transforming it.[105] His rhetoric also displays the recognition that racial intermarriage would never gain public acceptance if grouped with other disreputable marital practices, such as progressive polygamy and trial marriage. Not wishing to suffer the same abuses that other participants in conjugal misconduct faced, Schuyler aligned himself with the guardians of marital propriety in his efforts to bring respectable intermarried couples within their midst.

* * *

It would be easy to dismiss Schuyler as an anomaly in his outspokenness on the subject of racial intermarriage, the drama of his political rhetoric, and the controversy he seemed to court throughout his career.[106] While not reflective of the views that more mainstream race leaders such as Kelly Miller and W. E. B. Du Bois expressed on the subject, Schuyler's perspective corresponded with a small, if vocal movement that pushed for racial intermarriage as a legitimate romantic arrangement if practiced by the right people. Schuyler employed many of the rhetorical strategies utilized by the Penguin Club, an organization founded in New York in 1936, which provided a communal space for couples involved in black-white marriages. The Penguin Club was not the first of its kind; it was modeled after the Manasseh Society, an interracial marriage society that was formed in Milwaukee in the late nineteenth century and which established a second branch in Chicago soon after. By 1900 the society had reached a membership of seven hundred, and it became known for hosting a yearly ball that couples could attend only in black-white pairings.[107]

---

[105] Schuyler expressed a similar ambivalence about shifting marital trends in a 1931 column. He praised Pope Pius XI for writing a 16,000-word Encyclical that "ranted and raved at companionate marriage, divorce and birth control." Schuyler supported the Pope's "impassioned defense of chaste wedlock," and he encouraged black readers to familiarize themselves with this call for a return to the "old morality." "Views and Reviews," *Pittsburgh Courier*, 17 Jan. 1931, p. 10.

[106] See Jeffrey Ferguson, *The Sage of Sugar Hill: George Schuyler and the Harlem Renaissance* (New Haven: Yale University Press, 2005).

[107] Clotye M. Larsson, ed., *Marriage across the Color Line* (Chicago: Johnson Publishing Company, 1965), 59; W. Forrest Cozart, *The Mannaseh: A Story of Mixed Marriages* (Atlantic City: State Register Publishing Co., 1909), 28–29; G. Reginald Daniel, *More Than Black: Multiracial Identity and the New Racial Order* (Philadelphia: Temple University Press, 2002), 96–97; Kevin K. Gaines, *Uplifting the Race: Black Leadership, Politics, and Culture in the Twentieth Century* (Chapel Hill: University of North Carolina Press, 1996), 125; Carter, *The United States of the United Races*, 146–147; Ralph E. Luker, *The Social Gospel in Black and White: American Racial Reform, 1885–1912* (Chapel Hill: University of North Carolina Press, 1991), 174.

While the Manasseh Society had challenged convention by celebrating the existence of married black-white couples, its organizers insisted that it was a purely social organization. The society did not incorporate an explicit political strategy into its constitution, and its primary function was to provide leisure activities for intermarried couples and to offer charitable aid to interracial families in dire financial straits.[108] Manasseh Society member Lewis Proctor recounted the organization's founding in a speech before members at the first annual ball. He declared, "The marriage of colored men to white women has always been looked upon with criticism by both races, and it was for the purpose of removing this sting that the society was founded."[109] In order to serve this purpose, however, Proctor believed that the organization had to prove to the critical public that its members were upstanding citizens with healthy marriages. The society therefore instituted a Committee on Membership, which investigated all applicants and demanded that members be legally married. The society barred couples in common law unions, and it generally limited its membership to stable middle-class couples. It also required that members attend church regularly and raise Christian children. Procter argued that these restrictions were essential for the organization's success in proving its high moral standing to skeptics.[110]

The Penguin Club emerged nearly fifty years after the founding of the Manasseh Society. And while it maintained its predecessor's firm commitment to providing community for mixed-race couples, it displayed deeper attention to creating social and political change than had the Manasseh Society, likely due to its later date of origin. The Penguin Club was established in 1936 in an effort to protect the rights of intermarried couples and their children. It was named for the bird "[so] beautifully marked with white and black," and its founders hoped to create a social space for couples who had been shunned by both black and white society.[111] Following an announcement of the group's formation in *The New York Amsterdam News*, Penguin Club organizers were bombarded with applications from mixed-race couples, a hundred of whom were

---

[108] St. Clair Drake and Horace R. Clayton, *Black Metropolis: A Study of Negro Life in a Northern City*, revised and enlarged edition (Chicago: University of Chicago Press, 1993), 145–146.

[109] "Whites and Blacks," *Chicago Daily Tribune*, 2 Mar. 1892, p. 3.

[110] Ibid., 3; Daniel, *More Than Black*, 96.

[111] T.E.B., "The Feminist Viewpoint: The Penguin Club," *New York Amsterdam News*, 14 Mar. 1936, p. 6; "Mixed Couples Charge Ban by Both Races; Form Club," *Amsterdam News*, 22 Feb. 1936, p. 11.

granted entry following careful investigations seeking "proof of character." The club barred childless couples from membership, claiming that commitment to parenthood was essential to a stable relationship.[112]

While this decision to welcome only respectable and procreative couples indicates a dedication to traditional notions of marital and familial propriety, as displayed by the Manasseh Society at the turn of the twentieth century, the Penguin Club had a somewhat more progressive and political agenda than its predecessor. One *Amsterdam News* writer cited "militance" in the club's mission of "breaking down all barriers in both races which now ban interracial couples." This reporter had attended a Penguin Club meeting at the Harlem YMCA, and listed the resolutions put forth at the event: "The club wants whites in Harlem accepted in civic and community organizations on the same basis as Negroes. It wants Negroes to feel free to walk into the Y.M.C.A. or a similar organization in white sections without fear of embarrassment."[113] While they still billed the club as a social group for mixed-race couples, Penguin Club organizers suggested that the gathering of such couples could achieve significant political ends. Like Schuyler, the founders of the Penguin Club believed that intermarriage could serve as a gateway to residential and social desegregation, as well as improved communication between the races.

In its efforts to create spaces for interracial couples, the Penguin Club applied strategies that nodded to both the traditional and the progressive, in the same way that Schuyler toed that line in his writings. Clearly the club's appeals to monogamous, procreative matrimony were defining elements of its interracial agenda. This insistence upon respectable marriage coheres with efforts by prominent African Americans to produce successful, legitimate, and committed marriages as a means of attaining racial equality throughout the early twentieth century. In the words of historian Michele Mitchell, "Orderly homes, personal behavior, and thrift supposedly indicated black people's readiness for full participation in the national body politic, thus marriage could ostensibly obliterate the sexual legacies of slavery, especially concubinage."[114] In light of the belief

---

[112] Larsson, *Marriage across the Color Line*, 59; Joseph Golden, "Patterns of Negro-White Intermarriage," *American Sociological Review* 19, no. 2 (1954): 147; "Scores Seek to Join Club Formed for Mixed Couples," *Amsterdam News*, 14 Mar. 1936, p. 3; "Intermarried Couples Open Fight to End All Barriers," *Amsterdam News*, 18 Apr. 1936, p. 1.

[113] "Intermarried Couples Open Fight to End All Barriers," 1.

[114] Mitchell, *Righteous Propagation*, 202.

that successful and monogamous marriage could prove African
Americans' fitness for citizenship, it becomes clear what a risk founders
of the Manasseh Society, and later the Penguin Club, took in their public
support of interracial marriage. Calls for monogamy, legitimacy, and
childbearing no doubt excluded some who may have benefited from the
services these clubs had to offer. But too much focus on exclusions
obscures the great gambles these organizations took in celebrating racial
intermarriage within a climate that was anything but supportive.

At the same time, we cannot overlook the ways in which club organizers embraced exclusionary and, to a degree, eugenic principles in service
of this goal. While the members of the Penguin Club did not have the
authority to prevent couples from exchanging vows, they nonetheless ran
their organization like a marriage licensing bureau, permitting entry to
those couples who met a certain set of abstract qualifications and denying
it to those who failed to meet that standard. In drawing a line between
formally wed and common law couples, procreative and childless couples,
middle-class and working-class couples – in sum, between those who
could provide "proof of character" and those who could not – organizers
of interracial marriage societies distanced themselves from the couples
that did not fit their image of marital propriety. While they contended that
racial intermarriage could yield positive effects, they also suggested that
these effects would materialize only with the exclusion of couples who
were unfit to participate.[115]

In addition to fighting against racial discrimination, then, 1920s
and 1930s amalgamationist thinkers granted authority to the notion of
marriage as a legitimizing social force. They embraced the language
of marriage crisis, agreeing that modern marriage was in a state of disarray
and that it needed fixing. But they turned conventional logic on its head by
arguing that racial intermarriage could provide one necessary solution to
the problems at hand. Not only would it improve public policy by blurring
the color line and eroding the tensions that gave way to racial violence and
segregation; it would also bring new reverence to the institution of marriage, undermining the scourges of progressive polygamy, dysgenic unions,

---

[115] This approach would endure among racial intermarriage societies in subsequent generations. Groups modeled after the Manasseh Society and the Penguin Club emerged after
World War II, and like their predecessors, they provided social support and community
space for intermarried couples. Also like their predecessors, organizations such as the
Club of Tomorrow, Club Internationale, and Club Miscegenation urged members to
exhibit their moral uprightness, economic stability, and Christian devotion. Romano,
Race Mixing, 141–142.

and trial marriage by validating respectable unions between loving couples. Amid ongoing courtroom claims that consensual black-white marriage was impossible, amalgamationists insisted that proper and successful interracial unions were not merely possible but desirable. In making these claims, amalgamationists reinforced the notion that people's marriages were tied to the social and moral fiber of the nation.

From this angle, we see the complex role that amalgamationist rhetoric played. On the one hand, it sought to erase the arbitrary racial lines that divided the nation. On the other hand, it bolstered the public image of one marital minority at the expense of another, solidifying marriage's role as an arbiter of citizenship and social status, and drawing a firm line between those deemed worthy of its privileges and those whose sexualities rendered them unfit for state and social approval. In many ways, this strategy was an outgrowth of the backlash that intermarried couples faced. Recognizing the abuse that mixed couples incurred for their unconventional unions and aware that legal intermarriages could not always withstand the pressures of court officials and disapproving families, amalgamationists did what they could to bring higher social status to respectable black-white couples. In many cases, they did so by excluding the families they deemed less worthy of marital recognition – just as others excluded them from the popular vision of proper matrimony. In this way, while attention to the fight for racial intermarriage informs our understandings of racial discrimination in the early twentieth century, it also tells us about the role that marriage itself could play in driving a wedge between proper and improper family units. Rather than challenge the exclusionary nature of marriage, amalgamationists attempted to use it to their advantage.

This strategy would be useful to the originators of the marriage education movement, which came to prominence in the 1930s and was premised on the eugenic notion that respectable marriage ought to be limited to committed, physically and mentally fit couples with ambitions of child-rearing. Like amalgamationists, marriage educators believed that marriage had the power to improve society as a whole, and they encouraged the wider exchange of vows as a means of restoring order to a country that suffered from loosening morals and shifting gender roles. These marriage instructors promoted their vision of marital propriety by defining it in opposition to the romantic arrangements they deemed inadequate. Not surprisingly, they often held up racial intermarriage as a chief form of conjugal misconduct.

6

Averting the Crisis

The Birth of the Marriage Education Movement

Much of the backlash against conjugal misconduct examined thus far was legal in nature. Reactions to disreputable marriages included crackdowns on matrimonial bureaus and commercialized matchmaking, tighter regulations on remarriage after divorce, stricter eugenic laws, a push for uniform marriage and divorce legislation, efforts to craft a constitutional amendment permitting federal marriage legislation, the creation of stricter annulment laws, and the development of new anti-miscegenation bills. Each of these legal initiatives responded to a different set of marital challenges; together they reflected a broader effort to restrain couples from defying marital norms and to mandate permanent, monogamous, and respectable unions amid ongoing anxiety that the institution of marriage was in decline.

But alongside the legal push to contain conjugal misconduct was the fear that the law was insufficient to fight modern marital trends, particularly since disparate state laws prevented the creation of national marriage standards. Even as reformers fought to erect legal barriers to controversial marriages, many of them also argued that the law held limited reach in shaping romantic arrangements. For instance, Newell Maynard of the National Society for Broader Education gave a 1914 lecture to the Asheville Young Women's Christian Association, where he declared the need for stricter eugenic regulation and uniform marriage laws. He added, however, that these legal changes should be accompanied by increased education in parenting and marital relations to ensure children's long-term commitment to proper family life.[1] Similarly,

---

[1] "Series of Lectures Closed Last Night," *Asheville Citizen Times,* 25 Jan. 1914, p. 5.

Cincinnati clubwomen supported the push for more stringent and consistent divorce laws, eugenic health certificates, and a constitutional amendment permitting federal marriage and divorce law. In addition, they called for the requirement of a two-week lapse between the receipt of a marriage license and the exchange of vows, and for prohibitions on black-white intermarriage. Nevertheless, members of these organizations also recognized that such legal measures could only be effective if accompanied by a change in culture. Therefore, they also encouraged educational programs to warn children against inappropriate unions.[2] Even Charles Thaddeus Terry, president of the Uniform State Laws Commission, agreed that legal changes alone could not save the family from the forces that threatened it, arguing in 1914 that education was essential to creating stronger marriages and households.[3]

Religious leaders put forth similar arguments about the need for marriage education. In 1921, Baptist minister and writer Albert Beaven denounced the "fast, sporty, godless" people who were destroying the institution of marriage with their affinity for divorce and their indifference to proper family life. Preaching to his Rochester, New York, congregants, Beaven praised uniform divorce laws, eugenic regulations, and the publication of the banns as "wise" strategies. He nonetheless claimed that these measures failed to get to the root of the marriage crisis, declaring, "There are many advance steps that could be taken to safeguard the marriage altar, but after we have done our best along this line we need to realize that satisfactory relationships in the home are created not by law, but by the folks that make up the home." He continued, "We will do more to remedy the present difficulty in home life by fencing the marriage altar religiously than by fencing it legally. While the latter is valuable the former is indispensable." Beaven thus called for Christians to educate children on the value of healthy homes and families and to prevent them from rushing into inadvisable nuptials. He claimed that this training would reverse trends toward divorce and dysgenic marriage in a way that legislation could not do.[4]

In many ways, such sentiments aligned conservative clergymen like Beaven with the reformers they had historically shunned. For instance,

---

[2] Emma L. Fetta, "Federal Marriage and Divorce Law Logical, View of Cincinnatians, Backing Movement; Home Training Necessary," *Cincinnati Enquirer*, 14 Dec. 1922, p. 2.

[3] Charles Henry Adams, "New York Day by Day," *Eagle* (Bryan, Tex.), 28 Dec. 1914, p. 4; "Has It Justified Itself?," *Detroit Free Press*, 8 Feb. 1915, p. 4.

[4] "Divorce Courts Are Kept Busy by Sporty Set," *Democrat and Chronicle* (Rochester, N.Y.), 3 Oct. 1921, p. 19.

Judge Ben Lindsey, a frequent target of religious officials for his perceived advocacy of trial marriage, expressed similar views on the matter. Lindsey noted that the myriad laws intended to preserve marriage had failed in their objectives. He explained that "the law of the heart is more important than the law of the statutes," and therefore stricter divorce laws alone could never prevent couples from making poor marital decisions – and Lindsey did not hesitate to classify many couples' choices as poor. He agreed with Beaven that the institutions of marriage and family were in a state of crisis, asserting, "We've got to recognize the fact that we are face to face with one of the greatest social problems in modern time in this statistically proved failure of marriage." Despite their differences, these two men were united in their belief that new educational strategies were necessary to halt the deterioration of marriages across the nation.[5]

Family reform organizations also joined in this call for marriage education. As noted in Chapter 3, the Russell Sage Foundation's Committee on Marriage Laws worked to create uniform marriage legislation, outlaw common law marriage, raise the age of marital consent, and eliminate elopements across state borders. But in spite of that organization's legal approach, its chair Joanna Colcord embraced the logic of men like Beaven and Lindsey, contending that stricter marriage laws were an inadequate fix. Colcord explained these sentiments in the committee's 1923–1924 report, stating, "The committee feels that there is need for much educational work before adequate legislation regarding marriage can possibly be effected." Colcord believed that her organization, and others like it, needed to provide this training in proper mate selection and comportment in marriage.[6]

Colcord's call for educational solutions was a pervasive and influential one in the 1920s and 1930s. This era witnessed the creation of wide-reaching programs in marriage counseling and education, which sought to remedy the problems many believed had come to taint the institution of marriage. This new breed of marriage educators agreed that legislation was not sufficient to combat shifting marital values. Instead, they strove to eliminate alternative marital relations through education, individualized counseling, and cultural indoctrination. Their quest to instill proper values about marriage and heterosexual romance through matrimonial

---

[5] "Geraldine Discusses Divorce," *Oakland Tribune Magazine*, 21 Jan. 1923, p. 12.

[6] "Report of the Committee of Marriage Laws," 1923–1924, Family Service Association of America Records, Box 13, Folder 41, Social Welfare History Archives, University of Minnesota.

training was perhaps the most enduring response to the varied forms of conjugal misconduct profiled throughout this book.

In the eyes of many social scientists, the 1920s marked the point of no return for the nation's marriage crisis. As the divorce rate rose, the birth rate declined, as did the marriage rate among college-educated women. To the dismay of marriage scholars and eugenicists, the wider accessibility of contraception allowed married couples to limit the number of children they bore, and permitted single people to partake in sexual experimentation without facing the fear of unwanted pregnancy. Birth control also ensured the continuation of trial marriage as a viable option for noncommittal couples, and it allowed couples to view sex as a means of recreation, rather than an essential tool for procreation. Paul Popenoe, a renowned eugenicist, educator, and marriage counselor, addressed these changing marital tides with alarm in his 1925 book *Modern Marriage: A Handbook*. "That something is wrong with marriage today is universally admitted and deplored," he declared. "The number of celibates, of mismated couples, of divorces, of childless homes, of wife deserters, of mental and nervous wrecks; the frequency of marital discord, of prostitution and adultery, of perversions, of juvenile delinquency, tells the story."[7] Popenoe would devote his professional career to warning the public about these menaces to marital convention and to reversing them through the implementation of marital education in homes, churches, and schools.

In 1928, University of North Carolina sociologist Ernest R. Groves expressed similar concerns over the state of matrimony with his book *The Marriage Crisis*. Groves contended that the wider availability of contraception fundamentally changed marriage in the United States. Now that growing numbers of couples had the resources to postpone or eschew childbearing, procreation was no longer an expected component of romantic relationships. As a result, Groves argued, more and more couples based their unions on sexual attraction, rather than on the desire to raise families. This change marked a drastic shift away from traditional notions of sex as a tool for reproduction within marriage and toward a vision of marriage as merely a site for the hedonistic pursuit of pleasure. "By taking out the risk of undesired parenthood," Groves explained, "marriage ceases to be of social significance and becomes merely a private matter of concern only to those persons forming an alliance."[8]

---

[7] Paul Popenoe, *Modern Marriage: A Handbook* (New York: Macmillan, 1925), vi. Also quoted in Davis, *More Perfect Unions*, 27.
[8] Ernest R. Groves, *The Marriage Crisis* (New York: Longmans, Green, 1928), 43.

While Groves recognized that on the surface this application of a "pleasure philosophy" to married life did not appear to be the stuff of crisis, he expressed concern that the removal of reproductive expectations from matrimony would have dire social consequences. He worried that the wider availability of contraception was leading young people to reject marriage entirely, as they now had greater opportunity for sexual exploration outside the confines of matrimony. Even more troubling to Groves, the accessibility of birth control led a growing number of couples to form trial marriages. As contraceptive methods became more widely available, Groves feared that more couples would wed on a conditional basis, holding out the right to dissolve their unions as long as they remained childless. Groves did not approach trial marriage with the same outright disdain of some of its earlier critics. He did, however, worry that trial marriages were doomed to fail, for while provisionally married partners might share intense sexual attraction, they often lacked a true romantic connection, and they approached their unions without considering the long-term sacrifices marriage required. Groves feared that these noncommittal attitudes made divorce inevitable.[9]

Groves therefore hoped to eradicate experimental marriage practices. Unlike earlier anti–trial marriage crusaders, however, Groves did not believe that legislation was the appropriate way to reverse the trend, and he criticized those opponents of modern marital practices whose strategy was "to advocate stringent divorce laws, and, from every corner, more coercion as an antidote to the dangerous freedom of the present."[10] Groves believed that the law could never restrain the forces of sexual desire. Instead he argued that proper attitudes toward sex and marriage must be taught, and he encouraged parents and educators to adopt a program of marital training that would instruct impressionable youth on the importance of marriage and family. Adopting what he called a "preventative approach," Groves reasoned that matrimonial education would avert sexual experimentation and trial marriages down the line. He emphasized the role that social scientists could play in shaping public attitudes about marriage and family, arguing that specialists in sociology, psychology, and psychiatry held the knowledge and training to instill healthy attitudes about sex and marriage. This instruction would prevent trial marriages from forming, and it would reassert the centrality of childbearing to marital relations.[11]

---

[9] Ibid., 93–94.   [10] Ibid., vii–viii.   [11] Ibid., 196–203.

To carry out this mission, Groves taught the first ever university course in marriage education at Boston University in 1922, and he incorporated marriage training into the University of North Carolina's curriculum in 1927 (see Figure 6.1). These courses became immensely popular on university campuses throughout the 1930s, with one study estimating that by 1937, more than two hundred American colleges and universities offered courses on marital preparation. Groves also founded the Conference on Conservation of Marriage and the Family, through which he publicized courses on marital training and further pushed the argument that aid from experts in the social sciences could improve the quality of marriages and solve the marriage crisis that contraception and trial marriage had wrought.[12]

Popenoe agreed with Groves that successful marriage relied on the precise application of expert knowledge, calling for the wider implementation of marriage training as a means of preventing marital failure. This schematic approach characterized professional treatment of marriage in the 1930s, as social scientists, physicians, educators, clergy, and social workers united within the broad domain of "marriage counseling." These experts formed clinics that offered advice on successful marriage to young couples striving for marital success and to long-married couples hoping to reclaim the happiness that temporarily eluded them. They extended marital training into schools, encouraging healthy, procreative matrimony to students from elementary school onward. They debated the uses of contraception, the proper age for marriage, and the role of sexual pleasure in maintaining marital contentment. In sum, these counselors believed that there was indeed a science to successful marriage, and that with proper education, commitment, and communication, couples could endure whatever hardships came their way. In implementing their new model, marriage experts addressed the shortcomings of the law in shaping romantic practices and added innovative strategies to a long-standing battle against conjugal misconduct.

* * *

Much of the marriage education movement's success derived from Paul Popenoe's public relations skills. Popenoe's extensive correspondence

---

[12] Simmons, *Making Marriage Modern*, 116–117; Celello, *Making Marriage Work*, 32–33; Eva S. Moskowitz, *In Therapy We Trust: America's Obsession with Self-Fulfillment* (Baltimore: Johns Hopkins University Press, 2001), 84–87; Jeffrey P. Moran, *Teaching Sex: The Shaping of Adolescence in the 20th Century* (Cambridge, Mass.: Harvard University Press, 2000), 126–130.

FIGURE 6.1 Ernest Groves teaches his marriage course at the University of North Carolina at Chapel Hill, Newspaper Enterprise Association Reference Department, 7 May 1940.

with clergy, educators, and social workers; his organization of countless conferences, lectures, and workshops on the proper methods of marriage education and counseling; his copious publication of books, pamphlets, and articles on marital and sexual propriety; and his continued insistence that these subjects be incorporated into school curricula display the vigor with which Popenoe spread his message. Born in Topeka, Kansas, in 1888, Popenoe's original passion was for botany. He left Stanford University after his junior year to care for his ailing father and to collect and cultivate date palms. But Popenoe shifted his focus from plant breeding to human breeding throughout the 1910s, serving as editor of the *Journal of Heredity* from 1913 to 1918 and accepting the position of executive secretary of the American Social Hygiene Association in 1920.[13]

---

[13] Molly Ladd-Taylor, "Eugenics, Sterilisation and Modern Marriage in the USA: The Strange Career of Paul Popenoe," *Gender and History* 13, no. 2 (2001): 303.

Popenoe never completed college, but after receiving an honorary degree from Occidental College, he embraced the title of "Dr. Popenoe" for the remainder of his career. His lack of academic credentials led to some professional slights, including his exclusion from the American Association of Marriage Counselors.[14] Nevertheless, Popenoe's limited training did not hinder his rise to the top of his profession or his reputation as an expert in the fields of marriage and family.[15] Popenoe's earlier publications, among them *Applied Eugenics* (1918), *The Conservation of the Family* (1926), and *Sterilization for Human Betterment* (1929), were largely grounded in eugenic theory, and Popenoe devoted himself to proving the scientific bases for differences between men and women, the threat that immigration of Eastern Europeans posed to the survival of Nordic stock, and the need to hasten the reproduction of the fit and to halt the reproduction of the unfit.[16] Gradually these ideas coalesced into the preoccupation with marriage that would drive Popenoe for the duration of his career. Inspired by the matrimonial health consultation centers that spread through Germany and Austria in the 1920s, Popenoe appointed himself the American authority in the field when he founded the American Institute of Family Relations (AIFR) in 1930.[17] He viewed the AIFR as a "human laboratory where marriage problems were classified, studied, and solved" by "real scientists."[18]

In addition to offering therapy to married couples, Popenoe wished to provide lessons about matrimony to those who had yet to experience it firsthand. Sharing the mission of Ernest Groves, Popenoe was an outspoken advocate of marital training within university curricula. While he acknowledged that around half of American colleges and universities had begun to offer some sort of marital instruction by the end of the 1930s, he feared that these courses were "largely perfunctory," focusing most often on the history of the family so as to avoid more concrete, controversial,

[14] Ian Dowbiggin, *The Search for Domestic Bliss: Marriage and Family Counseling in 20th-Century America* (Lawrence: University Press of Kansas, 2014), 32–33.

[15] Of Popenoe and other self-proclaimed marriage experts, Celello writes, "What defines their expertise is not the extent of their education but the authoritative way in which they present their views, particularly in the popular media." *Making Marriage Work*, 6.

[16] Ladd-Taylor, "Eugenics, Sterilisation and Modern Marriage in the USA," 303–304.

[17] See Moskowitz, *In Therapy We Trust*, 76, and Kline, *Building a Better Race*, 142, for further information on Popenoe's indebtedness to the marriage consultation centers constructed in Prussian cities in the name of "race hygiene" and "race betterment." By 1934 more than a thousand of these centers offered eugenic and psychological advice to clients.

[18] Moskowitz, *In Therapy We Trust*, 76.

and prescriptive lessons on domestic living. But Popenoe believed that such hands-on training was essential, and not only for college students. He insisted that children's education for marriage start at an early age, both in school and at home, so that young people entered adulthood eager to wed and prepared for the responsibilities that marriage entailed. He considered it particularly essential for girls to receive this training, as he found that many young women completed elementary school, high school, and sometimes college without the knowledge of housekeeping that was essential for any competent wife. Too often, Popenoe argued, ignorance in the fields of cooking, home-making, and childrearing rendered otherwise healthy women unfit for marriage.[19]

In his early work, Popenoe displayed a clear rejection of marriage and reproduction across the black-white color line. Along with coauthor Roswell Johnson, Popenoe argued in *Applied Eugenics* that African Americans were eugenically inferior to whites and that racial intermarriage should not be permitted because it detracted from the purity and dominance of the white race.[20] Popenoe's condemnation of racial intermarriage persisted in his later works, albeit in a less forceful manner. In one 1935 piece he admitted that couples who married across racial lines could be happy together, but he also presumed that the overwhelming majority of them were not. While he continued to put forth the biological arguments he had made in *Applied Eugenics*, claiming that two upstanding members of distinct racial groups risked producing substandard offspring, he did more to emphasize the social and psychological consequences that mixed-race couples faced. He stated that overwhelmingly negative public opinions of interracial romance ought to discourage couples from marrying across the color line and that couples who defied this popular sentiment risked social ostracism and emotional strain.[21]

Another driving force behind Popenoe's marital education program was his belief that too many couples were entering marriage on a trial basis and subsequently divorcing. Rejecting the notion that marriage

---

[19] Popenoe, "A College Education for Marriage," American Social Hygiene Association pamphlet, April 1939, Paul Popenoe Papers, Box 126, Folder 4, American Heritage Center, Laramie, Wyo. See also Moran, *Teaching Sex*, 126–127.

[20] Paul Popenoe and Roswell Hill Johnson, *Applied Eugenics* (New York: Macmillan Company, 1918), 280–297. See also Popenoe, *The Conservation of the Family* (Baltimore: Williams & Wilkins, 1926), 144; Laura L. Lovett, "'African and Cherokee by Choice': Race and Resistance under Legalized Segregation," *American Indian Quarterly* 22, nos. 1–2 (1998): 216–217.

[21] Paul Popenoe, "Problems of Heredity," 1935, Popenoe Papers, Box 116, Folder 1.

could be a temporary contract to be dissolved at will if either party found the experience unsatisfactory, Popenoe strove to discourage divorce through sex and marriage education. One of Popenoe's key strategies for undermining divorce was to note the physical and mental inadequacy of divorcees. In one 1933 article Popenoe wrote, "A very slight consideration at once shows that the divorcees are on the whole biologically inferior to the happily married part of the population. They represent a much higher frequency of mental disease, a shorter expectation of life, and a high degree of sterility. Despite innumerable exceptions, then, it cannot be doubted that the divorcees as a group represent a population that is eugenically less desirable than the average [population]."[22]

Despite this professed belief in the innate inferiority of divorcees, Popenoe also argued that divorce could be eliminated through education. By instilling admiration of family life and contempt for the practice of divorce into the minds of young children, Popenoe hoped to create a generation of youth that valued marriage above all other social institutions. The law alone could not achieve this goal, and Popenoe doubted its effectiveness in averting the marriage crisis. "The conservation of the family is to be sought not through changes in divorce laws," he argued, "but through better education for marriage, a broader range of social opportunities for young people to enable them to find suitable mates ... and the provision of clinics or other facilities for giving people the necessary technical information and aid in adjustment of personality to the married state." In Popenoe's view, only expert intervention could steady the divorce rate.[23]

In later works, Popenoe continued to broadcast the benefits of marriage education by highlighting divorcees' anti-social qualities and by insisting that childhood marital training could prevent these pathologies from developing. He claimed that divorce was frequently the result of frigidity and sexual maladjustment, declaring that the common charges of "mental cruelty," "desertion," and "non-support" as grounds for divorce were most often euphemisms for the more humiliating lack of sexual compatibility. According to Popenoe, one in every four wives found marriage "physically distasteful," and when not addressed this aversion could lead to divorce. Popenoe argued that frigidity derived from

---

[22] Paul Popenoe, "Divorce and Remarriage from a Eugenic Point of View," *Social Forces* 12, no. 1 (1933): 48.
[23] Ibid., 48–50; Popenoe, "Remarriage of Divorce to Each Other," Popenoe Papers, Box 117, Folder 3.

insufficient knowledge about sexuality, and he blamed this ignorance on the lack of education in homes and schools. According to Popenoe, appropriate premarital education would prevent couples from separating due to sexual maladjustment, and effective post-marital counseling could solve couples' sexual problems after they developed.[24]

Popenoe was not alone in his quest to prevent divorce through marital education. Members of Washington, D.C.'s Home Defense League viewed divorce as a threat to moral society, and they encouraged "conversion and a sanctified Christian life" as means of overcoming the growing divorce trend.[25] Chicago's Commission on Christian Homes, a council of local Methodist Episcopal pastors, was also committed to the elimination of divorce. These pastors called for marriage training within the church as a strategy for preventing future divorces, and they urged churches to hire secular marriage experts who would help to accomplish this mission alongside religious authorities.[26] Like Popenoe, organizers of the Home Defense League and the Commission on Christian Homes believed that solid family foundations and marital education could yield sturdy partnerships, reversing the nation's growing reliance on divorce as a way to escape unhappy marriage.

As he waged his battle against divorce, Popenoe also hoped to do away with a variety of other sexual and romantic trends that he deemed "amoral, unmoral or conspicuously immoral, and destructive of the best products of the social order, chiefly the home."[27] Throughout his career Popenoe crusaded against premarital intercourse, which became all the more prevalent with the wider availability of birth control.[28] While he acknowledged that couples who had premarital sex were at high risk of pregnancy and venereal disease, Popenoe focused primarily on the psychological dangers that unmarried lovers faced, arguing that these risks could be even more serious. Among them, Popenoe highlighted early

---

[24] Paul Popenoe, "The Frigid Wives of Reno," 1938, Popenoe Papers, Box 133, Folder 5; Davis, *More Perfect Unions*, 37.

[25] Home Defense League Bulletin, June 1929, Popenoe Papers, Box 117, Folder 2.

[26] "Church Studies Trend toward 'Pagan Homes,'" *Chicago Daily Tribune*, 7 Dec. 1933, p. 2.

[27] AIFR Brochure, Popenoe Papers, Box 139, Folder 8.

[28] Paul Popenoe, "Premarital Sexual Experiments," American Institute of Family Relations, 1935, p. 2, Popenoe Papers, Box 116, Folder 1. See Katharine Bement Davis, *Factors in the Sex Life of Twenty-Two Hundred Women* (New York: Harper & Brothers, 1929), 19, on the marginally higher rates of premarital sexual experience among women with knowledge of birth control prior to marriage.

disillusionment from negative sexual experience and mental disturbance due to social pressures to have sex against one's better judgment.[29]

Like Popenoe, novelist and social worker Margaret Culkin Banning also sought to combat the growing acceptance of premarital sex by emphasizing the emotional and psychological damages it could cause. In a 1937 *Reader's Digest* article, Banning explained that many women who engaged in premature sexual relations were so damaged by the experience that they remained unmarried and childless throughout their adult lives. She also argued that clandestine sexual activity harmed the nervous system and that women who had early sexual experiences compromised their chances of matrimony later on, as the majority of young men were interested in marrying only virgins. Hoping to remedy the damages she believed to result from premarital sex, Banning recommended that couples be encouraged to marry early so that they could consummate their sexual desires within the realm of marital legitimacy.[30]

While Banning pushed for early marriage, she was careful to note that young couples should approach their nuptials with the full intention of permanency. This argument was in line with the philosophies of Popenoe and AIFR leaders, who sought to prevent couples from entering into too-hasty unions and trial marriages. Popenoe believed that one of the AIFR's most crucial missions was to eliminate "various illicit forms of cohabitation through bizarre, irresponsible unions as veritable false pretenses of marriage."[31] In a 1925 article he had raised the subjects of "trial marriage" and "companionate marriage" – he applied the terms interchangeably as he believed the two practices were identical in their commitment to childlessness and their embrace of divorce by mutual consent as a solution to domestic dissatisfaction.[32] In this early work on trial marriage, Popenoe claimed to reject the practice because of the physical harms he believed it could inflict. He argued that its tendency to delay childbearing was a "deep-seated evil" that could lead to sterility. When older couples did decide to conceive after years of a companionate

---

[29] Popenoe, "Premarital Sexual Experiments," 2.

[30] Margaret Culkin Banning, "The Case for Chastity," *Reader's Digest* 31, no. 184 (1937): 2–10. Popenoe strongly agreed with this case for early marriage, due in great part to his eugenically oriented hope that healthy women would give birth to as many children as they could. Popenoe, "Some Eugenic Aspects of Early Marriage," undated, Popenoe Papers, Box 125, Folder 5.

[31] AIFR Brochure, Popenoe Papers, Box 139, Folder 8.

[32] Paul Popenoe, "Family or Companionate," *Journal of Social Hygiene* 11, no. 3 (1925): 129; Davis, "Not Marriage at All," 1159.

arrangement, the wife risked increased pain and higher rates of miscarriage and stillbirth. Late conception was also detrimental to the wife's physical health because "a woman's body is organized for pregnancy as well as coitus, and an occasional pregnancy is necessary to her complete well-being." These "elementary biological facts," Popenoe argued, were rarely taken into account by individuals who fell prey to "modern schemes for adjusting marriage to the present economic and social conditions."[33]

Ten years later Popenoe would replace the pseudoscientific argument that trial marriage carried irreversible physical symptoms with the claim that the practice reflected psychological and emotional imbalances that could be cured only through marriage education. He stated that trial marriage was simply a euphemism for the sexual experimentation of "neurotics" and "radical reformers," who he believed set a negative example for naïve adolescents.[34] According to Popenoe, trial marriages were bound to fail because spouses entered them without committing themselves to success. He argued, "One of the things most needed in modern marriage is to get away from this psychology of intemperance, of experimentalism, and adopt a psychology of permanence and continuity in its place."[35]

Popenoe encouraged readers to study "We Try Trial Marriage," a 1930 *Forum and Century* article by Helen Conway, as proof of the "fatal psychological flaws" inherent in a couple's plans for trial marriage. Conway and her boyfriend Fred Stevens, a college professor, had decided to engage in an informal and unbinding trial marriage. Conway and Stevens were in love, but they did not yet know if their relationship would survive the challenges of cohabitation, and so they

---

[33] Popenoe, "Family or Companionate," 133, 137. However unsatisfactory Popenoe's explanation for delayed reproduction may have been, he at least attempted to offer one. Often he asserted that his theories were grounded in scientific reasoning without articulating what that reasoning was at all. In *Modern Marriage*, for example, he wrote that "before marriage a man cannot be more than one-third alive (I put this as a mere maximum, because some men are never alive at all, in any true sense of the word); after marriage he may be two-thirds alive; after he has children he can really live, if he has it in him" (26). While admitting to speaking "figuratively," his use of these quantities to argue for the superiority of fruitful marriage nonetheless suggests reliance upon data that he never in fact produced.

[34] Paul Popenoe, "Premarital Sexual Experiments," 1935, Popenoe Papers, Box 116, Folder 1.

[35] Paul Popenoe, "Discussing 'The New Morality,'" 1935, Popenoe Papers, Box 116, Folder 1.

decided to test out marriage before committing to it in law. The experiment proved challenging for them, and ultimately they parted ways, grateful that they had no legal bonds to dissolve, but convinced that had they entered into an official marriage they might never have drifted apart. In reflecting on the experiment, Conway concluded, "the way to liberty is not always by non-conformity to the accepted order." She continued, "I do not think individual happiness can be achieved by an arrangement which attempts to defy the existing order with impunity. It now seems to me that there would be so much more freedom in marriage."[36]

Popenoe used Conway's account as proof that trial marriage led only to unhappiness, instability, and identity crisis. He also warned that a woman who entered a trial marriage would most likely "(a) have no companion in old age, (b) have no children, and (c) have no feeling of permanence, security, and the dignity which goes with being a part of the great biological picture of man and woman continuing the life of the race."[37] In making these biological and psychological arguments against trial marriage, Popenoe sought to preempt couples from forming a type of domestic arrangement that he deemed contrary to the public good. He demanded that noncommittal couples work with marriage instructors and counselors who could steer them toward permanent marriage, and he broadcast the physical and psychological harms these practices could cause in an attempt to diminish their appeal.

* * *

While divorce, trial marriage, and unmarried cohabitation had long attracted intervention from legislators and cultural authorities, marriage educators such as Popenoe created new methods for combatting these trends. They also identified other behaviors that they believed needed to be deterred; in the process, they marginalized new and unsuspecting groups for their inadvertent challenges to the marital order. Among those defined by Popenoe and colleagues as enemies of the marriage state were childless couples, women who postponed marriage for the sake of college and career, and single men and women. Throughout the 1930s these practices fell deeper into the realm of conjugal misconduct, as educators publicly denounced the private lives of unmarried individuals and childless couples as threats to public policy.

---

[36] Helen Conway, "We Try Trial Marriage," *Forum and Century* 84, no. 5 (1930): 275–276.
[37] Popenoe, "Discussing 'The New Morality,'" 6.

The expression of hostility toward unmarried women was not a new phenomenon. As we have seen, Theodore Roosevelt's 1906 warning against "race suicide" reflected widely held concerns that educated white women were insufficiently committed to marriage and procreation. These anxieties intensified in the 1930s as single women gained greater responsibility and higher salaries in their workplaces. Some commentators were struck by the changing styles and attitudes they saw in this increasingly visible cadre of unmarried women. In contrasting single women of the 1930s to their nineteenth-century counterparts, author Margaret Culkin Banning noted remarkable differences in physical appearance. "The spinster of the last generation, that often pathetic figure, wearing clothes which must never be too conspicuous and were often a little shabby, the spinster for whom anything was good enough if it was warm and neat – because nobody was going to look at her twice anyhow – is gone forever," she wrote in 1934. Nowadays, Banning continued, the single woman was likely to be "as well dressed and well groomed as any woman in the world."[38] Due to this general change in dress and comportment, Banning explained, it was nearly impossible to distinguish married from unmarried women on sight.

More threatening than the altered physical appearance of single women was their growing self-sufficiency. In purchasing their own fashionable clothes and maintaining their own finances, these women revealed men's obsolescence in providing for women's material needs. Many women also learned to invest their money wisely, procuring modest sums that, in the words of Banning, "[took] the edge off that awful fear of dependence founded only too well on fact in the last generation, when unmarried women had to be taken care of like so many invalids."[39] In this vein, Banning also noted that with the erection of street lights in urban centers, women no longer needed male escorts for protection, and they therefore could maintain active social lives in the absence of masculine companionship. "What that has meant in widened horizons and enriched experience cannot be measured," she declared.[40] While Banning exaggerated the extent of single women's material wealth and social freedom, her argument empowered women to celebrate their self-sufficiency. It also sought to diminish the stigma so frequently attached to unmarried women, who were often denigrated for their

[38] Margaret Culkin Banning, "The Plight of the Spinster," *Harper's Monthly Magazine*, June 1929, 90.
[39] Ibid., 92.   [40] Ibid., 91.

independence from men and suspected of maintaining lesbian relations, whether or not this was the case.[41]

Eugenicists were concerned with the growth of this contented and self-sufficient class of unmarried and educated women, predicting that decreased marriage rates among the college educated would lead to race suicide. The number of women attending college had increased threefold between 1890 and 1910, and these rates continued to grow as the century progressed.[42] Katharine Bement Davis, the secretary of John D. Rockefeller's Bureau for Social Hygiene, was particularly bothered by the low rates of marriage among this growing mass of female college graduates. Drawing from several sociological studies, Davis approximated that the female marriage rate was 50 percent at both women's and coeducational institutions, although she admitted that she could not furnish the precise percentage.[43]

Davis explored women's motivations for remaining single in a 1928 study of 1,200 unmarried college graduates. The explanations these women provided in their questionnaire responses varied widely; the greatest number (28%) claimed that they simply had not met the right man, while only 2 percent attributed their single status to professional commitments. Seventeen respondents stated that lesbian relations had prevented them from desiring marriage, nine found sex distasteful, and seven blamed their mothers for instilling in them a resistance to marriage. Mining through these diverse responses, Davis was unable to generalize about the overall reasons women had for not getting married, although she acknowledged that only a minority of her respondents held strong opposition to the institution of marriage itself. Still, she agreed with eugenicists that more college-educated women ought to be marrying and producing children.[44]

[41] Simmons, *Making Marriage Modern*, 145–147; Simmons, "Companionate Marriage and the Lesbian Threat," *Frontiers: A Journal of Women's Studies* 4, no. 3 (1979): 54–59.

[42] Davis, *More Perfect Unions*, 21; Coontz, *Marriage, a History*, 192; Filene, *Him/Her/Self*, 28.

[43] Katharine Bement Davis, "Why They Failed to Marry," *Harper's*, March 1928, 460–469. According to one 1903 study, the marriage rate for women at Vassar, Smith, and Wellesley had decreased from 55.46 percent for the class of 1867 to 28.92 percent for the class of 1896. See Lovett, *Conceiving the Future*, 93–94. Filene indicates that in 1915, only 39 percent of all living alumnae from eight major women's colleges and Cornell University were married. *Him/Her/Self*, 30–31.

[44] Davis, "Why They Failed to Marry," 460–469. Apparently, Davis viewed herself as part of this problem group, as she too remained unmarried, although as historian Ellen Fitzpatrick argues, it is nearly impossible to tell this from her disapproving tone. Fitzpatrick, *Endless Crusade: Women Social Scientists and Progressive Reform* (New York: Oxford University Press, 1990), 205–206.

Popenoe had some concrete plans for addressing the issue, and while he was far from the first person to speak ill of single people, he took the argument to new heights in his efforts to systematically exclude unmarried women from public and professional life. His biggest targets were single teachers. Popenoe's marriage education campaign was grounded in the notion that all eugenically sound young adults should enter into procreative marriages, and he encouraged teachers to instruct students on this subject from kindergarten through high school graduation. If teachers were to be effective authorities on the superiority of married life, however, they needed to be able to teach through actions, and not just words. Popenoe thus argued that the American teaching force should consist exclusively of married individuals. Defying the common belief that married women must leave the teaching workforce to make room for single women who could not depend on a husband's wages, Popenoe insisted that single female teachers were the ones who needed to go.[45] A syndicated 1932 article articulated the problem that unmarried teachers posed to students, and credited Popenoe for waging a just battle against them. "Preparing girls theoretically for modern existence," the author argued, unwed teachers "still exemplify the medieval virtue of celibacy; and young girls are impressionable. Having themselves known no other life, the sisterhood of teaching spinsters tend to make the career idea glamourous or, at least, desirable." Often because their own unmarried teachers had failed to incorporate family life into their lesson plans, this new crop of single schoolteachers put yet another generation of students at risk of perpetual spinsterhood. Critics such as Popenoe feared that their decision to prioritize a profession over family would send a message that young girls could not afford to receive.[46]

The author of this article assured readers that Popenoe was not "anti-spinster," as he believed unmarried women teachers were the victims of the very educational system that now employed them and that they had pursued teaching careers only because they had never been properly trained to pursue marriage. Now, however, they were perpetuating the negative cycle, which Popenoe believed would cease only with their removal from the classroom. Popenoe's tone toward unmarried teachers

[45] On employment discrimination against married women, see Stephen Ewing, "Blue Laws for School-Teachers," *Harper's*, February 1928, 329–338; Cott, *Public Vows*, 172–174; Linda Gordon, *Pitied but Not Entitled: Single Mothers and the History of Welfare* (Cambridge, Mass.: Harvard University Press, 1994), 52–54.

[46] "Old Maid Teachers 'Menace Marriages,'" *Brooklyn Daily Eagle*, 17 Jul. 1932, p. 4A. See also Kline, *Building a Better Race*, 131.

had hardened three years later as he addressed the Phi Delta Kappa Society in Los Angeles in 1935. In this speech Popenoe claimed that schools had become "dysgenic" due to an overabundance of unmarried staff. He demanded that schools cease hiring "abnormal" women as teachers, for these women were inappropriate classroom role models. He also recommended that married women replace single ones in the fields of nursing, library science, and social work. He called for the removal of "neurotics and misfits," and he argued that the only way to achieve this goal would be to screen applicants more carefully before granting them teaching certification and to initiate annual evaluations that would weed out undesirable teachers from school faculties.[47]

Popenoe was not alone in his crusade to eliminate unmarried teachers from primary and secondary school classrooms. The ever-provocative George Schuyler made a similar case in his "Views and Reviews" column, declaring, "If I were king or dictator of this nation, I wouldn't allow *any* single young men or women to teach. I have nothing against people who are young and single, but I think it is absurd for children to be instructed by teachers who know little more about life than their pupils. A teacher's character makes a greater impression on pupils than his or her teaching. Teachers, to my way of thinking, should be men and women who have seen and experienced all sides of life; faced love and disappointment, success and failure."[48] While Schuyler's campaign did not prompt the removal of unmarried teachers, it cast single women as threats to the marital order, whose example must not be followed by impressionable youth. In making such arguments, men like Popenoe and Schuyler added yet another item to the list of romantic practices that could not be tolerated in a society that valued marriage and procreation.

Marriage educators also fought against single living by increasing opportunities for romance on college campuses. Popenoe often bemoaned the fact that college enrollment led women to delay marriage or to

---

[47] Paul Popenoe, "How Can the Schools Educate for Marriage," Popenoe Papers, Box 119, Folder 1; Popenoe, "Problems of Heredity," Popenoe Papers, Box 116, Folder 1. Popenoe was similarly committed to employing only marriage counselors who were happily married. Beyond this, he pursued counselors who were physically attractive, and he feared that hiring counselors who were "physically handicapped or defective in any way" might dissuade clients from marriage. Popenoe, "Memorandum on the Selection of Counselors," Popenoe Papers, Box 141, Folder 6.

[48] Schuyler, "Views and Reviews," *The Pittsburgh Courier*, 9 Feb. 1929, pt. 3, p. 8. Schuyler also proposed that schools exclusively employ those post-menopausal women who had birthed and raised children, even if they lacked formal training. In his view, academic credentials were less valuable than life experience.

sacrifice it entirely for the sake of a career. He feared that the postponement of marriage would weaken a woman's reproductive functions and that the longer she waited to wed, the less likely she would be to fulfill her procreative responsibilities. "If a healthy, intelligent American girl of 20 wants to marry," Popenoe wrote, "there's no biological reason for discouraging her. And those who encourage her to postpone marriage until after she is 25 are, from a biological point of view, doing both her and the nation an injury."[49] Hoping to decrease the population of college-educated spinsters, but recognizing that female college enrollment would continue to rise, Popenoe and his colleagues attempted to incorporate marriage training into higher education.

Academic coursework in marriage contributed to this goal. While marriage training classes were open to all students, above all they encouraged women to prioritize marriage over career following their graduation.[50] Campus marriage promoters also looked beyond the curriculum in their quest to foist matrimony upon students. We can see such efforts in the work of Roswell Johnson, who coauthored *Applied Eugenics* with Popenoe in 1918. Concerned that American colleges and universities actively discouraged marriage, Johnson sought to transform the university into a "marriage bureau." In a 1934 paper cowritten with Gertrude Chittenden, Johnson cited a study showing that fraternity members married at 1.7 times the rate of nonfraternity members. Noting the heterosexual socialization inherent in fraternity life, the authors called for universities to initiate social programs that offered similar opportunities for coeducational mixing. "Our universities and colleges could well afford to improve their social programs for the purpose of encouraging courtship and marriage," they wrote, noting, however, that these programs need not fashion themselves in the image of the social fraternity. "There are many other means of promoting social contacts among men and women. School dances, dramatic clubs, combined Y.M.C.A. and Y.W.C.A. groups, religious groups, informal gatherings of all kinds which include members of both sexes would help to solve the problem."[51]

In another paper, Johnson and collaborator Ann Rudd further laid out universities' obligations to reverse decreasing marriage rates among the

---

[49] Paul Popenoe, "Some Eugenic Aspects of Early Marriage," undated, Popenoe Papers, Box 125, Folder 5.
[50] Dowbiggin, *The Search for Domestic Bliss*, 24
[51] Gertrude Chittenden, in collaboration with Roswell Johnson, "Marriage of College Graduates: Its Relationship to Membership in the Social Fraternity," 16 Jul. 1934, American Philosophical Society, Eugenics Record Office Records, Series I, Box 17.

most educated classes. Basing their claims on a University of Pittsburgh study, Johnson and Rudd argued that universities were doing very little to encourage matrimony among students. The authors viewed this deficiency as a failure in undergraduate education. Nevertheless, they believed that college students were impressionable and that with appropriate effort the problem could be fixed. They reasoned, "It should not be an extremely difficult matter for a college or university to obtain eugenically desirable results in increasing the marriage rate by organizing a program of positive eugenics, to interest students in marriage and to make them feel that they have a definite duty towards society in marrying and having as large families as they can possibly afford."[52] Fifty percent of the study's undergraduate respondents claimed to have been influenced either for or against marriage through their coursework, particularly in the fields of psychology, eugenics, sociology, biology, economics, history, and genetics. Johnson and Rudd thus encouraged concerted efforts to strengthen marital education in these disciplines.[53]

The authors also proposed that university officials incorporate lessons on the significance of marriage into freshman orientation proceedings and that they increase the number of Greek organizations on campus and lower their entrance fees and dues so that more students could access the heterosocial contact such groups facilitated. Whatever methods universities employed, the authors argued, it was crucial that they place marriage at the center of undergraduate training. "Since college students are a fairly well selected group as far as ambition and intelligence are concerned, and should be valuable citizens later in life," they explained, "for the benefit of the race they should have a high marriage rate."[54] Above all other forms of professional and intellectual training, education toward that familial ideal ought to be universities' top priority.

While these scholars were most committed to encouraging marriage among the college educated, and particularly among those intelligent

---

[52] Ann Rudd and Roswell Johnson, "The Effect of a University in Influencing Students for or against Marriage," 26 May 1933, American Philosophical Society, Eugenics Record Office Records, Series I, Box 17.

[53] Ibid. Only three respondents claimed that coursework had influenced them *against* marriage, and the writers were generally dismissive of their viewpoints. For example, regarding one student who claimed he opposed marriage "because he does not think that he can find a person with whom he would care to live," the authors argued that this was "no doubt due to the fact that he himself would be extremely difficult to get along with because he is, I believe, slightly neurotic."

[54] Ibid.

women who delayed marriage and motherhood for the sake of education and professional life, they also hoped to spread marriage to the wider American population. The marriage rate decreased by 13.5 percent between 1930 and 1932, and marriage scholars sought to reverse this alarming trend by publicizing new methods of mate selection.[55] Throughout the 1930s the AIFR incorporated workshops on mate selection into many of its conferences on marriage education, while other organizations devoted themselves exclusively to this function.[56] They employed methods developed by social scientists, who devised mathematical formulae for determining the likely success of a match between two people. New York's Personal Relations Institute (PRI), for example, which billed itself as "an independent and self-supporting foundation devoted solely to the study and application of scientific means for increasing the success and happiness of the individual in his personal relationships," centered its activities on these studies. In a 1937 bulletin, the Institute boasted that it employed the methods of Dr. Lewis Terman, "Stanford University's brilliant psychologist," to locate ideal mates for its clients. Touting the PRI's use of psychological testing to ensure marital harmony, the bulletin boasted of Terman's research methods, which it guaranteed would unite compatible couples.[57]

University of Chicago sociologist Ernest Burgess was another innovator in the field of quantitative marriage counseling, which he laid out in his 1938 book, *Predicting Success or Failure in Marriage*. With graduate student Leonard S. Cottrell, Jr., Burgess analyzed survey responses from 526 married couples to determine which factors – among them "philosophy of life," "intimate relations," and "table manners" – were most crucial in generating marital happiness. With this information, Burgess believed he could devise a formula that would alert couples to their chances of success in matrimony *before* they exchanged vows. Proponents of these formulas believed that premarital compatibility tests would

---

[55] Beth L. Bailey, "Scientific Truth . . . and Love: The Marriage Education Movement in the United States," *Journal of Social History* 20, no. 4 (1987): 712.

[56] Program, "The Department of Education, Institute of Family Relations, Los Angeles, California, Has Arranged an All-Day Southern California Conference on Problems of the Modern Family at Occidental College," 28 Oct. 1933, Popenoe Papers, Box 140, Folder 6.

[57] "Your Personal Relations," *The Personal Relations Institute: Science Service Publication No. 5*, 1937, Popenoe Papers, Box 139, Folder 8; see Kline, *Building a Better Race*, 40–41, on Terman's 1938 book, *Psychological Factors in Marital Happiness*, which argued that the most successful marriages were between masculine men and traditional, feminine women.

preempt the formation of unsuitable marriages, and thus temper the divorce rate.[58]

Proponents of marriage compatibility tests hoped that in addition to raising the quality and the duration of marriages, they might also increase their quantity – a much desired goal in light of the Depression-era decline.[59] As promotional materials for the PRI explained, many marriageable Americans were not acquainted with like-minded members of the opposite sex, and as a result they married inappropriate partners or remained single. The PRI hoped to improve their marital prospects. To receive suggestions for an ideal mate, a client would fill out a questionnaire describing physical, emotional, and intellectual qualities. The staff would then search its files for a mate whose profile complemented the new client's. The inquiring client would then receive information about the matching individual, as well as a detailed interpretation of the couple's potential compatibility. The PRI would forward communication between the two parties until the couple was ready to proceed unassisted.[60] While this procedure sounds remarkably similar to the work conducted by matchmaking agencies in prior decades, the originators of marital compatibility testing were driven less by the desire to profit than by an urge to create enduring unions among as many fit clients as they could entice. In that sense, their work bore a closer resemblance to the not-for-profit matchmaking bureaus discussed at the end of Chapter 1. Like the bureaus run by religious and charitable organizations, Terman and Burgess modified a controversial courtship model to suit their more conservative ends: an increase in marriage and procreation, and a decrease in the rates of divorce and nonmarriage among fit Americans. In other words, they believed that scientific courtship methods could temper the marriage crisis.

* * *

Efforts to increase rates of marriage through the removal of unmarried teachers from classrooms, the implementation of social and curricular

---

[58] Celello, *Making Marriage Work*, 30–32; Ernest W. Burgess, "Predictive Factors in the Success or Failure of Marriage," *Living* 1, no. 1 (1939); Dowbiggin, *The Search for Domestic Bliss*, 35–36.

[59] The marriage rate fell from around ten per every 1,000 persons in the mid-1920s to 7.9 in 1932, likely the greatest decline in the nation's history. It was estimated that between 700,000 and a million couples postponed their marriages between 1930 and 1935. Paul H. Jacobson, *American Marriage and Divorce* (New York: Rinehart & Company, 1959), 23–24; Wilson H. Grabill, Clyde V. Kiser, and Pascal K. Whelpton, *The Fertility of American Women* (New York: John Wiley and Sons, 1958), 360–361.

[60] "Your Personal Relations," Popenoe Papers.

programs to encourage heterosexual socialization at universities, and the use of scientific formulas to predict success in marriage all served to highlight the undesirability of unmarried life and to increase marriage rates among the physically and mentally fit. But nonmarriage was not the only status that marital educators sought to erase; Popenoe was also committed to stigmatizing deliberately childless married couples as selfish and lazy, depicting their private decision to not have children as a threat to the public order.

Part of this hostility toward childless couples derived from Popenoe's disapproval of nonprocreative sex. Popenoe was not unequivocally opposed to birth control, specifically because he believed that "unfit" couples should utilize it to prevent undesirable procreation.[61] He rejected the use of contraception among healthy, white, middle-class couples, however, arguing that their reproduction was necessary for the proliferation of a vigorous white society. Driven by these eugenic principles, Popenoe castigated healthy couples who did not make concerted efforts to spread their genes, and he incorporated voluntary childlessness into his expanding list of disreputable marital practices.[62]

In criticizing voluntarily childless parents, Popenoe reacted to a national shift toward smaller family units, the growing public acceptance of birth control, and the broadening cultural embrace of childless couples as legitimate partners in marriage. Census figures shed light on the increasing popularity of childlessness, particularly among affluent urban couples. The 1910 census revealed that in Chicago, 34.1 percent of the most affluent families had no children, and these numbers showed no signs of diminishing.[63] Of the one thousand married women that Katharine Bement Davis questioned for her 1929 study, *Factors in the Sex Life of Twenty-Two Hundred Women*, 730 claimed to use available birth control techniques with their husbands.[64] Meanwhile, studies conducted in Cincinnati, Minneapolis, New York, and Philadelphia also

---

[61] While he approved of the use of birth control by the unfit, he believed that sterilization was a preferable method of preventing their reproduction. Ladd-Taylor, "Eugenics, Sterilisation and Modern Marriage in the USA," 305.

[62] Davis, *More Perfect Unions*, 33; "Aims and Objectives," Pamphlet of the American Eugenics Society, c. 1933–1936, Popenoe Papers, Box 114, Folder 3.

[63] Paula S. Fass, *The Damned and the Beautiful: American Youth in the 1920s* (New York: Oxford University Press, 1977), 59, 388 fn. 10. According to Elaine Tyler May, the proportion of childless American-born wives grew from 14 percent in 1910 to 21 percent in 1940. *Barren in the Promised Land*, 63.

[64] Fass, *The Damned and the Beautiful*, 76. Katharine Bement Davis, *Factors in the Sex Life of Twenty-Two Hundred Women*, 13.

revealed an increase in illegal abortions in the years immediately following the stock market crash of 1929.[65] These numbers were discouraging to eugenically driven marriage counselors like Popenoe, who viewed increases in contraceptive use and abortion as threats to the future of white American civilization.

For many women, these statistics reflected an acknowledgment, particularly among the college educated, that parenting was not a required path. As journalist and writer Dorothy Dunbar Bromley explained in 1929, new women were no longer beholden to the notion that the inability or unwillingness to bear children rendered them incomplete persons. Some of these women were too committed to their work to take on the responsibility of raising children, while others found such great satisfaction in their marriages that they did not wish to upset the balance. Bromley recognized that these perspectives were not typical of American women in the 1920s, but she believed that they displayed "how perfectly natural it is for a woman to consider herself and her own happiness – and little else when she faces the ordeal of having a child."[66] In challenging the notion that women held an instinctive desire for childbearing, writers like Bromley toppled the worldviews of eugenic marriage proponents, who believed that the future of civilization depended on aggressive procreation by America's most intelligent people. Popenoe was surely not pleased, then, with Bromley's claim that graduates of Smith, Barnard, and Wellesley who had been out of college for fifteen years or more had an average of "considerably less than two children."[67]

The Great Depression would only exacerbate this problem for Popenoe. In one 1934 article, Bromley revealed a dwindling birth rate among the middle and upper classes in the post-Depression years. Citing a study conducted by the Milbank Memorial Foundation in cooperation with the United Public Health Service, Bromley explained that the birth rate of poor families receiving government relief had remained constant throughout the Depression, while the birth rate of couples affluent enough to attain contraceptives had fallen.[68] Bromley also cited a study by biologist Raymond Pearl, whose research showed that the birth rate among poor mothers was about 66 percent higher

[65] Reagan, *When Abortion Was a Crime*, 134–135.
[66] Dorothy Dunbar Bromley, "This Maternal Instinct," *Harper's*, Sep. 1929, 427.
[67] Ibid., 431.
[68] Bromley, "Birth Control and the Depression," *Harper's*, Oct. 1934, 563–564.

than among affluent mothers in the 1930s.[69] These were the very trends that Popenoe wished to reverse.[70]

Popular culture also influenced some couples to opt out of childrearing. According to historian Elaine Tyler May, couples were influenced to remain childless by the glamorous images of real-life childless couples such as Mary Pickford and Douglas Fairbanks and by the romantic child-free marriages of couples depicted in the films of Cecil B. DeMille. Positive media representations of modern childless couples informed consumers that parenting was not the only route to happiness, and encouraged couples to pursue their own paths to marital satisfaction, whether or not children factored into the equation.[71] In response to the growing acceptance of childlessness, Popenoe toughened his stance throughout the 1930s, replacing his call for childrearing as an essential component of marital contentment with a verbal attack on those couples who chose not to reproduce.

While Popenoe estimated that one in five educated American couples was childless, he distinguished those struggling with infertility from those who had made the decision not to procreate. "And why don't certain couples want a baby in the home?" he asked in a pamphlet entitled *The Truth about Sterility*. "They will usually explain their flight from fecundity by taking unto themselves credit for some lofty motive. It would not sound so well to say, 'Gosh, no! We don't want to be bothered with kids. It would break up our bridge club!'"[72] Of the 862 cases of child-free marriage that Popenoe encountered in his research, he claimed that 280 were involuntary and 582 were voluntary. Of the latter, he attributed 180 cases to self-centeredness, 128 to the wife's career, and 96 to economic pressure. While Popenoe praised those 27 couples who had elected to stay childless out of "eugenic conscience," or the desire not to pass on genetic flaws to the next generation, he disparaged the others, whose self-centeredness prevented them from making healthy reproductive choices.[73]

---

[69] Ibid., 564; "Differential Birth Rate Ascribed to Birth Control," *Science News Letter* 35, no. 10 (1939): 151.

[70] On the rising popularity and commercial development of contraceptives, see Andrea Tone, *Devices and Desires: A History of Contraceptives in America* (New York: Hill and Wang, 2001).

[71] May, *Barren in the Promised Land*, 88, 91.

[72] Paul Popenoe, "The Truth about Sterility," AIFR Pamphlet, 1939, Popenoe Papers, Box 133, Folder 3.

[73] Ibid. Popenoe described the couples who rejected parenting as "social climbers" who "wanted to be free to travel" or "thought children would interfere with their own pleasures." Of those who stayed childless for the sake of the wife's career, Popenoe noted, "This was a deliberate choice; the family did not need the wife's earnings but she desired to be 'unencumbered' for work outside the home."

Popenoe knew that he could not encourage procreative marriage through mere proselytizing, so in addition to the direct appeals he made to readers, clients, and conference attendees on the merits of matrimony and childrearing, he also proposed government intervention to incentivize the creation of large families. He believed that married men should receive extra income so that their wives would not have to work, and he proposed that couples receive an additional sum for each child. Popenoe saw this "family wage" as a way to ensure reproduction among fit couples who might otherwise limit their offspring out of economic necessity. He was troubled to observe that childless couples held higher standards of living than those with children, and he argued that a system of equal work for equal pay "placed a premium on sterility."[74] He thus proposed an "adjustment of the economic burden of parenthood" so as to remove incentives toward childlessness, particularly among the educated. "Where a childless bachelor is given the same salary for a job that is given to a married man with four children," he wrote, "it means that the family man must adopt a standard of living about one-fourth as high as that of the bachelor. No wonder that in such circumstances educated couples refrain from producing children . . . [S]ome form of selective family wage must be adopted which will cease to penalize people for bringing up families."[75]

Popenoe did not wish to compensate all families with children equally, however, as he was committed to maintaining class hierarchy in rewarding white-collar families with more money than working-class ones. He explained this by arguing that it cost a college professor much more money to raise a child than it did a ditch digger. "Hence," he asserted, "if you give the same amount in each case you either give the ditch digger too much, making it profitable for him to raise children 'for revenue only,' or else you offer the college professor so little that it is of no help."[76] We can see from these statements that Popenoe's family wage was grounded in his ubiquitous eugenic agenda and that more than anything else he wanted to guarantee that those he considered the fittest would be the ones to contribute their genes to the greater population.

But the zealotry of Popenoe's eugenic objectives should not suggest that the family wage was merely a fixation among hardline eugenicists,

[74] Paul Popenoe, "Marriages Without Children," from *The Childless Marriage*, unpublished, 1930s, Popenoe Papers, Box 172, Folder 1.

[75] Paul Popenoe, "Problems of Heredity," 1935, Popenoe Papers, Box 116, Folder 1.

[76] Letter from Paul Popenoe to William A. Shannon, 13 Dec. 1937, Popenoe Papers, Box 121, Folder 2. Popenoe repeated a similar argument in a letter to Ruth Hall Chatfield, 27 May 1938, Popenoe Papers, Box 121, Folder 2.

since at least two college presidents adopted Popenoe's model. William
Ernest Wells, president of Wells College in Aurora-on-Cayuga, New
York, offered an additional yearly $1,000 to male instructors after they
married, and $250 for each dependent child under the age of twenty-
one.[77] Robert Leigh, president of Bennington College, implemented a
similar plan, granting a yearly allotment of $500 to any employee with
a nonearning wife or husband, and an additional $500 for up to two
children under the age of twenty-one.[78] The cap at two children defied
Popenoe's quest to encourage limitless childbearing among those he
considered the worthiest. Furthermore, Leigh's gender-neutral language
suggested that in some cases wives would be the ones to work, and the
dependent husbands would rely on their financial contributions. This was
not an idea that would have met with Popenoe's approval, and Leigh's
system thus indicates a departure from the pronatalist concerns that drove
Popenoe's thoughts on marriage.[79]

At the same time, all of these models demonstrate the institutionalization of heterosexual marriage and childbearing as practices worthy of
encouragement and reward; this was a belief on which the marriage
education movement hinged, even among those marital specialists who
steered clear of Popenoe's eugenic agenda. These marriage educators,
among them Emily Hartshorne Mudd, Abraham and Hannah Stone, and
Lester Dearborn, spread a considerably different message than did Popenoe. They encouraged the wider use of birth control, and they withheld
judgment in their discussions of premarital sex, nonmarriage, and voluntary childlessness. Rather than embrace a eugenically driven campaign to
fend off "race suicide," they encouraged counseling out of a desire to
improve the physical and emotional lives of married couples. These counselors nevertheless gave currency to the argument that a marriage crisis was
under way, claiming that their methods could help clients to alleviate the
marital struggles that accompanied changing cultural and sexual mores.
While they treated clients with sensitivity and respect, their writings illustrate a continued belief that harmonious marriage was the supreme social
arrangement, which clients could attain if they were willing to put in the
work. Those who failed to reach this stage, on the other hand, were shown

---

[77] Letter from W. E. Weld to Paul Popenoe, 14 Oct. 1936, Popenoe Papers, Box 121,
Folder 2.
[78] Letter from Robert D. Leigh to Popenoe, 2 Mar. 1936, Popenoe Papers, Box 121,
Folder 2.
[79] For more discussion of debates over the "family wage," see Gordon, *Pitied but Not
Entitled*, 55–59.

to be poorly adjusted and abnormal, lacking the mental and emotional stability to maintain a steady partnership. Though these marriage educators displayed little of Popenoe's disdain for unconventional marital practice, their commitment to providing therapy for the sole purpose of improving the quality of heterosexual marriage only further marginalized those persons who were unwilling or unable to take part in it.

In the tradition of Groves and Popenoe, Abraham and Hannah Stone, the husband and wife team who founded the Marriage Consultation Center at the New York City Labor Temple, insisted that education for marriage should start in the home, from early childhood onward. Through the Marriage Consultation Center, the Stones hoped to provide the marital training that parents neglected to deliver to their children. Among these offerings were premarital consultations, in which clients could receive information from staff about the psychological differences between men and women, about human anatomy and reproductive functions, and about the use of birth control.[80] In their efforts to instruct clients on the pleasures of sex in marriage, they drew new boundaries between acceptable and unacceptable female sexual behaviors. Advising wives to occupy a middle ground between ravenous sexual desire and Victorian repression, the Stones maintained that successful marriage depended on the wife's ability to achieve this sexual balance.[81] In spreading their message, the Stones drew a firmer line between proper and improper female sexual expression within marriage, marginalizing over- and undersexualized women by assigning them blame for marital failures.

Emily Hartshorne Mudd founded the Marriage Counsel of Philadelphia in 1932 in an effort to increase couples' happiness within marriage and to educate potential brides and grooms about married life. Still a student in social work at the University of Pennsylvania at the time of the Marriage Counsel's founding, Mudd used her growing professional knowledge to stress the importance of preparation for marriage. "Let us combat the bogies of ignorance, superstition and fear with knowledge and truth," she pled in a 1932 article in *Birth Control Review*. "Let us make available to the youth of our country, men and women who are to be married or have recently married, the facts about sex and marriage."[82] Mudd attempted to

---

[80] Hannah M. Stone and Abraham Stone, "The Premarital Consultation," *Birth Control Review* 4, no. 4 (1936): 3–4.

[81] Davis, *More Perfect Unions*, 43.

[82] Emily Hartshorne Mudd, "Is Preventive Work the Next Step?," *Birth Control Review* 16, no. 2 (1932): 42–43.

spread this message with a staff of counselors who offered aid to couples that were considering marriage, in the thick of it, or barely staying afloat. In 1936 Mudd claimed that her clients ranged from nineteen to forty years old and that they came to the Marriage Counsel through references from social workers, ministers, doctors, and educators. While there was no official fee, Mudd believed that clients received a "psychological advantage" when they paid for services received, and she therefore asked for voluntary payments, the average sum being one dollar per session.[83] Mudd welcomed counselors from varied professions. Her descriptions of their credentials were somewhat hazy, and the only clear standards she laid out were that counselors "have themselves experienced marriage and that they have some knowledge of normal physiological processes, of organic disease, and of nervous symptoms and disorders." In some cases, Mudd was even willing to employ staff members with less-than-stellar knowledge of these physiological phenomena, as she believed that counselors' compassionate demeanor was more significant than the content of their words.[84]

Despite downplaying the significance of her counselors' academic knowledge, Mudd did see value in scholarship on marriage and family, and she made frequent reference to the Marriage Counsel's library, which contained approximately 300 books on such topics as preparation for marriage, sex technique in marriage, and birth control. Mudd did not wish to convey the same message to each client, and instead she suggested the use of this literature only to the couples she believed would respond to it.[85] In many instances Mudd's refusal to dictate the course that couples should take in their relations flew in the face of the allegedly fact-based training that eugenicists like Popenoe incorporated into their marital instruction. Her organization sought not to dictate proper marital comportment, but rather to spread knowledge to those who lacked it.

Mudd was troubled above all by her observation that many college and professional school graduates entered adulthood without sufficient knowledge of human physiology and the "psychology of marriage and parenthood."[86] With the Marriage Counsel of Philadelphia, Mudd

---

[83] Emily Hartshorne Mudd, "Brief Descriptions of Typical Marriage and Family Counseling Services," *Parent Education* 3, nos. 1–2 (1936): 18.

[84] Ibid., 18.

[85] Emily Hartshorne Mudd and Jean L. Whitehill, "Use and Misuse of Books in Counselling," *Parent Education* 4, no. 3 (1938): 139–144.

[86] Emily Hartshorne Mudd, "Has the Marriage Counsel a Place in Community Activity? A Report of Two Years' Work of the Philadelphia Marriage Counsel," *Marriage Hygiene* 1 (1935): 414–418.

sought to remedy this limitation and to prepare young people for the matrimonial state that likely awaited them. More than anything, it seems that Mudd wanted to teach clients to feel comfortable discussing and thinking about sex, a subject she believed Americans learned too little about in family and school training, later leading them to suffer from unhappy and uncommunicative marriages. In many ways, these efforts to demystify sex, even among the young and uninitiated, were great departures from the premarital training offered in prior generations.[87]

And yet some of Mudd's actual commentaries on the cases she encountered challenge the suggestion that her marital ideologies departed radically from those of marriage counselors who broadcast their eugenic motivations.[88] While Mudd called for frank dialogue on anatomy and sexual adjustment, she offered these suggestions primarily in service of long-lasting and monogamous marriages. Mudd acknowledged that under present circumstances marriage was not always the desirable route for all persons; she nevertheless sought to make it so by providing physiological and psychological training to those who were unprepared. Mudd displayed this reverence for marriage above all other social arrangements when she described the plight of "Mrs. F.," a "timid, pitifully scared-looking little woman," who came to the Marital Counsel after nine unhappy weeks of marriage. Mrs. F claimed to have prepared for marriage through books, but she now found it unbearable – her husband, who told Mrs. F that she acted just like a little girl, agreed. The two had met after the death of Mrs. F's mother, with whom she had lived happily for her entire young life. They wed after six months of acquaintance, and while Mrs. F. admitted that her husband was perfectly kind to her, she did not like his personality, resented his physical advances, and viewed him as merely a "meal ticket."[89]

---

[87] Emily Hartshorne Mudd, "Some Aspects of Counseling in a Marriage and Family Consultation Service," *Family* 16, no. 10 (1936): 303. For more information on the motivations behind Mudd's practice, see Dowbiggin, *The Search for Domestic Bliss*, 14–29.

[88] Though less outspoken about eugenics in her marriage counseling than Popenoe, Mudd was nonetheless a supporter of the movement. She attended the London eugenics conference in 1930. After that, she toured several German marriage counseling centers, praising these organizations – and the German government in general – for being more enthusiastic in providing eugenic sterilization to unfit populations than their American counterparts. Dowbiggin, *The Search for Domestic Bliss*, 19–22.

[89] Emily Hartshorne Mudd, "Young People and Marriage: The Development of Capacities for Effective Family Life," *Science and Society* 1, no. 3 (1937): 131–140.

In recounting this case to readers of *Science and Society*, Mudd reserved her harshest criticism for Mrs. F's late mother, whose overprotectiveness and failure to provide marital training to her daughter had produced a poorly socialized young woman. "As we think of the tragedy before this frail little lady," Mudd observed, "we may perhaps wonder if her mother ever thought of such a future during those formative girlhood years when she so absorbed and filled her daughter's life that her daughter was not able to become normally interested in and attracted by members of the opposite sex ... as she had remained a child surrounded by the security of a perpetual mother."[90] With this comment on the necessity of proper attraction to the opposite sex, Mudd revealed that her efforts as a marriage counselor were driven not purely by a longing to improve the quality of individual marriages, but also by a belief that heterosexual desire and marriage were the types of natural and normal phenomena that all young people could experience if trained properly.

In a 1937 article in *Mental Hygiene*, Mudd shared another case that displayed these priorities. In recounting the experiences of a client named "Mrs. H," Mudd described a frail and timid nineteen-year-old who was paralyzed by her fears of sex and intimacy. Though she had been married for several months, this woman resisted her husband's touch and dreaded the thought of pregnancy. Upon a referral from her physician, Mrs. H met with Marriage Counsel staff on several occasions. According to Mudd, the young woman's remarks "indicated repeatedly an almost complete rejection of her feminine rôle and the possibility of normal sexual relations." Through her sessions at the Marriage Counsel, however, the woman developed a greater understanding of how to perform this "feminine rôle," shedding some of her fears of sexual activity and even claiming that she would like to have children if her husband's income increased. Mudd was encouraged by this progress, and she believed that Mrs. H might now possess the knowledge and stability necessary to experience happiness in marriage and motherhood.[91]

By using this woman's case to illustrate the Marriage Counsel's success in steering clients from sexual maladjustment to marital contentment, Mudd laid out a firm definition of what "normal sexual relations" indeed were; they included happy marriage, enjoyment of monogamous sex, and the desire to procreate. In the process, Mudd also presented nonmarriage,

[90] Ibid., 133.
[91] Emily Hartshorne Mudd, "An Analysis of One Hundred Consecutive Cases in the Marriage Counsel of Philadelphia," *Mental Hygiene* 21, no. 2 (1937): 209–210.

the lack of sexual yearning, and the wish to remain childless as decidedly abnormal behaviors, or products of improper socialization that might be remedied by instruction from experts on marriage and the family.[92] In addition, she and Lester Dearborn, the director of the Massachusetts Society for Social Hygiene, were invested in reversing and preventing homosexual urges through a process referred to by psychiatrists as "heterosexual adjustment." Through this method they endeavored to ward off homosexual impulses by educating clients on the merits of courtship, marriage, and childrearing. As historian Rebecca Davis notes, amid widening recognition that same-sex sexual attraction was a relatively common phenomenon, the task of marriage educators was "to guide the psychosexual development of children and adolescents toward heterosexual object choices despite children's plurality of desires."[93]

Mudd was very much invested in this process. Her frank discussion of sexual matters and her openness to a wide variety of opinions from counselors marked a departure from the one-size-fits-all approach to marriage counseling espoused by Popenoe and his by-the-books colleagues. Nonetheless, her need to problematize and then remedy all behavior that did not lead clients in the direction of marital harmony reveals an enduring belief in the centrality of marriage to proper human socialization. The Marriage Counsel thus played a part in reifying procreative heterosexual matrimony as the most legitimate adult social relationship, consequently contributing to Popenoe's efforts to marginalize the unmarried and childless amid declining marriage and birth rates.

Whether grounded in eugenic fears of race suicide or in genuine desires to improve the marriages of unhappy couples, marriage counseling was effective in reinforcing one particular marital ideal above all others. As different as their approaches may have been, together marriage experts functioned under the assumption that happy marriage was a manifestation of proper human adjustment and that barriers to long-lasting matrimony should thus be eliminated. By infiltrating schools, churches, newspapers, and airwaves with lessons about the necessity of preparation for marriage, the urgency of eugenic compatibility, and the folly of provisional or experimental marital arrangements, these experts strove

---

[92] On efforts to cure "hysterical" women who rejected sexual contact with men, often due to histories of abuse, see Elizabeth Lunbeck, *The Psychiatric Persuasion: Knowledge, Gender, and Power in Modern America* (Princeton: Princeton University Press, 1994), 209–228.

[93] Davis, *More Perfect Unions*, 50–53.

to erase the disreputable marital practices that the law alone could not thwart. While infinitely helpful to some couples in need of guidance, this movement also served to stigmatize and combat acts of conjugal misconduct, in drawing firmer lines between reputable and disreputable marital practice and in solidifying a hierarchy that placed procreative heterosexual marriage above all other social arrangements.

***

It may seem curious to center so much of a book about marriage law on the counseling movement – especially given my focus on Paul Popenoe, whose views appear misinformed, pseudoscientific, and even fanatical with the benefit of hindsight. But those views, however fanatical, were extremely influential. For one, Popenoe's own career flourished in the decades that followed the founding of the AIFR. He was known throughout the 1950s and 1960s as the nation's foremost marriage expert, due in great part to his regular appearances on television and the popular *Ladies' Home Journal* column he edited, "Can This Marriage Be Saved?"[94] But beyond Popenoe's personal legacy, his work sparked a broader marriage education movement that has thrived ever since. Still, the newness of that movement's form should not suggest newness of content. While Popenoe, Groves, Mudd, and other marriage educators founded the profession in their own right, their work also embodied a much longer struggle to contain challenges to early twentieth-century marital norms.

In this sense, restrictive marriage laws and a repressive marriage counseling movement were two sides of the same coin in their mutual efforts to combat conjugal misconduct. We have seen the power of legal backlash in the form of legislation, the pursuit of uniform statutes, and judicial decisions intended to eliminate marital nonconformity in the name of public policy. Collectively, these varied forms of legal backlash led to a new form of cultural backlash in the 1920s and 1930s. Through the marriage education movement, teachers, counselors, and social scientists worked to avert challenges to marital norms not through legal means, but rather through education and cultural indoctrination. The questionable science, exaggerated claims of expertise, racial and class bias, and moralistic superiority at the heart of many marriage counselors' initiatives did not

---

[94] Ladd-Taylor, "Eugenics, Sterilisation and Modern Marriage in the USA," 298. As Ladd-Taylor notes, the influence Popenoe's eugenic program had on the 1933 Nazi sterilization law has typically been omitted from this celebratory narrative.

detract from their impact. Rather, marriage educators' appeals to real or embellished academic expertise, their frankness in discussing sexual topics, and their allure among audiences who longed for advice on matters of the heart and the loins allowed them to maintain positions of authority.

Furthermore, counselors' faithfulness to the script that lawmakers, judges, medical professionals, religious leaders, and journalists before them had created allowed this new crop of reformers to introduce their program without great controversy. In their opposition to divorce and remarriage, dysgenic marriage, trial marriage, and interracial marriage, counselors like Popenoe joined a long-running initiative to suppress marital arrangements that defied traditional morality. Meanwhile, in their desire to promote healthy heterosexual marriage as a goal to be reached at all costs, counselors like Mudd and Dearborn also fed into a long-brewing conversation about the threats of increasing divorce rates, delayed marriage, and race suicide. These reformers also used their platforms to heighten the stigma on unmarried college-educated women and childless couples, thus expanding the pool of suspects who could be targeted for failing to adhere to marital convention. While they did not have the authority of the law behind them, in many ways they created a method of marital surveillance that was impervious to the shifting tides of legislation.[95]

The work of marriage counselors in the 1920s and 1930s had a wide influence on American conceptions of matrimony. As Kristin Celello has argued, self-described marriage experts planted the long-held assumption

---

[95] In this sense, Ian Dowbiggin's desire to prove that counselors like Mudd were radicals due to the sympathies some of them held toward left-wing movements seems misguided. The reactionary goals behind marriage counselors' programs, as evidenced by the professional practices described above, seem more significant to the study of the industry than whatever political views they harbored. Dowbiggin's urge to label marriage counselors "radicals" appears to be motivated by his sense that there is a current marriage crisis under way in couples' willingness to abandon unions that are unsatisfying, and his desire to attribute that crisis to a liberal source. He blames early twentieth-century marriage counselors for the creation of this "me-marriage" model. But Dowbiggin's eagerness to attribute the problems he sees in marriage today to "radicals" seems to be the driving force behind his book, with historical concerns taking a secondary role (for example, his narration emanates in great part from the current work of William Doherty, a conservative therapist who rejects his colleagues' embrace of divorce as a solution to marital incompatibility). It would be disingenuous for me to claim that any historian of marriage could remove the influence of present-day marriage debates from his or her historical scholarship. But Dowbiggin's hostility toward marriage counseling in the present leads him to draw some unsound conclusions about marriage counselors in the past. Dowbiggin, *The Search for Domestic Bliss.*

that it was the responsibility of heterosexual couples – and particularly of married women – to put in the hard work required to uphold their nuptials. From the start, experts encouraged wives to consult counselors and advice literature to keep their marriages intact; in the wake of World War II, they pushed recently wed women to prioritize their marriages above all other commitments once their husbands returned from military service; and in the 1950s, they urged women to tolerate their husbands' abuse, infidelity, and alcoholism in the name of preserving family unity and avoiding divorce.[96] Experts' warnings entered into many venues; for instance, as Elaine Tyler May has shown, the message that wives must sacrifice their own ambitions to tend to their husbands' needs was a staple in popular cinema and movie magazines during and after World War II. Meanwhile, college curricula doubled down on the promotion of mothering and homemaking to female students.[97]

Postwar marriage experts also amplified their claims that marital harmony required adherence to strict gender roles. According to Rebecca Davis, their insistence that women exit the workforce en masse and accept housekeeping as their primary avocation paved the way for the widespread closure of public day care centers and the dismissal of female employees.[98] Furthermore, as Wendy Kline argues, experts' push for marriage and procreation contributed to the baby boom. This postwar celebration of matrimony, family, and childbearing – and the disproportionate jump in fertility among middle- and upper-class whites – derived in part from counselors' insistence that marriage and procreation were the expected life paths for educated, affluent women.[99] Legislation alone could not guarantee the spread of these family values, but the marriage counseling and education industry helped to ensure that marriage would remain the defining American social institution, in spite of the forces that challenged its dominance.

The creation of a marriage education industry thus marked a new space for the ongoing backlash against conjugal misconduct. If experts'

---

[96] Celello, *Making Marriage Work*.

[97] Elaine Tyler May, *Homeward Bound: American Families in the Cold War Era*, revised and updated edition (New York: Basic Books, 1999), 54–58, 65–72.

[98] Davis, *More Perfect Unions*, 83–100. On 1950s efforts to reassert marital gender roles in primary and secondary education, see Moran, *Teaching Sex*, 143–145.

[99] Kline, *Building a Better Race*, 152–156. See also Wini Breines, *Young White and Miserable: Growing Up Female in the Fifties* (Boston: Beacon Press, 1992), 50–51; James T. Patterson, *Grand Expectations: The United States, 1945–1974* (New York: Oxford University Press, 1996), 76–81, 360–361.

arguments tended to rely on eugenic pseudoscience, their messages were no less evidence based than judges' unsubstantiated claims that marital nonconformity defied public policy. And unlike judges and lawmakers, whose influence was restricted by state borders, marriage counselors and educators were not beholden to the legal codes of a single state. As such, these experts strove to create a national marital culture that resisted changing models of marriage, family, gender, and sexual expression. They utilized counseling, education, advice literature, and popular media to impart a commitment to permanent, procreative, and monogamous marriage among affluent white heterosexual couples. In so doing, they took calls for preserving public policy beyond the legal realm and into an even more pervasive cultural sphere. Heeding the pleas of uniform state legislation promoters such as Charles Thaddeus Terry, they incorporated education into the broader push for legal reform. Along the way, they brought new life to a long-running quest to halt the perceived marriage crisis.

But ironically, the marriage education industry thrived on the very crisis it sought to eradicate. Alarmist rhetoric about the deterioration of marriage allowed Popenoe and others to build their own careers and simultaneously to reassert the centrality of long-term and procreative marriage to a nation that was exploring other options. Experts' ceaseless claims that marriage was falling out of favor helped to ensure that it would do no such thing. Once again, this strategy was not a bold innovation on the part of marital experts themselves. As we have seen throughout this book, vocal outcries against marital nonconformity served as reliable strategies for maintaining marital tradition. In this sense, marriage educators drew from a dependable toolkit, mimicking those opponents of commercialized matchmaking, progressive polygamy, dysgenic marriage, trial marriage, and interracial marriage. While their methods were original, their insistence that marriage not bend to individualistic whims was well established. By adding therapy, education, and promises of academic training to preexisting legal models, they found a winning strategy in the battle against conjugal misconduct.

Epilogue

The many forms of conjugal misconduct on display throughout the early twentieth century sparked just as many forms of backlash. The expansion of courtship through personal advertisements and matrimonial agencies led to the criminalization of commercialized matchmaking and sparked efforts to create state-run marriage bureaus that might discourage bachelorhood, support healthy matrimony, and assimilate Native American populations. Growing incidences of "progressive polygamy" and evasive out-of-state remarriages inspired campaigns to criminalize hasty remarriage and to forge uniform marriage and divorce statutes. Similarly, the defiance of eugenic marriage laws led to increased surveillance of nuptials exchanged across state lines and prompted the creation and passage of uniform marriage evasion legislation. Trial marriages provoked widespread condemnation from religious, judicial, and journalistic commentators and encouraged legislators to tighten underage annulment statutes in several states. Meanwhile, black-white marriages sparked consistent efforts to pass new anti-miscegenation laws and led various judges to declare that interracial unions could not be formed consensually, but must rather be the product of deceit or insanity. Collectively, these practices inspired a marriage training movement in the 1930s, by which educators, counselors, and social scientists sought to avert challenges to marital norms through education and cultural indoctrination. Troubled by the marriage crisis they perceived before them, professionals hoped that new generations would abandon the boundary-pushing marital behaviors that had become all too prevalent.

It goes without saying that these legal and cultural responses, which tended to stigmatize and criminalize marital nonconformists, were not consequences that participants in unconventional marital arrangements desired. But in recognizing that these couples were often victimized for breaching marital convention, we must also acknowledge the role they played in shaping and reshaping cultural and legal definitions of marriage throughout the first four decades of the twentieth century. Their acts encouraged legislators to impose new limits on the types of marriages that couples were permitted to form, at the same time that they exposed the limitations of the law in governing matters of the heart. In sum, their unconventional marital arrangements pushed the boundaries of matrimonial possibility, shaped the parameters of marital inclusion, and called for consistent reevaluations of the definition of marriage itself.

At the same time that these conflicts drew and redrew the boundaries of marital participation, they never weakened marriage's ascendency as the defining social organizer. To the contrary, the unconventional domestic relations examined here helped in many ways to *strengthen* the institution of marriage. Challenges to marital norms emboldened traditionalists in their quests to preserve marriage as the exclusive site for romantic intimacy and as an essential force for the propagation of the human race. The rise of alternative marital arrangements sparked new laws and restrictions that reinforced the centrality of marriage to American social life. While the nonconforming couples examined in the preceding pages ignited this fear that the institution of marriage was unraveling, they were also deeply invested in that institution; they certainly pushed the boundaries of marital convention, but they did so in an effort to incorporate their alternative romantic arrangements within those boundaries. At the same time that their relationships inspired new laws and cultural programs to avert a perceived marriage crisis, these nonconforming couples displayed reverence for the institution of marriage and a strong desire to be a part of it.

In many cases, nonconformists defended their right to proper matrimonial recognition by contrasting their own relationships with those of other unconventional couples or by stating that their relations were in fact superior to normative marriages. Persons seeking partnership through matrimonial advertisements often highlighted their qualities of decency, respectability, and sexual modesty, and they emphasized that they were seeking stable matrimony, and not the tawdry adventures that less civilized people pursued through personal ads. Prominent couples involved in trial marriages, among them Fannie Hurst and Jacques Danielson, tried to prove the legitimacy of their unusual arrangements by contrasting them to the noncommittal affairs of free lovers and unattached bohemians. Outspoken proponents of racial intermarriage pushed for public acceptance of upstanding black-white couples by excluding poor, childless, and nonchurchgoing spouses from their ranks and by emphasizing the low rate of separation among intermarried couples.[1] And while couples who defied state remarriage and eugenic regulations did not often denigrate other romantic arrangements, they dodged such laws out of a deep desire to take part in the institution of marriage, at times with the accompanying claim that restrictive marriage laws challenged the sanctity of marriage by limiting its occurrence.

The lawmakers, journalists, scientists, and clergy who hoped to preserve the marital status quo accused nonconformists of demeaning the institution of marriage with their unconventional arrangements. They responded to nontraditional marriages with legal and cultural imperatives that would protect marriage from these assaults and block unwelcome imposters from receiving marital sanction. But their acts of resistance should not obscure the fact that the marital nonconformists addressed in this book were invested in the institution as well. That is to say, they performed acts of conjugal misconduct in service of, and not in opposition to, the institution of marriage. They therefore strengthened marriage by continually inciting authorities to draw firmer lines between married and nonmarried status and by persisting in their efforts to fall within the former category.

* * *

The historical patterns on display throughout this book have continued to manifest themselves in recent decades. Backlash against conjugal misconduct adopted complex forms in the 1990s as growing rates of divorce, unmarried cohabitation, and single motherhood generated new state-sponsored strategies for reversing what many perceived to be a revitalized marriage crisis. These initiatives included the introduction of covenant marriage laws in Louisiana (1997), Arizona (1998), and Arkansas (2001). Couples entering into covenant marriage must undergo counseling before exchanging vows and endure a two-year

---

[1] Barbara Young Welke explores this general phenomenon in her work on race, gender, ability, and citizenship throughout the long nineteenth century. The marginalized populations she studies sometimes sought to improve their legal status by defining themselves against even more marginalized groups. See, for example, her discussion of the ways in which women and racial minorities strategically distanced themselves from the category of disability. Welke, *Law and the Borders of Belonging in the Long Nineteenth Century United States* (New York: Cambridge University Press, 2010), 78–79.

waiting period if they wish to divorce. Though covenant marriage did not become a popular nuptial option, it was one of many political efforts to boost the nation's flagging commitment to marital commitment at the turn of the twenty-first century.[2]

Efforts to preserve marriage as a gateway to social citizenship have also persisted in academic realms. Sensing danger in shifting marital norms, a group of social scientists has devoted itself to proving that procreative and long-lasting heterosexual marriage remains the cornerstone of functional society. Adopting methods introduced in the 1930s by Paul Popenoe and colleagues, present-day researchers such as Barbara Dafoe Whitehead, W. Bradford Wilcox, Linda Waite, Maggie Gallagher, and David Popenoe, the son of Paul Popenoe, ceaselessly insist that deviations from these marital norms will yield terrible social repercussions. These writers argue that married couples are happier and healthier than single people; they warn that unmarried cohabitants have less satisfying relations than do legally married spouses; and they insist that childless couples are not fulfilling a social obligation to procreate. They also contend that couples who engage in premarital sex and cohabit before they wed are less content in marriage than those who do not.[3]

The younger Popenoe, a retired sociologist, founded the National Marriage Project (NMP) at Rutgers University in 1997. Now housed at the University of Virginia and directed by sociologist W. Bradford Wilcox, the NMP continues to pursue its mission of assessing the health of marriages in the United States, devising strategies for improving their quality and informing the public about the (inevitably declining) state of matrimony in America. While the NMP boasts of its "nonpartisan, non-sectarian, and interdisciplinary" approaches to research and instruction in marriage, the organization's findings consistently reflect the traditional values once promoted by the elder Popenoe, now rearticulated in the NMP's efforts to suppress any intimate arrangements that stray from a monogamous, procreative, and heterosexual standard. NMP publications

[2] Davis, *More Perfect Unions*, 238–240. Davis also traces the varied marriage promotion initiatives that emerged from President Bill Clinton's 1996 welfare reform measures and culminated with the George W. Bush administration's laundry list of programs that incorporated marriage into antipoverty aid (240–252). See also Pleck, *Not Just Roommates*.
[3] Nancy D. Polikoff, *Beyond (Straight and Gay) Marriage: Valuing All Families under the Law* (Boston: Beacon Press, 2008), 63–82; Kline, *Building a Better Race*, 156–164; Davis, *More Perfect Unions*, 247–259; Galena K. Rhoades and Scott M. Stanley, *Before "I Do": What Do Premarital Experiences Have to Do with Marital Quality among Today's Young Adults?* (Charlottesville: National Marriage Project, 2014).

bemoan the rise in divorces, the decline in nuptials, and the increase in out-of-wedlock childbearing among working-class persons with only high school diplomas. On an abstract level, NMP contributors worry about the negative social consequences that might derive from individuals' decisions to "live apart from the civilizing power of married life."[4] More concretely, they express concern that by not getting married, working-class Americans deny themselves an opportunity to achieve economic security by combining resources with a spouse. The NMP also criticizes any behaviors that threaten familial stability, citing studies to argue that divorce, unmarried cohabitation, and single-parenthood are detrimental to children's emotional health.[5]

Like Paul Popenoe, these marriage enthusiasts couch their moralistic arguments in academic language and social scientific research. Meanwhile, dozens of scholars have disputed these studies, noting their tendency to ignore questions of class, race, education, and earning potential in order to present marital status as the lone determinant of happiness and emotional stability.[6] It should come as little surprise that the children of married parents are often on steadier footing than the children of unwed parents. In addition to the financial and emotional benefits that accompany a two-parent, dual-income household, marriage provides couples with state and federal income tax advantages, the right to share pensions and Social Security benefits, greater access to insurance through a spouse's employers, and a host of other legal and financial privileges; these material benefits offer married families more opportunities to thrive

---

[4] W. Bradford Wilcox, ed., *The State of Our Unions 2010: When Marriage Disappears: The New Middle America* (Charlottesville: National Marriage Project and the Institute for American Values, 2010), 15–16.

[5] Wilcox, *The State of Our Unions* (2010), 93–97; National Marriage Project, *The State of Our Unions 2012: The President's Marriage Agenda* (Charlottesville: National Marriage Project, 2012), 89–96. Wilcox, "Why Single Men May Not Be Having the Most Fun," *Washington Post*, 13 Feb. 2016, www.washingtonpost.com/news/in-theory/wp/2016/02/13/why-single-men-may-not-be-having-the-most-fun.

[6] Polikoff, *Beyond (Straight and Gay) Marriage*, 70–75; Bella DePaulo, *Singled Out: How Singles Are Stereotyped, Stigmatized, and Ignored, and Still Live Happily Ever After* (New York: St. Martin's, 2006), 28–61; Davis, *More Perfect Unions*, 248–249, 256; Michael Wald, "Adult's Sexual Orientation and State Determinations Regarding Placement of Children," *Family Law Quarterly* 40, no. 3 (2006): 403 fn. 56; Frank Furstenberg, "Can Marriage Be Saved?," *Dissent* 52, no. 3 (2005): 76–80; Wendy D. Manning and Susan Brown, "Children's Economic Well-Being in Married and Cohabiting Parent Families," *Journal of Marriage and Family* 68, no. 2 (2006): 345–362; Tamara Metz, *Untying the Knot: Marriage, the State, and the Case for Their Divorce* (Princeton: Princeton University Press, 2010), 181, fn. 34.

than unmarried ones.[7] But while some scholars have sought solutions for bringing economic stability to families that do not fit a traditional marital mold, the NMP markets marriage as a one-size-fits-all remedy to family vulnerability – in many ways deflecting much-needed conversations about class inequality with alarmist rhetoric about the devaluation of marriage.[8]

This anxiety over conjugal misconduct surged as the debate over same-sex marriage came to occupy a central place in American law and culture. Long on the backburner of the gay liberation movement, a series of incidents in the early 1990s brought the issue to the front lines of America's culture wars. In 1990, three same-sex couples applied unsuccessfully for marriage licenses in Hawaii. The couples then filed a lawsuit alleging that the state's refusal to grant licenses to same-sex couples was unconstitutional. In 1993, the Hawaii Supreme Court's plurality opinion held that the exclusion of same-sex couples from the institution of marriage was indeed a form of sex discrimination, opening the door to future marriage equality victories and inspiring both proponents and opponents of same-sex marriage to fight for their clashing causes.[9]

The early legal backlash against this growing push for gay marriage was robust. In 1996, the US Congress passed the Defense of Marriage Act (DOMA), which prevented the federal government from recognizing

[7] Andrew J. Cherlin, *The Marriage-Go-Round: The State of Marriage and the Family in America Today* (New York: Alfred A. Knopf, 2009), 114; Metz, *Untying the Knot*, 128–129; Lisa Duggan, "Holy Matrimony!" *Nation*, 15 Mar. 2004, pp. 14–19; Michael Warner, *The Trouble with Normal: Sex, Politics, and the Ethics of Queer Life* (Cambridge, Mass.: Harvard University Press, 1999), 117–119.

[8] For studies that explore possibilities for granting legal and economic rights to nontraditional families, see Metz, *Untying the Knot*; J. Herbie DiFonzo and Ruth C. Stern, *Intimate Associations: The Law and Culture of American Families* (Ann Arbor: University of Michigan Press, 2013); Elizabeth Brake, *Minimizing Marriage: Marriage, Morality, and the Law* (New York: Oxford University Press, 2012); Judith Stacey, "Forsaking No Others: Coming to Terms with Family Diversity," in *Marriage at the Crossroads: Law, Policy, and the Brave New World of Twenty-First Century Families*, ed. Marsha Garrison and Elizabeth S. Scott (New York: Cambridge University Press, 2012), 201–223.

[9] Carlos A. Ball, Introduction to *After Marriage Equality: The Future of LGBT Rights*, ed. Ball (New York: New York University Press, 2016), 2–3; Ball, *From the Closet to the Courtroom: Five LGBT Rights Lawsuits That Have Changed Our Nation* (Boston: Beacon Press, 2010), 151–198; Michael D. Sant'Ambrogio and Sylvia A. Law, "*Baehr v. Lewin* and the Long Road to Marriage Equality," *University of Hawai'i Law Review* 33 (2011): 705–753; Daniel R. Pinello, *America's Struggle for Same-Sex Marriage* (New York: Cambridge University Press, 2006), 25–29. For a comprehensive discussion of the marriage equality movement from its origins to its completion, see Nathaniel Frank, *Awakenings: How Gays and Lesbians Brought Marriage Equality to America* (Cambridge, Mass.: Belknap Press, 2017).

same-sex marriages and protected states from having to recognize same-sex unions conducted in other locations – thus preempting the legal confusion that has historically resulted from disparities in state marriage laws. After President Bill Clinton signed DOMA into law, many other states enacted their own laws denying the recognition of same-sex nuptials. In subsequent years, the conflict between supporters and detractors of marriage equality intensified. In 2003, the Supreme Judicial Court of Massachusetts legalized same-sex marriage, and soon after the supreme courts of California, Connecticut, and Iowa followed suit. In response to these judicial victories, voters in more than half of the states supported constitutional amendments restricting marriage to one man and one woman – including California's Proposition 8, which overturned the California Supreme Court's prior ruling in favor of same-sex marriage. Ultimately, thirty-one states passed measures to exclude gay and lesbian couples from legal matrimony.[10]

Likely responding to this barrage of antigay legislation, some marriage equality advocates adopted the rhetoric of their conservative opponents. Countering oft-repeated claims that the legalization of same-sex unions would weaken the institution of marriage, these activists insisted that opening the gates of matrimony to committed gay and lesbian couples would in fact *improve* the institution of marriage and bolster the nation's flagging sexual morals. This argument often relied on a strategy that emphasized the decency and respectability of same-sex couples who sought marriage, while maligning those who did not aspire to matrimony. For instance, in a 2004 presentation sponsored by the Brookings Institution, gay journalist Jonathan Rauch argued that the legalization of same-sex marriage would encourage persons of all sexual orientations to move "back toward the expectation of marriage as a universal norm."[11] Rauch justified his attachment to marriage as the "gold standard for committed relationships" by asserting that marriage helped the state to monitor public health in a way that no other romantic arrangement could do. Applying rhetoric that sounds strikingly similar to the justifications for eugenic laws in the 1910s, Rauch argued that same-sex marriage was "one of the most important ways that society has to

---

[10] Ball, *After Marriage Equality*, 3–4; Katherine Franke, "What Marriage Equality Teaches Us: The Afterlife of Racism and Homophobia," in *After Marriage Equality*, ed. Ball, 238–239; Polikoff, *Beyond (Straight and Gay) Marriage*, 92–97; John D'Emilio, "The Marriage Fight Is Setting Us Back," *Gay & Lesbian Review* 13, no. 6 (2006): 10.

[11] Brookings Institution, "Can Gay Marriage Strengthen the American Family?" 1 Apr. 2004, www.brookings.edu/wp-content/uploads/2012/04/20040401.pdf, pp. 6–8.

regulate sexual conduct in order to prevent the threat of sexual diseases and all the other problems that go with promiscuity. I think that [if] we had accepted and established same-sex marriage in the 1970s, we would have seen nothing like the horrific AIDS crisis that we saw."[12]

While jettisoning the eugenic rhetoric applied by Rauch, other early twenty-first-century proponents of marriage equality also argued that same-sex marriage could improve the institution of marriage as a whole. The Human Rights Campaign (HRC), the nation's largest LGBTQ advocacy group, contended that same-sex marriage "would open the doors to more supporters, not opponents [of marriage]. And it would help keep the age-old institution alive."[13] In its promotional materials, the organization quoted conservative columnist David Brooks to make this point, reproducing Brooks's claim: "We shouldn't just allow gay marriage. We should insist on gay marriage. We should regard it as scandalous that two people could claim to love each other and not want to sanctify their love with marriage and fidelity."[14] By citing Brooks's column as an effective argument for marriage equality, the HRC in essence joined him in condemning those romantic and sexual arrangements that do not include or aspire to marriage.

Amid these debates over whether gay couples promised to save or destroy the institution of marriage, and in the wake of the much-publicized blow that the passage of Proposition 8 dealt to the marriage equality movement, public opinion began to shift. In 2012, President Barack Obama voiced his support for marriage equality, and voters in four different states passed measures to permit same-sex marriage, triggering the rapid overturning of state marriage bans in subsequent years.[15]

[12] Ibid., 37. See also Rauch, *Gay Marriage: Why It Is Good for Gays, Good for Straights, and Good for America* (New York: Times Books, 2004); Polikoff, *Beyond (Straight and Gay) Marriage*, 83. Rauch was not the first person to encourage same-sex marriage as a means of tempering promiscuity in gay male communities. As theorist Michael Warner has explained, the predominately white and male writers who led the push for same-sex marriage in the 1990s highlighted the worthiness of matrimonially inclined gay men and lesbians by contrasting their virtue to the depraved behaviors of a promiscuous queer community. According to Warner, these activists believed that marriage held the power to civilize gays and lesbians and to do away with what Andrew Sullivan labeled in 1998 their "proclivity for quick and easy sex." Warner, *The Trouble with Normal*, 135.

[13] Human Rights Campaign, "Answers to Questions about Marriage Equality," http:// gaymarriage.procon.org/sourcefiles/HRC-answers-to-questions-about-marriage-equality .pdf; Ayumu Kaneko, "The Same-Sex Marriage Campaign in the Age of Neoliberalism," *Japanese Journal of American Studies* 26 (2015): 175.

[14] David Brooks, "The Power of Marriage," *New York Times*, 22 Nov. 2003, p. A15.

[15] Ball, *After Marriage Equality*, 4–5.

The state-by-state legalization of same-sex unions generated familiar complications, as couples who wed out-of-state were often denied the rights of matrimony upon returning home.[16] Such conflicts added ammunition to the fight for federal recognition of same-sex marriage. Eventually this fight gained enough force that some hardened critics of the movement became allies – to a degree. On the surface, the most stunning change of heart came in the form of a 2012 *New York Times* op-ed by David Blankenhorn, in which the longtime opponent of same-sex marriage expressed his newfound support for marriage equality.

Up to this point, Blankenhorn had devoted much energy to blocking gay partners from exchanging vows. As founder and president of the Institute for American Values and as the author of a 2007 book arguing against same-sex marriage, Blankenhorn insisted that gay unions weakened the institution of marriage by eliminating the expectation that children be raised by their two biological parents.[17] In 2010, Blankenhorn served as a witness for the defense in the federal lawsuit against California's Proposition 8, rearticulating his belief that the legalization of marriage between same-sex partners would weaken the institution of marriage on the whole.[18] In the district court's ruling against Proposition 8, Judge Vaughn Walker noted that Blankenhorn lacked the expertise necessary to be a reliable witness on the matter and that he "provided no credible evidence to support any of the claimed adverse effects" of same-sex marriage.[19] Despite these limitations, Blankenhorn filled the role of a modern-day expert, whose lack of scholarly credentials did not diminish his self-proclaimed authority on proper family structures.

To the surprise of many, two years after serving as Proposition 8's most prominent defendant, Blankenhorn declared his conditional support of same-sex marriage. In his *New York Times* piece, Blankenhorn explained that he had formerly opposed marriage between gay and

---

[16] Franke, "What Marriage Equality Teaches Us," 240–241.

[17] David Blankenhorn, *The Future of Marriage* (New York: Encounter Books, 2007); Blankenhorn, "Protecting Marriage to Protect Children," *Los Angeles Times*, 19 Sep. 2008, http://articles.latimes.com/2008/sep/19/opinion/oe-blankenhorn19.

[18] He did acknowledge, however, that marriage would also provide benefits for same-sex parents and their children. *Perry v. Schwarzenegger*, 704 F. Supp.2d 921 (N.D. Cal. 2010), court transcript available at www.afer.org/wp-content/uploads/2010/01/Perry-Vol-11-1-26-10.pdf; Karin Klein, "Proposition 8's Witness for the Defense – No, the Plaintiffs," *Los Angeles Times*, 22 Jun. 2012, http://articles.latimes.com/2012/jun/22/news/la-ol-blankenhorn-proposition-8-20120622.

[19] *Perry v. Schwarzenegger*, 704 F. Supp.2d 921 (N.D. Cal. 2010). Judge's decision available at www.wsj.com/public/resources/documents/080410prop8ruling.pdf.

lesbian couples because such unions deprived children of the right "to know and to be cared for by the two parents who brought them into this world." In his view, marriage between heterosexual partners granted children the "gift" of a legal connection to their two biological parents; the children of same-sex couples could never receive that gift, and thus were at a deep disadvantage. Blankenhorn maintained that unions between gay couples contributed to the "deinstitutionalization" of marriage, which he defined as "marriage's steady transformation in both law and custom from a structured institution with clear public purposes to the state's licensing of private relationships that are privately defined." Blankenhorn bemoaned the diverse purposes marriage had come to serve, waxing nostalgic for an imagined day when its lone role was to ensure that children received care and legal protections from their biological parents.[20]

At the start of his 2012 column, Blankenhorn assured readers that his definition of what constitutes proper family and parenting configurations had not wavered, but he now voiced tepid support for same-sex marriage. He stated several reasons for this change of heart. First, he believed the cultural tide had shifted beyond the point of no return in favor of marriage equality. In this sense, same-sex couples' enduring push for the legal recognition of their unions had borne fruit, and efforts to halt this progress were futile. Second, Blankenhorn admitted that his past efforts to recenter debates over marriage equality on the topic of parenting had failed. Instead, he realized that the issue at the crux of the marriage debate was gay people's access to equal legal rights and protections. Expressing regret that most of his fellow critics of same-sex marriage were driven by "an underlying antigay animus," Blankenhorn was ready to form a new set of allies.[21]

This is where the most compelling and troubling elements of his argument lie. At the end of his op-ed, Blankenhorn laid out what appeared to be his central objective: to recruit respectable gay and lesbian couples into his fight against a twenty-first-century marriage crisis. He expressed hope that his begrudging acceptance of same-sex unions, and their inevitable legalization, might restore reverence for the institution of marriage itself. Abandoning his past efforts to block gay and lesbian

---

[20] David Blankenhorn, "How My View on Gay Marriage Changed," *New York Times*, 22 Jun. 2012, www.nytimes.com/2012/06/23/opinion/how-my-view-on-gay-marriage-changed.html.

[21] Ibid.

couples from the altar, Blankenhorn now argued that conceding marriage rights to those partners might indirectly lead more heterosexuals to follow suit. "Instead of fighting gay marriage," he explained, "I'd like to help build new coalitions bringing together gays who want to strengthen marriage with straight people who want to do the same. For example, once we accept gay marriage, might we also agree that marrying before having children is a vital cultural value that all of us should do more to embrace? Can we agree that, for all lovers who want their love to last, marriage is preferable to cohabitation?" As these concluding remarks reveal, at the heart of Blankenhorn's initiative was an effort to address rising rates of nonmarital cohabitation and procreation – not by devising initiatives to support unmarried families, but by promoting marriage as an end-all solution to the challenges of contemporary family life. Recognizing that his battle against the legalization of same-sex marriage was a losing one, Blankenhorn courted gays and lesbians to help him enforce his narrow vision of family, with the new concession that that vision could include respectable gay couples if need be.[22]

David Blankenhorn's evolution on same-sex marriage illustrates some familiar historical patterns in the response to conjugal misconduct. His initial criticism of same-sex marriage and his support for Proposition 8 embody the conservative backlash that we have seen throughout this book, as authorities sought to suppress challenges to marital norms through proposed legislation and courtroom intervention. His subsequent reversal on same-sex marriage reflects, on one hand, an acknowledgment that the institution of marriage can expand to include new characters – in this case committed gay and lesbian couples. On the other hand, however, Blankenhorn used his capitulation as a tool to reassert the centrality of marriage to American family life and to further marginalize the unwed.

With this revelation, Blankenhorn roused the fury of his former allies in the anti–marriage equality cause.[23] He also incurred criticism from left-wing detractors such as Richard Kim, editor of *The Nation*, who

---

[22] Ibid. See also Cary Franklin, "Marrying Liberty and Equality: The New Jurisprudence of Gay Rights," *Virginia Law Review* 100, no. 5 (2014): 820–823. On other prominent conservatives who embraced same-sex marriage on the premise that it helped to strengthen the institution of matrimony, see Franke, "What Marriage Equality Teaches Us," 244, 248–250.

[23] Five board members of Blankenhorn's Institute for American Values resigned after the publication of his op-ed. The institution lost half a million dollars in donations during the six months that followed. Mark Oppenheimer, "In Shift, an Activist Enlists Same-Sex Couples in a Pro-Marriage Coalition," *New York Times*, 30 Jan. 2013, p. A19.

denounced Blankenhorn's statement as a cynical ploy. "Blankenhorn once thought gay marriage could be a useful instrument to instill his regressive, archaic, and punitive views on marriage in the public and in the law," Kim reasoned. "He still thinks that. He's just made a political calculation that gays are more valuable now as recruits than scapegoats."[24] Other commentators were more supportive of Blankenhorn's change of heart, presenting it as a hopeful sign that that political rivals might learn to see eye to eye on a just cause. In a *New Republic* piece, John Corvino, a philosopher and longtime supporter of same-sex marriage, declared that Blankenhorn's announcement was "a victory for reason and nuance." Though Corvino had previously criticized Blankenhorn's opposition to marriage equality, he now praised Blankenhorn's willingness to modify his stance, concluding, "I appreciate having him, finally, on both the pro-children *and* pro-equality side."[25]

This perspective ultimately found favor in the nation's highest court. In its 2013 ruling on the *United States v. Windsor*, the court declared DOMA unconstitutional. Supporting Corvino's claim that marriage equality was a pro-child phenomenon, the majority opinion discussed the injustices that children of unmarried parents faced in comparison to children whose parents were legally wed. In the opinion, Justice Anthony Kennedy noted that unmarried families faced higher health care costs, reduced inheritance benefits, and diminished access to federal financial aid. By denying thousands of same-sex couples the right to marriage, DOMA ensured that the children of gay and lesbian parents faced numerous disadvantages.[26]

---

[24] Richard Kim, "What's Still the Matter with David Blankenhorn," *Nation,* 24 Jun. 2012, www.thenation.com/article/whats-still-matter-david-blankenhorn/.

[25] John Corvino, "From Prop 8 Advocate to Gay Marriage Supporter: In Praise of David Blankenhorn's Nuanced Evolution," *New Republic,* 22 Jun. 2012, https://newrepublic.com/article/104256/john-corvino-prop-8-advocate-gay-marriage-supporter-praise-david-blankenhorns-nuanced. See also Paul Harris, "Gay Marriage Supporters Welcome Leading Critic's Change of Heart," *Guardian,* 23 Jun. 2012, www.theguardian.com/world/2012/jun/23/gay-marriage-critic-david-blankenhorn. Six months later, Corvino joined Blankenhorn, Rauch, and seventy-two other writers and activists of all political stripes in signing a pamphlet entitled "A Call for a New Conversation on Marriage." This document, sponsored by Blankenhorn's Institute for American Values, bemoaned declining marriage rates among middle- and working-class individuals and sought new strategies for marriage promotion: "The current question is: 'Should gays marry?' The new question is: 'Who among us, gay or straight, wants to strengthen marriage?" *"A Call for a New Conversation on Marriage": An Appeal from Seventy-Five American Leaders,* Institute for American Values, 2013, http://americanvalues.org/catalog/pdfs/2013-01.pdf.

[26] *United States v. Windsor,* 133 S. Ct. 2675 (2013).

Two years later, the Supreme Court applied similar logic in *Obergefell v. Hodges*. In this landmark case, the court declared that state laws barring same-sex marriage were unconstitutional, in essence granting same-sex couples the right to marry throughout the nation. Justice Kennedy's majority decision provided numerous justifications for the legalization of same-sex marriage, including the familiar idea that it was unreasonable for a union to be valid in one state and invalid in another.[27] But one of his most forceful points concerned the influence of marriage on children. Specifically, Kennedy emphasized the suffering he believed the children of unmarried couples faced:

> Without the recognition, stability, and predictability marriage offers, their children suffer the stigma of knowing their families are somehow lesser. They also suffer the significant material costs of being raised by unmarried parents, relegated through no fault of their own to a more difficult and uncertain family life. The marriage laws at issue here thus harm and humiliate the children of same-sex couples.[28]

According to Kennedy, the exclusion of same-sex couples from marriage created a class of illegitimate children who lacked material support and personal dignity. If same-sex parents could marry, Kennedy asserted, their children would attain the economic benefits and the sense of self-worth that having unmarried parents denied them.

The court's desire to grant economic and legal protections to the children of same-sex parents was an admirable one, and countless families have benefited and will continue to benefit from the decision. But the intangible costs that the court attributed to nonmarriage – namely, children's sense of humiliation and the belief that their families are somehow lesser – are more difficult to assess.[29] It is certainly possible that many children feel shame over their parents' unmarried status or, conversely, pride in their parents' legitimate marriages. But if young people are in fact humiliated by their parents' nonmarriages, one has to wonder if the

---

[27] *Obergefell v. Hodges*, 135 S. Ct. 2584 (2015). Petitioner James Obergefell had wed John Arthur in Maryland, but they lived in Ohio, where same-sex marriage was unlawful. Obergefell brought suit after Arthur died and the state of Ohio would not list him as the surviving spouse on Arthur's death certificate. Coplaintiffs Ijpe DeKoe and Thomas Kostura had married in New York, but their wedding was similarly held void in their home state of Tennessee.

[28] *Obergefell v. Hodges*, 135 S. Ct. 2584 (2015).

[29] Kennedy made similar points in his *Windsor* decision, stating that DOMA "humiliates tens of thousands of children now being raised by same-sex couples." *United States v. Windsor*, 133 S. Ct. 2675 (2013).

court's rhetoric did not reinforce that sense of stigma. For in celebrating the material and emotional stability that children with married parents might encounter, the ruling underscored the notion that the children of unmarried parents are prone to instability and suffering due to their family arrangements. Moreover, by reinforcing the role of marriage as the primary provider of children's legal and economic protections, not to mention their sense of dignity and self-worth, the court stifled discussion of strategies for protecting *all* children, and not merely the children of married parents, gay or straight.[30]

In this sense, the court's majority ruling further entrenched Blankenhorn's logic into law. It fortified the belief that marriage is essential to the positive development of children, while simultaneously deepening the divide between the children of married and unmarried parents. Rather than dwell on the specific legal and economic benefits marriage grants to children, it relied on abstract notions about the harm and humiliation caused to the children of unmarried parents. In prioritizing the abstract over the concrete, Kennedy asserted the moral superiority of marriage rather than acknowledge the inequality it helps to perpetuate.

He also took many other opportunities to praise marriage as the ultimate, perhaps even the exclusive, sign of love, commitment, and family. For instance, Kennedy expressed skepticism that unmarried individuals might ever escape solitude and despair, stating in one particularly dramatic line, "Marriage responds to the universal fear that a lonely person might call out only to find no one there. It offers the hope of companionship and understanding and assurance that while both still live there will be someone to care for the other." This statement virtually erases the possibility of camaraderie and caregiving among unmarried people, instead presenting marriage as the ultimate path to forging human connection. Similarly, Kennedy began his concluding paragraph with these already-famous words: "No union is more profound than marriage, for it embodies the highest ideals of love, fidelity, devotion, sacrifice, and family. In forming a marital union, two people become something greater than once they were." In declaring authoritatively that marriage is the most profound union there is, Kennedy belittled the countless family structures that do not depend on marriage for their sense of profundity.[31]

---

[30] Melissa Murray, "*Obergefell v. Hodges* and Nonmarriage Inequality," *California Law Review* 104, no. 5 (2016): 1216–1217.

[31] *Obergefell v. Hodges*, 135 S. Ct. 2584 (2015). As Melissa Murray notes, "The majority's rhetoric suggests that the prospect of willingly being unmarried is utterly unimaginable.

Legal scholar Melissa Murray has laid out some of the potential negative consequences of Kennedy's "love letter to marriage."[32] Above all, Murray worries that the ruling undermines the protections courts had granted to unmarried families in prior decisions, highlighting several cases from the past five decades that offered rights to unwed individuals and their offspring. These rulings granted inheritance rights to the children of unmarried parents, validated the use of contraception outside marriage, eliminated household zoning laws that discriminated against nonnuclear families, and decriminalized sodomy; Murray views this last act, a product of the landmark 2003 case *Lawrence v. Texas*, as a clear endorsement of nonmarital sexual relations.[33]

Murray expresses concern that in its excessive celebration of marriage, *Obergefell* risks undoing some of these advancements for unmarried persons and alternative family units:

> *Obergefell*, with its pro-marriage rhetoric, preempts the possibility of relationship and family pluralism in favor of a constitutional landscape in which marriage exists alone as the constitutionally protected option for family and relationship formation. In this regard, *Obergefell* does far more than venerate marriage for the purpose of democratizing access to that institution. Instead, it forecloses on the promise of greater constitutional protection for nonmarriage that *Lawrence* and its ilk offered. In so doing, *Obergefell* leaves nonmarriage and its constituents in a constitutionally precarious position.[34]

These critiques of the *Obergefell* decision do not minimize the protections it provides to couples and families that had long been deprived of them due to antigay animus. But in celebrating the legalization of same-sex marriage as a civil rights victory, we must also consider the ways in which the elimination of one type of family discrimination can help to

---

And it is this incredulity – and its underlying faith in the rightness and goodness of marriage – that fuels *Obergefell*. It leads Justice Kennedy and the majority to the right conclusion – that same-sex couples have the right to marry. But the price for securing the right to marry and 'equal dignity' for same-sex couples is, perhaps ironically, the inequality and indignity of nonmarital life." "*Obergefell v. Hodges* and Nonmarriage Inequality," 1216.

[32] Murray, "*Obergefell v. Hodges* and Nonmarriage Inequality," 1211.

[33] Ibid., 1216–1229.

[34] Ibid., 1211–1212. See also Melissa Murray, "Accommodating Nonmarriage," *Southern California Law Review* 88, no. 3 (2015); Deborah A. Widiss, "Non-Marital Families and (or after?) Marriage Equality," *Florida State Law Review* 42, no. 2 (2015); Serena Mayeri, "Marital Supremacy and the Constitution of the Nonmarital Family," *California Law Review* 103, no. 5 (2015); Nancy D. Polikoff, "Concord with Which Other Families?: Marriage Equality, Family Demographics, and Race," *University of Pennsylvania Law Review Online* 164, no. 1 (2016).

accentuate others, specifically in the Supreme Court's strong division between upstanding families united in marriage and those degraded families that lack marital ties.

Moreover, the same-sex marriage victory has given rise to other forms of discrimination against conjugal misconduct, sometimes emerging from the very people who waged a political battle in name of "marriage equality." In the lead-up to the *Obergefell* decision, and in its immediate aftermath, a number of prominent supporters of same-sex unions sought to bolster support for gay marriage by contrasting it with polygamy, or plural marriage. This was in many ways a defensive strategy, as it responded to one of the most popular conservative arguments against same-sex marriage: that bringing gay and lesbian couples within the boundaries of marital legitimacy created a "slippery slope," in that it paved the way for the legalization of polygamy, bestiality, and marriage to children and inanimate objects.[35] While proponents of marriage equality typically refuse to engage with allegations that same-sex unions will lead to the validation of nuptials between adults and minors (or nonhumans, or nonorganisms), they seem less comfortable when it comes to arguments that the legalization of same-sex marriage opens the door to the legalization of plural marriage. Some seek to deflect criticisms against same-sex unions by castigating polygamy as an immoral practice and contrasting its immorality with the respectability of marriage between two loving partners of the same gender.[36]

Scholars have voiced varied opinions on the feasibility of efforts to legalize polygamy in the wake of *Obergefell*, and it is beyond the scope of this study to confirm or deny their logic.[37] What I am interested in instead

---

[35] In his *Obergefell* dissent, Chief Justice John Roberts wrote, "It is striking how much of the majority's reasoning would apply with equal force to the claim of a fundamental right to plural marriage." *Obergefell v. Hodges*, 135 S. Ct. 2584 (2015).

[36] See Joseph J. Fischel, "A More Promiscuous Politics: LGBT Rights Without the LGBT Rights," in *After Marriage Equality*, ed. Ball, 181–211.

[37] For the argument that rulings in favor of same-sex marriage pave the way for the future legalization of plural marriage, see Ronald C. Den Otter, "Three May Not Be a Crowd: The Case for a Constitutional Right to Plural Marriage," *Emory Law Journal* 64, no. 6 (2015); Den Otter, *In Defense of Plural Marriage* (New York: Cambridge University Press, 2015); Mark Goldfeder, *Legalizing Plural Marriage: The Next Frontier in Family Law* (Lebanon, N.H.: Brandeis University Press, 2017). For opposing arguments, see John O. Hayward, "Plural Marriage: When One Spouse Is Not Enough," *Journal of Constitutional Law Online* 19, no. 1 (2017); Joanna L. Grossman and Lawrence M. Friedman, "Is Three Still a Crowd? Polygamy and the Law after *Obergefell v. Hodges*," *Verdict*, 7 Jul. 2015, https://verdict.justia.com/2015/07/07/is-three-still-a-crowd-polygamy-and-the-law-after-obergefell-v-hodges.

is the rhetoric that proponents of marriage equality have used to discuss polygamy, often in an effort to deny its connection to same-sex marriage. Some have emphasized gender inequality in polygamous communities as a warning against plural marriage. For example, political theorist Stephen Macedo notes that the majority of polygamous households have been composed of one husband with multiple wives and that polygamy is thus "a patriarchal and hierarchical union – a system of male headship – that is fundamentally at odds with our constitutional values." He asserts that such arrangements are synonymous with the oppression of wives and children and that in contrast, a nation's embrace of monogamy is a sign that that nation is embracing gender equality and gay liberation as well.[38]

In addition to harming women, Macedo argues, polygamy decreases the marital prospects of nonelite men. Were polygamy permitted in the United States, women would choose men of higher means, thus leaving lower-class men wifeless. And without wives, Macedo projects, these men would be "much more prone to substance abuse, violence, and risky behavior."[39] Jonathan Rauch reiterates this argument that plural marriage would lead to competition among men for wives, with wealthy men ultimately proving victorious. He writes, "This competitive, zero-sum dynamic sets off a competition among high-status men to hoard marriage opportunities, which leaves lower-status men out in the cold. Those men, denied access to life's most stabilizing and civilizing institution, are unfairly disadvantaged and often turn to behaviors like crime and violence." Rejecting claims that *Obergefell* has raised the prospect of legal polygamy, Rauch states definitively that "gay marriage and polygamy are opposites, not equivalents."[40]

Some post-*Obergefell* arguments against polygamy veer on the conspiratorial. Journalist Cathy Young has embraced a strategy popular among opponents of same-sex marriage, who maintain that the legalization of gay marriage negatively affects heterosexual marriages and the

---

[38] Stephen Macedo, "From Same-Sex Marriage to Polygamy?," *American Prospect*, 11 Jun. 2015, http://prospect.org/article/same-sex-marriage-polygamy. See also William N. Eskridge, Jr., *The Case for Same-Sex Marriage: From Sexual Liberty to Civilized Commitment* (New York: Free Press, 1996), 148–149.

[39] Macedo, "From Same-Sex Marriage to Polygamy?"

[40] Jonathan Rauch, "No, Polygamy Isn't the Next Gay Marriage," *Politico*, 30 Jun. 2015, www.politico.com/magazine/story/2015/06/polygamy-not-next-gay-marriage-119614. Rauch draws some of his conclusions from Joseph Henrich, Robert Boyd, and Peter J. Richerson, "The Puzzle of Monogamous Marriage," *Philosophical Transactions of the Royal Society B* 367, no. 1589 (2012): 657–669.

institution at large. Young notes the failure of this argument in the marriage equality debate, right before taking a similar tack against polygamy. She writes, "Legalizing multiple spouses ... would immediately affect every couple by opening a potential door to new partners in the marriage." In other words, legalized polygamy would mean that a partner in a monogamous marriage could bring new partners into that union against the will of his or her original spouse.[41] Moreover, Young predicts, the rise of plural marriage will send an unfortunate message to impressionable individuals who have been taught to revere monogamy. "A movement for plural marriage rights would be accompanied by a push to destigmatize other forms of non-monogamy such as open marriage," she warns. "The message that sexual exclusivity in marriage is optional – accompanied by visible and positive images of non-monogamous unions – could have a ripple effect. Before long, the spouse who insists on fidelity could be forced to justify such an old-fashioned preference."[42] Young's words evoke the arguments that Corra Harris and Edwin Slosson made a century earlier, as they denounced celebrity trial marriage for fear that it would influence laypeople to form unconventional unions that suited their individual needs.

Atlantic writer Conor Friedersdorf raises similar concerns about the potential influence of legalized polygamy on American marital culture. While assuring readers that if a polyamorous family moved next door to him he would treat those neighbors with respect, he nonetheless claims that it would be "imprudent to include their arrangement in civil marriage, with its incentivizing benefits, because if group marriage were to become normalized and spread beyond a tiny fringe the consequences for society could be significant and negative." Those negative consequences could include increased opposition to same-sex marriage in foreign countries that have not legalized it, as the growth of American polygamy would confirm the "slippery slope" argument to gay marriage skeptics

---

[41] Cathy Young, "Polygamy Is Not Next," *Time*, 30 Jun. 2015, http://time.com/3942139/polygamy-is-not-next/. John O. Hayward makes a similar assertion: "Although same-sex marriage does not impinge on traditional marriage, plural marriage threatens every existing marriage, including same-sex marriage, by destroying the exclusivity of the marriage bond." Hayward, "Plural Marriage," 11.

[42] Young, "Polygamy Is Not Next." Young writes in another piece, "In a free society, multi-partner relationships should not be criminalized. But neither should they lose their stigma in the name of tolerance." Young, "Polyamory Pushes the Bounds of Relationships," *Newsday*, 13 Jan. 2014, www.newsday.com/opinion/columnists/cathy-young/polyamory-pushes-the-bounds-of-relationships-cathy-young-1.6790959.

abroad. Like Young, Friedersdorf raises the possibility that in the world of legalized polygamy, one supposedly monogamous spouse might coerce his partner into forming a plural marriage: "'Either she joins us,' a husband might say, 'or I'm out.'"[43]

Attention to these farfetched hypothetical arguments against plural marriage should not detract from some of the valid concerns its legalization would entail. For instance, the multiple economic benefits attached to marriage – including spousal access to health care, Social Security, and inheritance – are premised on the notion that a marriage is between two individuals. Incorporating additional parties into the boundaries of marriage would require the rewriting of countless statutes.[44] But what is striking about the majority of arguments used by proponents of same-sex marriage to disavow plural marriage is that they are grounded *not* in legal reasoning, but rather in moralistic assumptions about the value of polygamous relations. Arguments that polygamy is a lesser marital arrangement, that it is bad for children, that it sends an unfortunate example to impressionable individuals, that it diminishes men's marital prospects, and more broadly that it damages and transforms the institution of marriage as a whole resemble the sorts of justifications that have long been used against historical forms of conjugal misconduct – and most recently against same-sex marriage itself.[45]

Furthermore, although some opponents of polygamy rely on empirical data to support their claims, they often neglect to consider studies that counter the assumption that polygamy is inherently harmful to society.[46]

---

[43] Conor Friedersdorf, "The Case against Encouraging Polygamy," *Atlantic*, 9 Jul. 2015, www.theatlantic.com/politics/archive/2015/07/case-against-polygamy/397823/.

[44] Young addresses these legal questions, though she does nothing to challenge the assumption that two-partner unions are deserving of such benefits while larger units are not. Young, "Polygamy Is Not Next."

[45] As journalist Michael Brendan Dougherty argues, proponents of same-sex marriage who disavow polygamy "rely on class and religious prejudices, as well as on rationales that were deemed illegitimate when launched at same-sex couples." "How Gay Marriage Paves the Way for Legal Polygamy," *The Week*, 6 Jul. 2015, http://theweek.com/articles/564178/how-gay-marriage-paves-way-legal-polygamy. See also William Baude, "Is Polygamy Next?," *New York Times*, 21 Jul. 2015, p. A27; Fredrik DeBoer, "It's Time to Legalize Polygamy," *Politico*, 26 Jun. 2015, www.politico.com/magazine/story/2015/06/gay-marriage-decision-polygamy-119469.

[46] For example, sociologist Elisabeth Sheff argues that the legalization of plural marriage would provide social and economic support to the children in polygamous families. Sheff, *The Polyamorists Next Door: Inside Multiple-Partner Relationships and Families* (Lanham, Md.: Rowman & Littlefield, 2014). Cited in William E. Smith, "Marriage May Lead to Polygamy, but So What?," *Religion Dispatches*, 7 Jul. 2016, http://religiondispatches.org/same-sex-marriage-may-lead-to-polygamy-but-so-what/.

Plural marriage detractors also evoke historical narratives to strengthen their arguments. For instance, Macedo notes that in nineteenth-century Utah, the children of monogamists often enjoyed better health than the children of polygamous families as one of many pieces of historical evidence to discourage the legalization of plural marriage. Macedo dismisses counterarguments by noting that his case against polygamy is grounded in the sort of historical knowledge and empirical data that his opponents lack. "Why should we expect future generations to look favourably on radical social experiments conducted in the absence of supportive evidence?" he asks in response to the suggestion that polygamy may eventually become a popular and well-regarded phenomenon. "History's arc, as best we can now tell, bends away from the plural marriage and toward monogamy, gender equality, and same-sex marriage."[47]

Some historical scholarship challenges Macedo's suggestion that the embrace of monogamy has gone hand-in-hand with progressive shifts toward gender and sexual equality. For instance, historian Nwando Achebe reveals that polyandry, or the marriage of one woman to multiple husbands, helped grant social, economic, and sexual autonomy to women in precolonial Nigeria. As Achebe indicates, British colonial control disrupted this process, imposing patriarchal authority over Nigerian households by demanding that families be monogamous and male-headed.[48] Still, Macedo has studied polygamy extensively, and it would be unreasonable to dispute each of his specific examples of the harms plural marriage has caused.[49]

But in evoking unflattering historical examples of polygamy in order to contrast it with respectable marriage practices, Macedo and like-minded critics prioritize one set of historical narratives at the expense of others. They use history to show the abuses that have occurred within polygamous communities, but they give less attention to the abuses perpetuated against polygamists or, more broadly, against marital nonconformists at large. By ignoring the backlash that individuals faced for utilizing matchmaking services, remarrying too hastily after divorce, defying eugenic marriage statutes, forming trial marriages, and exchanging vows across

---

[47] Stephen Macedo, "The Case for Monogamy," *Economist*, 9 Jul. 2015, www.economist .com/blogs/democracyinamerica/2015/07/marriage-and-civil-rights.

[48] Nwando Achebe, "Woman-to-Woman, Polyandrous, and Child Marriage: Expressions and Contestations of Marriage Rights in Colonial and Independent Nigeria," in *Domestic Tensions, National Anxieties*, ed. Celello and Kholoussy, 170–191.

[49] Stephen Macedo, *Just Married: Same-Sex Couples, Monogamy and the Future of Marriage* (Princeton: Princeton University Press, 2015), 145–203.

the color line, these critics neglect to see the historical patterns that they themselves have perpetuated by castigating one form of conjugal misconduct in order to bolster another. Like their predecessors, they rely on the studies of experts to argue that they are seeking not to repress, but rather to uphold public policy and preserve public health. But in their vocal refrains against polygamy, these critics have also reanimated the backlash against conjugal misconduct in the post-*Obergefell* era.

In addressing these subtle forms of backlash, I do not intend to equate the anti-polygamy rumblings emerging from supporters of same-sex marriage with the blatant expressions of antigay sentiment that have increased since the *Obergefell* ruling. For instance, the legalization of same-sex marriage made a celebrity of Kim Davis, the county clerk for Rowan County, Kentucky, who famously defied the Supreme Court's decision by refusing to issue marriage licenses to same-sex couples.[50] The embrace of same-sex marriage has also prompted a spate of bills intended to permit discrimination in the name of "religious freedom." Among these is Indiana's Religious Freedom Restoration Act, signed into law in 2015 by then-governor Mike Pence and widely supported on grounds that it forbids the government from forcing businesses to provide cakes, flowers, and photography services at weddings for gay and lesbian couples.[51]

But in addition to the acts of flagrant discrimination that have accompanied the legalization of same-sex unions, the marriage equality movement has yielded other harmful consequences, particularly in creating new outlets for hostility against the unwed and the improperly wed. We see this hostility in Justice Kennedy's homage to marriage as the most valuable human relationship available, and his devaluation of nonmarital families. We see it in the retrenchment of legal protections for the unwed, and in the reinforcement of marriage's exclusive ties to tax benefits, inheritance rights, and health care access. We see it in the elimination of domestic partnership benefits to those couples who do not marry; indeed, state governments and private businesses have taken this route en masse in the wake of the *Obergefell* decision, implying that the only families worthy of protection are married ones, and ignoring the many social and

---

[50] Adam Liptak, "Justices Deny Bid to Resist Gay Marriage in Kentucky," *New York Times*, 1 Sep. 2015, p. A11; Alan Blinder and Richard Pérez-Peña, "Kentucky Clerk Defies Justices on Marriage," *New York Times*, 2 Sep. 2015, p. A1; "Kentucky: Defiant Clerk Loses Again," *New York Times*, 6 Nov. 2015, p. A15.

[51] "Indiana Gov. Pence Defends Religious Objections Law: 'This Bill Is Not about Discrimination,'" *Chicago Tribune*, 26 Mar. 2015, www.chicagotribune.com/chi-indiana-religious-freedom-bill-sb101-pence-20150326-story.html.

economic reasons why some same-sex couples might still opt for nonmarriage in the age of marriage equality.[52] And we see it in strident efforts to define the decency of same-sex marriage at the expense of other controversial arrangements, such as polygamy.

My purpose is not to challenge same-sex marriage or to defend polygamy, but rather to suggest that historical knowledge of backlash in the face of perceived marriage crisis should give us all pause in our assessments of what constitutes proper marital and familial arrangements. Through the present-day example of same-sex marriage, we see the role that acts of marital nonconformity continue to play in both transforming and reinforcing the basic tenets of marriage. Gay and lesbian couples' efforts to wed have given way to legislation and judicial decisions that open the gates of marriage to same-sex couples, as well as legislation that doubles down on anti-LGBTQ discrimination. Same-sex marriage has led more people to understand that romantic love cannot be constrained by boundaries of gender and sexual orientation, at the same time that it has drawn new lines between reputable and disreputable domestic arrangements. It has also led many gay and lesbian couples, so often criticized for their perceived desire to redefine the institution of marriage by seeking inclusion in it, to become conservative defenders of the authority of the monogamous, two-person marital relation.

This is the power that marriage wields. Its ability to grant political and legal privileges to some domestic arrangements while denying them to others ensures that there will continue to be battles waged over the boundaries of marital inclusion. In the early twenty-first century, as in the early twentieth, efforts by new groups to gain access to marriage have resulted in both the demolition of old barriers to legal matrimony and the creation of new ones. Again and again, acts of conjugal misconduct have sparked perceptions of a national marriage crisis, yielding a mixture of backlash and accommodation to shifting marital trends. But ultimately the biggest victor in these crises is the institution of marriage itself. Each debate over the shifting parameters of marriage serves to keep marriage front and center and to strengthen its grip on American family law. The

---

[52] Tara Siegel Bernard, "With Marriage a Right, Domestic Partner Benefits Come into Question," *New York Times*, 29 Jun. 2015, p. A11; Sara Warner, "How Gay Marriage and Wedding Culture Threaten Other Couples," *Time*, 11 Feb. 2016, http://time.com/4213175/gay-marriage-domestic-partner-benefits/. As Warner notes, couples who live in states that lack anti-bias protections for sexual orientation are vulnerable to many forms of discrimination – including job loss and eviction – when they out themselves by filing for a marriage license.

undying perception that the institution of marriage is in crisis has helped
to keep that institution relevant, in part by guaranteeing that there will
continue to be parties seeking entry into its borders, and by ensuring that
formerly excluded parties will guard those borders once admitted inside.
Just as early twentieth-century controversies over marital nonconformity
helped marriage to remain a marker of status and social citizenship, the
battle over same-sex unions has reasserted marriage's role as "the gold
standard for committed relationships." These varied acts of conjugal
misconduct have sparked ongoing claims that marriage is a dying entity,
but then as now, predictions of marriage's demise have allowed its
supreme reign to persist.

Index

Continued from page ii...

Davison Douglas, *Jim Crow Moves North*

Andrew Wender Cohen, *The Racketeer's Progress*

Michael Willrich, *City of Courts, Socializing Justice in Progressive Era Chicago*

Barbara Young Welke, *Recasting American Liberty: Gender, Law and the Railroad Revolution, 1865–1920*

Michael Vorenberg, *Final Freedom: The Civil War, the Abolition of Slavery, and the Thirteenth Amendment*

Robert J. Steinfeld, *Coercion, Contract, and Free Labor in Nineteenth Century America*

David M. Rabban, *Free Speech in Its Forgotten Years*

Jenny Wahl, *The Bondsman's Burden: An Economic Analysis of the Common Law of Southern Slavery*

Michael Grossberg, *A Judgment for Solomon: The d'Hauteville Case and Legal Experience in the Antebellum South*